CW00732744

2007

THE PUBLICATIONS OF THE BEDFORDSHIRE
HISTORICAL RECORD SOCIETY
VOLUME 86

# THE BOUSFIELD DIARIES

# A MIDDLE-CLASS FAMILY IN
# LATE VICTORIAN BEDFORD

*Edited by*

Richard Smart

THE BEDFORDSHIRE HISTORICAL RECORD SOCIETY

THE BOYDELL PRESS

First published 2007


A publication of
Bedfordshire Historical Record Society
published by The Boydell Press
an imprint of Boydell & Brewer Ltd
PO Box 9, Woodbridge, Suffolk IP12 3DF, UK
and of Boydell & Brewer Inc.
668 Mt Hope Avenue, Rochester, NY 14620, USA
website: www.boydellandbrewer.com


ISBN 978-0-85155-072-5


ISSN 0067-4826


The Society is most grateful for financial support
from the Simon Whitbread Trust and other donors who
have helped make the publication of this volume possible.


Details of previous volumes are available from
Boydell and Brewer Ltd


A CIP catalogue record for this book is available
from the British Library


This publication is printed on acid-free paper

Printed in Great Britain by
Biddles Ltd, King's Lynn, Norfolk

# Contents

# Plates

Maps and illustrations are reproduced by courtesy of John Hamilton for nos 1, 2, 13–15 and 17; Bedfordshire and Luton Archives and Records Services for nos 8–10, 18–23; and Bedford Borough Council for nos 5–7 and 11. The cover illustration and other photographs are the property of the author.

# Tables

# Acknowledgements

First must come Charlotte Bousfield herself, for it is her words describing the experience of eighteen years in her life, their joys and sadness, that form the body of this volume. Next, I would thank Guy and Marjorie Bousfield, who were aware of the value and interest of her diaries, and so saved them for posterity. Without the devotion and scholarship of John Hamilton who edited them, and of Hilary Hamilton who transcribed and typed the 375,000 words of the three volumes, they would have been visible only to a restricted audience.

For help in the presentation of this text, I would thank most of all Barbara Tearle, the Society's General Editor, for her huge commitment to the task of bringing order and consistency to my first efforts at abridging the text. She was as meticulous in her attention to detail as she was thoughtful in suggesting ways of approaching the diaries themselves. Barbara was also gentle but firm in her admonitions as to the need to proceed with a speed which was slightly less relaxed than that to which I had become accustomed.

I would also like to express my appreciation of the help of three people whose knowledge of the history of Bedford and the county is unparalleled: Patricia Bell, former Bedfordshire County Archivist and for some years Bedfordshire Historical Record Society's General Editor; James Collett-White, archivist of Southill Park, a member of staff at the Bedfordshire and Luton Archives and Record Service, and editor of the previous volume to this, no. 85; and Richard Wildman, well-known local author and archivist of Bedford Modern School.

Thanks to Jennie Clarke and the staff of the Cecil Higgins Art Gallery, Bedford, for their help in making available some of the illustrations, to David Stubbs, for preparing them and other images for publication, and to Margaret Evans for her work on the family trees; to Christopher Smart for his help in processing the images. Thanks are due also to the Revd Brian Trudgian, the minister of Southend Methodist Church.

Finally, thanks to the staff of the Bedfordshire and Luton Archives and Record Service, especially Trevor Cunnick, who are always expert and helpful.

# Abbreviations

| | |
|---|---|
| BA | Bachelor of Arts |
| BHRS | Bedfordshire Historical Record Society |
| BLARS | Bedfordshire and Luton Archives and Record Service |
| BR | Blue Ribbon |
| B Works | Britannia Iron Works |
| BWTA | British Women's Temperance Association |
| CEB | Charlotte Eliza Bousfield |
| CETS | Church of England Temperance Society |
| CEWU | Church of England Women's Union |
| COR | Crown Office Row, where Will had his chambers |
| GF | Greyfriars Blue Ribbon Room |
| L&NW | London and North Western Railway |
| LNWR | London and North Western Railway |
| LRCP | Licentiate of the Royal College of Physicians |
| MA | Master of Arts |
| M Hall | Memorial Hall, London |
| MM | Mothers' Meeting |
| M Meeting | Mothers' Meeting |
| MP | Member of Parliament |
| MRCS | Member of the Royal College of Surgeons |
| Mr FH | Frederick Howard |
| Mr JH | James Howard |
| OKR | Old Kent Road, Ted's home and surgery |
| PC | postcard |
| QC | Queen's Counsel |
| S Army | Salvation Army |
| WTAU | Women's Total Abstinence Union |

# Introduction

> If Oscar Wilde is to be believed, keeping a personal diary was a common activity among middle class women in the late nineteenth century, but the two he satirises so delightfully in *The Importance of being Earnest* are young and unmarried. Charlotte Bousfield was long married and not far off being a grandmother when she first took up her pen.

These words are appropriate, not only because they encapsulate what this volume is about, but also because they were written by John Hamilton, the great-grandson of Charlotte Bousfield, the diarist herself, as the introduction to his own transcript of her diaries.

Diaries were written and read long before the nineteenth century, and they come in many forms. The Paston letters are the earliest English example, dating from the fifteenth century. Although a collection of letters, rather than strictly a diary, they are similar to the Bousfield diaries in that they constitute a record of the events in the lives of a middle-class family, largely from the point of view of the woman who is in many ways at its centre, Margaret Paston. One of the fascinations of reading both of these accounts, so far apart in time, is the way in which the personality of the writer gradually emerges.

Another similarity they share is that the audience, the readership, is defined. The Paston letters are each addressed to one person. Charlotte's diaries begin in 1878 with the expression of her hope that they 'will be profitable to myself & perhaps interesting to my children'.[1] This seems to have been the case, as her entry for 26 February 1883 states that although she has considered giving it up 'my children seem to be so much interested in listening to some of the records of the past with which I occasionally amuse them that for their sakes more than by my own wish in the matter I will continue a remembrance of the chief events of our family life'.

And so she did, and the audience for whom she was writing would understand what she was saying. They would put faces to names, and call up contexts unconsciously and without effort in order to bring to the text a subtext of shared experience, and so to make full sense of it. It is the purpose of this introduction and of the notes (which are profuse) to attempt to achieve for the reader today something of the richness which Charlotte's diaries would have had for her own family. She would have been surprised to know that her words have reached a much wider audience than that which she envisaged. One wonders what opinion she would have had (and she would certainly have had one) about the web logs, or blogs, which are the twenty-first century's contribution to the concept of a diary?

It is with pleasure, therefore, that the Bedfordshire Historical Record Society (BHRS) is publishing the Bousfield diaries because they not only paint a vivid picture of the lives of a large family centred in Victorian Bedford, but they extend

---

[1] See Plate 2.

beyond both family and local history to document national and international events, covering the period between 1878 and 1896.

### Charlotte Collins and Edward Bousfield – their early lives

Charlotte Bousfield, the diarist, was born Charlotte Eliza Collins and married Edward Tenney Bousfield in 1853.[2] Charlotte herself came from a family whose lives were centred in a county much further west than Bedford. In the early years of the nineteenth century Charlotte's grandmother, Mrs Cox, a widow, was living with her only unmarried daughter, also named Charlotte, in Seaton, on the south coast of Devon.[3] Mrs Cox was a nonconformist and as the only place of worship in Seaton was the Anglican church, she attended the nearest nonconformist chapel which was in the nearby village of Beer. As she grew older she could no longer manage the walk, and offered her own home for worship, and then was instrumental in having a little chapel built for herself and her neighbours, applying to the local ministerial training college[4] for a preacher. As a result in 1823 Robert Collins, a young man of 21, was sent to visit Seaton every Sunday to take the services. Charlotte herself[5] writes:

> Both the work and the Widow's Daughter so interested him that the end of his Term of 5 years in college, during which he ministered in his frequent <u>turn</u> in the Widow's home as Preacher, [was] concluded by his marriage with her Daughter Charlotte E Cox.

The wedding took place in 1827 in Seaton church,[6] and soon afterwards Robert was moved to Braunton, a village on the north Devon coast near Barnstaple. Here the couple lived in the manse, and this is where Charlotte the diarist was born on 10 July 1828. Her early years were marked by the birth of her six siblings, and by the regular changes of home occasioned by her father's ministry in the Congregationalist church. They moved from Braunton to Hindon in Wiltshire (1830), to Newnham-on-Severn (c. 1835), then to Tetbury in Gloucestershire (1841), and on to Stockbridge in Hampshire in 1854. Here it was that her mother died in 1858. Charlotte reflects in the diaries that her mother's last words were 'my sins are forgiven; I'm going to glory'. In a letter written much later[7] she writes to a young relative: 'If by any chance you should go to or through Stockbridge in the little burying place of the Congregational Chapel [is] to be seen my dear mother's grave & headstone. My Father lived at Stockbridge at the dates on it, & I lost my Mother & one dear Sister (who are both buried there) during his residence in the last house on the right hand side, at the lower end of the village.'[8] She was to lose all but one of her remaining siblings by 1863, the last of them, her brother Alfred, dying some time before 1881.[9] In view of this history of early mortality in her family, it is not

---

2   See Plate 1 for Charlotte's portrait, painted by her daughter Hattie.
3   See family trees in Appendix 1.
4   The Axminster Nonconformist Academy.
5   in a paper written after the diaries entitled 'How My Parents Met'.
6   Before 1837, only Quakers and Jews were exempt from being married in the Anglican parish church.
7   to Violet, her grandson Alec's wife, undated but probably from December 1924.
8   See diary entry for 10 July 1879.
9   See diary entry for 1 October 1884.

surprising that Charlotte was always concerned about the health of her own husband and children.

Little is known of Charlotte's childhood, except that she was brought up in a strict nonconformist household, and remained throughout her life true to its principles, however difficult it might be. 'Am "I", as I am sure my children think me, narrow-minded, strait laced & puritanical?' she asks herself in the entry dated 18 January 1882. To which she answers: 'Or do I so love my Lord & Master as to desire in all I do to serve & please Him? I do trust the latter is the case.'

Certainly, as the oldest child, Charlotte would have had to start earning her living early in life in order to support her younger siblings. She began work aged 16 in 1844 in Buckingham as a governess, the only career open to a middle-class woman at this time. Two or three years later she moved further north to take up a post as a teacher in Newark, at a school known rather grandly as Mrs Bousfield's Ladies Seminary. Mrs Frances Bousfield, the proprietor of the school, and her husband William, both Methodists, were the parents of seven children, coincidentally the same number as the Collins children. The third of these was Edward Tenney Bousfield, Charlotte's future husband.

The years of Edward's childhood were ones of varied fortunes for the family. From 1832, his father, William, and William's elder brother Edward Little, were partners in the family's ironmonger's business, set up by their father, also an Edward.[10] Edward Little, however, was ambitious to make his mark in local politics, and the next years were to prove his political abilities. He became a councillor in 1836, and eventually in 1842 was elected mayor, Newark's first citizen.

But success in local politics was not mirrored in the business field, and three years later the family business failed, and was taken over by a local lawyer, a process which avoided formal bankruptcy proceedings. Edward Little, disgraced, then disappeared from Newark, and has not been traced. William, with seven children to maintain, the youngest only eight years old, managed to rent premises and carry on the family business.

The rapid rise and equally rapid fall of his uncle must have been a disturbing experience for the young Edward Tenney, but soon after this he met Charlotte Collins when she arrived in Newark to work for his mother. Charlotte was one year older than Edward, both of them in their early twenties. In 1853 they were married in the Congregational chapel in Tetbury where the bride's father was minister at the time, and then settled in Newark, where their first two children were born, William Robert, named after his grandfathers and known as Will, in 1854, and Edward Collins, named after his father and mother, known as Ted or Eddie, in 1855, and referred to as such here in order to distinguish him from his father, Edward.

Charlotte's husband not only set up a new home in Newark at this time, but also a business, of which the only record located is of its termination, which took place on the 11 March 1857. The firm was named in the *London Gazette* as Nicholson and Bousfield, and its business as 'iron founders, engineers, and agricultural implement manufacturers'.[11] Edward's partner was William Neuzam Nicholson, whose father was also the owner of an iron foundry, and a more successful one than the Bous-

---

[10] See family tree in Appendix 1.
[11] *London Gazette*, 1 May 1857.

field's. The Nicholsons were beginning to make a reputation for themselves, winning prizes for their products and showing them at the Great Exhibition of 1851.[12]

The interpretation of these events is problematical. Perhaps Edward wanted to restore his family's reputation, and to start a new business incorporating the Bousfield name. In any case it failed, and in 1856 the family moved to Sticklepath, a village on the northern edge of Dartmoor. It seems a strange move, because the Bousfields had no connections in the west country (though of course Charlotte had). It was in this small village that once again Edward attempted unsuccessfully to set himself up in business: after two years he lost money, gave it up and sought employment elsewhere. Some twenty years later, after they had settled in Bedford, Charlotte reflected that she 'could write quite a history of how [Edward] came here a young man ... after having been made willing to become a servant instead of a Master, by his losses as one in the two short years preceding our coming to Bedford from Sticklepath'.[13] And so, with the success of his application to join a well established agricultural machinery manufacturing company in Bedford, he became, reluctantly, 'a servant instead of a Master'. The business Edward joined was known as J. & F. Howard Ltd.

The family, with their third son, John Ebenezer, just one month old, moved to Bedford in September 1858, and were to stay in the town for 45 years.

*The Bousfields' Bedford*

In the 1850s, when the Bousfields settled there, Bedford was a small rural market town, with a population of some 12,000.[14] Perhaps it reminded them of Newark, a market town of similar size, also centred around a medieval castle and straddling a river. In Bedford, there was hardly a trace of the industrialisation which was already far advanced in other towns and cities. Industrialisation in the nineteenth century involved both the use of a centralised production system using steam driven machines in factories to produce goods with maximum efficiency; and also effective transport facilities to move coal to the sites of production and to take the finished products to their markets. Bedford had neither of these, though both were present in an embryonic form.

The introduction of industrialisation in Bedford is largely the contribution of the imaginative and ambitious Howard family. The business which Edward joined in 1858 was founded by John Howard, 'old Mr Howard' as Charlotte refers to him in the diaries. Howard was schooled in Bedford, then apprenticed as an ironmonger, and in 1835 set up a shop at 35 High Street, with an iron founding workshop behind it, in what in 2007 is used as a car park. Agricultural implements soon became an important part of their trade. John's eldest son James joined the business and developed an interest in designing improved ploughs. In 1850, James' youngest brother Frederick also joined the business and the two brothers took it over from their father (hence, J. & F. Howard Ltd).

Progress at Howard's was rapid, for the middle years of the century were a golden age for farming in Britain. The rapid rise in population and its increasing concentra-

[12] This was nothing compared with the reputation of William Nicholson's son and grandson, who were the artists Sir William and Ben Nicholson.
[13] See diary entry for 7 October 1879.
[14] Pictured on the dust cover.

tion in urban centres resulted in growing demand for food and particularly grain. The rural economy in Bedfordshire was basically an arable one, and the workshop behind the High Street shop was kept busy supplying the increasing demand for agricultural implements to maximise the productivity of the land and its tillers. First came ploughs. The 'Howard plough' had become well-known, and in 1851 it won a prize at the Great Exhibition, but soon a number of new implements were developed: hoes and harrows, mowing machines, horse drawn rakes, seed drills.

The workshop was now no longer large enough to enable the level of production to match that of demand and in 1856 work began on the construction of a new factory, the Britannia Iron Works, which was completed in 1859.[15] It was the pride of Victorian Bedford, and represents a triumphant example of the entrepreneurial instinct. Its presence marked the arrival of industry to the town, and it soon acquired national and international renown, visited by the Italian Nationalist leader Garibaldi in 1864, and by a Japanese Prince (Satsuma) in the late 1860s, both of whom were interested in modernising their respective countries.

What gave it this reputation? The factory was remarkable for the use it made of what are now known as machine tools – a journal in 1860 commented on the 'extent to which they [Howard's] carry out moulding by machinery ... a visit to the Howard factory would amply repay those interested in the extensive production of castings of iron of one particular pattern'.[16] The Britannia Iron Works was one of the largest factories of its kind in the world, covering some 20 acres. Its growth continued throughout the 1870s, and by 1881 it employed 650 men and apprentices[17] and produced some 10,000 finished implements a year, which were exported from Bedford nationally and internationally.

Such an enormous undertaking required an efficient system of rail transport to transport heavy and bulky goods, bringing in coal and iron ore for the foundry and taking the finished products for delivery. Bedford had come late to this aspect of industrialisation, as it had to the factory system. The first railway line was opened by the London and North Western Railway (LNWR) in 1846. It ran from St John's station, south of the river, to Bletchley – very limited in its direct coverage.[18] It took eleven years before the next development occurred, the Midland Railway line from Bedford to Hitchin, whence the trains would join the Great Northern Line to London. Bedford's Midland Station was opened in 1859,[19] and the Midland's direct line to London via Luton was finally completed in 1868, along with the magnificent St Pancras Station.[20]

The opening of the Britannia Iron Works in 1859 occurred just after the line to Hitchin had become available. The factory had its own internal railway and goods station, with connections to the Midland and to the LNWR line. The lithograph of the Britannia works from the north side (Plate 11) shows this clearly, together with the barges on the River Ouse, which could transport materials to and from places as far downstream as the port of Kings Lynn.

---

[15]  See Plate 11.

[16]  *The Engineer*, 20 July 1860, and quoted in Hamilton, *Glad for God*, p. 162.

[17]  The figures are those given by Frederick Howard which appear in the census of 1881.

[18]  See Plates 18 and 20.

[19]  See Plates 19 and 20.

[20]  See F.G. Cockman, *The Railway Age in Bedfordshire*, BHRS vol. 53 (Bedford: The Society, 1974).

One important result of the new opportunities for employment provided by the Iron Works was an increase in the population, as individuals and families moved to Bedford, and particularly to the areas south of the river to live close to the works. This continued until the late 1870s as the factory steadily expanded its floor space and the number of its employees. Table 1, below, shows the numerical size of, and the percentage increase in, the population of Bedford itself and of the parish of St Mary's, one of the five within the town, in which the Iron Works was situated. The increase in the population of both is very rapid, but this is particularly pronounced in St Mary's, which saw a three-fold increase between 1851 and 1891, a much more rapid increase than that of the population of the nation as a whole, which increased by a factor of less than two in this period.

**Table 1.** Population of Bedford and the parish of St Mary's Bedford, 1851 to 1901

| Year | Bedford | % increase | Decade | St Mary's | % increase | Decade |
|------|---------|------------|--------|-----------|------------|--------|
| 1851 | 11,693  |            |        | 1670      |            |        |
| 1861 | 13,413  | 14.7       | 1851–60 | 1869     | 11.9       | 1851–60 |
| 1871 | 16,850  | 25.6       | 1861–70 | 2574     | 37.7       | 1861–70 |
| 1881 | 19,533  | 15.9       | 1871–80 | 3565     | 38.5       | 1871–80 |
| 1891 | 28,023  | 43.5       | 1881–90 | 4878     | 36.8       | 1881–90 |
| 1901 | 35,144  | 25.4       | 1891–1900 | 5615   | 15.1       | 1891–1900 |

Who were these new employees? A survey of the census returns for St Mary's in 1881 shows that only 27% of Howard's employees were born in Bedford. Of the remaining 73%, 28% moved into the town from the county, and the remaining 45% were born out of county. With a total workforce of 650 in 1881, this suggests that some 475 men (i.e. 73% of the total), most of them skilled engineers, had moved to Bedford to work at the Iron Works. These men with their families would certainly amount to several thousands of new residents, and new houses for them sprang up near to the factory, such as the patriotically named Britannia and Victoria Roads.

Table 2, below, reveals that it was the lowest level of workers, the unskilled labourers, who formed the largest category (30.8 % of the total workforce). Of these, almost half (44%) had been born in Bedford itself. The remaining categories, consisting of the more highly skilled workmen, were all recruited largely from outside the town, and in the case of the boiler makers, all were born outside the county itself. There is a strong correlation between the level of skill of each employee and the distance between the birthplace and the Iron Works.

It was in the decade of the 1870s that agriculture in the county together with the fortunes of Howard's business reached the peak of their success, both of them marked very strongly in 1874 by two significant events in Bedford. The first was the opening in April of the new much larger Corn Exchange on the north side of St Paul's Square, a more fitting and practical setting for the buying and selling of grain, and an excellent venue for public meetings and concerts, as it still is.[21] It replaced

---

[21] Pictured on the dust cover.

its much smaller predecessor which then became known as the Floral Hall, and was demolished in 1904.[22]

**Table 2.** Employees of Howard's Britannia Iron Works living in the parish of St Mary's Bedford in 1881

| Category | Number | Percentage of total | Place of birth as a percentage for each category of worker | | |
| | | | Bedford | Beds | Out of county |
| --- | --- | --- | --- | --- | --- |
| Labourer | 52 | 30.8 | 44 | 42 | 14 |
| (Engine) fitter | 40 | 23.7 | 25 | 18 | 57 |
| (Black)smith | 18 | 10.7 | 22 | 28 | 50 |
| Iron moulder | 10 | 5.9 | 40 | 10 | 50 |
| Clerk (inc. apprentices) | 6 | 3.6 | 34 | 16 | 50 |
| Boiler maker | 6 | 3.6 | 0 | 0 | 100 |
| Others | 37 | 21.7 | 15 | 30 | 55 |
| Total | 169 | 100.0 | N/A | N/A | N/A |

Figures extracted from the census of 1881, Bedford St Mary's parish. The sample comprises all 169 men in this parish who are identified in the census as employed by Howard's. 'Others' contains the remaining job categories in which there were fewer than six people: they were skilled workers such as engine drivers – and also Edward and John Bousfield. The table shows: in columns 2 and 3 the number and percentage of employees in each job category; and in columns 4 to 6 the percentage in each job category who were Bedford-born or in-migrants from elsewhere in Bedfordshire or out of county.

The second event that summer was the staging of the Royal Show, held every year in a different location by the Royal Agricultural Society (RAS), as a showcase for agricultural products, implements as well as livestock. Founded in 1838, the RAS played a leading role in the development of British agriculture and of a vibrant rural economy through the dissemination of a scientific approach and the promotion of new ideas. The view of Bedford printed in the *Illustrated London News* of 11 July 1874, and chosen as the dustcover for this volume, demonstrates overtly the confidence and pride of the town and covertly the prominence of the Britannia Iron Works nationally in producing innovative agricultural implements and machinery.

Only four years later saw the beginning of the prolonged period of agricultural depression which ended the 'Golden Years of Farming' as they are sometimes known. The problem was that the price of corn was being undercut over much of Europe by cheap grain flooding the market from the USA, the product of the opening up of the fertile prairies by the Union Pacific Railway, which was completed in 1869, connecting the eastern and western seaboards. In 1877, before the effects had made themselves felt, the price of corn on the English markets was 56s per quarter. From then on it dropped steadily until in 1886 it was selling at 31s per quarter, and declined even further until in 1893 it reached a trough of 26s. Some arable farmers converted land to pasture: most were forced to reduce their costs to take account

---

[22] See Plate 10.

of the lower income they were receiving. This meant both cutting the wages of their agricultural labourers, and reducing the number of those employed. Some went bankrupt, or simply gave up farming.[23]

As a result, many of the 'ag. labs' lost their tied cottages as well as their jobs, and moved into towns seeking work there as general labourers and swelling the urban proletariat. Businesses like Howard's suffered as farmers reduced their expenditure on new implements and machines. Charlotte comments on this in 1884: 'Farming was never so un-remunerative, & the free trade which has over stocked the corn market seems not an unmitigated blessing since with cheapness of many articles of food there is great scarcity of work both in fields & Factories.'[24] Farming began to recover in the mid-1890s, but never reached the success it had enjoyed in the mid-Victorian years.

Another important development in the history of Bedford in the 1880s also involved new families attracted to live in the town, English families who had spent their working lives abroad, in India particularly, as civil servants or in the army. This migration had already started earlier, but it was given a great boost when the Harpur Trust charity changed its rules in 1873 to allow families from abroad to educate their sons and daughters at a heavily subsidised rate, even if neither they nor their parents had been born in the town. Residents objected, but the 'squatters' (as some derisively called them) came and stayed. They settled predominantly in three areas north of the river: the Waterloo area on the north bank of the river, close to the newly improved Embankment; the large houses on either side of Kimbolton Road, north of the Union workhouse, on the northern edge of the town; and the area east of the railway line and north of Bromham Road, known as 'the poets'. Each family employed several servants, and the influx of both classes is demonstrated in Table 1. The population of Bedford rose by a massive 43.5% between 1881 and 1891.

The squatters brought with them a whiff of the exotic. 'You invited friends to "tiffin" rather than to lunch; you said you were going down to "the bazaar" when you were going shopping in the High Street.'[25] The raffish dandy made his appearance:

> In Bedford, you're aware, for *Dandies such as I!*
> The proper thing is, every day, to toddle up the High –
> Sundays may do for Cads, but not for me or you,
> So titivated in our best, we show them "who is who",
> Walking up the High, Walking up the High,
> Is *the* thing every afternoon, for Dandies such as I!!![26]

The two groups were very different. The Anglo-Indians were middle- or upper middle-class Anglicans, living north of the river, while the Britannia's employees were largely working class, with a small number of professionals, such as Edward Bousfield, many living south of the river. The Anglo-Indians were a visible part of Bedford life, but the Bousfields never mention them, even though their grandson

[23] See James Collett-White, *Bedfordshire in the 1880s* (Bedford: BLARS, 2006).
[24] See diary entry for 25 November 1884.
[25] Patricia Bell, 'Aspects of Anglo-Indian Bedford', in *Worthington George Smith and Other Studies*, BHRS vol. 57 (Bedford: The Society, 1978), p. 191.
[26] Ibid., p. 182. See Plate 8, a view looking north from the bridge.

George attended Bedford School in the 1890s, where the vast majority of the squatters' sons were educated.

The spirit of the 1880s was encapsulated in the person of Joshua Hawkins. He was himself a squatter (though not an Anglo-Indian) in that he came to Bedford (in 1879) in order to educate his sons at Bedford School. Up to this point he had been a Methodist minister, but in Bedford until his death in 1892 he gave up this part of his earlier life and identified himself with the town. He became co-proprietor (with Edwin Ransom) of the *Bedfordshire Times and Independent* and was an outstanding Mayor, serving five terms in that office between 1883 and 1890. He was a speculative builder, responsible for many of the large villas in Lansdowne, Dynevor and Linden roads. Hawkins' greatest achievement was to promote Bedford, to its own citizens, as much as to others outside the town. In 1883 the new bridge over the river was opened, to extend Prebend Street over the river, easing the pressure of traffic over the town bridge, which increased as Southend developed. In 1888, another important development was the opening of Bedford Park in the north of the town, described at the time as 'Bedford's Bois de Boulogne', and the impressive De Parys Avenue leading up to its main entrance gates as 'Bedford's Champs Elysees'.

The *Bedfordshire Times* office published a pamphlet, *Bedford in 1888*, to mark its opening by the Marquess of Tavistock. It is euphoric in its tone and bursting with energy and confidence:

> High Street affords clear evidence of the giant-like strides of trade and enterprise in Bedford. In the principal streets of the town it may almost be said that a shop is not to be got for love or money. The handsome new business premises that are constantly erected, the palatial shop fronts that are ever being inserted ... together with the stagnation in the Bankruptcy Court so far as Bedford is concerned, all betoken great commercial activity.[27]

Charlotte's diaries cover much the same period as that of Hawkins' residence in Bedford. She met him and comments favourably on him,[28] but the picture she paints of the plight of the underclass, the alcoholics and the vagrants in the casual wards of the workhouse, is completely the reverse of Hawkins' promotion of the buoyant state of Bedford's commercial and business life. So is the situation in the countryside, suffering from the baneful effects of the depression in agriculture – poverty, unemployment and, indeed, bankruptcy. Both accounts are true, but both are partial. Hawkins' picture is the more visible: Charlotte's the more grounded in experience, and the more fundamentally significant.

*The family in Bedford before the beginning of the diaries, 1858–1878*
On their arrival in Bedford in September 1858 the Bousfields lived at 43 Cauldwell Street, on the south side of the river, convenient both for the town centre, which was just north of the bridge, and for the Britannia Iron Works, where Edward was employed.[29] The first of their daughters, named Charlotte after her mother and known as 'Lottie', was born here. Five doors away, at no. 53, lived another family with growing children and a father employed by Howard's: these were the Mortons,

27  Ibid., p. 187.
28  See diary entry for 24 April 1880.
29  See map on Plate 23.

who were to remain close friends of the Bousfields for years to come: one of the Mortons' sons some 30 years later was to marry Lottie.

In 1863, the Bousfield family moved to the new house which was to be their home throughout their time in Bedford. Edward had bought several plots of land from the estate 'formerly occupied by the County Asylum'[30] which was closed in 1860,[31] and whose land became the first building estate south of the river. As Charlotte put it in her diary entry for 12 September 1883:

Twenty years ago this very month this house was finished, & we took possession of it as our own, calling it 'Alpha Villa', because [it was] the very first house built in a neighbourhood newly divided into building sites, most of which are now covered by streets of houses, inhabited probably by more than 800 people.

The photograph in Plate 3 shows the house today. It was large, appropriate to the size of the family.[32] In 1871, it housed no less than twelve people. Eight were family – Edward and Charlotte; the three sons, of whom the two younger ones were described as scholars. Will (aged 17) was described as an apprentice agricultural engineer – he had left Bedford Modern School, 'with every first prize in the Modern School except that for writing',[33] and he was working for Howard's until he won a scholarship to Caius College Cambridge in the following year. By 1871, there were three daughters: Charlotte, known as Lottie; Harriet Mary known as Hattie, born in 1865; and the youngest child, Florence Jane, known as Edris, born in 1869, who died at the age of three in 1872. In addition, there was one boarder, sixteen-year-old Lee Osborn, born in Bradford, whose occupation was described in the same terms as Will's. Three young women (all aged 20) served the household; one as a dressmaker, a second as cook and kitchen maid and the third as housemaid. All of them were born in villages within ten miles of Bedford. Finally, the Bousfields employed a man who acted as gardener, coachman and odd job man, who lived out (Howcutt is the first of these mentioned by name in the diaries). Edward's status had gone up, or perhaps he had been promoted, as he now describes himself as 'engineer, manager of iron-works', whereas in 1861 his occupation was simply stated as 'mechanical engineer'.

It was a busy and a lively household, but Charlotte resolved to take on an extra responsibility: she and Edward undertook to provide for the religious needs of the growing population of what was becoming a new suburb. Charlotte was mindful of what her grandmother had done in Seaton fifty years earlier, in holding services in her own house, an action which must have resonated with her, in that it had led to the marriage of her own mother and father. And so, in the late 1860s, she and Edward began to do the same.

Perhaps it was the death of Edris in 1872[34] which inspired them to take the next step – to build a church. Trustees were appointed, and in 1873 Edward sold them some of the land which he had bought on the other side of Offa Road from Alpha

---

[30] *Bedfordshire Times and Independent*, 3 June 1873.
[31] Its 422 patients were moved to the newly built Three Counties Asylum at Arlesey.
[32] See family trees in Appendix 1.
[33] See diary entry for 1 July 1880.
[34] See Plate 16.

Villa. The building was begun in May, and with Edward's financial help completed within the space of six months and opened on 12 November 1873.[35]

The project drew in family members as well as friends and business associates. John Howard was chairman of the trustees, Edward's sister, Sarah Jane Barker (aunt Jenny), laid one of the foundation stones, and the tower was dedicated to John Moore, the recently deceased husband of another of Edward's sisters, Frances Mary (aunt Fanny). It was dedicated as the Southend Wesleyan Chapel, and so gave its name to the new suburb, which was, as the *Bedfordshire Times and Independent* put it, 'a more agreeable name than "The Old Asylum Ground" hitherto in vogue'.[36] Charlotte referred to it fondly many times throughout her diaries as 'our little chapel'. It formed a focus in her life, involved the whole family, and is still today an active place of worship.[37]

When the diaries begin, five years later, they open not in Bedford, but at the resort of Ventnor in the Isle of Wight, in the middle of a family gathering to celebrate Charlotte's and Edward's Silver Wedding in March 1878. Ventnor was well known to the family, and well loved, the change of scene and climate usually proving beneficial to their health. By this time the children were often living away from home.

Of the five, Will is 24. He has had a distinguished academic record at Cambridge, where he read mathematics, and graduated in 1876 as sixteenth Wrangler (that is, sixteenth in rank order out of all the mathematics undergraduates in his year). He was awarded a scholarship to work for Joseph Whitworth's engineering works in Manchester, and later lectured in Mathematics and Engineering at University College, Bristol, but decided to take up the law as a career, and is living away from home in Clifton, Bristol, where he is tutoring the son of a retired army officer (Captain Alcock) while reading for his law examinations. His engineering background, and his father's experience of many patent applications, were useful ones for a barrister who would specialise in patent law, though he may not have anticipated this at the time.

Ted, aged 23, is living at home, and commuting to London where he is studying medicine, having spent some time as assistant to a Bedford doctor, James Coombs.[38]

John, the youngest of the three boys, aged 20, is staying with the Mortons in Chelmsford. Alfred Morton is now a partner in the firm of Coleman and Morton, so it is likely that John was working for him, perhaps as an apprentice.

Lottie, the elder of the two girls, is seventeen, and is spending time with her brother Will in Clifton.

The youngest is Hattie, a thirteen-year-old school girl in Bedford.

Charlotte is concerned about the love affairs which the two elder boys have recently begun. Will's girl friend and later wife was Florence Kelly, the daughter of a wealthy advertising agent and parliamentary printer, with homes on the Isle of Wight (Clarendon Lodge, Shanklin) as well as in Maida Vale in London. The first contact between the families was a chance meeting of Florence's father and Will's

---

[35] See Plate 4 and map on Plate 23.
[36] *Bedfordshire Times and Independent*, 3 June 1873.
[37] See Plate 4.
[38] Dr Coombs (1813–1905) MD, alderman and Mayor of Bedford 1871, 1889 and 1891.

mother on the 'tramway car' from Ryde Pier.[39] Will and Florence were married in 1879. Ted's girl friend, who also became his wife, was Clara Henman, who lived with her widowed mother in Bromham, then a village, now a suburb, north of Bedford. They met through attending services at the St Paul's chapel in Bedford (Harpur Street),[40] and were married in 1882.

### Edward Bousfield

The life of Charlotte's husband Edward certainly does not take centre stage in her diaries, yet in his career he made an important contribution both locally and nationally to the prosperity of Bedford's first and major industrial plant through his hard work and inventive genius.

The major factor in the success of Howard's was the innovative nature of its products, and Edward's contribution to the flow of inventions was very significant. Between 1861, when his name first appears on a patent application, and 1889, when James Howard died, 74 patents had Edward's name on them, and from then until 1898, when he took out his last patent, 14 out of the 21 were in his name alone.

The range of implements in whose development he played a part is very wide. It includes horse-drawn ploughs, rakes, hoes and harrows; reaping and mowing machines; steam boilers, including 'Howard's Safety Boiler'; a steam-driven tractor, 'Howard's Farmer's Engine', and steam ploughs, i.e. ploughs drawn by two steam engines, one at each side of the field. Edward's name is on the patent application for this important invention, for which he probably takes the credit. When the diaries begin, in 1878, Edward was occupied with the task of designing a sheaf-binding reaper, for harvesting corn and hay and binding the sheaves and this continued until 1884. Other manufacturers were also producing reapers, and the Royal Agricultural Society decided to hold trials at the Royal Show held in 1884 at Shrewsbury. Edward was bitterly disappointed that his reaper only came second. Charlotte reports her husband's despair and his decision to retire from Howard's in the following year, in her diary for 20 October 1884, where he also hints at 'half formed plans' for his retirement, which must allude to his undertaking training for the Bar, in which he succeeded in 1887.[41]

Edward's plans were not, however, fully realised. He did become a barrister, but seems only to have had two briefs, and his retirement from Howard's did not take place until 1898, though he worked part-time as a consultant for a while.[42] He clearly loved mechanical engineering more than anything else, and turned to new challenges in this field in the 1890s, when he became interested in 'explosion engines' as they were known – i.e. internal combustion engines. What made him disillusioned was not simply the disappointment of the trials; it was his belief that his work was not properly appreciated by the Howard brothers[43] – he chafed at being an employee. The depression in agriculture must also have been worrying: Howard's were having to dismiss employees, or put them on short time.[44] Edward's years at

---

[39] See diary entry for 23 October 1878.
[40] See Plate 5.
[41] See diary entries for 24 October and 5 November 1887.
[42] See diary entry for 6 March 1889.
[43] See diary entry for 7 October 1879.
[44] See diary entry for 25 November 1884.

the Britannia Ironworks were its golden years, and he may well have recognised that they were coming to an end. All that is left of it now is the archway, pictured in Plate 12.

*The Diaries*

Charlotte Bousfield's diaries, reflective, lively and personal, describe the lives of the members of her middle-class family, based in Victorian Bedford. The study of the diaries straddles both family and local history: though the close focus is on the family, the social and political background is always present. There are a number of major themes which it is appropriate to highlight in this introduction to their vivid portrayal by Charlotte herself.

The first is the family's religious life. The Bousfields' fervent Methodism must have found the religious climate in the town congenial. Bedford itself was after all 'Bunyan's Town', and not far from Huntingdon, the birth-place of Oliver Cromwell. The Ecclesiastical Census of 1851 provides the best evidence for this, even though it records the situation some years earlier than the Bousfields' arrival in the town. It shows that 40.5% of the population of England and Wales attended a religious service on that day (Bedford registered slightly more, 43%). Of those who attended, just over 50% nationally were Anglicans (Bedford's Anglican congregations were much less numerous – only 33% of the total). In the national census Methodism was by far the strongest of the nonconformist denominations, 18% of the total; in Bedford it was the Congregationalists who were the strongest of the dissenting groups, numbering 26%, the Methodist following on with 19% of the total.[45]

The Bousfields' religious activities were naturally centred on their own church, just over the road, but they attended most of the other Methodist chapels in the town, and Edward was an active lay preacher, travelling to many local villages. Charlotte, assisted by her daughters when they were at home, was involved in a range of activities, among them the Sunday School and Mothers' meetings, and a variety of fund-raising projects.

It was a blow to her in 1879, therefore, when her work for Southend was criti-cised as being too interfering – 'we took too much upon us' as she paraphrases the criticisms of some of the congregation.[46] She was forced to accept that 'we may never again take an active part in managing its affairs'. It was not easy for her to withdraw completely, and in January 1881 she got herself involved in attempting to settle a seating dispute at Southend.[47] By this time, Edward had taken on admin-istrative responsibility for the local Methodist churches, as Circuit Steward, and in the following month Charlotte became involved again in stirring up trouble in a meeting to discuss raising funds for the circuit, which appears to have embarrassed her husband and to have rumbled on through the summer.[48] Charlotte was not able to devote herself to the cause which was so dear to her heart.

---

45 These figures are taken from D.W. Bushby, *Elementary Education in Bedford, 1868–1903* and *The Ecclesiastical Census, Bedfordshire, March 1851*, BHRS vol. 54 (Bedford: The Society, 1975) and Joyce Godber, *The Story of Bedford* (Luton: White Crescent Press Ltd, 1978).
46 See diary entry for 22 June 1879.
47 See diary entry for 13 January 1881.
48 See diary entry for 20 February 1881.

She was further disappointed when in the following year John followed his two elder brothers in moving to London to work. She writes on 1 July 1882 'To-day another has flown our home nest. I had hoped we might have had one Son living in Bedford who could have been a comfort near to us ... in years to come.' Her diary entry for 28 September 1882 reveals her despondency:

Of late I have not felt much inclined for writing in my Diary. Amidst much to be thankful for as ever, many of the circumstances surrounding the daily routine have not been joyous & I have often a feeling of depression amounting to sadness, the cause doubtless partly in myself.

But, at this low point in her life, at the age of 54, Charlotte was about to embark upon a cause which would dominate her life and fully occupy her time and energies for years to come – the temperance movement, the second of the major themes. In her diary for 7 October 1882 she writes somewhat tentatively: 'I do not remember that I have written of the fact that some weeks since I allowed my name to be put on the Committee of the Mission of the "Blue Ribbon Army" which has as yet been little more than talked about in Bedford.'

There is no doubt that alcoholism (or intemperance as it was called at the time) was a serious social problem. In the 1880s, when Charlotte joined the Blue Ribbon army, the average working-class family spent about a quarter of their total income on alcohol, and there were frequently voiced fears that many were 'drinking themselves to death'.

But the origins of the temperance movement in England date back some fifty years earlier to the 1830s, when intemperance began to be seen as a problem, increasingly evident with the spread of industrialisation, where factory owners demanded punctual, alert and efficient workers. The temperance movement first appears in the northern industrial towns, introduced by middle-class men who saw drunkenness not as a disease, but as caused by moral weakness. Their aim was to curb widespread drunkenness in working-class men; not to cure drunkards, which they believed to be impossible, but to control drinking. Many working-class men believed that the leaders were hypocritical, as heavy drinking was often equally a part of the lives of their middle-class brothers. The view began to spread, particularly among working-class political groups, that the real problems that were the cause of alcohol abuse were social ones. In contrast to the middle-class explanation, they believed that it was problems such as poverty, bad sanitation and housing conditions that caused the misery from which alcohol provided a temporary escape, and that must be addressed first.

Another interpretation of the most appropriate solution to the problems was introduced by Joseph Livesey, a working-class cheese seller from Preston, in the later 1830s. He believed that drinking in moderation, as supported by society in general, and by the medical profession in particular, actually increased the incidence of drunkenness. Only total abstinence was acceptable, and his followers were called upon to sign a pledge promising to abstain from all alcoholic beverages. Since its foundation in 1935 the work of Alcoholics Anonymous has always taken this line: 'all available ... testimony indicates that alcoholism ... cannot be cured in the ordinary sense of the term, but that it can be arrested through total abstinence from alcohol in any form'.[49] The story has it that it was one of Livesey's followers who coined one of the most famous words to be connected with the temperance movement. A reformed drinker, he was one day fervently advocating total abstinence when he is said to have stuttered over the word 'total'. The result 't-t-t-total' was picked up by Livesey and very soon came into the language as the word 'teetotal'.

The third approach to the problem was that of prohibition. Copying activity in the USA, British temperance advocates founded the United Kingdom Alliance in 1853, pledging to work through Parliament to outlaw liquor in England – shades of the America of the 1920s and 1930s. The leader of the group, which thought of itself as a political party, was Sir Wilfrid Lawson, who introduced the first of his Permissive Bills in 1864. This was intended to introduce what is known as a 'local veto'. Its principle was to give to the local electors in small areas such as the parish in rural districts, or small boroughs, the power to control the liquor traffic in their areas, though this was never passed into law.

Most of Charlotte's work in the temperance movement falls within the second of these three approaches. In 1882 her introduction to the movement was through the Blue Ribbon Army, an organisation which had been founded in the USA by an immigrant Irishman, Francis Murphy, and whose message was that of total abstinence, which it combined with evangelical preaching and singing, an approach known as Gospel Temperance. Murphy arrived from the States in 1881 to introduce it to the UK. Working initially in northern England, he went on to campaign in Manchester, Dublin and Norwich as well as undertaking a lecture tour through Scotland before returning to the USA. The (in)famous poet William McGonagall heard him in Dundee, and lauded his campaign, as follows:

*A Tribute to Mr Murphy and The Blue Ribbon Army*

ALL hail to Mr Murphy, he is a hero brave,
That has crossed the mighty Atlantic wave,
For what purpose let me pause and think –
I answer, to warn the people not to taste strong drink.

And, I'm sure, if they take his advice, they never will rue
The day they joined the Blue Ribbon Army in the year 1882;
And I hope to their colours they will always prove true,
And shout, Hurrah ! for Mr Murphy and the Ribbon of Blue.[50]

Charlotte's diary entry reports on 14 November 1882 that she took Mr McGonagall's advice and with it the pledge. The words she would have said, those of the Blue Ribbon pledge, were:

With charity to all and malice toward none, I promise by divine help to abstain from all intoxicating liquors and beverages, and to discountenance their use by others. The Lord help me to keep this pledge, for Jesus' sake.[51]

---

[49] Alcoholics Anonymous General Service Conference-approved literature: *The Twelve Steps of AA*.

[50] McGonagall in his Reminiscences describes an entertainment he provided in a public house in Dundee in the holiday week after New Year's Day 1882, while the Blue Ribbon army were based in the town. During the course of this he provided 'a good recitation' in which it is likely that this poem received its first performance. It is included in his first volume of collected verse, *Poetic Gems* (1890).

[51] Quoted in Lilian Lewis Shiman, *Crusade against Drink in Victorian England* (Basingstoke: Macmillan, 1988), p. 116.

The blue ribbons which signified having taken this pledge were pinned on to the dress or coat, as poppies are for Remembrance Sunday.[52] The significance of the symbol was a biblical one. In the Book of Numbers, God exhorts Moses to persuade the children of Israel to 'put upon the fringe of the borders [of their garments] a ribband of blue ... that ye remember all the commandments of the Lord ... and that ye seek not only after your own heart ... after which you used to go whoring [but] that ye be holy unto your God'.[53]

In September 1883 Charlotte joined another temperance organisation, one specifically focused on the problems for women which were posed by alcoholism – the British Women's Temperance Association (BWTA). This was also founded in the USA, and first appeared in England in 1876. Its purpose was specifically to help women fight the evils of drink and encourage their children to abstain. It was politically active and lobbied politicians and submitted petitions. Charlotte was instrumental in forming a branch in Bedford. She continued to be involved with both these organisations, though more closely with the BWTA, as she herself chronicles. She spent many days travelling the country (York, Liverpool, Nottingham, Gloucester etc.) attending meetings and speaking.

Charlotte's most demanding undertaking, however, was the establishing in London of a home for inebriate women, which opened in 1886. At the time, there were very few of these in existence, particularly for women, and Charlotte gave herself heart and soul to the task of attempting to cure the women, mostly middle-class, like herself. For three months, indeed, she ran the home herself. It must have been an eye-opening experience for her to live with chronic alcoholism, such as she saw there, with the patients' desperate and degrading attempts to smuggle drink in. The plight of middle-class women was in some ways worse than that of working-class women, for they had to keep up appearances, and not let their addiction show if possible. Nor were there any easy excuses for their condition – they were not poor, they did not live in cold, cramped or uncomfortable homes. There were other reasons, of course – a loveless marriage, boredom, lack of a fulfilling life, but these were not topics which ladies such as these would be able to discuss. Perhaps they may have been able to talk about it to each other and to Charlotte while they were patients, and this may have helped some of them. She showed them compassion and attempted to understand the reason for their sad state.[54] In 1890 her handling of an incident at the home led to criticism of her, and she resigned. This seems, at the least, a most ungrateful attitude on the part of the other members of the committee in view of the great commitment both she and Ted had made to the welfare of the patients over the previous four years.

Three years later, the BWTA split when a radical new President, influenced by developments in the USA, persuaded members to change the Association's policy, by including a raft of other social and political issues in its work, including women's suffrage. Charlotte and other members left to form a new grouping, the Women's Total Abstinence Union (WTAU).

All of this work was related to the total abstinence aspect of temperance, but

---

[52] See diary entry for 26 February 1883.
[53] Numbers xv 37–40.
[54] See diary entry for 6 September 1886.

Charlotte also became involved with the third approach, that of prohibition, and the control of supply of alcohol. The affair of the Southend Hotel in 1886 is an example. With the wife of the Mayor of Bedford, Mrs Ransom, she was successful in taking out a summons against the landlord of a local public house, the Southend Hotel, for selling liquor out of hours. This resulted in a fine and the endorsement of his licence, but unfortunately Charlotte wrote a letter to the local press suggesting that the defending solicitor, who happened to be a Methodist himself, had been acting unworthily and had been serving not God but mammon. The diary entries for 4 and 7 September, 29 October, 22 November and 7 December 1886 record the whole saga. In the following year, Charlotte also began to take part in the Brewsters' Sessions, in opposing the extension of licences and the granting of new ones.[55]

A late example of Charlotte's concern for the underclass in Victorian society is the part she played in the reform of the corrupt management of Bedford workhouse. The last few pages of her diary record this, starting with the entry for 19 December 1894.

Charlotte Bousfield's diaries deal with a variety of themes in addition to the principal ones of religion and temperance (summarised above), and reveal many facets of life in the late Victorian period. Some of these are surprising, for example, the efficiency of communications, in the years before the telephone, email and the internal combustion engine. The postal system was excellent – telegrams were delivered within a few hours and letters and postcards very quickly – for example, 'John went back to his work Tuesday morning & the same day we received a letter' (16 April 1884).

Most important was the railway, which made possible the extensive travelling which the Bousfields enjoyed. Bedford was gradually developing into a commuter town and Ted was able to live at home in 1878 and travel to London every day to study for his medical qualifications. The service was neither as quick nor as frequent as it is today, however. Fast trains took 1 hour 20 minutes to St Pancras, twice as long as they do today, and there were only four or five trains in the morning rather than four or five every hour.

For many people in the county, it was the local lines connecting towns and villages which were more useful than the main line. The map in Plate 20 shows how extensive the railway system was, with a station within reach of most of the Bedfordshire villages. Blunham, Sandy, Potton and Gamlingay all had stations on the LNWR, as did Ampthill, Sharnbrook and Oakley on the Midland line until Dr Beeching's reforms of the early 1960s cut so many of them, as lamented by Flanders and Swann:

> I'll travel no more from Littleton Badsey to Openshaw.
> At Long Stanton I'll stand well clear of the doors no more.
> No whitewashed pebbles, no Up and no Down
> From Formby Four Crosses to Dunstable Town.[56]

Horse-drawn vehicles of various sorts were the daily form of transport for many, including the Bousfields, who used both a barouche (a four-wheeled closed carriage

---

[55] See diary entry for 4 August 1887.
[56] From *Slow Train* written in 1964.

driven by a coachman) and also a smaller two-wheeled chaise, which Charlotte could drive herself, sometimes using it to travel to the family's second home in Aspley Heath (a village near Woburn, close to the Buckinghamshire border)[57] in preference to the train. Bicycles[58] and tricycles were also used and people were accustomed to walking much greater distances than has become normal in recent times. The diary entry for 28 January 1880 illustrates the variety of transport modes chosen according to the purpose – including skating.[59]

The Bousfields were typical of many middle-class families of the time in that the female members of the family were not employed in earning a living, whereas the male members were, but they were well educated up to the age of 18. Charlotte and her daughters were able to spend time away from home, visiting and staying with relatives and also in holidays at home and abroad. This is not evident in the abridgement, because most of the extensive coverage of visiting and holidays has been excised. In 1880, for example, Charlotte spent six weeks between mid February and early April at Ventnor, which she describes as 'our sanatorium', with the two girls who were unwell, and another fortnight at Jersey in October.

In later years, as Charlotte became heavily involved with the BWTA, she spent much more time away from home, visiting and speaking at branches all over the country. She had already an extensive network of friends in Bedford and relatives in London and Southport, but now she began to develop many more. She writes on 26 September 1887 from Aspley Heath, 'Since we came here I have been away so many times that I have had no opportunity of engaging in any work (beyond helping a little at the Bazaar) & this will continue … until the middle of Nov$^r$.'

In October 1887 alone she visited London, Nottingham, Gloucester and Yorkshire, travelling around each county, and staying several days in each place with BWTA members. Her network was not only on a national scale, but an international one: she hosted a visit from an American barrister and temperance supporter, Mrs Foster,[60] and from friends living in South Africa and Europe.

The censuses well illustrate the mobility of other members of the family as well as Charlotte. On census day in 1871 (Sunday 2 April) only Edward, Will and John were at home. Ted was living in Gorton, a suburb to the east of Manchester, apprenticed to a chemist, and Lottie was staying in Chelmsford with the Mortons, who had recently moved there. Charlotte and Edris, aged two, were staying with Charlotte's father and step-mother, the Rev. Robert Collins and his wife Mary. Hattie, aged only six, was staying in Hayes, Middlesex, with an unidentified family.[61] In 1881, most of the children were staying away from home. William was married and living in Cricklewood, Ted was practising in Bristol, and Lottie was staying with him. Harriet was at school in Jersey. In 1891, the numbers at Alpha Villa on census day had increased. By then, the three boys were all married and living in London, but father Edward and the two daughters were there, together with their old friend Emma Morton and

---

[57] See Plate 14.
[58] See Plate 13.
[59] See Plate 9.
[60] See diary entry for 21 June 1890.
[61] Hattie was staying with a widow, Emma E. Hewins, registered as having been born in Balderstone, a village near Newark, and her occupation, unusual for a woman then as now, as ironmonger. Perhaps she had been an employee of the Bousfields in their ironmonger's business.

Charlotte's eldest grandson George. Charlotte herself was on holiday with Will and his family at Shanklin in the Isle of Wight. Edward was the only member of the family who was residing at Alpha Villa on all three days.

Charlotte's relations with her children were good, though they sometimes challenged the strictness of her religious beliefs.[62] Will was certainly the most vigorous in his arguments with his mother. As a lawyer and a politician, he could hardly be more practised in the art. In October 1890 she writes:

> Each time Will comes I determine I will not be drawn into argument, but the mention of a book, or an opinion, leads into it before we are aware, & often throws a cloud over the happiness of his visits, because our ideas seem to me to grow farther & farther apart, & I love him so much I cannot bear to feel this.[63]

Charlotte's fundamentalist approach to biblical texts and to the gospel of total abstinence obviously provoked strong words from her outspoken eldest son. But Charlotte was enormously proud of Will's achievements and that made the increasing differences between them all the more bitter for her. Will had become by this stage an Anglican, but he had also become a Conservative. Charlotte was strongly Liberal in her sympathies, as a nonconformist, an advocate of temperance and a great admirer of Gladstone. It was difficult for her to support the Liberal MP who most frequently represented the borough, a member of the Whitbread family, because they were brewers, and after Gladstone's conversion to Home Rule in 1885, it was also difficult to support him, because for her 'Home Rule in Ireland would be Rome Rule.'[64]

Other aspects of the lives of the family are so familiar to Charlotte that they need no comment from her, and so may escape the notice of the diaries' readers in the twenty-first century. The clearly defined differentiation of the social classes is one of these. Both in the work place and at home the working classes and the middle classes did not mix except in the context of master and worker or mistress and servant. That is not to say that relations between the classes were strained or unpleasant in any way. The only time that a confrontation of any kind took place was during the Southend Hotel dispute, when, after the conviction of the landlord, the 'wives and families ... made a noisy demonstration in his favour ... threatening and hooting' outside the house of the woman who had reported the out-of-hours drinking. Charlotte confronted them and bested them, 'despite some saucy speeches about "lady detectives" '.[65] It is interesting to note that this episode seems to have involved the women more than the men (many of them presumably employed by the works) despite the fact that it was the men's drinking and noisy behaviour that caused the problem. In other respects, it reflects a frequent working-class response to the prohibition aspect of temperance, that the middle classes were seeking to deprive the working man of his simple pleasures by denying them their use of public houses, which provided not only the facility to buy and consume drink, but also a

---

[62]  As already noted on p. xiii.
[63]  See diary entry for 3 October 1890.
[64]  See diary entry for 25 December 1890.
[65]  See diary entry for 29 October 1886.

warm, lit, social club, providing a comfortable contrast to their cramped and uncomfortable houses.

There are some surprising omissions from the diaries. Charlotte very rarely comments on the servants, despite the fact that without their support, she would not have been able to pursue the good works to which she devoted so much time over so many years. She was certainly aware of their importance. In her diary entry for 15 October 1878, she was awaiting the first visit of Flo to Alpha Villa when both of the servants were taken ill and left. She was about to send Flo a telegram to ask her to defer her visit, but was persuaded by Lottie that they could cope. 'We had therefore to entertain our visitors as best we could ... They were rather amused than anything else at the dilemma.' Even so, she had a charwoman to assist.

She rarely if ever comments on domestic affairs, such as clothes and food, or the pregnancies of her daughters-in-law (there were fourteen of them before the diaries conclude in 1896), though sickness is a recurrent theme. She hardly ever refers to her mother-in-law, Frances Bousfield, who had moved into the house in Cauldwell Street vacated by Charlotte and her family in 1863, though Charlotte had known her since the 1840s when she had taught at Mrs Bousfield's Ladies Seminary in Newark. Most surprising of all is that except for noting her grandson George's arrival[66] and his impending departure[67] she ignores his presence completely, despite the fact that he was living at Alpha Villa as a day boy at Bedford School for four years, from October 1890.[68] It would be hard to imagine a grandmother today behaving in a similar way in these circumstances.

Some aspects of the diaries, however, seem familiar. The Christmas problem of who hosts the family get together,[69] concerns about the low level of church attendance, and about 'the difficulty & discouragement of carrying on the Bible Class' with often from twenty to thirty boys, 'many of whom are so ill-behaved that it seems almost impossible to do them good'.[70]

Charlotte Bousfield's diaries reveal something of the lives of a multi-talented Bedford family at a time of rapid change in the town, whose members contributed greatly to its industrial development and to the betterment of its less privileged citizens.

*Editorial Method*

Charlotte's main diaries comprise over 500,000 words in four manuscript volumes, covering some forty years, starting with her silver wedding celebrations in 1878, and ending in 1919, by which time Charlotte and her husband Edward had moved to Nottingham. The first three of these, centred in Bedford, form the basis of this volume and extend over a period of nineteen years, from 1878 to 1896. Within this period they are uneven in their coverage. The general pattern is an increase in the word length of the entries year by year from 1878 to 1885, then a slight decline in the next two years (1886 and 1887), followed by the shortest yearly entries of the

[66] See diary entry for 3 October 1890.
[67] See diary entry for 15 December 1893.
[68] See Plate 7. George began his time at the School in the building pictured here, though in the following year the new buildings were opened on their present site just south of Bedford Park.
[69] See diary entry for 29 December 1889.
[70] See diary entry for 3 November 1890.

nineteen-year period for the final years from 1888 to 1896. The four-year period between 1884 and 1887 is the most prolific, comprising 42% of the total content, and the last four years consist only of a few fragmented entries.

The first task in preparing these diaries for publication was to abridge the text in order to bring its length into line with the normal length of the BHRS series of volumes, that is down to about 125,000 words. That meant cutting out just over two thirds of the material. It was not easy to do this, and I was concerned that such a large-scale amputation would destroy the quality and flow of Charlotte's style. I can only say that I hope that this is not the case! Because of the extent and frequency of the cuts that have been made, it has been decided not to indicate where material has been excluded from the abridged text, as, if this were done, it would fragment the narrative to the detriment of the reader's enjoyment of the text.

The principles which were adopted in choosing text to include or exclude were few and simple, but flexible. Material which refers to Bedford or Bedfordshire always has its place, unless it is repetitious, something that is almost inevitable in a diary. This is partly because some similar events recur regularly, and are not conducive to much variety in their recording, and partly because the distance of time between one entry and another clouds the clarity of the diarist's recollection of what has been written earlier and what has not.

Another quality which is persuasive is, of course, readability. Examples of this are the visit to Dartmoor, with Charlotte's reflections on the nature of criminality (September 1884), and the visit to Paris (30 June 1878). Both of these examples also reveal an appealing aspect of Charlotte's character. And finally, I have included some descriptions of occasions and events which are interesting in themselves, even if not directly relevant to the county. An example of this is the extensive treatment of the events at the homes for inebriate women which Charlotte set up in London. The attempts of the patients to introduce alcohol into the home are sad but comical at the same time (6 June 1886). More seriously, her accounts of the introduction of Will as a QC (23 January 1891) and of the election process (canvassing, the counting of the votes, the declaration of the results, and the introduction of the new MP to the House, 14 May 1892) could not be omitted – and have not been.

The negatives include the reverse of the positives. I was prejudiced to exclude the material which was not directly connected with Bedfordshire. There was a lot of this. I have only included a few of the many lengthy entries detailing the family's holidays, so that there is at least a sample available. I have also excluded repetitious material, including religious reflections and accounts of sermons. Again, I have adopted the sample approach. All the material which describes unique events which refer to Bedfordshire are thus included.

The original diaries are, of course, manuscripts.[71] In preparing this volume, I have used the transcript made by John Hamilton and typed by Hilary Hamilton. In any cases of doubt, I have checked the original manuscript. My editorial method, as far as the treatment of the text that has been selected as outlined above, has been identical to that of John Hamilton.

The main principle is to retain as much as possible of the original, while ensuring that the result in print will be easy to read as far as its layout is concerned. This applies

---

[71] See Plate 2.

to paragraphing: Charlotte's manuscript is not generally paragraphed, but this has been done. Her use of hyphens, superscript letters (as in 'Dec$^r$ 28$^{th}$'), contractions, initial capital Letters for Nouns (and other Parts of Speech) and underlining for emphasis have been left in. Spelling has been corrected where necessary, but where she uses acceptable alternatives, they are left: examples are the style of 'favor', 'labor', common in the mid-nineteenth century, and the contraction 'Gloster'. The spelling of personal names has been made consistent, and punctuation has been altered where it clarifies the meaning. Square brackets have been inserted, according to the standard convention, to indicate editorial additions to the original text. The headings for each entry have been italicised, and notes have been added to assist the reader to understand what Charlotte's family, the intended readers of the diaries, would have understood without any assistance. In these notes I have chosen to refer to Charlotte by her initials, CEB. Although somewhat impersonal, this style of address serves to distinguish her, the diarist, from all the other characters who populate her diaries.

# THE BOUSFIELD DIARIES

## Volume 1

## March 1878 to January 1883

### 1878

*At Undercliff House, Ventnor, March 24<sup>th</sup> 1878*

I celebrated my Silver-wedding, & it occurred to me that from that event would be
a favorable time for keeping a record of the principal occurrences of my daily life;
if it should please God to spare me some years longer, to recall them may, & will,
be profitable to myself & perhaps interesting to my children. Although I wish to
express my thoughts & feelings in reference to those circumstances which I think it
worth while to chronicle as freely as if I knew no other eye than my own would rest
on what I write, I feel it will not be easy to do this, yet I must be strictly truthful
both in reference to myself & those of whom I may have somewhat to record.

With the 25 years that have flown past since my wedding day, I feel the summer
of life has gone, but it has been crowded with mercies & its sun-shine far exceeded
the clouds & storms. I have under some sort of inspiration for which I can scarcely
account (for I know I am no poetess or I should often write verses when I cannot)
written some lines, which grew into many more than I intended, but in which, dedicated to my dear Husband, I epitomized better than I can in prose just what our life
together thus far has been, & this I think I shall write at the beginning of this journal,
hoping & believing that our dear ones may, when they have reached our time of life,
find in them some expression for themselves of the same loving kindness & tender
mercy which followed their Parents so far on their pilgrimage.[1]

*March 27<sup>th</sup>*

With my eldest child over 24 & my youngest on earth 13 years old,[2] it is probable
that the most important events of their lives may occur in a much shorter space of
time than our married life has been, therefore although over 49 years of age seems
late to begin a diary, I do so that I may keep in remembrance the way by which they
may be led by the same Guiding Hand which has so wisely & wonderfully brought
us to this stage of our journey & also, now that my memory is not so good as it
once was, to keep a reminder of my own special mercies, & be able to recall them
as I could not without aid if I should live to be really old or even for years whether
many or few.[3]

---

[1] CEB (henceforth used in footnotes to refer to Charlotte the diarist) apparently did not carry out her
intention, as the verses have not survived.
[2] CEB alludes to her sixth child, Edris, a little girl who died at the age of three in 1872.
[3] CEB did indeed live to be 'really old': she died in 1933 at the age of 105.

To account for dating this at the beginning from Ventnor I must say that I left Alpha Villa with Hattie more than a month ago for this place, where Lottie joined us from Clifton the next day, and John from Chelmsford a few days later, all being out of health, the girls from coughs and John from weakness consequent on his long illness just as he was leaving home at Xmas. Ventnor has again & again been our resort when change was needed, with the result desired.[4]

After we had been settled here a few days Will gave us one of the surprises of which he is fond by making his appearance most unexpectedly. Capt$^n$ & M$^{rs}$ Alcock & family visited Ryde & he accompanied his pupil, coming on to us to stay & returning to him for a few hours daily; his spare time was spent with us or in geological searches, in which Hattie was generally his companion. He remained in the Island about a fortnight & returned to Clifton[5] only a few days before the time all had arranged to meet to commemorate our Silver wedding day. However not to disappoint me he came back Saturday 23rd on which day Papa & Ted also joined us. It was a great pleasure to me that my dear Husband was able to come, & to us both to have all our five children with us; except for the thought that one dear one had gone from us that would otherwise have been there also, there was nothing to mar my joy & pride & thankfulness at being so surrounded.

March 24th was a glorious Sabbath morning as bright in sunshine as our wedding morning 25 years ago. I felt so glad that it was Sunday & that we could in God's house offer our praise & thanksgiving for his great goodness to us from that day until the present. We all sat down to breakfast with a wedding cake gaily decorated, flowers etc on the table, & our silver presents from the children & others spread near. Will had brought us a beautiful antique salver, & John, Lottie & Hattie had united to present me with a silver bracelet. I felt even prouder than I did when I sat down as a Bride to our wedding-breakfast, & not without reason, for not only did I feel as much pride as ever in looking on my Husband, but my three tall boys & two girls were an additional source, of which I must not write all I (their Mother) think.

As I looked around on each, restored to health & strength, within, and then without on the grand & glorious ocean sparkling & heaving in the rays of the sun, my cup of earthly happiness was filled to the brim, & seemed even running over when we went together to worship in the Congregational Church where, sitting so that we could see the faces of all our children, my dear Husband & I joined with glad & grateful hearts in public thanksgiving, for good M$^r$ Davis knew why we had all assembled on that day & did not forget to offer it on our behalf. As we left the Church we were met by several of our Bedford friends who were staying here, amongst them D$^r$ Coombs & M$^r$ & M$^{rs}$ Hobson.[6]

---

[4]  Ventnor, a seaside resort in the Isle of Wight, was well known for its microclimate which it was claimed was ideal for the treatment of pulmonary disease. At a time when tuberculosis was rife, sufferers came from all over the country to the Royal National Hospital for Diseases of the Chest.

[5]  Clifton, a suburb of Bristol.

[6]  Mr and Mrs Hobson were Bedford's Mayor and Mayoress in 1881.

*April 1st*

The boys have confided some of their love affairs to me, but will not I dare say take my opinion in reference to them if they have an opposite one of their own.[7] I tell Will & Eddie, as professional men, they cannot marry & keep their necessary position in society as early as their Father did; at their age his future course was tolerably settled & income not uncertain, & what was ample for us when we began life together would not suffice now to bring them an equal amount of comfort & respectability. We have never lacked not only the comforts but many of the luxuries of life & did not marry until we had a reasonable prospect of having them. Eddie is fond of saying what Papa did when I advise him, as I think for his good, & he is so warm in his love affairs that I fear if his affections should get <u>fixed</u> where his love is returned (which I think can scarcely be said at present), his prudence should be outrun or set aside.

My first anxiety for my boys is that they shall choose Christian women & next that they may not bring upon themselves & us anxieties which love only cannot keep off. But I find I am chronicling ideas rather than facts, which however I shall sometimes allow myself to do that I may in the future be able to compare events with my thoughts in the past in reference to them.

*April 8th*

Our intention of leaving Ventnor last Wednesday was altered by a pouring wet morning & Hattie's having taken a bad influenza cold – a bottle of medicine from Dr Williamson & keeping her in bed for the day did her so much good that I thought it best to take advantage of the warm sunny morning which succeeded the previous day's down-pour &, hastily packing what was not already done, left Undercliff House about noon. After a delightful little passage across the Solent & a pleasant journey in a carriage all to ourselves the whole way to London, we crossed from Victoria to St Pancras in a cab & thence on to Bedford arriving at 'home sweet home' soon after 7 o'clock.

I found Papa had prepared a pleasant little surprise for me by having the breakfast room fresh papered & new turkey carpet & rug & the stove taken out & replaced by a Dog-grate with tiled hearth & sides. Howcutt was busy finishing the setting of the latter when I got in.[8]

*April*[9]

I went to [St. Paul's] Chapel[10] with Ted & remained to the sacramental service, as this was the first opportunity I had ever had of doing so with him. I was disappointed that it was not one of unmixed pleasure. Thoughts of anxiety for his future so filled my mind as to almost unfit it for God's worship. Clara Henman sat before us, & I find he continues to think more of her even than he did when a correspondence

---

7    CEB refers to the 'love affairs' between Will and Florence Kelly, and between Eddie (or Ted, as she usually calls him) and Clara Henman, discussed further in diary entries for 9 and 10 April and 15 and 23 October.
8    Howcutt is the odd-job man whose duties included gardening, looking after the horse and carriage and household repairs.
9    No specific date is given, but it is presumably 9 April, as it appears between entries on 8 and 10 April.
10   St Paul's Chapel, in Harpur Street, built in 1804.

began between them in some way last Nov$^r$, of which he told me on my return from Hastings when passing through town & greatly to my surprise, as it began in the fortnight of our absence from home, & without their having met in the meantime.

*April 10$^{th}$*
Eddie left us yesterday after having been living at home three months, he has had a season railway ticket & instead of lodging in London has been daily to the Hospital returning each night. I had proposed his doing this principally because I did not wish him to share lodgings with O Coombs who wished to live with him when Mr Hayward[11] left, the difference between the two as companions was that one was a Christian man (with whom I was glad for him to associate) & the other was not; if anything can show the value of religion it is the restraining power it influences over young men left unrestrained by anything else in a great city.

Ted's stay at home has done him good in some ways, but I fear his premature attachment is strengthened; his Papa & I have pointed out to him the imprudence as we both think of engaging himself before he has completed his studies, & he promised to keep himself free. If he likes Clara as well as he now thinks he does when he has been further abroad in the world, & a long engagement is contemplated by them, all may be well, but I had hoped his mind would have been more absorbed by the ambitions which he seemed to have in his profession for some time to come. Papa thinks exactly as I do in the matter. I have been to Mrs Henman & told her that we cannot give any countenance to the correspondence which is, we hear, going on under the circumstances in which they are both placed.

*It is now far in May*: several weeks have elapsed since I have written in my journal. I have been very busy from the time of returning home from Norwood where I stayed until Thursday.[12] Papa only spent Sunday at Grandpapa's, returning to Bedford on Monday morning, although it was Bank Holiday, to make trial of some machines which the rain prevented his being able to do on Saturday before he left. I was very much disappointed that he could not be with me in the Crystal Palace where we had intended spending Easter Monday together.

I accompanied him to the station after breakfast & did my best as he begged me to enjoy myself without him. G-papa & G-mama promised to come to me at 2 o'clock, but by some mistake we did not meet. After waiting for them a long time I determined to get a seat where I could see the vast concourse of people that thronged the centre of the Palace & at the same time hear the Concert which was about to be held. Getting into as advantageous position as possible in the Orchestra in front of the great Organ, I found ample occupation for eyes & ears.

Amongst the attractions for the day was the Phonograph which was being exhibited & explained for (I believe) the first time. I heard the sounds & songs that were said or sung into it re-produced by the instrument in a muffled sort of tone, but quite sufficient to show that when perfected it may be as wonderful & useful as

---

[11] The Haywards were cousins of CEB.

[12] with her father (referred to as Grandpapa) and step-mother (Grandmama). The house was named Penrith Lodge, in Belvedere Road, conveniently close to the re-sited Crystal Palace.

the Telephone, which I hear is really used as a medium of communication between persons at immense distances.

During the next week we had a succession of visitors. Will was the last of them; he went to Ventnor for his Easter holiday & to continue the geological researches which he began when with us in the Island earlier. Mr Derham was still there. Staying in London to eat his dinners at the Middle Temple, he afterwards came home to take Hattie with him to Clifton; he prefers the company of one of his sisters in his lodgings &, thinking it good for him to have one of them with him, we have been willing that they should go. Lottie went first after Xmas, but our intention of letting her study at the High School, opened there at that time,[13] was set aside by her taking cold directly she went; she continued to go two or three days but was too unwell to take the walks from Will's rooms to the school after that time & did not regain her usual health until her visit to Ventnor.

Hattie had begun the same term with Mrs Brown & for the same reason had to leave school.[14] After our return to Bedford Lottie began again with Mrs Brown & as Hattie seemed the stronger of the two, I was more willing for her to go from home with Will & for him to regulate her studies, although I scarcely think she will feel sufficient interest in them alone or be ready to pass the junior Cambridge exam at Xmas as she had hoped to do with Mrs B. However, it will do her good to be thrown more on her own resources & be away from us; as the youngest (on earth) we are apt to do too much for her.

I never mention 'the youngest' but the words recall my precious one that passed away more than six years ago; she has a place in my heart that can never be filled by any other, I think of her still as my babe.

*May*[15]

Ted's final exam for his MRCS is over; it has been the subject of alternate hopes & fears for some weeks for it was not until the time for it drew very near that he really realized that he must work much harder than he had been doing to get through. This however he has done, & the next morning came home triumphantly flourishing the tin case containing his diploma. I had no fears for him in anything in which skilful use of his fingers would lead to his success; surgery & practical anatomy have been his delight since he began at St Bart's;[16] he inherits to some extent his Papa's mechanical powers which I have often thought may make him great as a Surgeon if he will specially devote himself to his favorite branch of the Medical profession as he has expressed his intention of doing. Hard reading is not what he likes & has not occupied his time as systematically as it ought to have done, so that he had too

13  Clifton High School, one of several being established at this time by the Girls' Public Day School Company (now the Girls' Schools Association), was opened on 1 January 1878.
14  Ada Haydon Brown was the wife of Dr John Brown, pastor of the Congregational Chapel in Bedford, better known as the Bunyan Meeting, in Mill Street. She had been involved in the establishment of the Cambridge Higher Local Examinations in the 1870s. She started her own school in the Manse, situated opposite the Harpur Trust Almshouses in Dame Alice Street. She was the grandmother of the influential economist John Maynard Keynes.
15  No specific date is given to this entry, but the previous entry (deleted here) is for 19 May, and the subsequent one (also deleted) is dated 30 June.
16  St Bartholomew's Hospital in Smithfield London is the oldest in the country. Ted would have studied at the Hospital's Medical College, founded in 1843, for his MRCS (Member of the Royal College of Surgeons) qualification.

much to do the last few weeks & has been reading early & late. He got through with more ease than he expected. He returned to Town with the determination of reading for his medical qualification in Oct$^r$, & in the mean time taking some work that he could do without much interrupting it.

*June 30$^{th}$ /78*

Arrived home from Paris to which place Lottie, Ted & myself have paid a somewhat unexpected visit with Papa.[17] When he found he would have to go so early we gave up the idea of accompanying him as we had intended both the girls should do if he could leave in their vacation. This he found it would be impossible for him to do, but seeing that he did not anticipate much pleasure in going alone, & when I thought of going without him later, I lost almost all inclination for doing so, so we suddenly made up our minds to go together, & begged M$^{rs}$ Brown to consent to Lottie's accompanying us &, as Ted's visit to Clifton was just over, we thought he might not have another opportunity of visiting the Exhibition when real work began & so telegraphed to him to bring Hattie with him & join us in London, which he did, but Will was not willing to spare Hattie thinking it better that she should accompany him in the holidays, so that he came alone.

We left London together (Papa, Ted, Lottie & myself) on Monday 17$^{th}$ about 8 o'clock, & arrived in Paris at 10 o'clock Tuesday morning. The weather was delightful on arriving in Paris but we spent the remainder of the morning in searching for private apartments as Papa did not wish to go to an Hotel. He had to leave us before we had succeeded in getting them. Soon after we had settled our place of abode it began to rain & the next day poured almost incessantly until 5 o'clock p m. To make the best of the wet day we thought it best to spend it in the Exhibition. Every thing beautiful & wonderful that could be carried seemed brought together [there].

The first day we took a general look round walking through without stopping much, but in subsequent visits Lottie & I spent our time in the departments that interested us, the jewellery particularly we stayed some time in & Lottie had several conversations with the attendants at the different cases, nearly all Frenchmen, all of whom were most polite & ready to tell us anything we wished to know.

One evening we took the Steam-boat from the Pier within the Exhibition enclosure & went down the Seine as far as the bridge close to the Place de la Concorde, the grand centre of Paris, spent some time in the gardens of the Tuilleries [*sic*], walked up to the grand front of the Palace which, when I last saw it was in all its glory but is now only stone walls & empty window frames & has so been since the wanton wickedness of the Communists set it on fire.[18]

---

[17] His purpose was to visit the Paris Exhibition of 1878. Modelled on the Great Exhibition of 1851 in London, the Paris Exhibition was much larger, and displayed early models of some of the most important features of life today, among them Alexander Graham Bell's telephone and Edison's phonograph, all matters of interest in the Bousfield household. Perhaps the most interesting for Edward would have been the first demonstration of electric lighting used in a large outdoor area. Such lighting had been installed all along the Avenue de l'Opera and the Place de l'Opera, and in June, a switch was thrown and the area was lit by electric light bulbs.

[18] The Tuileries Palace, which had been the residence of Napoleon III, was set on fire and destroyed by the Socialists of the Paris Commune in May 1871, in protest against the actions of the new government of the Third Republic in seeking peace terms with the Prussians at the end of the Franco-Prussian War.

Papa could not be with us until evening when we all returned to our lodgings & had a walk at night, this I generally did when he returned from the Exhibition if we had not been there. Lottie was frequently too tired to do so, but she & Ted were with us more than once to see what I must call night street life in Paris, so totally different to anything we ever see in England. The principal Boulevards seemed almost as light as day, not only from the street lights but from the innumerable Cafés brilliantly illuminated; in front of these are placed as many little tables & seats as the broad pavement will allow, so as not to obstruct the way, & around these are seated in the street people of all classes it seemed to us, as calmly eating & drinking as if in their own houses. Crowds of foot passengers filled the rest of the pavement, indeed all Paris appeared to turn out into the streets from dusk to near midnight, either to walk or sit.

The very hot weather we were having may to some extent have accounted for the throngs through which we had to make our way. The manner in which Parisian houses are built, in flats occupied by different families, most of them with no means of getting out of door air except perhaps from a front balcony, is doubtless also a reason why the people crowd into the streets, though this can scarcely hold good at night. With no word to express 'home' they seem to have no idea of the cosy evening gatherings in families which we English love so much, but prefer the out of door bustle & excitement.

The shops in some parts are not closed until very late which is another attraction. One night we spent an hour or two in the Palais Royale which is now a large square of shops all with covered causeways under which in all weathers the people walk to gaze on & admire the brilliant jewellery, real or other, sparkling in the gas light in nearly every window. Almost all were jewellers' shops & we could only wonder how all found customers sufficient to keep them open.

June 30th we reached home after a rather shorter stay in Paris than we intended. Papa had arranged to come back the previous Wednesday or Thursday, leaving me with Ted & Lottie to finish the fortnight for which we took our rooms, but the intense heat, our weariness of the continual fatigue & bustle of sight-seeing & the fact that the next Sunday was to [be] the grand national fête day in honor of the Exhibition, made us all more than willing to return earlier, so he stayed for us until Friday afternoon when, starting together, we travelled all night to London & had a much more pleasant journey than in going, as far as Calais, having a carriage to ourselves the whole way.

I was glad to have a real Sabbath the next day instead of a Parisian Sunday. We had made the best of the last by going to the Scotch Presbyterian Church (which is a large round room at the top of some buildings in the Rue de Rivoli) for morning worship. We heard an excellent sermon & much enjoyed the service. This was one of several Protestant mission places distributed over Paris through the agency of Revd McAll, a good devoted man who, with Mrs McAll, has given his whole energy to the work which has gradually increased until its influence has become so marked in the worst quarter of the City that he has received public acknowledgement & thanks for it. In Belleville, the Communists' principal district, he has his chief place of worship & lives himself close to it.[19] Another hymn & prayer in French by Mr

---

19   Belleville, a working-class neighbourhood of Paris, was one of the districts which had resisted most

M<sup>c</sup>All concluded the service, the whole of which was conducted in the most orderly manner & without the slightest interruption amidst a population where but a few years ago terror & destruction reigned, but where the preaching of the Gospel of Peace was beginning to produce its legitimate fruits. Truly 'where sin <u>abounded,</u> grace did much more abound' or God would not have put it into good M<sup>r</sup> M<sup>c</sup>All's heart to preach to the sinners in Paris beginning at Belleville.

We were on the whole satisfied with & thankful for this Sunday, but the preparations we saw going on for the next made me especially anxious to avoid the dissipation of mind it must have produced on us unless we had shut ourselves up the whole day.[20] I was very pleased that neither Ted nor Lottie were at all tempted by the sight of the tens of thousands of gas globes hung in festoons between the lamp posts around the Place de la Concorde & up the chief Avenues to the Arc de Triomphe etc, & other preparations for the grand illumination, & wished to leave instead of remaining to see a spectacle which it would have given us all great pleasure to witness on any other day.

*July 10<sup>th</sup>*

<u>My birthday: is it possible that that was fifty years ago!</u> I began this by looking back on the way by which I had been led 25 years, & now I must double that period in telling of my Heavenly Father's goodness to me all the way by which he has led me through the wilderness; sometimes a cloudy pillar has seemed to obscure it, & even in earlier years a shade of doubt & despondency for some time made the path at times seem dark, but I have had so little of the trial & suffering to which so many, yes & those dearest to me, have been the subjects of from childhood upward, that I cannot but wonder why I have been spared this. My three dear sisters, all younger than myself, have all passed away after years of weakness, my brothers too! I the eldest of all have scarcely recollection of anything but health, this I regard as one of my special mercies; then for my earliest surroundings as the child of a Christian minister, the restraining influence of my home education to keep me from the desire even for those pleasures & follies of youth to which so many are trained, & the leadings by which my future course in life was marked out for me until I left my Father's house, all these I look back upon with a grateful heart, & from then until now my mercies have been continued in an unbroken chain.

It is true the dear ones of my early home have all passed away, except one, but my dear Mother's almost last words were 'My sins are forgiven, I'm going to glory'[21] & each of those who have followed her have left a testimony that their only hope & trust was in Christ, & with such a good hope for them what can I record but that 'loving kindness & tender mercy have followed me all the days of my life', & even

---

strongly the attack on the Commune by the government forces in May 1871. It was in this troubled year that Mr M<sup>c</sup>All first visited Paris and began his mission to bring reconciliation to a city which had hardly emerged from its bitter civil war.

[20] CEB's objection is primarily Sabbatarian, that such an event should not be taking place on a Sunday.

[21] In a letter CEB writes: 'If by any chance you should go to or through Stockbridge (9 miles distant from Winchester) in the little burying place of the Congregational Chapel [is] to be seen my dear mother's grave & headstone. My Father lived at Stockbridge at the dates on it, & I lost my Mother & one dear Sister (who are both buried there) during his residence in the last house on the right hand side, at the lower end of the village now inhabited by a Dr.'

in my last fiery trial when my precious lamb was taken from me, I know that in faithfulness was the stroke sent & the love that dealt it I shall some day understand, so in this my jubilee year I desire more than every to consecrate my 'residue of days' to His service who has done such great things for me, & with a thankful heart record His goodness.

## Shanklin Oct$^r$ 15$^{th}$

What a number of events have transpired in the three short months since my birthday. On that very day my dear Husband came home in the middle of the morning looking dreadfully pale & holding up his left arm with his right hand. I was frightened & fearing a bone was broken sent at once to the Infirmary[22] for Mr Johnson & in the mean time kept it fomented with hot water to relieve the pain & swelling. Whilst doing this I found that he had attempted to shorten the way to the field to which he was going to look at a machine by jumping over an old wall, in doing so a stone must have given way just as he was on it, & he fell heavily with his arm bent under him. Mr J pronounced the injury to be a bad sprain which was a relief to my mind, but he had to go to bed instead of leaving home in the evening as he fully intended for the Royal Show at Clifton.[23]

This was a great disappointment to Will who was hoping to have entertained his Papa during the time of the Show, as also to John who, having finished his time at Chelmsford, had returned home a few days previously & gone to Bristol to await his coming at Will's rooms.[24] Papa had to carry his poor arm in a sling for some time & even now feels the effect of his accident. John's return to Bedford was the next family event; he is now quite settled at the Works & the idea of having one of my boys living at home again is a great pleasure to me.

I must go back again now to August 3rd when Papa's arm was well enough to allow him to leave home[25] for Clifton to attend the trial of mowers which was to take place after the Royal Show.[26] In the afternoon of the same day Florence Kelly came to pay us a visit which had been promised for some time. It seemed very unfortunate that she was coming just then for both the servants had to leave that very week, one with a bad eye, the other a lame knee, & as she had never been to see us before, I was unwilling for her to do so at such an unusual time of domestic disquiet & began writing a telegram the morning Annie left to explain the state of affairs & beg her to defer her visit. Lottie was however very anxious she should not

---

22   Bedford Infirmary was opened in 1803 and is sited between the Ampthill and Kempston Roads, where the South Wing Hospital now stands. It was funded by subscription.

23   The Royal Show provided an important showcase for the innovations in agricultural machinery in which Edward played a leading part as described in the Introduction. It was held in a different place each year – in 1879 it would be held in London.

24   John had been staying at Chelmsford with Mr and Mrs Morton and their son Alex. The Morton family were old friends of the Bousfields, as they were neighbours in Cauldwell Street, Bedford, before the Bousfields moved to Alpha Villa in 1863. In Chelmsford, Mr Morton was partner in the agricultural machinery manufacturers Coleman and Morton. It is not known what the purpose of this long visit was, nor what was meant by the 'time' which John was 'finishing', but he may have been serving an apprenticeship in the business.

25   CEB is writing from Shanklin about Bedford.

26   Mowers were machines used for cutting hay. The project occupying Edward at this time was the development of the sheaf-binding machine, used in the harvesting of corn. In fact, a contemporary described the introduction of reaping machines as 'the most striking feature of agricultural progress in the last twenty years' (see Hamilton, *Glad for God*, p. 178).

be put off & was sure from what we saw of her when she spent a few days with us at our lodgings at Ventnor in the spring that she would be quite willing to make the best with us of our unforeseen position, so that I consented not to telegraph & met her on Saturday evening at the Midland Station.

Mr Hayward too had written to say that he would spend Sunday with us & came later that night. We had therefore to entertain our friends as best we could, with the help of a char-woman. They were rather amused than anything else at the dilemma & both very assiduous in rendering help & waiting on us & each other. Mr H left on Monday; we managed pretty well until Wednesday when Elizabeth's eye was so far better that she could come back & wait at table etc which was all the more fortunate as Papa returned home on that day with Will, John & Hattie, the latter I forgot to say had been living with Will since leaving Ventnor in April going on with her studies with him as he wished for her company.

On Saturday John was taken suddenly ill in the same manner as at Xmas & we had to call in M$^r$ Coombs[27] for him; fortunately the attack was not so violent as before but kept him in bed nearly a week & very weak from the effects of it nearly another.

My own illness also increased at the same time & for several days M$^r$ C was in constant attendance on me & I had more suffering than ever in the same number consecutively in my life before. It was most fortunate at this juncture that Will was at home & almost worth being ill to have all the gentle care which he gave me, tending me day or night to relieve my pain. Lottie too was a capital manager of domestic affairs for me & with one poor one-eyed servant & the char-woman kept me from all anxiety about house-keeping; and our <u>visitor Florence, that I had wished to keep away when matters were far less complicated, moved backward & forward between John's room</u> & mine, doing anything she could for each of us <u>like another daughter.</u>

### Will & Flo's Engagement

At the end of a fortnight both John & myself were rapidly getting better but I was scarcely prepared for the unexpected turn which events then took. We had all liked Florence very much before her visit to Bedford, but it was not until her goodness at the time we needed help so much that we loved her. The infection went entirely round & affected Will so seriously that he told her of his ailment, & as she seemed willing to undertake his cure, they so far & so soon settled matters between themselves that before Florence's return home the beginning of the next week, she had consented to his visiting her in London & formally obtaining Papa's & Mamma's consent to their engagement, which was cordially given. This fact Florence announced to me in a few hasty lines to which Will added as PS an 'All right' that would have been a merry chuckle if I could have heard him say it instead.

In a day or two after I received a very kind letter from Mr Kelly & now the affair seems quite old & I am spending a week with my future daughter-in-law at her Shanklin home, on my way from Clifton (where I have left Hattie with Will) to Ventnor where I hope to meet my dear Husband to-morrow. Florence & I have had

---

[27] Dr James Coombs was an Alderman and elected Mayor of Bedford in 1871, 1889 and 1891. Ted was articled to him for a time.

a nice cosy time together & some chats about the past & future; she knows she has not promised herself to a rich man, but believes she sees something above money worth in her choice, & is content to wait until Will has finished his reading & can be called to the Bar which cannot be for more than two years. God bless them both together & make their way plain.

### Undercliff House, Ventnor Oct<sup>r</sup> 23<sup>rd</sup>

I left Shanklin last Saturday and came here as arranged before I left home. Mr & Mrs Kelly invited Papa to come to me at Clarendon Lodge, but he wished to carry out our first idea which was to be quite free to come in & go out as we would without interfering with the order or comfort of others. I got here in the afternoon in time to have tea & a cheerful fire ready for him on his arrival about 6 o'clock. It was very funny that he met with Mr K at the same place in which we first saw him, the tramway car from Ryde Pier to the Station, & that he was immediately recognized as Will's Father from his likeness to him, so that the introduction which I expected to give them to each other was quite unnecessary, & they at once began to converse after Mr K had accosted Papa somewhat to his surprise.

My first meeting with Mr Kelly when I brought Lottie & Hattie to Ventnor in the spring of last year & our short journey together from Ryde to Shanklin seemed very accidental, & but for our mentioning the name of the house to which we were going here, he would never have known even our name, but driving to Ventnor he determined to enquire at 'Swiss Cottage' after his fellow travellers, to whom he had been very kind & attentive for the little time we waited & travelled with him. Mrs K was rather displeased at his making friends with strangers but called with him, which call we returned with Will (who had joined us & come in just as they were leaving).

This was the beginning of an intimacy which bids fair to end only with life, seeing that we became so mutually pleased with each other as to continue to visit during our stay in the Island, & our children afterwards both in London & Bedford, & that it is now a settled matter with two of them that they will spend their lives together: on how small a thing does the weal or woe of human destiny often seem to turn. I do hope & believe it will be for the former in this case & that Florence & Will in years to come may never regret what appeared such an unimportant circumstance to their Parents, but is likely to be far otherwise to themselves.

### Nov<sup>r</sup> 5<sup>th</sup>

Once more after my wanderings, arrived at our own dear home on Saturday afternoon, having been away from it nearly five weeks. Papa would gladly have returned at the same time but had to go to Paris before doing so, & for this our stay at Ventnor was shortened several days as he was anxious to get to the Exhibition again before the packing up had begun on Nov<sup>r</sup> 1st, the date at which it was permitted.

A letter from Florence to Lottie to-day tells us that she has been to the Temple & finds Will's name in the list of those who have successfully passed the exam in Roman law at which doubtless she is, as we all are, very pleased. He has now time to turn his mind to the subject in which his Papa just now is specially interested – Electric Lighting, & at his request is giving attention to it. He has bought a Battery etc for experimenting, & if the two lay their wise heads together they may do something. Papa's great forte is simplifying what others do by more complicated means, & he thinks he has a good idea in reference to this new method of lighting which many seem to think will supersede gas some day.

*Friday Nov' 8th*

On Wednesday evening Papa arrived home after his second trip to the Exhibition where he spent the greater part of three days; he had a quiet day with Grandpapa & then a few hours in London on his way to Bedford, which he tells me he spent in the Lawyer's office in Chancery Lane & in a visit to the Polytechnic where he heard a lecture on Electric Light which pleased him greatly. His journey seems to have been rather uneventful as he has not told us much about it, & he did not enjoy staying alone in the Great City he said in his letter to Lottie.

When he came home to dinner to-day he told me he had been paying for the horse which he has got for us. We have many times debated whether we should keep one in years past, but whilst the children were young & at school I never cared sufficiently about it to drive alone. Now however that Lottie has nearly finished school, & one or other of the boys will be occasionally coming home, I can have company when my dear Husband cannot be with me, & he has so little time to spare in drives for pleasure himself that I think it is very good & kind of him so to indulge myself & his girls. The time is not I hope very far distant when we shall be able to enjoy it together more frequently than we shall at present.

I do not yet feel altogether that it is more than a matter of enjoyment, but the time cannot be far distant when I shall feel less able than I now do to walk everywhere, & if we are spared to grow old together a snug ride when we desire it may add both to the health & happiness of the old folk, although if I am like Father it will not for many years be a necessity.

*Nov' 11th*

John & I have been together to the London Missionary Society's meeting at Bunyan School-room. I have still an affection for the old Society for which I was a collector for years, even when a child, & to which I hope to contribute as long as I live, although having just taken Mrs Durley's collecting book for the Wesleyan Missions, my work is now in another corner of the Vineyard; still it is for the same Master & if for Him it matters little to me under what name it is done.

I remember the trial it was to me when we first came to Bedford twenty years ago to dissociate myself from the Congregational church in which I was born & bred for the Wesleyan into which the force of circumstances seemed to thrust me, but having conjointly with my Husband been able to accomplish some little work in it for God that neither would have done separately, & having the satisfaction of knowing that all our children have under its ministry (& I trust & believe our added efforts to train them up in the way they should go) been led to be 'stepping heavenwards', I have no regret that it was so.

*Nov' 29th*

Yesterday was Ted's birthday. I sent him a letter of good wishes accompanied by a money present expressing the hope that this might be the last birthday on which such a one might be more acceptable to him than any other, as I believe it will, seeing that he has now been just three months at Tewkesbury[28] so that his first quarter's salary is scarcely due & has not yet been paid.

In his last letter he tells me that he will only be able to come home for a single day, the 26th Dec[r], which he says is Clara Henman's birth-day, & from that day he intends to be formally engaged to her; to this too I have now no objection to offer, she is I believe a truly good girl; he has remained unchanged in his attachment to her over a year, & being assured of hers to himself, if his future prospects are as fixed & favorable as he believes, they may be contented & happy without riches.

*Dec[r] 4th*

I have been wanting for days past to have half an hour's chat in my journal but have not found time what with Mothers' meetings, & work-men & going into the town (for pleasure last night in the Ladies' gallery at the Corn Exchange[29] to a political meeting), I do not seem to have had a minute to spare for this. I see it is not quite so long as I thought since I wrote, but events thicken around me & when I measure the time by them it seems longer, although I have said more than once lately that the end of the week never seemed to come so quickly as now.

But these boys of mine (bless them) nearly take away my mental breath! On Monday morning before I was scarcely down (having been in all Sunday & had breakfast in bed that morning for my cold), who should come to the gate in a Cab but Will & Florence. I could scarcely believe my own eyes as I believed one to be in Bristol & the other in London, but there they were together. The explanation was that Will's stopped tooth had been giving him such pain that he must needs go to the dentist who filled it in London to take it out. I suggested there might have been one in Clifton, to which the reply was that it would be done 'for nothing' by the London man (NB journey to Town 30/- at least), & that he had come down with Florence for an hour or two, returning with her home & thence to Clifton the same night.

The real secret of their hasty visit was soon made known. Will took the opportunity of going to the Works to meet his Papa to have a few words with him alone, which I thought must refer to the thought he had expressed of doing something in Electricity on his own account after Xmas, but to my astonishment the current of it was diverted into an entirely new direction, & he came to tell us that he wanted to be married! I really had always thought him a sober fellow who, if he were engaged, would discreetly wait until he had made some way in the world after he had done with his law studies & had been 'called', such an idea as his marrying before this never entered my head, but it had evidently got into his. We had some talk with him & having heard what he had to say in the matter, I promised to do what he said Mr Kelly suggested, see & converse with him, before doing which it would be impossible for us to give any opinion.

His present income is ample for him to begin housekeeping in the modest way which he wishes & says Florence is quite willing for, & having spoken to Captn Alcock as to the probable length of time he intends his son's education to continue, which it appears is a year & half longer, for that time his income will be good &

---

[28]  where Ted was working as assistant to a doctor.
[29]  CEB refers to the new Corn Exchange, opened in 1874, and much larger than the old Corn Exchange which remained in situ and was now known as the Floral Hall until it was demolished in 1904.

certain, but he must then give up other occupation to be for some length of time with a Barrister or Solicitor, which will be spending instead of earning, & how then?[30]

I had a letter from him on Wednesday morning telling me I must do all I could to help him when I saw Mr K & that he has quite made up his mind to be married at Easter if he would give his consent to let Florence. He says he is quite tired of living in two rooms; I fear for the next four or five years he will increase his anxieties as much as his comfort by having more. He looked very unwell on Monday & has some cough which always, after the experiences of my past life, gives me concern, but I hope it is only a cold & that now his tooth is extracted he will soon be better. He promised to begin taking Hydroline or Cod liver oil. I should be glad for him to have Florence to take care of him if he could afford it, but cannot help thinking it would have been wise for them both to have had patience in waiting until he had made more provision for the future.

### Dec' 12th

I have been busy this week, Monday my usual Mothers' meeting & getting the women's books made up for the Coal club, Tuesday morning making a few preparations to receive Fanny & Mr Clulow[31] who came at night from Plymouth (Mr C preaches the first anniversary sermons at Bromham-road Chapel next Sunday), the whole of the afternoon & evening was spent in helping to arrange the tables for the Zanana Mission Sale which occupied the whole of yesterday & was a success in spite of the very inclement weather & the absence of many of those on whom we had depended for customers.[32]

Lottie & all her schoolfellows were very active at their Stall which was entirely filled by articles that they had themselves made & got together, most of which were sold, realizing more than ...[33] Mrs Brown & myself had the children's clothing & worked together very pleasantly in selling it; the whole proceeds of the Sale were over ... which was nearly double what was first expected, a result obtained by the energy of a few ladies, in addition to the work done at our monthly meeting, which had before been sent away & excited little interest in the workers & very small returns at the central place for selling them for the same object.

It does the young people especially so much good apart from this to be spending their leisure moments in thinking of & working for others, & a more suitable one for them to engage in could scarcely be found than the enlightenment of their Indian sisters (most of them about their own station) who are shut up in the prison homes of their Fathers & Husbands, not allowed to see a male Missionary & only to be reached by Christian ladies, many of whom are now in India devoting their time, & some of them their whole means also, to this work.

---

[30] Will had already decided to become a barrister, having been admitted to the Inner Temple on 23 November 1877. He would have to spend up to three years in pupillage with a barrister, not a solicitor.

[31] Fanny Clulow was Edward's sister, and Mr (Rev.) Clulow his brother-in-law. He was the minister of the Wesleyan Methodist Chapel in Harpur Street, known as St Paul's, immediately to the left of the Assembly Rooms, now the Harpur Suite.

[32] The Zanana mission was dedicated to the plight of women in India, particularly those who were forced to live in seclusion. Women's groups, such as those CEB supported, found this an appealing cause.

[33] Spaces are left here, and lower down, which CEB failed to fill in with the amount raised.

*Dec$^r$ 17$^{th}$*

This afternoon Lottie came home much disconcerted; she began her Senior Cambridge Exam on Monday & got through her first three papers with tolerable satisfaction to herself, but although she had before felt more sure of her Arithmetic than any other subject, she got so nervous & excited over her paper (although she says it was not particularly difficult) that she could not collect her ideas sufficiently to work the sums correctly, & trying the most difficult first, feels sure that she has not in the time allowed done enough to pass in this. The poor child was dreadfully vexed with herself & fearful that I should be so also with her, but I comforted her with the assurance that with the knowledge I had of how much she had worked during the two terms she has been at school this year, I was quite satisfied she had done her best & would reap the advantage of the study although she might not pass the exam which at least in this paper will scarcely be a true test for her. I tried to show her that disappointment was part of the discipline of life, & hoped she might never have a keener one.

Mrs Farrar has just sent me as she promised a little book which she has written containing a story of a boy who was sent to the Children's Home by her last Xmas.[34] I have amused John & Papa by reading it through to them before they went to bed. Papa is still thinking about & working at Electric Lighting & is making a machine for it at the Works where he & John went together again after tea until near supper time. In a letter this morning Will says he has constructed a simple & cheap lamp for it which he is waiting to show Papa when he comes home. He intends to leave Clifton for London to-morrow with Hattie on his way home, but first to accompany Florence & her sister to a party at Sir Sidney Waterlow's to-morrow night.[35]

*Dec$^r$ 22$^{nd}$*

Another of our quiet Sabbaths has just come to a close. Papa did not go to Chapel with John, Lottie & myself this morning as he was appointed to preach at Wilstead in the afternoon where John walked with him. To-night we have been to our little Chapel; dear old Mr Howard was to have preached but has been very ill all the week, & when John called at his house after this morning's service to ask after him, & whether any arrangement had been made for to-night's at Southend, he was told that it was feared he was sinking fast.[36] There cannot be any hope that we shall hear his voice again where he always seemed to feel an especial pleasure in preaching, & where I have again & again listened to him with as much pleasure; he delivered his message always feeling from his great age that it might be his last opportunity

34 Mrs Farrar was the daughter of 'old Mr Howard' – see diary for the following days, and next footnote.

35 Sir Sydney Waterlow (1822–1906) started his career in business working as an apprentice in his family's printing business. He became a banker and entered public life as a London councillor. He introduced telegraph links between police stations, and in 1867 was knighted for his work as a juror in the Paris Exhibition of 1867. He was Lord Mayor of London from 1872 to 1873, and a Liberal MP from 1874 to 1885. Waterlow worked for many charities, including the Improved Industrial Dwellings Company which built model low-rent housing for the poor similar to the Peabody buildings, and is perhaps best remembered for his donation of Waterlow Park, near Highgate in north London, to the public as a 'garden for the gardenless'.

36 'Old Mr Howard' was John Howard, who began the family's association with iron founding and the manufacture of agricultural implements. Born in 1791, he was four times Mayor of Bedford (1858–1862).

& with earnestness entreated the people as an old man to flee to that Saviour who had been his strength & support through so many years.

As he had been too ill to think of his work now probably finished here, & no provision being made for it, my dear Husband has had to preach again to-night. He took occasion to speak of the circumstances in which the good old man then appeared to be to the people, & prayed earnestly for him. He also spoke very nicely in reference to the death of the Princess Alice & of the sorrow that had entered the highest family in the land, & then preached from the text 'Be ye therefore also ready etc'.

The congregation was not as large as usual owing probably to the inclement weather in part, but it is sad to think that with a population surrounding the Chapel of more than five times as many as would fill it, so few comparatively feel delight in God's worship & allow any trifle to keep them from His house, but it cannot surely be that the faithful appeals which have been made in it for more than 6 years shall be without its influence for good on our neighbours. 'My word shall not return to me void' is a promise.

### Dec' 25th

This is a sad Xmas day for many we know. Mr Howard died on Monday morning. I have not yet heard the particulars of his last moments further than Mr F Howard[37] told Papa his almost last word was 'beautiful' looking up, as if his dying eyes saw sights those around his bed could not see, & who can tell 'How bright were the realms of light, Bursting at once upon the sight'!

My dear old cousin Mrs Tarry passed away last month & her only son William from his letter seems to feel deeply his Mother's loss, although doubtless too her death was great gain, she was over 70 years of age & the last of the same generation as my dear Mother, that I knew in her family. Alfred & Clara Lyddon lost their dear little three year old babe last week & feel the blow very keenly. I know what their trial must be. The poor Queen too is keeping sorrowful Xmas at Osborne.[38]

Many who have not lost friends have little room for joy. The Glasgow Bank failure, & since that the West of England Bank failure also, have suddenly reduced to the depths of poverty many whose all was invested in them, or will be swallowed up to meet the calls; for some weeks past the papers have given sad accounts of the distress of many who were depending upon or connected with them.[39]

Amidst so much suffering what cause have we as a family for gratitude that no great calamity has befallen us to bring a cloud of sorrow on our home to-day. I have not had the pleasure of having all my boys & girls together as I love to do on Xmas day, for Will is spending it with Florence in London & brings her down to us to-morrow, and Ted, having decided to leave Tewkesbury finally on Jan^y 11th, cannot come home as he at first intended at the same time. Hattie however came home on

---

[37] Mr F. Howard was Frederick Howard, third son of John, and co-founder of the Howard business in 1851 with his brother James, the eldest son. He was later knighted.

[38] CEB refers to the death on 14 December of the Queen's daughter Princess Alice, wife of the Grand Duke of Hesse.

[39] Bank failures were becoming less frequent since the spectacular failure of Overend and Gurney in 1866 stimulated the conversion of private banks into limited liability companies. The Glasgow Bank was not a limited liability bank. Some directors were convicted of fraud, and its failure led to several others, including the West of England Bank.

Monday from London where she stayed a few days with the Kellys on her way from Clifton. John & Lottie too are at home so that we have been very quietly happy. After breakfast all the three started off with baskets containing a few Xmas gifts of puddings, tea, sugar, etc to some old people & widows that we thought would feel happier for a little unexpected help, which they all needed, & the pleasure they showed in receiving gave the children much also. John finished the morning skating on the river, Lottie chose to be at home, & Hattie accompanied Papa & myself to the Cemetery,[40] whither we went to visit our darling Babe's grave & place another wreath on it.

After early dinner the three young ones went skating together; it is some years since they have had such opportunities for it as the last week, the frost has been severe for a fortnight & for a week the river has been frozen & hundreds of people have been on it both skating & walking. Lottie could only begin on Saturday when she really left School, finishing as I tell her the first stage of her education. Her examination finished on Friday & she seems to have done well in it from her papers which Mrs Brown has examined at the end of each day during the week; she fears her unfortunate arithmetic paper will, notwithstanding this, prevent her passing, which there is otherwise little doubt but she would have done with some honors; anyway she will have had the benefit of the preparatory study which is what I thought most of & she needed the incentive to persevere as much as she has.

To return to Xmas day, Papa & I spent the afternoon together alone until near 4 o'clock when it began to snow fast & we started for a little walk to meet the girls with umbrellas. The evening we passed sitting around the bright fire all together & family worship & conversation finished our quiet day. I had forgotten one source of pleasure & amusement, the arrival of the Xmas cards which were numerous, & ranged on the picture frames crowned with holly made the dining-room look very gay.

*Dec' 31st*
The last day of this first year of keeping my diary has come & what a record of continual blessings it is; as a family we have been kept from the inroads of death, the girls' health is so good that I am quite hoping there will not be a need to leave home as we have before had to on their account. John's health seems quite re-established although he began the year with much suffering & a long illness. Then not only are we brought to the close of the year without loss, but with the prospect of a happy addition to it in another Florence, instead of the dear one of the same name that I was nursing in pain & weakness 7 years ago. God is very good to us, both in taking & giving, for our little one is beyond this, & dear Florence Kelly will I believe be another daughter & a good loving wife for Will. He came from London (after having spent Xmas there with her) on Thursday, bringing her with him. I am glad to see that their attachment to each other seems to have mutually much increased, & believing as I do that they have the firmest foundation of all true affection, the love of God in the heart, & because of this love each other so much, I cannot but rejoice in their happiness & be thankful that there is a prospect of their so soon being united.

---

[40] Bedford Cemetery was opened in 1855, situated on rising ground north of Bedford, next to what was thirty years later to become Bedford Park.

Ted's letter of this morning has all the old ring of affection in it which has been somewhat wanting since we have had to see differently from him in some of his movements. He has now become formally engaged to Clara, & when he can afford to marry will I believe have as good and amiable a wife as Will. I have met & talked with Clara more than once since she came home for her holidays & have invited her to come & see us before Ted's return next month (if he comes), but she seems to prefer waiting until then, further than calling, which she did with her Mother yesterday. Eddie says in his letter to-day that he is making application for the post of Assistant House Surgeon at the Bristol Hospital, which I should be very glad for him to get because he would be living near Will & Florence & would have many friends beside, & also because it might lead to something better; at all events he would not be shut up in such an out of the way corner as at Tewkesbury, & as his way there has been closed, I believe that it will be made for him elsewhere.

Papa is going to conduct a 'watch night' service in the School-room of our little Chapel; before it was built we for several years had one, as well as the Sunday night service, in this room, where our neighbours who chose have often assembled for worship. I trust & believe our one great desire is to benefit them & serve God, & I am sure this influences my dear Husband to-night for he would rather enjoy being together at home to 'watch & pray' the new year in. Will & Florence are having a few moments alone together before they go, if thus they begin all their future years, our God will be their God.

## 1879

*Jan^y 16^th*
Florence Kelly came last Saturday (11th) for Will's birthday; her sister Julia accompanied her & both remained until Tuesday morning. The same day Ted also returned from Tewkesbury, his application for the appointment in Bristol having been unsuccessful. Clara Henman paid us her first visit as his fiancée on Monday; they seem much attached to each other & I hope will be wise enough to be satisfied with occasionally meeting until Ted can well afford to marry. It was a real pleasure to me to look on all my children sitting around the dinner table, & with two intended daughters-in-law also, I felt glad & happy to see them all looking so. Clara stayed with us until Wednesday afternoon & left to prepare to go with Ted on a visit to his Grandpapa at Norwood Thursday morning, on which day he left home & accompanied her thither where they now are.

Since Florence left, Will has been almost continually occupied at the Works helping Papa with the Electric light machine which he is making, & perfecting his own lamp, which he thinks has the advantage of being more simple in principle than any he has yet seen. Papa has also an idea for a lamp with one Carbon, & they will probably combine their ideas in one. I like to hear them talk together about their Electricity & am sanguine that between them they may do something to the advantage of both.[41]

---

[41] The genesis of the electric light bulb was a long one, extending well into the twentieth century, when tungsten replaced carbon as a longer lasting material for the filament.

*Jan^y 24^{th}*

Will left us yesterday afternoon for the treble purpose of visiting Florence for a day or two before returning to Clifton, eating his dinners at the Temple, & taking some preliminary steps for Papa & himself conjointly in patenting both an electrical machine & a lamp at which they have both been working very hard, having been at the Works several times until 10 o'clock at night. Will intended to have gone to London earlier in the week, but has been very much engrossed with his lamp & has been sitting pencil & paper in hand a good part of his time when in the house. I hope the time he has spent at home has been useful to him; he could scarcely have gained as much information on the subject of electric lighting anywhere in the same time as he has done from reading up the subject thoroughly to go into the matter with his Papa, talking about it with him continually & seeing what he has been doing at the Works before he came home.

John has been the constant helper of both in the evenings when they have been making trials & experiments & I have been with them late twice, waiting to see the expected result of their efforts. Will's stay with us has been a pleasure to me. I enjoy listening when he & Papa are talking together, although of course I only partially understand a good deal they converse about. This is in all probability the last visit he will pay as a bachelor in his old home, & I shall only be too glad when he has one of his own & a loving companion with him in it.

Lottie has now entered upon her duties as my helper in domestic matters & has left school, much to her satisfaction. She has begun very diligently to help, spending all her mornings, excepting an hour for her music, either in assisting with the cooking or other household work. I tell her she has only entered upon another stage of her education; when we get quite settled I want her to read Ancient History with me in the evenings & join Mr Demar's music & singing classes.[42]

*Feb^y 17^{th}*

To recount briefly the circumstances that have transpired; the most important are Papa's disappointment that the idea he had of an electrode kept cool by water for the new lamp which he was patenting with Will has been adopted by Siemens & patented by him, & this is the more vexing as the model embodying this idea was made & tried early in Dec^r by Papa & might have been secured then, a month before the date of Siemens' patent which he knew nothing of until it was found by the Patent Agent.[43]

*March 26^{th}*

I little thought when I began my journal just a year ago that this first one would record such a rapid march of events as have already transpired, nor that Will would be its prominent topic. Monday (March 24th, another anniversary of our wedding day) I returned home from Bristol where I have been more than a fortnight on busi-

---

[42] CEB mis-spells the name of the locally well-known organist, music teacher and founder of the Bedford Musical Society, Philip Henry Diemer (1836–1910).

[43] Edward's disappointment is understandable. Siemens, which was established in London as well as Germany, were in the forefront of developments in electric lighting. They were responsible for setting up the first electric street lighting in 1881, in Godalming, and later co-founded the Osram light bulb company.

ness little anticipated by either himself or us when we were together at Ventnor at the same date last year to celebrate our Silver-wedding. I went to Clifton a fortnight last Saturday to meet Mrs Kelly & Florence at Will's rooms in East Shrubbery & spend a few days with them there before beginning my real work of getting his house ready for his Bride. Mrs K & F arrived an hour or two before myself & the latter with Will were at the Station to meet me.

After dinner we had a carriage & all went together to look at the house at West-bury,[44] Mr Kelly & I for the first time. Will showed us his purchases & arrangements with some satisfaction & was both displeased & annoyed when I did not express mine, but the reverse. He had evidently thought that if he could make the temporary home which they expect to have there look as comfortable as his rooms used to do at Cambridge, it would be all he & Florence would need for the present; his chief and wise end had evidently been to expend as little as possible & keep his money for the time when to expend instead of earn before he can be called to the Bar.

Mr K had told him he might be 'as economical as he liked' but neither of us were prepared for the extent to which he wished to carry this. He had been to sales & bought many good articles cheaply but so mixed in sorts & in some things so ponderous that I was dismayed at the thought of having to arrange such a home as I thought they ought to have out of them. However after laughing & crying & arguing over matters with him, & with Mr & Mrs Kelly to second me (Florence had little to say on the subject) I succeeded in getting him to consent to the removal of a great book-case that nearly reached the ceiling in the upper sitting room to the lower one, to taking up the floor-cloth which he had himself most carefully nailed down in it & putting it below, also rearranging the furniture generally so that with the addition of some kind presents from Mr & Mrs K & from myself, the place soon bore more the aspect I wished for.

Will was not however grateful to me for my suggestions nor to Mr K for his presents, but would have preferred all being as he intended. He told me he should have done more himself if he had felt justified in doing so, if the liberality of the latter had taken the form of a settlement on Florence instead of her usual allowance (which he has promised to continue), & gifts which will probably amount to more than he would have been satisfied with, judging from Mr K's generosity as far as he has known him.

Sunday morning we all went to the Westbury parish Church & heard Will's & Florence's banns published 'for the first time of asking', which did not matter as we were strangers, but if we had not been, I think he would not have cared in the least. The Vicar read the prayers & preached but as that is not the mode of praying in which I can join with pleasure & the sermon was almost unintelligible to me from the preacher having lost all his front teeth, I did not feel much edified; my chief regret at Will & F not living nearer Clifton is that they will have no near place of worship where they are likely to be profited if I may judge from that morning.

Monday morning returned home thankful & satisfied that I had been able to help the first that had taken final flight from the home nest to build one for himself.

---

[44]  A town some twenty miles west of Bristol.

*April 12th*
The last day of an eventful week in our family annals. On Monday began Eddie's exam for the LRCP[45] for which he has been so long preparing & about which I have for a longer time been anxious; it finishes by a viva voce to-night after which he will know the final result of the whole. He had more than twelve hours' examination during Monday, Tuesday and Wednesday, & as there was nothing more until this evening at 7 o'clock, he came home for the intermediate days. He seems to think he has done pretty well so far, but we shall not know that our hopes are realized until Monday morning when surely we shall not be disappointed.

*April 14th*
My hopes are realized. I have received a short letter from Eddie this evening which he signs 'Edward C Bousfield LRCP & MRCS', the only intimation he gives me that his examination is successfully over but quite sufficient, but I am satisfied & thankful.

*April 18th*
The event which has occupied so much time to prepare for is over & Will & Florence are married. To detail all the events of that day would fill several pages in my journal, but the most prominent I must record.

Leaving Norwood with Papa, Lottie & Hattie by an early train (which we only caught by the Guard stopping it for us after it had really begun to move for starting), we arrived at Sutherland Gardens in good time to dress in the wedding garments.[46] Florence's dress of white satin with stripes of brocaded white flowers, with pearl ornaments & orange blossom wreath, & the veil thrown over all looked very pretty, as indeed was the toute ensemble of the bridal procession.

The Bride looked as if she felt the dignity of her position as she walked up the Church leaning on her Father's arm & held her head very erect; her eldest sister followed closely behind them & then four couples of bridesmaids, the last two little girls. Ted was Will's best-man but the male portion of the assembly were quite eclipsed by the long white train of girls that walked apart from them. The Church had been decorated for Easter & many shrubs & flowers remained which added to the pretty effect of the scene. I stood near to Will with Papa behind me, Mr & Mrs K near to Florence, & many of her Aunts, Uncles & friends around.

A company of friends & relatives numbering about 60 sat down to the Wedding-breakfast, during which I presented to Will a card on which were some verses which I had prepared for him on his marriage, with the motive I usually have when I attempt poetry, to put into a more lasting form than prose often is some sentences which I hope may influence him in future years. He looked surprised & pleased & laughingly prophesied a place in Westminster Abbey for me. When he had read them, or rather when Canon Duckworth did so, for Mr Kelly passed them to him, & without my leave or licence he made them part of his speech in proposing the health of the Bride & Bridegroom; I sat next to him at the Breakfast & when he sat

---

[45] Licentiate of the Royal College of Physicians.
[46] The Kellys' London residence is now known as Sutherland Avenue, which is in Maida Vale, West London. The change of name from Gardens to Avenue occurred in the 1880s or 1890s.

down told him he was very naughty for so doing, however he only smiled at me & begged for a copy of them.

His conversation at the table was more delightful to me than any of the tempting viands with which it was loaded. Will's remark about Westminster Abbey caused him to tell me a funny story relating to Dean Stanley,[47] when at a public entertainment at which his health was proposed by an individual who, having exhausted all the compliments he could think of to pay him for his universal goodness, brought them to a climax by saying 'And he'll bury anybody', the worst possible compliment he could have paid the Dean who he (Canon D) told me had experienced some annoyance at remarks that had been made on some of the Public funerals he had permitted in the Abbey, Charles Dickens's for one.[48] This led to remarks on Dickens's deserts as a literary man from his country, and he joined with me in thinking that he deserved great respect for morality but little for real religion, & so fell short of what he might have accomplished for the benefit of mankind by his clever writings. The Canon left the table just before 3 o'clock to go to his Bible-class, he told us, at that hour; he seems as good as he is a charming man.[49]

Will made a nice little speech in returning thanks to the toast for Florence & himself, & later on quite a facetious one in proposing the health of the Bridesmaids, saying that although he could scarcely call them the nine Muses, yet he certainly could from the knowledge he had of them designate them 'the Musical Nine' & as such drank to them, & it was very funny to hear 'the Musical Nine' re-echoed all around the tables.

Papa's speech in proposing the Host & Hostess was very good, its only failing was that for fear of being too long he sat down before he had said all he wished & intended as a Christian father on the occasion. Ted returned thanks for the Bridesmaids & gave Florence a welcome into our Family on behalf of the younger members of it.

We left Sutherland Gardens about 7 o'clock, Papa, John & Hattie with Ted for Bedford, I & Lottie for Norwood until next day. Will & Florence had a short journey as far as St Albans, they left about 4 o'clock amidst a shower of rice, but fortunately no rain.

*May 5th*

On Thursday morning Mr & Mrs K, Will, Florence, Lottie & myself left by the early train for Cambridge to see Will take his MA degree in the Senate House. The ceremony was not very imposing & does not awaken the same amount of interest amongst the Undergraduates as taking the BA degree after the Tripos.[50]

---

[47] Dean of Westminster. He set up the Palestine Exploration Fund, which supported archaeological excavations in the Holy Land.

[48] Dickens died at his house, Gad's Hill Place, near Rochester in Kent, and it was presumed that he would be buried at Rochester Cathedral. But public opinion demanded that he be buried at the Abbey, and Dean Stanley agreed. The funeral, on 14 June 1870, was a very private one, as he had requested in his will. Only twelve mourners attended, made up of family and close friends, together with the Abbey clergy. So Dickens was buried in the almost empty and silent Abbey, the funeral service being read by the Dean.

[49] Charlotte seems quite taken with the Canon, who was Sub-Dean and a Canon of Westminster Abbey.

[50] The degree of Master of Arts at Cambridge, as at Oxford, is awarded automatically to students who have gained a first degree after a period of seven years has elapsed since they matriculated.

The Galleries (which were quite filled by them when we went four years ago when Will took his, as sixteenth Wrangler[51]) had only half a dozen lookers on & the whole affair was almost a dumb show; the mumble of sound which came from two officials in cap & gown who stood on one side of the dais (which we supposed to be some Latin sentence said in connection with each candidate's name) & the Vice Chancellor's solemnly taking his seat in the front of it, & each advancing as his name was called, & kneeling on a stool at his feet, placing his hands as if praying between the VC's & listening to some sounds (so inarticulate that Will, who looked up at him as if he intended to understand, failed to do so) was all that was to be seen or heard; & the chatter that was kept up on all sides, although in a low tone, made the scene very unimpressive. There were about 150 to receive their degree, some of them by no means young men.

After a rest Lottie & I went to Kings College to meet the others for the evening prayers there, but were a few minutes too late to go with them into the Chapel & remained in the outer one to hear the Organ & singing, after which we all returned to Caius for tea,[52] & then to the station, Mr & Mrs K, Will & Florence going to London, & Lottie & myself returning home. Mr K especially seemed much pleased with the whole day's proceedings & Florence was I think a little proud of her Husband in his new stiff silk MA gown.

*May 9th*

The events of this week are chiefly of a very domestic character, spring cleaning, every corner supposed to be turned out, much to Lottie's annoyance; she declares she will never have spring cleanings in her house when she has one. This is her first year from school & I am glad for her to take domestic lessons, although they are not all to her taste, she will profit by them in days to come, & if she remembers will be amused at what she now says & thinks about them.

*May 19th*

On Sunday week Papa had to preach twice at Turvey & I went with him, driving together for the first time in the chaise, which we enjoyed riding in much more than the Brougham although there was occasional rain.[53] I am so glad he has a carriage that he will always use instead of walking when he has to go out on Sunday, as he has preferred doing to taking a man with him. He preached with much more freedom than he does here, & very nicely. The people seemed very pleased to see him especially those with whom we had tea who made much of me also. I promised to go again on a week-day when Father & Grandma are here & take them to see Leigh Richmond's church. When we came from the afternoon service in the chapel we went to it & remained some time to hear the choir practise as they do every Sunday after prayers in the afternoon. The old man who took care of our horse at

---

51  i.e. he came sixteenth in the rank order of all undergraduates taking the Mathematics Tripos in his year.
52  Gonville and Caius, Will's college at Cambridge.
53  The chaise is a small open carriage with a movable hood: the Brougham a larger four-wheeled closed carriage, usually driven by a coachman.

the Inn told me he well remembered Leigh Richmond & how he used to like to listen to his preaching as a boy.[54]

The past week has been a very busy one in domestic matters, but I have now the satisfaction of feeling that cleanliness & order prevail in our home. Papa has scarcely grumbled once at the necessary interference with the usual state of things, & took down & put up the dining-room pictures without a murmur, which he has not always before done, although he does not like anyone else to touch them. Lottie has been very useful & much more willing to help than I expected; I am quite as pleased for her to have had the training as I am to have had her assistance, I want her to be as clever in household duties as in any accomplishment so called. Last week she joined Mr Demar's piano forte class, also Mr Stannard's drawing class[55] & went for the first lesson with a sketching party. She has now abundant occupation in the house & in practising for both Masters, but I want her to help in distributing tracts when we can get further aid to make Southend into a District, she must not be too busy to have no time to work for God's cause.

On Friday called on Mrs Pike, a widow lady who has just come to the town with her daughter, the former has been several times to our Chapel (St Paul's); the latter only was at home & told us she preferred going to Church, her reasons for doing so seemed to be those of many who feel there is a loss of social position in not belonging to the Establishment, & if this consideration is the first, there is undoubted worldly advantage in being connected with it, but to be classed with 'not many mighty, not many noble' is to occupy a position of which He, whose life was but a pattern of humility, was not ashamed, & the desire for worldly influence which it is so difficult to repress cannot be pleasing to Him in those who profess to be His followers, but these are to be found in all communities that confess Him, their motives are known to Him & by these shall they be judged.

## June 5th

Have taken advantage of another really fine day to fulfil my promise made to the good people of Turvey when I went there with Papa, to take Grandma Bousfield & Grandpapa to see them. After dinner I drove them through Kempston & Bromham, the longer route, Grandma Collins also accompanied us. Everything around us was dressed in brightness & beauty, the delicate tints of the young foliage & the brilliant green of the fields made a charming picture whichever way we looked, & all were delighted with the ride. We alighted at the Church, which was the place we were specially interested in, & went round the interior to look at the monuments, particularly the tablets in memory of good Leigh Richmond & several members of his family. The woman who was busy cleaning in the Church told us that one of his daughters had been staying a week or two at the vicarage where her home had been in her Father's life time, & had left only the previous day. He died in 1827 at the comparatively early age of 55.

After we had taken tea at Mrs Wright's, she went with us to the house of an old

---

[54] Revd. Leigh Richmond was Rector of Turvey from 1805 until his death in 1827. He wrote and preached on family and village life.

[55] Henry Stannard (1844–1920), born at Woburn, was a member of the Norwich School of landscape artists whose leaders were Crome and Cotman. Lottie's drawing classes were based at Mr Stannard's Academy of Arts, situated in Prebend Street.

widow who was converted under Leigh Richmond's preaching. We found the old lady in bed & complaining of great weakness which she told us she felt increased every day; she seemed delighted to talk with us of the good man & very pleased for Father to pray with her. She looked much older than he does, although she is a year younger. She is now a member of the Congregational Church which was formed the year after Revd L Richmond's death by many who were dissatisfied with the teachings of the Clergyman who succeeded him.

I have forgotten to say that on coming out of the church we went to see the tombstones of two graves side by side which both recorded the ages of 105 years, one of a male, the other a female, but of different names. Whilst we were looking at these, old Mr Higgins (who is the organist at the Church & who we heard training the choir when Papa was there) came up to us & remarked on the circumstance & how seldom such a one occurred. We had a little pleasant chat with him; his appearance is very singular, his long white hair almost reaching to his shoulders. He is the owner & occupier of Turvey Abbey & spends most of his time in church matters.[56]

*June 11th*

To-day Father & Grandma Collins left us, the former is a marvel of youthfulness, he has been as active & cheerful as many are twenty years younger, playing & laughing with the girls even more than Papa does, & frequently walking into the town twice in the day.

Yesterday was a very fine day & in the afternoon I drove them to see Clara's Mother.[57] Grandma's pleasure however was interrupted by an accident which happened on Monday morning after she had been into the town & bought for me some strong ammonia. The chemist had not properly secured the cork & on Lottie's breaking the wax which fastened the wrapper of the bottle, it flew out & the liquid also into both their faces, principally in Grandma's, so that one eye was burnt both inside & out, fortunately without injuring the sight. The oil which we applied did it a great deal of good & she was able to go out with it tied up, as it was for travelling to-day.

I have had a letter from Ted to-day after waiting nearly a fortnight for it; in some particulars it has not given Papa & myself pleasure. He replies to my request that he will not make a practice of taking wine by saying that I need be under no apprehension on that account as he never takes 'more than one glass of port at dessert' (how I wish he did not take any), but he confesses that he is smoking more than ever; not having a great deal to do is his excuse for this, but it is a poor one. I have done my utmost to train my boys to eschew these things but what habits they have or may form in this way I cannot now control & can only pray that they may be kept from their 'dominion'.

Last night Papa invited the two Grandmas with Father & myself to the Works to show us the lamps which he has been making for the Electric light. He is still persevering in this matter but his machine, like his first lamp, has been to some extent superseded by a patent which has been published before his, so that he will

---

[56]  Charles Longuet Higgins (1806–1885) was a member of the Higgins family, Lords of the Manor of Turvey. He was a benefactor of the village, the first chairman of the Board of Guardians, and High Sheriff of Bedfordshire in 1860.

[57]  The Henmans lived at Sutton Cottage in Kempston, at that time a village just south of Bedford.

probably have to alter to steer clear of it. One lamp in particular which he showed us pleased me much, the consumption of the carbons was so divided, by placing a number side by side & quite near each other, on a kind of endless chain, which continually but very slowly revolved, that by increasing the length of chain the carbons may be kept burning for a very much longer time than any single one alone however long could possibly be. I think this will be his lamp. Will writes that he has been hard at work on the one which he is making & has tried it with tolerable success but has discovered some defects which he is now working to remedy.

### June 12th

The Head Master of the Grammar School[58] sent Papa & myself a card of invitation for the Speech day to which I went with Lottie & Grandma Bousfield at the Corn Exchange this afternoon. The Lord Lieutenant of the county, Earl Cowper, was present together with the Mayor & corporation. The boys who had gained prizes received them from the Head Master. It seems but a short time since I was a far more interested spectator in such a scene. When Will left the Modern School Earl Cowper presented the prizes, & as he carried off the first prize for everything but writing, I remember his lordship specially complimented & shook hands with him, & I believe we sent a wheel-barrow to bring his books home. The sight to-day recalled all this very vividly & Mrs Richards[59] and Grandma who were with us to-day say they were also present on that occasion.

### Sunday June 22nd

Just returned from the little Chapel with Grandma B, Aunt Jenny[60] & Hattie; John & Lottie have gone into the town to hear an old minister from London (Mr Hargreaves) who preaches to-night. Papa has gone to Haynes[61] since dinner to take two services there. To-day what on the printed bills is called the 'fourth Anniversary' of the Sunday school, which I began the year after our little Chapel was built,[62] with John, Lottie, Hattie & Miss Hulch as teachers, has been celebrated, & whilst looking around on the children & the congregation this evening I had mingled feelings of thankfulness & annoyance, the former to think that we had been permitted to carry out a work in its erection, which must live after we have passed away, & the latter to see those who had no part of the labor putting themselves in places of prominence & making themselves important without cause; but although I felt this I am almost surprised that I feel as satisfied & thankful as I do that we took the course we did when Papa & I were found fault with by those who 'love to have the pre-eminence' that we did too much to carry on what we had been at so much pains to get.[63]

---

[58] Ted and John had been pupils at the Grammar School, now known as Bedford School. The Head-master was James Surtees Philpotts.

[59] Mrs [Fanny] Richards was the daughter of Edward's youngest sister, Hannah Maria, who married George Cato, a South African business man and politician, who rose to wealth and power (Mayor of Durban, vice consul for Denmark, Norway and Sweden), and was known as King Cato.

[60] Aunt Jenny was one of Edward's sisters, who lived in Southport.

[61] A village south of Bedford.

[62] The 'little Chapel' was built and opened in 1873, the year after the death of their last child, Edris.

[63] CEB refers to opposition which she met which led to her 'giving up the work'. There were to be other examples of this. The reason cited here is that she and Edward 'took too much upon themselves'. Was CEB too domineering and lacking in sensitivity in dealing with colleagues?

Old Mr Howard asked me how it was we had altered in our activity & labors for the place that he always admired & loved to preach in, & when I told him we had given up the work to those who thought we 'took too much upon us', he replied 'Ah, that was what they said to Moses, & the earth opened her mouth & swallowed them all up', to which I answered I did not wish such a dreadful doom to fall upon those who were jealous of us, & laughed at the dear old gentleman's wit.

But although we may never again take an active part in managing its affairs, nothing can alter our affection for the place that stands upon the ground which Papa gave for it, & of which I turned the first sod the morning it was marked out for beginning to build on it, & for which we both begged & worked until it was paid for; one motive I know actuating us, not what others would say or think, but that those who lived around us might have opportunity of hearing the Word of Life; this they have & will have as long as it stands.

*July 5ᵗʰ 1879*
The last night of another busy week, but more of pleasure than business. Monday evening went to the Midland Station to meet Mʳ Clulow & Family. Jenny accompanied me & remained to wait for the next train as they did not reach Bedford until the last train. Mʳ C as genial & good as we have always found him.

The Royal Show began June 30th that same day & a week earlier than usual. Papa decided not to go until the second day when I was obliged to leave my four visitors to each other's & Lottie's care, or not carry out my wish & promise to Mr Kelly to accompany him during the time he would be in London, making their house our home for that time. John & indeed all of us were invited to stay at Sutherland Gardens. Starting with Papa on Tuesday after tea we were kindly welcomed on our arrival by both Mr & Mrs Kelly.

Next morning Papa & John left immediately after breakfast for the Show & business; an hour later the Brougham was at the door to take Mr & Mrs K, Julia[64] & myself. We left the house in the midst of sunshine, which was succeeded by a shower of rain almost as soon as we reached the ground, this was but such weather as had been day after day for weeks past, & the scene around us as we entered the Show-yard was that of a dismal swamp. The unprecedented quantity of rain that has fallen almost prevented the exhibition being opened at the time named, & quite precluded things being in their usual order on such occasions. On all sides were to be seen waggons, engines, etc buried to the axles in the deep mud, or in some cases half turned over just where they stuck fast on their way to their different positions. Between the long rows of Exhibitors' sheds & around & through the centre of the show ground great efforts had been made to make a tolerably dry path-way for visitors by laying down planks & hurdles, & for a time by taking care to keep on these we managed to get about without much discomfort for an hour or two, but found the pleasantest thing would be to get seats under shelter of the awning over the stand erected for viewing the horses which were all brought out to be paraded in a large enclosed space in front of it. Here we remained through the afternoon & saw not only the horses but the Dukes of Edinburgh & Connaught who with the two Duchesses drove past where we sat to their places in the centre of the semi-circle.

---

64  Julia Kelly, Florence's sister.

A thunderstorm & torrents of rain at intervals compelled us several times to use our umbrella under the awning, but in spite of the rain & mud we got back to the carriage without much injury except to boots, but had quite enough of the Show under such difficulties.

### July 14th

I have been spending a good deal of time to-day reading the account of the funeral of the poor young Prince Napoleon who but a few weeks ago left his widowed Mother & his exile home to follow the fortunes of the British army in Zululand; strange what motive could induce him to leave her, and place himself in circumstances of danger where duty did not call him, and stranger that she, & those who regarded him as the hope of France, should have permitted him to run a risk which had such a possible if not probable termination as has come to pass.[65]

Mrs Richards has this evening brought me some Natal papers of June 11th, which have just arrived, to read, & the account which these give both of his death and the deep feeling of sorrow which pervades the whole Colony, shown by the honor paid to his remains along the whole route from the spot where he fell to the point where they were embarked for the sad return to England & his Mother, shows how he was esteemed. Poor husbandless, childless Mother! How little can all the pomp & sympathy which was shown from the Queen & Royal family (all the sons pall-bearers, & the Queen with the poor Empress whilst her 'boy' was being carried out to his burial) to the poor French workmen & women who loaded his coffin with flowers, or showed their love by their tears, assuage her grief; 'the only balm', one of the Roman Catholic preachers said in his sermon yesterday, 'that she has is the blessed hope that her son has found acceptance with his God & Saviour'. July 12th (my Mother's birthday 80 years ago was on that date) he was laid by his Father's side in the little Chapel at Chislehurst. The 'Telegraph' correspondent says it had been his lot in less than forty years to witness the carrying to the tomb of three Napoleons, the First to the Invalides, the Third in the little Kentish chapel, & 'his poor brave boy in the same receptacle to-day'.

### July 18th

I have had two letters from Florence this week written from Malvern where Will still is, they say they will spend the first part of their vacation with us, coming August 5th. Florence apologizes in the second letter for not having remembered my birth-day, which Will ought rather to have done; he thinks their joint signature at the end makes up for not having written to me himself! When he has children of his own he will better understand how much Parents value the expressed as well as silently manifested love of these.

---

[65] Napoleon III, his wife the Empress Eugenie, and his only son, the Prince Imperial, fled to England after the defeat of the Imperial French army in the Franco-Prussian War in 1870 and the consequent fall of the Second Empire, and settled at Chislehurst in Kent. After the death of Napoleon III in 1873, the Bonapartists named the Prince Imperial Napoleon IV, and he was certainly the hope of this group if not of France as a whole. His decision to take part in the British war against the Zulus was motivated by a combination of gratitude for the support given to him and his family, and his need to live up to the reputation of his family name.

*August 3rd*

To-day has been a real Sabbath, quiet & restful, although it was not ushered in very peacefully. John went last night to meet Papa on his return from London by the late train & drove him from the Station in the chaise. Whilst waiting a heavy storm of hail & thunder came on & I was thankful to see them come in safely although they got wet. The lightning did not cease before our going to bed, but about half past 1 o'clock this morning the storm seemed to return with great fury & kept us awake more than two hours. I never remember having seen such vivid & incessant lightning as continued for that time, accompanied by thunder, wind & rain; it was truly awful, & lying in bed as I was I felt deeply awed, knowing what mighty forces were let loose around our dwelling. I committed myself & my dear ones to His keeping who rules the storm & felt secure, but realized how in an instant one stroke might sever soul & body & that the only real security in life is to live prepared for the end whenever it may come, as it does to so many, if not most, unexpectedly.

*August 13th*

Will is spending part of every day at the Works, carrying out with Papa their joint ideas in electrical lighting which are yet far from perfected, although the latter has from the time they began working at it continued to experiment & devote nearly all his leisure to it.

The thunderstorm which I mentioned in the last page was spoken of in the Papers as the most terrific that had occurred for many years & the 'Telegraph' in a leader on it said it would be remembered as the great storm of August 3rd 1879.

The next day (Monday Bank Holiday) we were at the river-side at the Works to see a large Balloon ascent from a field on the opposite side. Whilst waiting there, some men in a boat with drags accosted us & asked whether we knew where the boy had been overturned from a canoe into the water, which was the first we heard of the accident, & whilst watching these men another very similar occurred by the heedless dashing & splashing about in the river of people with boats who did not know how to manage them, only in this case the two (an old & a young man) that were turned over in a little boat were picked up immediately and landed on the bank near to us.

In the afternoon all of us except Ted went to Ampthill Park & had tea in it. John rode the Bicycle in turn with Will, & Papa & myself with the girls & Florence rode & walked by turns; the afternoon was delightful & we thoroughly enjoyed our meal in the open air.

Papa has tonight (Wednesday) been to the Sale of the remainder of dear old Mr Howard's property at the Swan[66] & bought another of the houses in Victoria Terrace which adjoins the two he bought a few weeks since.[67] He has done this chiefly, he says, because I wish it; I trust I am not greedy of gain but I shall be glad when my dear Husband can live without some of the business annoyances he now has, & all that helps to bring this nearer I am thankful for, but trust we shall be faithful stewards in all that we have.

---

66  The Swan Hotel is an old coaching inn situated on the Embankment overlooking the Town Bridge.
67  From old Mr Howard – see entry for 7 October, below.

*August 15th*

This has been a delicious summer day & we have taken tea (as we did yesterday) on the lawn, since which Florence & I have walked into the town with Lottie, who has been to the practice of the choir at the Chapel. Since supper I have had my harp & with Will, Ted & Lottie have been singing some of the children's songs I used to sing with them years ago when, with the dear one now joining in the chorus above, they used to sit around me & join their voices in one I loved to hear, 'Why do I love Jesus', Baby calling to Papa to sing too 'Shout, shout the victory, we're on our journey home', but the tones have all changed & 'The children, where are they?'

*August 28th*

Florence & Will's visit has ended, the former left us on Tuesday morning, the latter this evening. I think Florence has felt happy & at home with us as we have with her, not a word on either side has marred the pleasure of her first stay with us as Will's wife. I forgot to say that Florence would have gone on Monday (as Will wished her to get some London visits paid whilst he was finishing his work here) but she remained over the afternoon to be present at & help me with my Mothers' meeting tea. The day was fortunately fine & we laid the tables for the women on the walk behind the house which was sheltered from sun & wind. They seemed to enjoy their meal very much; after tea all went into the field for an hour for croquet, bowls, etc & then returned to the breakfast-room where, seated in rows, we entertained them with music. Will, Florence, Ted, Clara & Lottie sang to them, accompanying them the piano or my harp, then they joined in some tunes of their own selection, after which Papa came in, talked very appropriately to them for a little while & then read & prayed, after which they left seemingly thankful & happy.

*August 29th*

This morning old Mrs Hutchence came to wish me good bye before going to Kempston to live. I got Ted to prescribe for her rheumatism which has come on since I last saw her. He had scarcely finished for her when a stranger called to ask if I could give him an in-patient ticket for the Infirmary,[68] again Ted's medical knowledge was called for to look into his case, & finding it one that will probably benefit, he has been to see the House Surgeon who has promised to take him in to-morrow. I am very much interested in the old man who is an intelligent Scotchman who has for years been getting a living as a Hawker until unable to pursue his calling owing to a bad leg which, with rest & good living the Drs tell him will get better. He told us he had spent nearly his last shilling to get from St Neots to Bedford by the carrier, hoping to get admission into the Infirmary & was apparently by chance directed here. Perhaps He who cares for the sparrows sent him.

*Sept* *1st*

After Lottie left this evening I called for Mrs Richards & took her for a drive as I came from the Station; we met Papa driving to the harvest field not far from home; he got into the carriage & went with us, or rather we went with him, to see

[68] Subscribers were allowed to nominate a number of in- or out-patients according to the amount of their subscriptions.

his 'binder' at work. He is following up last year's experiences, following it in the field whenever he can, as he will continue to do until he has got it to his mind. The weather has been fine since Friday & the harvest now seems fairly begun, but how late!

*Saturday Sept' 6th*
Wednesday, Tract Distributors' meeting at Moravian School-room; called to see Mrs Rose, drove home to tea & walked into the town after to wish Mr & Mrs Broadbent adieu; they left for Ramsgate on Friday. Thursday morning called at the Infirmary to see the old Scotchman, found him very contented & pleased with everything, his chief occupation sitting up in bed must be writing, at which I found him, & he has sent me by post enough to have taken him some hours, a long poem in my honor, another for Papa & a letter of thanks & requests for a little money for his washing, some old newspapers, etc. The old man is grateful & is getting better.

Saturday, as soon as possible after dinner, Papa drove us to Ampthill Park to the same spot where we had tea three weeks before with Will & Florence. We spread our tea things, as then, on the stumps of the old trees under a great beech tree; a slight shower of rain came on from which we were quite sheltered & went on enjoying our tea, after which Papa stretched himself on the rug with a basket for his pillow & had a short nap. Then John & Alec[69] went to the 'Ossory Arms' for the chaise whilst Papa walked with me through the fields to Millbrook Church where they met us. These little Saturday outings are a real recreation to Papa after his week's thinking & working & I shall try to keep up the custom.

The wire Binder he has about made right, & is now trying to get one out to tie the sheaves with string as they are cut by the reaper. This is much more difficult & will I dare say occupy his mind as long as the harvest lasts.

*Sept' 27th*
This afternoon we have been (John & myself) in the cornfield with Papa to see the 'Binder' at work; it is now taking much of his time & attention as it is not yet quite to his mind, although it worked very well; several people came to the field to see it [including] Mr & Mrs Nutter & Mr J Howard;[70] the latter came up to me & shook hands & chatted awhile very pleasantly, after riding up the field on the Reaping-machine to save his leg which is still lame.

*Oct' 7th*
I had another letter from Will soon after his former one to say that having seen Capt[n] Alcock (who was ill in bed), he had come to a conclusion with him & had at once finished with his pupils; he says that they & their Mother are exceedingly sorry but, all things considered, he has I believe done what will be an ultimate gain, although present loss. His occupation with them made his law reading too secondary a matter & he is now earnestly pursuing it as he never has done before.

Papa & I have had a drive to-day to Pavenham where he had sent a reaping & binding machine to try it, after further alterations, in a field of wheat which at this

---

69 CEB refers to John's friend as Alec, but he was generally known as Alex, and will be cited as such.
70 James Howard, head of the firm after the death of his father.

date is still uncut. I walked round the corn after it with Papa & he was much more satisfied than before; if it had not been for the sodden state of the ground after the excessive rains it would have worked quite satisfactorily, but the weight of the machine often caused it to sink & clog & so stopped it until cleared again.

Papa has promised if possible to leave for his holiday on Saturday the 18th, of course I am to go with him & am quite anticipating the change & a visit to West-bury. Mr F Howard called Papa into his Office a few days since & made him an offer at a reduced price of the house immediately adjoining this, rather than put it up to auction for the third time; he would not give him a reply until he had talked with me about it; as he seemed anxious for Papa to have it & left the payment quite at his convenience, we concluded to do so & now have four out of the six houses that old Mr Howard owned in Victoria Terrace. Papa has sold some Chinese Stock to buy them but this has been at a good profit & makes up a little for his losses in Turkish Bonds in past years.

I think we are not actuated by a desire 'to add house to house' but these seemed to come into our possession so easily, & even after deciding not to buy them that I hope it is providential. God has indeed been good in giving us enough of this world's goods to place us beyond the probability of need in case Papa should at any time determine to do what he has often been tempted to, finish his more than 20 years connexion with the Britannia Works.

I could write quite a history of how he came here a young man just as they were built, after having been made willing to become a servant instead of a Master, by his losses as one in the two short years preceding our coming to Bedford from Stickle-path.[71] What seemed to others the greatest mistake of our lives has been over-ruled for our temporal prosperity, & I believe usefulness as Christians.

### Nov 18th

After being at home for some days with a bad cold Hattie went back to school on Thursday (13th) & is to be a Boarder with Mrs Brown during the remainder of this term. The Cambridge Exam which is now drawing near & for which she is preparing seems to be the chief subject of her thoughts by day & dreams at night.

I have to-day bought 10 shares of £1 each in the 'Bedford Coffee Tavern Co'. I think it will be a benefit to the working men of the town & I wanted to have a little interest in it. Papa was not willing to take shares as he was quite disgusted with the little support the Teetotallers gave 'the British Workman'[72] which, with a few other gentlemen, he did his best to promote but which had to be given up some months since. I believe however this will be a success & have taken the shares on my own account; he did not seem to disapprove when I told him what I had done. Mr Halliley (the solicitor at whose office I bought them) told me he was at school with my two Sons; I think I have heard Will speak of him when they were school-boys together

---

[71] Edward and CEB lived in Sticklepath, a village on the northern edge of Dartmoor, for two years before they moved to Bedford in September 1858. It would appear that Edward's apparently unsuccessful business, as Master, was in the manufacturing of agricultural tools of some kind.

[72] *The British Workman* magazine started in 1855. Its aim was to 'promote the health, wealth and happiness of the working classes' and it was broadly both Temperance and Evangelistic.

but I never remember to have seen him before; he is a very gentlemanly young man & gave me a good deal of information about the Coffee Co.[73]

### Nov 26th

Just a week ago I made up my mind quite suddenly after breakfast (Thursday 20th) to go to London to get papers for the houses being renovated in Victoria Terrace, carbons for Papa's electric light, & to see Will & Florence who have been at Sutherland Gardens since a few days after we left them at Westbury.

Calling first at Mr Kelly's I found Florence at home & Will away making arrangements & enquiries relative to the course he has to pursue when he begins his legal studies with a Barrister as he intends to do after Xmas. I intended to have returned the same night, but finding that in spite of all the efforts they have been making ever since they came to London to find a house to suit them, they had not succeeded in doing so until the day or so before, & had not then decided, I accepted Mrs K's invitation to stay the night & accompany them next morning to look at one at Cricklewood which seemed more desirable than any other they had seen. After breakfast with Mr & Mrs Kelly we went & all agreed that it was what would be for the present just what they needed. Mrs K is pleased that she is within twenty minutes drive of the house & I that they will be nearer Bedford than I thought possible to be living in London, the station being some miles nearer than St Pancras & close to the house so that it will be always easy to go to see them.

Returned home Friday night by the last train, being just too late for the earlier one by which I hoped to have come. Will met me at the station (St Pancras) with the carbons which he went to get for me, as the snow & cold prevented my going anywhere after our return from Cricklewood in the morning.

### Dec 4th

In the fortnight that has elapsed since I was in London I have had need of patience. Elizabeth has again had to leave to go to the Infirmary. I thought myself fortunate in getting her place filled immediately, but at the end of little more than a week her successor suddenly complained of illness & I had to let her go at once. Mrs Billingham told me of a very young girl who had just come to see her & wanted a situation; being then at her house I told her to fetch her & she is now (aged fifteen) my house-maid until I can meet with a suitable one.

During this period of deranged domestic affairs, Florence, Will & Lawrence Kelly have been with us. They came the day following my return from London & left this morning for Westbury. Will has again spent most of his time at the Works about the electric light & stayed longer than he intended to complete another lamp which he got finished & tried last night, & with which both he & Papa seem very satisfied. Lawrence is reading & getting ready for an examination under Will's Tutor-ship; he is a very pleasant youth, but I fear found our sober ways & country life dull. I went to the Station with the three this morning & saw them off for Bristol by Midland.

---

[73] This entry marks the beginning of CEB's close involvement with the temperance movement, which was to play such a large part in her life over the next few years.

*Dec<sup>r</sup> 17<sup>th</sup>*

Having been without visitors a fortnight & without much difficulty obtaining another house-maid who seems likely to suit, matters domestic have taken a very even course, & I can scarcely tell how it is that I have been almost continually occupied; collecting the annual subscriptions to the Foreign Missions, journeys to Victoria Terrace to look after the workmen who are preparing No 3 for the new tenants who have entered upon it to-day, & going into the town on ordinary business & for the Mothers' meeting coal club, has kept me from home a great deal. This year, having a smaller number than usual in the two clubs, I have got Mr Curtis to get & distribute the coal for me instead of as before getting Papa to order it from the Colliery.

This day seems but a sample of many others. This morning after giving directions for dinner etc at home, went into town about 11 o'clock, ordered beef & suet for to-morrow, then to Mr Curtis to send coal to two women whose names had been omitted in the list; thence to the Terrace to see that the woman had finished her cleaning at the house & to get a fire lighted in one of the sitting rooms for the new comers this cold day; after this to class, where I was a quarter of an hour late but preferred going part of the time. Mr Elton asked me to pray before I had been in the room five minutes, which I tried to do with I fear a not very collected mind. Returned home in time for dinner. After a rest went into the kitchen with Lottie to help Mrs Billingham make mince-meat; wrote one letter before tea & another after to Ted, then went into the school-room to hear Mr Vine preach, which, with a little newspaper reading, has finished its occupation. All days are not so varied but I wonder sometimes when I shall feel quiet & sit at needlework or some in-door pursuits at which some ladies accomplish so much. If I have a sense that what I do is duty I am always contented, but I must grow older or weaker I believe before I shall prefer what is not active duty.

Before returning home this morning Lottie wished to call at Mrs Brown's to make enquiries after Hattie; she is now in the midst of her Cambridge examination. On Tuesday she was in a sad trouble; after leaving the room where the exam was held, she found one of the Arithmetic papers which she ought to have handed in to the Examiner amongst her waste paper. Knowing that without this she could not possibly pass, she gave up all for lost & indulged in very bitter tears. Mrs Brown had little hope of getting over the difficulty for her but went to the Examiner & explained her mistake to him; seeing that the sums were on the paper provided, that they were well done & could not have been tampered with, he very kindly consented to take the paper, much to her joy as well as Mrs B's. She seems to think she has done very well in geography & grammar yesterday & all were in very good spirits as we met them coming out of the house this morning to continue their exam. Six of her school-fellows have gone in for it also.

Papa was elected to the Circuit Stewardship at the Quarterly meeting last week, & I was congratulated in the street on the event & on being 'Stewardess'. I hope I may do anything that may be my part for him, & for God's cause, well but the work is not likely to be subject for congratulation as far as I can see.

**1880**

*January 5th 1880*

On New year's day I went to the opening of the first 'Bedford Coffee Tavern', a ticket was sent to me as a Shareholder. Papa did not feel inclined to take any shares in the Co, but thinking it a good movement & wishing to see a little of the inner working of it, I took 10 shares on my own account a month or two since. The Lord Lieutenant, Duke of Bedford, High Sheriff & other notables met in the coffee-room where the first named formally opened the Tavern by a little speech & all adjourned to the New Corn Exchange where a public meeting was held. Will met me there with his sisters & Florence, at the end they returned home & I to see Mrs Richards; after tea went with her, to the Missionary meeting at Clapham,[74] Mr Elton & Miss Cornforth[75] accompanied us in the Cab. This little Chapel was one in which Mr Clulow was very much interested as it was built & opened during the time of his residence in Bedford to take the place of the little old place that had until then served as one.

Sunday was a bright fine day; it was quite a pleasure to walk to & from Chapel where I went with Papa, the girls & John. The Chapel was nearly full below & Mr Cornforth conducted the service in a very suitable manner but occasioned Papa a momentary annoyance by motioning him to take off his glove which he had, contrary to his usual custom, forgotten to do, before kneeling at the Communion table. I cannot but regard this as a remnant of Popery, or at least of popish adoration of the elements used in the Sacraments, & in the simple way in which Christ himself gave it first to His disciples find a model of how it should be given & received. 'Take ye all of it.' 'Divide it amongst yourselves.' Taking it from the hands of minister or priest, kneeling in its reception & paying attention to gloved or ungloved hand in so doing I regard as quite apart from & unworthy of the spirit of 'This do in remembrance of Me'. The bread & wine are the materials through which this is done, & I do not pretend to venerate them, which it seems to me can be the only meaning implied.

*Jany 6th*

Florence left us this morning with rather a sorrowful countenance that she was going without her Husband; Will is still working at electric lamps & since he came has made another at the Works which is not quite to his mind & which he stays to make so. As Florence is so near home, or rather Sutherland Gardens, she will only call at Cricklewood to see that all is right at their house (which is nearly in order) & sleep in London until Will can join her. Lottie & myself accompanied her to the Station, from whence we called on Mrs Richards & then went on to see what the men were doing at No 6 Victoria Terrace which was begun yesterday to be prepared for the tenants who are to come into it next month. After dinner the Mothers' meeting in Butt St, & since tea Lottie has been with me to the United Prayer meeting at the Bedford Rooms.

---

74  A village to the north of Bedford.
75  The daughter of the Minister of Southend Methodist Church.

*Jan^y 16^th*

We heard from Will on Wednesday that he had begun to read & work with a Barrister at his Chambers[76] & that his first-class season railway ticket was less than he expected so he should be able to go home for early dinner sometimes which, for Florence's sake, I am glad of.

On Wednesday the annual Society tea was held at the School-room St Paul's, after which the meeting in the Chapel. Papa came to the latter at 7 o'clock & took his seat in the corner of the pew, but was speedily espied & fetched out of it by Mr Cornforth who came to him & requested him to take his place where he could address the people; at first he looked as he felt, I am sure, as if he would much rather have remained where he was. After Mr Elton & Mr Bonser had spoken, he was called upon &, without any apparent difficulty of hesitation, said well & wisely words that seem to fix everyone's attention to them & every eye on him, & will I trust be remembered through the coming year. This is the first public act of his Circuit Stewardship, which [if] these are tokens will be a more arduous one than he expected.

*Jan^y 19^th*

On Saturday night Dr Rigg came to be our guest for Sunday & left before 9 o'clock this morning.[77] His visit to Bedford was to preach a funeral sermon for dear Uncle Clulow which he did last night to a very crowded congregation in St Paul's Chapel; it was computed that 1000 persons were present. I failed to appreciate his sermon from 1st Corinthians Chap ... verse ...,[78] but the paper from which at the end he read a sketch of the character of his late friend & former colleague was what all came to hear, rather than the preaching, & in this none were I think disappointed. His account of Mr Clulow's work all through his ministerial course, both as a worker & a man of business, were all that could be desired of a 'good & faithful servant' & his character as a Christian, as he described it, most truthful, 'firm as a rock wherever a principle was involved, but genial & full of kindness withal'.

*Jan^y 28^th*

In the afternoon on Thursday I called for Mrs Richards & a friend who is visiting her from Cape Colony (Miss Driver) & took them for a drive in the chaise. Miss D is in England for the first time & is much pleased to have seen our winter, which she has done to perfection, as also in Scotland where she went first; it is long since we have had so severe an one, the river has been frozen over sufficiently for skating four different times. I took them to Ampthill after very early dinner on Monday, put up the horse there & walked with them into the park to look at the old oaks etc, after which had tea at Mr Rushbrook's & returned home immediately after, reaching before dark as the moon was nearly full & made the day seem longer.

---

[76] In order to qualify, Will needed to keep 12 terms by eating dinners at his Inn (the Inner Temple) and to pass two examinations, one in Roman and one in English law. Will is here describing the beginning of his pupillage, in which he was working for a barrister at the same time as reading for the exams.

[77] Dr J.H. Rigg was a prominent Wesleyan minister and educationist. He was Principal of Westminster Training College, a Wesleyan foundation, and a member of the London School Board from 1870 to 1876.

[78] Spaces left here in the text.

Florence Brown[79] took tea with Lottie. Papa was in London for the day; Mrs R, Miss D & FB stayed to supper & went home in the Brougham when it went to the station to meet Papa.

He had been in Chancery Lane on business & so was close to the 'Chambers' of Mr Browne[80] with whom Will is; there he found him in what appeared to him almost an underground room dignified by that name in Stone Buildings, Lincoln's Inn. They returned to Cricklewood together for late dinner; this is Papa's first visit to their new home which is he says all that he & Florence could desire or need for some years to come.

Papa made me feel rather dismal on Will's account, first by telling me that he did not think him looking at all well, & then by talking about another young Barrister in the same Chambers with Will who was 'called' some time ago & had since that got three briefs value altogether 5 guineas! When I think of such a slow process of getting a living as such seems to be, I feel as if we had made a mistake in advising Will to make the law his profession, but all Barristers have had the same difficulties to contend with & I flatter myself he has more strings to his bow, as a scientific man and an engineer, than most of them & so a better hope of earlier success.

The most important event of last week was a visit which Papa received from his co-circuit-steward, who had been requested to see him by the Chapel Steward (Mr Moulton) to ask him to have a meeting in reference to the invitation which will be given to Mr Cornforth at the next Quarterly meeting to remain in Bedford a third year, which Mr M it appears is anxious should not be done. This is the quarter from which I feared the troubles would arise that would make his new office more difficult than it need have been. Papa wrote to Mr M as a member of his class expressing his regret that he should desire any steps to be taken with such an end in view as injurious to the prosperity of the Circuit; the only reply to this was a request that he would call a meeting 'to consider the working of the Circuit' as early as possible & appending the names of more than a dozen Leaders who united with him in the requisition.

On Saturday night after tea Papa went out to call on as many as he could of the most influential of these to enquire their real motive & reasons for signing, & found that nearly all had done so under a wrong impression & with no desire to interfere with Mr C's re-appointment. Under these circumstances he has written to Mr M that he can find no necessity for so unusual a course & that the only proper place for such a discussion before the Quarterly meeting must be the Leaders' meeting; to this he has not received a reply. I hope Mr Cornforth may not hear of all this or he will not accept an invitation with such pleasure & will feel much hurt & annoyed.

*Jan^y 29^th*

Yesterday evening the new organ which has been put into Bromham-road Chapel was opened by a musical service at which Papa, at the repeated request of the Chapel Steward etc, consented to preside. Music is not very much in his way & his address as Chairman was slightly too solemn for the occasion but was short & did not keep the people long from what they came most to hear. Mr Austin deserves

79  Mrs Brown's eldest daughter.
80  Probably Mr C. Browne, an experienced barrister who had been admitted to the Bar in 1846.

great credit for what he has made the choir able to perform by his training & they sang some pieces very well, but I did not enjoy listening to them as much as I should if their music had been much more simple & the organ the only accompaniment, instead of several violins, violoncello etc with it. It is a nice little organ & will be valuable if it leads the singing rightly.

When we came out of the Chapel the fog was so intense that it was not possible to see the length of the horse before the Brougham and Billingham[81] drove against the kerb-stone before we had gone many yards, so that John had to lead the horse & stoop down towards the ground to see where we were going & prevent our doing so again. We got home safely but I never saw anything like such weather in Bedford before as it was freezing at the same time; every tree this morning was laden with a splendid hoar frost, the near ones looking like gigantic branches of coral & the distant ones looked clothed in foliage of the purest white instead of green, & in the bright sunshine the prospect from our windows this morning was truly magnificent. After dinner I had a ride to Oakley, partly tempted by the splendid weather, in spite of the continued frost.

*Feb^y 10^th*

On Wednesday night Papa proposed my going to London the next day to do a little business for him & anything else I might wish. I left home Thursday morning after very early breakfast, to the Station before 8 o'clock taking my ticket for Child's Hill where I arrived about half past 9 o'clock & found Florence on the platform to meet me as she had received my Post card sent late the previous night to say I should call on Will & herself on my way through.[82] Will usually goes into the City by that train but remained to the next just to see me. I left again with him at 10 o'clock promising Florence to return at night to spend the next day with them. Will left me in the train at Farringdon St (which is the Station to which he always goes for Lincoln's Inn).

I went on to Camberwell to see the Mary Datchelor schools which Dr Rigg recommended to me for Hattie & of which his daughter is Head Mistress; saw her & went into several of the class-rooms. I was not at all prepossessed in Miss R's favor, a little cold consequential lady that doubtless could smile when she chose, but did not give me an opportunity of seeing her do so. The elder girls were having a dictation when I went into their room & the three words which I heard the teacher who was reading to them pronounce as the door was opened, 'against the cold', which sounded to me as if spelt 'cowld', did not give me a favorable impression of her, so that altogether I was not very sorry that the schools were too far from the station & Ted for Hattie to go to them, if he could have had her to live with him as he once named to me.

*March 13^th*

How little I thought when I began this diary less than two years ago that in that time I should have to chronicle the fact that I am Grandmama! Yet so it is. A letter from Will received this afternoon announces the birth of a son last evening about 5

---

[81] The successor to Howcutt as gardener, coachman and odd-job man.
[82] Child's Hill station is now much enlarged and renamed as Cricklewood Station. Note the efficiency of the post: the card posted on Wednesday night was delivered before 9.30 the following morning.

o'clock & that Mother & babe are doing well.[83] The girls are quite excited to think they are Aunts, & have been counting up that the little one will have 6 Grandparents & 9 Uncles & Aunts! May its Parents have wisdom to train it not only 'for the life which now is, but for that which is to come'. Will describes it as a very pretty baby with dark hair & eyes & altogether 'a wonderful creature'; it seems not so very very long ago that we thought the same of him, & yet Papa in his letter to-day by the same post reminds me that it is nearly thirty years since we began our letter-writing, which he calls 'more than half a long working life'. Truly it is so & I can only wonder at & be thankful for the strength & vigour which makes us smile at the thought of being Grandma & Grandpa, & not feel old enough to be so called, & Great-grandpapa will hardly realize his antiquity!

*March 16th*
Hattie's birthday: she has to-day completed her fifteenth year & is delighted at the thought that she cannot any longer be looked upon as a little girl, but more than this, at a Telegram which Papa sent to her this morning containing birth-day good wishes & congratulations that she has passed the Cambridge Examination; this after the narrow escape she had with her Arithmetic paper (in mistaking it for a waste paper) is all the more satisfactory, & the news coming on her birth-day has much increased her pleasure for the day.

*April 2nd*
The General Election of which we had seen some signs at Ventnor in posters to 'Vote for Cotton' or to 'Vote for Ashby' & political squibs (one of which was 'Tory waste makes woeful want') became more apparent as the absorbing idea in every place we passed on our journey to, & through, London. The Conservative candidates seemed in high favor at most of the Beer-houses & Gin Palaces, walls & windows being covered with flaring entreaties to vote for them, which probably most of their frequenters will do that can; very many of the private houses too we saw, in passing in the Cab through the streets, were decorated inside, on the windows, as well as outside, with bills for their special favorites.[84] Papa reached Bedford in time to give his vote for the two Liberal members who have been returned for the Borough, & will do the same for the Marquis of Tavistock & Mr J Howard who are contesting the county with Colonel Stuart.

*April 15th*
Almost all the elections have taken place & every one is surprised at the wave of Liberalism which has swept over the country.[85] Mr J Howard is returned for the County.[86] Changes have taken place in the Government that none can understand but

---

[83]  He was baptised Edward George Paul, and known as Georgie.

[84]  The Conservatives were seen as the party favouring the interests of brewers and publicans.

[85]  The Liberals were returned to power with a large majority – 137 seats in the Commons over the Conservatives – and Gladstone became Prime Minister for the second time in April 1880.

[86]  James Howard was active in farming politics. He ran a 600 acre farm himself (Clapham Park, north of Bedford), which he used to test prototypes for new machines from the Howard factory. He stood in this election as a representative of the Farmers' Alliance, which he had founded to promote the interests of tenant farmers, who were undergoing the difficult economic conditions which had begun in the late 1870s.

He who rules over all. Mr Waddy is rejected at Sheffield[87] & the Atheist Bradlaugh elected at Northampton.[88]

*April 24*[th]

I went with Miss Rogers to the old Corn Exchange which has been engaged by Mr Hawkins, the new Proprietor of the 'Bedford Times', as a reading & amusement room for the Militia who are now in the town for their annual training. The place was a good part filled by the men, & the ladies & gentlemen who had gathered to amuse & instruct them. About a dozen very large circular deal tables were placed in two rows down the centre, around which the men sat, some writing on slates or ciphering, others reading to themselves or being taught to read, in nearly every case by ladies. Against the walls writing-desks were fixed & at these the soldiers sat in rows writing in copy books if they wished for instruction, or letters to their friends. Bagatelle & chess-boards also were provided & on a platform at the top of the Exchange a Piano & Harmonium were placed at which, after the reading & writing were supposed to be finished, there were performances & songs given, in the choruses of some of which last the men heartily joined. Altogether it is a most successful movement to benefit the men & keep them from the public-houses.

I met Mr Finlinson[89] in the room & was introduced by him to Mr Hawkins who is a benevolent looking comely man of about 40 & deserves great credit for inaugurating the whole thing as I was told he had done. It is said too that he is an ex-Wesleyan minister, but has turned to literary pursuits here & is unknown in his old denomination, but he seems a very good man.[90]

After hearing Revd G O Bate preach at St Paul's Chapel on Sunday night, 25th, I went into the Corn Exchange alone & found perhaps 150 red-jackets again there, many of them had been engaged at the Bible classes & Mr Hawkins was about to begin a short service with them to conclude the day. After singing led by the Harmonium, he prayed & then gave an excellent short address, then Dr Goldsmith a still shorter one.

---

[87] Samuel Waddy was a Liberal MP, son of a former President of the Wesleyan conference. He became a barrister at the Inner Temple in 1854.

[88] Despite her support for the Liberal interest, the party where nonconformity was strong, CEB had only disgust for the atheism of Bradlaugh, who refused to take the oath of loyalty on the Bible (see the entry for 19 May below). He was rejected from the Commons and re-elected four times. In 1886 he was finally accepted when he was permitted to affirm the oath of allegiance without reference to God or the Bible.

[89] Until 1877, Wilkinson Finlinson was Headmaster of the Commercial School, now Bedford Modern School.

[90] Joshua Hawkins, a former Wesleyan Methodist minister, had arrived in Bedford in the previous year where he was to make his mark in local politics for the Liberal cause. He announced his intentions in the paper (whose correct title is *The Bedfordshire Times*) in an editorial of 5 April 1879: 'at present strangers to Bedford, we are determined to identify ourselves with the locality, and we hope that we shall ... be able to acquire a position among local philanthropists and leaders of opinion'. There is little doubt that Hawkins achieved this and much more. He was Mayor of Bedford five times between 1883 and 1891 and was closely associated with many developments – the opening up of De Parys Avenue, the Park, St Mary's Gardens, and the Prebend Street bridge. In view of the closeness of his interests with those of the Bousfields, it is surprising that he does not figure more frequently in CEB's diaries.

*April 26ᵗʰ*

Whilst my small affairs of cleaning, white-washing etc indoors & working-meetings etc out were occupying my time & thoughts, grand events were filling the heads & hands of our great men & wise. The greatest of them, Mr Gladstone, is again Prime Minister & Chancellor of the Exchequer. The Queen did not seem particularly anxious to bestow the honor upon him & sent first for Lord Hartington & then Earl Granville, but neither seem to have been willing to accept office before Mr Gladstone; his age, experience & marvellous influence & popularity point to him as the man of all others. Since he was last in his present high place he has thrown off the dubious character which his High Churchism gave him & has come out as a thorough Protestant by his writing against the Vatican, so that none will now distrust him as some were before ready to do & enquire if he were really a Catholic.

*May 4ᵗʰ*

A week since this evening I went into the town and took Mrs Brown's table at the Old Corn Exchange as I promised her. There were not many of the men of the militia in the room when I reached it about half past 6 o'clock, but they soon came in numbers & before the night had passed, three or four hundreds must have been present. Seating myself there was soon an opportunity for asking a passer-by whether he would like to read or write with me. The first two who accepted the invitation wrote letters on a slate after I had ruled lines & set a copy for them, & at length five or six were so occupied, all of whom could do little more than letters or very simple sentences. After the writing several did simple sums & then some remained to read. I was surprised to find so many in so short a time so ignorant of the first rudiments of education; one or two were young married men; the behaviour of all was very good. At 8 o'clock singing & music began & several left the table, but even then a few remained & continued their sums & reading. The time was entirely filled until 9 o'clock when 'God save the Queen' is sung & all disperse. For one youth I wrote a letter at his request to 'a young lady' but had to suggest a part of it as his ideas did not flow very freely. A proof of the benefit of the counter attraction to the public-house is that the publicans are complaining of the 'loss' to them.

When I met Will at the train Friday evening, we saw that Mr J Howard arrived by the same, he saw us also. Yesterday in the middle of the morning Papa came home to tell me that he had been talking with Mr J about Will; it appears his seeing him had reminded him that Mr Samuelson MP had asked him whether he knew a suitable man as Secretary for the Iron & Steel Institute & that he had not thought of any one until happening to see Will.[91] He advised Papa to write to Mr S at once thinking the occupation & duties not at all incompatible to his present pursuits. This done he finds, on seeing Mr H again this evening, that the letter addressed to Mr Samuelson in Devon cannot reach him for a day or two as he has returned to Town. Mr H has therefore written himself to-night, wished Papa to repeat his letter

---

[91]  Bernhard Samuelson was a Liberal MP whose interests centred on the promotion of technical education. He had wide experience in the industrial field, and had built an ironworks at Middlesborough in 1870 which was at the time the largest and most up-to-date plant of its kind. He is best known as the Chairman of the Royal Commission on Technical Instruction which sat between 1881 and 1884. The Samuelson Report, which summarised its findings in 1884, was influential in the development of technical education at all levels.

& to furnish him in the morning before he leaves for London with a copy of the testimonials which he had printed when he was a candidate for the Head Mastership of the Modern School.[92]

## May 19th

The District meeting was held in Bedford last week. Mr Spooner, the second Preacher at Aylesbury, was allotted to us for entertainment & came to tea the first day, Monday 10th, remaining until the following Friday morning. The previous Sunday the annual Missionary sermons were preached by Revd Gervaise Smith at night at our Chapel & the meeting the following evening when Dr Prinshon & Mr S both made speeches, the ministers who had come to the D meeting being also present. One of them we knew at Sticklepath when we lived there 21 years ago & had never spoken to him since, until as he was passing our pew I shook hands with him & invited him to come to see us, which he did with his colleague: both are Wesleyan Ministers at Northampton. They gave us a good deal of information as to the influence of the notorious infidel Bradlaugh who has just been returned as one of the members of Parliament for that town, & told us that only one Dissenting Minister beside themselves voted in opposition to him, & that they were marked men & would have suffered for it from the crowd if he had not been successful. From such Liberalism, & such representatives of it, may we be delivered in this country.

## May 29th

The examination is over & the result was made known to Will on Wednesday.[93] A letter from him to Papa, & from Florence to myself, gave us the welcome intelligence that he has passed. He tells us that he has written to Mr Waddy QC to 'ask him to introduce him on call' so that when the heavy fees are paid & that takes place, he will be a fully fledged Barrister.[94] How long a briefless one remains to be seen. The present Secretary of the Iron & Steel Institute has not it seems resigned, & Mr S told him the matter was for the present in abeyance.

## June 5th

John left home on Tuesday for Worcester whither he has gone to the West of England Show. Papa went the next evening & returned last night leaving John to return next week. Ted has to-day come home for his holiday; he left Wandsworth on Wednesday for Cricklewood to be present at 'christening' of his little nephew & to act as 'godfather'. The simple baptismal service in which each of my children were dedicated to God publicly, & always by my own Father, would have much more accorded with my wishes & feelings for the dear little one, but I think Will feels & has no desire to shift the responsibility of caring for its spiritual welfare & so himself was

---

[92] If Will had applied for the head mastership of his old school, this must have been in 1877, when the vacancy occurred, and in that year he would only have been 23 years of age – a highly unlikely age for this position, even though men were appointed to such posts much earlier than is the custom now.

[93] This was Wednesday 26 May, two days before they were made public in the pages of *The Times*.

[94] CEB refers to the process of being called to the bar, by which the would-be barrister was introduced by a Bencher of the Inn, as described below (21 June) and it would seem from CEB's previous reference to Mr Waddy on 15 April, that Will was probably already acquainted with him.

the second male sponsor, as it is I suppose customary to have two for a boy. The principle of having a special friend who is supposed suitable for this in case of a Parent's death is not objectionable, but to make such promises as are contained in the church service, for a child, is so beyond the power of any creature to perform that I cannot but regard that part of it as so, & am sorry that Will's training has not led him to see it in the same light.

Ted has also vaccinated Baby during his stay with Will. Clara met him in London where he took her to the Royal Academy etc. After returning with him to Cricklewood they came on here & she spends a day or two with us.

*June 21st*

I have not had much opportunity or inclination the last fortnight for my diary and so have not chronicled the fact of Will's call to the Bar at the Inner Temple, June 9th. In a letter to his Papa he says he was one of about forty other 'aspirants for the woolsack'. The ceremony only involved a speech from one of the Benchers who then drank to them & then a response from the senior Student, after which they drank to the Benchers & filed off. The 'call' has been very much louder to Papa than to Will, above £100 for fees & £6–3[95] for wig & box! This last rather vexed him as he thought Will must have ordered it where all the big wigs were supplied, at a fancy price; it seemed so preposterously dear. How long will it be I wonder much before the bare fees come back again.

One result of his correspondence with Mr Samuelson about the Iron & Steel Institute is that he has recommended him to the Society of Mechanical Engineers as 'eminently qualified' to give them a paper; this will bring him before some of the men whom it will be well to know.

I have been indulging in a little poetizing during the past week. A poem from 'Punch' copied in the Bedford Times on 'Our Sunday' & intended for the benefit of 'Sabbatarians' incited me to reply in the same sarcastic strain in which that was written & in the like rhythm. I scarcely thought the same Editor would insert two such opposite sets of ideas, but he has done so, & if it only makes any enemy of the Sabbath see the folly of trying to raise men 'out of their sink' as 'Punch' has it, by museums & giving them 'rest' from labor in picture galleries to prepare them for six days' labour more, my end will be answered, but I trust & believe the Sabbath, the Day of Rest, is too valuable to us as a nation to be sneered out of it.[96]

*July 1st 1880*

Last evening I went with John & Hattie at Mr Philpott's invitation to the Grammar School 'speeches' at the Corn Exchange. The speeches consisted principally of recitations from plays from the elder boys dressed in character & is quite a new institution since the days when Ted was a Grammar School boy when a concert, after the giving away of the prizes, was the entertainment. Some 'old boys' were present &

---

95  In decimal coinage, £6.15.
96  CEB refers here to the idea of providing museums, libraries and art galleries as an antidote to the spread of more damaging and potentially subversive recreations by the working classes, such as drinking and gambling. Her objection is not to these 'rational recreations', as they are called, but to the fact that they may be open on Sundays, and perhaps prove more attractive than the church or chapel.

made short speeches before the recitals, amongst them Sir Erskine May[97] & Captn Burnaby[98] the author of 'A Ride to Khiva'. I do not feel the interest I once did in the School celebrations when my boys were to me the objects of all others around which they centred, & I can now recall the feelings of maternal pride with which I saw Will go up to receive every first prize in the Modern School (except that for writing which he certainly did not deserve) from the hand of the Lord Lieutenant of the County, who then shook hands with him, awarding him also in addition to the books (for which we had to send a wheelbarrow) the £200 prize with which he left the School just ten years ago. His old Master, Mr Finlinson, is still very proud of him & we generally have a little chat about him when we meet.

*July 7th*
This evening John, Hattie & myself have been to a large meeting in the New Corn Exchange held to celebrate the Centenary of the establishment of Sunday Schools by Robert Raikes in 1780. Mr Poole the Head Master of the Modern School took the Chair. There were present a representative of the Sunday School Union in America (who amused us by saying how much he felt at home in this country although he had only been in it a week or two, one reason of which was that 'we spoke the American language, although somewhat imperfectly!'), Pasteur Brocher from Brussels, with Mr Kempson,[99] Mr Brown,[100] & others who all made good speeches. Sunday school work seemed to me more important than ever.

*Thursday July 23rd*
Papa left Bedford for Carlisle for the Royal Agricultural show Thursday evening (July 8th) travelling all night; John followed him on Saturday morning by a very early train so that my birthday was a very quiet one, Hattie only being at home. I had a kind letter from dear Father containing beside his good wishes a cheque for a birthday present, also a letter & memorandum-book of her own making from Lottie; both my boys forgot the day, or I believe would not have let it pass unnoticed, at Eddie I was most surprised, he used to be the one of all the others to write & often accompany his good wishes by what he could scarcely afford as a boy.

*Septr 4th*
On Friday I received a telegram from Ted begging that he might be met at the station with Clara at the 4–40 pm train. I had the horse put in the chaise & at once drove into the town with Florence & Hattie, doing a little shopping before meeting the train. Clara has been very unwell lately & with her Mother went to London to consult a Physician. Ted returned with them & we gave up the chaise to him to drive them to Kempston where he remained to tea. He came home to supper, & for that meal and an hour afterwards I had the pleasure of seeing all my

---

[97]   Thomas Erskine May (1815–1886) was a distinguished lawyer and Parliamentarian, known today as the author of the standard guide to Parliamentary procedure. He was clerk of the House of Commons from 1871.
[98]   Colonel Burnaby, as he became, was a senior officer in the expedition which was sent out in 1884 to raise the siege of Khartoum in the Sudan and rescue General Gordon and his force. Burnaby died a heroic death at Abu Klea when close to the beleaguered town.
[99]   The Rev. Mr Kempson was the Vicar of St Cuthbert's, Bedford (Church of England).
[100]  The Rev. Dr John Brown, Minister of the Mill Street Chapel, and husband of Mrs Ada Brown.

children assembled around our table once more. Before separating for bed, Baby was fetched to complete the circle &, although awakened out of a sound sleep, came good tempered and laughing, & for half an hour kept all eyes admiringly fixed on his antics & pretty ways.

Ted left again by early train after staying the night here. This afternoon was oppressively hot & as we could not all drive together, we determined to take a boat which would hold the whole family & have our tea on the river-bank. John & Will rowed us nearly to Kempston where we landed, boiled the kettle over the little lamp stove, & after some difficulties in finding a place to suit us, getting & boiling the water etc, all of which helped the afternoon's diversions, succeeded in getting a meal, & after a little further row turned homewards just in time to get in before dark. Baby was with us and behaved well as usual until he was too tired and sleepy to look about him.

### Oct[r] 7th (Thursday)

Friday went with Papa for a long drive to Wilden to see the Binder; it worked tolerably at first, but a slight alteration intended to improve, made just as Mr J Howard was entering the field, spoilt all for the time & it did not bind a sheaf whilst he was there, much to Papa's annoyance.

### Oct[r] 14th

The last few days of fine weather have enabled Papa to be in the fields & a behind-handed Farmer, who ought to have gathered in his crop of wheat weeks since, has given him another opportunity of working his String-Binder which to-morrow will have done its last work for this season.

I have had a delightful drive this afternoon with Papa to Colmworth, & rambled round the field in search of blackberries whilst he was having some alterations made in his machine, which he now thinks is 'on the way to perfection'.

### Nov[r] 20th

Will has had his first Brief & won his cause. This Florence tells me in a letter received on Thursday; she says she wanted to send us a PC to tell us but that he said oh, no, he would add it as a PS to his next letter. So he is not a 'briefless' Barrister entirely, we did not expect he would have made a beginning so soon.

### Nov[r] 30th

Ten days have passed since I sat down to write in my diary, & in that time events have transpired which will probably settle another of our children's future course. I had great hope when Ted left home for Langport that he might be led to something better in the neighbourhood of Bristol during his stay with Mr Lyddon at Cotham, & my hope is to a great extent realized. His reply to his Papa's letter to him was a telegram on Monday, saying 'something fresh had turned up' & a letter the next morning explained that he had heard of a house just about to be vacated by a medical man, which he thought it would be an excellent situation & opportunity for him if he could take it, but was undecided between that & some furnished rooms in another position. Papa was obliged to leave home for London with Mr JH before the postman came, so knowing he would wish me to go, I complied with

Ted's intimation that it would be well to come as soon as possible & left for Bristol before dinner. He so much expected me that, somewhat to my surprise, he was at Montpelier station to meet me when I arrived about 8 o'clock.

After breakfast next morning we walked out to look at several places he had thought of. First the rooms: these seemed to me so in a corner that to take them & wait for patients would be a very slow & dismal process. After looking over a very dirty house in a better position that was for sale by Auction in a little time, we went on to the shop of a chemist who first mentioned to Ted the house of which he had told us & which was exactly opposite to it. The position was everything to be desired, at an opening to six different streets, four of them good thorough-fares. The chemist encouraged him to endeavour to take it & said he would guarantee that he would make £200 the first year. After two interviews with Mr Fendick, who appeared not at all anxious to let another medical man into the house (near which he still has consulting rooms), he agreed to let him take it for £100 to include a few fixtures.

On our return home Saturday night, after talking together, Papa drew up the agreement & Ted wrote accepting his terms. This evening the former has been returned signed & so the matter may now be considered settled & I am satisfied & thankful that his lot will be cast, not only where he will have a fair prospect of worldly influence & success, but where he will have every opportunity of religious life & influence. He expresses his intention to make himself useful in connexion with a new & beautiful Wesleyan Chapel not far from his house, & if he does this with a single eye 'seeking first the Kingdom of God', all needful things will be added to him.

As we were coming from the Station on Saturday night in the Brougham, Ted said how much often resulted from a little & that he little thought when he went into the Chemist's shop for a trifle what it would lead to; I asked him whether he need wonder, when he thought of the prayers that had been offered for him that his course may be directed, added to his own, that he was sent to just the very spot. He is to enter at 'Wellesley House'[101] Jan^y 1st 1881. Sunday last 28th was his 25th birthday, the first time he tells me that he has been at home on that date for seven years.

*Dec^r 21^st*

Few events have transpired worth recording since I last wrote; Annie Morton came as expected & is still with us.[102] Kate came from Cambridge last Friday;[103] they will return home on Thursday. John seems much pleased to have his Chelmsford friends but is more marked in his attentions to Annie than I have ever seen him with any other girl; he is very fond of ladies' society, but I have always before said of him that he makes himself generally agreeable to all. To-night all have gone to the amateur concert, John & Lottie to help, Kate & Annie to hear the 'Messiah' at the Corn Exchange.

Contrary to my expectations Will & Florence with baby are to be with us on Friday. Knowing Mr Kelly's objection to sparing F, I asked Will in any case to come,

---

101   The name of Ted's new home and surgery.
102   Alex Morton's sister.
103   Another of Alex Morton's sisters.

as probably Ted will not be with us next year & there seemed little chance of the brothers being together for some years again. The request gave rise to a discussion which has ended in Mr K's conceding what he before refused & Will's wife is to accompany him, which will much add to our pleasure. I would not be selfish & wish always to have them, but felt very unwilling to give up the gratification which it is to have Will with us sometimes for Xmas-day.

## 1881

*Jan^y 3^rd 1881, Wellesley House, Bristol*
Since I last sat down to write Xmas & all its meetings have come & gone & the old year has slipped away. Will & Florence with Baby came to Bedford the day before Xmas-day, the latter much grown & improved & getting quite a wise little man.

*Jan^y 13^th*
I have now indeed quiet & time for everything that has to be done & some unexpected work I have found since my return home on Saturday. On Sunday morning very soon after Papa, John & myself had taken our seats in Chapel, a couple who usually sat a few seats in front of us came in & took places in the aisle; feeling sure something was wrong, I begged Papa to invite them into our seat, but Mr Henman did the same at once, much evidently to their relief. On enquiry we found the Stewards had refused to re-let the seat to them; on Monday morning I went to see them, & met the Chapel Stewards on the way, heard the case from each party & tried to soothe the offended individuals, which I think I succeeded in doing, by offering them a seat in our pew on Sunday nights until they could get another to suit themselves. After luncheon Papa thought I had better see Mr Cornforth & explain why we had done this, & although both I think were disposed to question the step, the whole matter seems more likely to be amicably settled & the public scandal of members of the same church at variance avoided.

As soon as I got back from the town I found the women of my Mothers' meeting waiting for me & to partake of the tea to which I had invited them at 4 o'clock. 18 came; we had a very pleasant & I hope profitable time together & separated at 6 o'clock. One woman who was absent amongst others I was told had a little boy very ill; this afternoon I called to see her, & whilst I was there watched with the poor Father & Mother whilst he passed away; the first they had lost & a sad case, the illness brought on a month ago by a blow on the head from a teacher at school!

*Thursday Jan^y 20^th*
I have to-day been driven into the town, having been weather-bound since Sunday morning. A frost set in very suddenly a week ago, in about three days the river was frozen over & skaters on it, a little snow having also fallen. Monday evening I noticed the wind was rising, was disturbed in the night by its increasing violence, by noon on Tuesday it had reached a climax and became such a storm as I never before remember to have seen & heard. About the same time the air became filled

with the finest snow like thick white dust which penetrated every crack & cranny through which the wind could come. When John came home to dinner he said the tiles & chimney-pots were flying about; towards night the wind subsided, whilst the snow fell thicker, but it was strong enough to blow the latter into the breakfast-room curtains as they were drawn over the doors so that I had to have them shaken & the snow swept up during the evening. It made its way in the same manner through all the windows facing the east.

Whilst remedying our small inconveniences we little thought of the amount of desolation which the storm had brought & which the newspaper in the morning revealed in every part of the country, but worst of all in London. There, in addition to the furious gale having driven the snow into drifts which stopped the street traffic & blocked many of the railways, it drove the waters of the Thames which were at high tide entirely beyond the usual level, not only inundating the streets of houses near the river, but bringing with them masses of ice that were dashed through these, shattering the furniture of the poor homes & spreading destruction as far as they reached. The correspondent in the 'Telegraph' describes the scene & says the water mark in the saturated houses measured six feet six inches from the ground & that the misery of the poor creatures who inhabited them seemed to paralyse them beyond making effort to repair their shattered dwellings, & not that only, but thickly covered (in many cases even the beds where they slept on the ground floor) with a layer of slimy mire which the muddy tide had brought with it.

After the wind fell, the snow increased very quickly all day yesterday &, adding to the tremendous drifts, has blocked road & rail in all directions. At the Works cart loads of snow were cleared out of the workshops which had a layer blown over them. As few letters arrived & business was almost at a standstill, John walked down to the station of the Midland Railway & found the lines filled with trains, one behind the other, that ought to have passed hours before; in several cases we hear of trains snowed in, in others of their not having arrived & from the telegraph wires being broken their whereabouts not known. There are eight cases in the paper to-day of persons who have perished in the snow wreaths, & many more are missing.

The disasters by sea are beyond all computation; the accounts of the wrecks & loss of life & of the gallant attempts of the life boats fill columns. Fishing boats have been lost by the score & hundreds of barges sunk in the rivers, some of them being dashed against piers & landing places & causing an immense amount of damage. The calamities & accidents on land & water are beyond anything I ever remember reading; Tuesday Jan^y 18th 1881 will be remembered as the day of the great Storm.

Whilst in the town I heard that Mr Elton had met with an adventure through the storm that might have been more serious than it ended. He had preached at Turvey on Tuesday night, intending to return home by the train calling there soon after 8 o'clock. Not a train arrived, & as no intelligence of any stoppage was received, he waited several hours expecting it, but none came through the whole night during which he remained at the Station. At daybreak he started to walk home, & with great difficulty succeeded, having at one part of the road got up to his neck in snow, but fortunately was near a stile which he crossed & got round the drift in some way through the fields. He reached Bedford about 9 o'clock in the morning. Mrs Elton told me how fearfully alarmed she was & during the night sent men with a horse

& cart to meet him, but they only got as far as Bromham where the road was so blocked that they were obliged to return.

*Tuesday Feb^y 1^st*

The almost unbroken quiet of the last fortnight gives me very few family events to chronicle. The newspaper & the postman have furnished almost all the intelligence I have received during that time. The former gives sad details of the various disasters that accompanied the storm of what one Paper calls 'Hurricane Tuesday' & yesterday's 'Telegraph' relates that over thirty bodies of persons frozen to death during the snow-storm have been found on the stretch of exposed downs in Wilts & West Berks since the thaw set in.

Last Tuesday, having to go into the town, I called to see Mrs Hobson & finding her a little better & alone stayed to tea with her. Mr H had gone to London in his capacity as Mayor to head a deputation consisting of the town MPs & other officials who were received at the House of Commons to obtain sanction for the appropriation of some of the 'St John's Hold' lands near St Peter's Church for a public Park & pleasure ground.[104] On his return Mr H showed me the plans which he had taken with him which looked very pretty & will be much greater benefit to the living than the income of them could have been to the dead donor, in providing paid prayers for his soul.[105]

Papa accepted an invitation to the Mayor's dinner on Wednesday, but a telegram from Mr J H summoned him to London on the morning of that day, & he was I think very glad to have so good a reason for excusing himself, & going to Cricklewood to dinner instead. Will's Briefs do not come in fast, but Mr Wheeler's do; he told Papa nine had come the previous day.[106] All this is good experience for him & fills his time at Chambers, he can scarcely hope to be gaining so much & making money for himself at the same time. We fear he is trying to do too much at home in the evening, sitting up until morning writing articles for 'Engineering' etc.

*Sunday Feb^y 20^th*

Last Wednesday at my suggestion Mr E called a meeting of the ladies who united with me for the Circuit fund sewing-meeting to determine how we should further organize ourselves to be prepared for a sale of the work in the summer. Thinking to enlist larger sympathy for us, he announced that any gentlemen who were interested in the movement would be welcome to come. Three accepted his invitation, Messrs Shepherd, Clare & Maxwell. After I had at Mr Elton's request stated the objects we had in view & expressed them as threefold (to renovate the Ministers' houses, meet deficiency in the Circuit funds, & provide a surplus fund for future contingencies in the same), Mr S at once said the houses were in good condition & the money not required; Mr C that if £50 were needed it would be at once forthcoming & proposed

---

104  Bedford Park was laid out on 61 acres of land owned by St John's Hospital and set apart for public recreation by a private Act of Parliament which followed the meeting attended by the Bedford delegation.
105  The Park was, and is, an important contribution to the quality of life in the town. It was opened in 1888, and was described at the time as 'Bedford's Bois de Boulogne', and the impressive De Parys Avenue leading up to its main entrance gates as 'Bedford's Champs Elysees'.
106  Will was probably in Wheeler's chambers at the Inner Temple. Mr Wheeler had been called to the bar in 1865, so he was older and more established than Will.

that 'no sale be held', & so influenced the meeting that only 8 hands were held up for my proposition to go on as we had been intending.

This, after all the efforts of months past & my hopes to get more than sufficient so that Papa might give up his Stewardship with a balance in hand, is a great disappointment & mortification, & I would at once give up all further effort only that my Husband has promised the invited minister that the house (which is now miserably shabby) shall be put into good order, & I should not be showing Christian 'gentleness' by doing what has been done by others in our society of late, withdrawing from all work when I could not do it my own way.[107]

As Circuit-Steward's wife, the preparation of the house rests with me & money to that extent must be found. Papa is very much annoyed at the rejection of what appeared such an easy method of getting out of the increasing embarrassment of the funds & made up his mind at first to resign, but after talking the matter over quietly together he concluded by saying we must either live above or below the spirit of opposition shown, & we decided that the former should be our course & that we would go on doing the duty which God had given us to do as unto Him, & when that was accomplished leave the responsibility with those who are probably anxious for the honor of his Office, which I have promised not to ask him to keep after the end of the year.

I am very thankful I was kept from saying, or rather showing, anger during the meeting which seemed to bewilder every one but those who came with the intention of doing what they fancied they achieved. It was proposed by the juvenile dictator that we should continue to meet for work & sell as we could from 'time to time'. I have engaged to be at the meeting next Thursday & shall make propositions which will I think be dignified & I trust at the same time only so because of the 'gentleness' which may reflect something of the character of Him to imitate whom alone is to be 'great'.

### March 3rd

Tuesday March 1st was a red-letter day for Will. On that day he had a grand opportunity, being retained in a patent case for the first time. He had to appear with Aston,[108] Goodeve & others before the Privy Council for the prolongation of a Patent which, however, the QC's argument was not successful to obtain. The men amongst whom Will must get known were called as witnesses & he had the opportunity of conversing on the case with Bramwell & Hopkinson who were of the number. The 10 guinea Brief was not even of so much importance as the fact that he acquitted himself to the entire satisfaction of the Agent through whose influence he got it.[109]

Papa went to London yesterday to take out some American patent with the same & he told him how favorably he was impressed with the remarks he made, or rather interposed, in the Solicitor General's pleading[110] & the evident effect it had on three

---

[107]  CEB seems to have stirred up opposition once again: an earlier example is referred to in the entry for 22 June 1879.
[108]  Theodore Aston QC was possibly the leading patent barrister of this period.
[109]  The Agent who helped Will to get his first brief is identified in the next paragraph but one as Mr Lake, of Haseltine Lake & Co of 8 Southampton Buildings.
[110]  The Solicitor General was Sir Farrer Herschell QC MP. He became Lord Chancellor briefly in 1886.

of the [a space is left here] out of four, even after the QC Aston had concluded his say, which he seems to have been anxious to prevent being followed on the same side, telling Will he would only have to concur, which however it was well he did not simply do.

Papa is very pleased at the opening that this has made in what he considers Will's special course & at the opinion Mr Lake gave him that he would be sure to succeed. And I can only thank Him whose interposition I see in every event of my children's life as of my own. Papa called for Will at Mr Wheeler's chambers yesterday afternoon; the latter came forward to shake hands laughing & saying 'here we are, fresh from the breezes of the Privy Council', an honor by the bye which he, Mr W, has never had.

### March 24th

I have spent the afternoon which I should like to have had at home on this day at the Circuit sewing-meeting at Bromham Road Chapel. At the last I fear the discontented ones who came to it in full number did not think me as 'gentle' as I intended to be. I told them that the meetings would be continued as before until the teas promised me were expended & that those ladies who had been & were collecting articles for a Sale would decide for themselves what they would do with these when that time came. This raised quite a tempest which I allayed in some measure by giving up all the Sewing-meeting proper into the hands of those who evidently wished to manage it, except the proceeds which it is only right to hand over to my Husband as C Steward to be used for the minister's house, or towards the growing deficiency.

After asking to take & giving Mrs Samuel the account book at the Committee meeting I called yesterday, & talking matters over with half a dozen instead of a room full, I simply told those who were present to-day that Mrs S had consented to become Secretary &, as no remark was made by any one, the meeting passed off as quietly as the last did the reverse & was only noticeable for the extremely subdued tone which pervaded it throughout the evening; about 16 were present.

### May 21st

Father & Grandma Collins came yesterday, the former looking well as usual & in excellent spirits. This afternoon Papa has driven us to Warden, where we put the horse up & had tea in the arbour of the only Inn in the place. The weather to-day has changed from the gales which have prevailed all the week to calm sun-shine & could not possibly have been more delightful for our ride which we all thoroughly enjoyed. John went before us on his Bicycle.

### May 31st

On Thursday the Circuit tea & sewing meeting was held at Bromham Road, a pretty good attendance of what Mr Cornforth called 'the elect ladies'; the discontented element being altogether absent the gathering was a pleasant one. Grandma Collins went with me; we were to have gone to the Zanana meeting the next day but Mrs Hobson came to tea unexpectedly & we did not go. After she left I went down to meet the 10 o'clock train by which Papa returned from London after calling at Cricklewood & dining with Will & Florence; he thinks them both looking thin & not well; Baby is well & now runs anywhere alone.

This evening we have been to a place of worship that I had never before seen, built by the Plymouth Brethren[111] in one of the lowest parts of the town. In this, called 'the Bedford Hall', it was announced that Lord Radstock would 'preach the Gospel'. As I had often heard of him & his work both in this country & in Russia, I was curious both to see & hear him. As to his appearance, a more unostentatious 'Lord' could not be imagined. Rather tall & of very pleasant countenance & voice, he gave out a hymn & prayed in a very simple & unassuming way, then read part of a Chapter, & in the same manner spoke from it with great earnestness to the people, many of them poor & many militia men who are now in the town. He told us of some striking instances of conversion resulting from personal conversation with those he happened to meet, some in railway carriages, or on the way as he found opportunity. Oh that there were more 'Lords' & Christians like him.[112]

*June 17th*

I must not close my Diary to-night without recording the special providence that has been about me to-day. This morning I went across to the field where the grass had been cut. Billingham was there alone hay-making. Taking his fork I told him he might fetch the horse for the Hay machine which was standing in the field; he did so, & after a few turns up & down with it, the driving over the hay looked so easy that I asked him to let me take his seat on the machine & try it. I had only taken it, & the reins in my hands, whilst he stood at the horse's head, when it took a step backward, which strained a weak place in the breeching sufficiently to snap it, & in some way that I cannot account for the wooden bar to which my elevated seat was fixed instantly snapped too, throwing me backwards over the machine, still however on it, until it reached the ground & the open iron-work of which it was made cracked like glass under me. Most thankful was I to regain my feet & to find myself free of the forks, which I thought of as I fell but of which I was quite clear, & altogether unhurt.

I sent Billingham at once for Papa who, when he had enquired whether I was hurt, or the horse, & found both were right, came laughing at my adventure & said I had discovered a weak place in his machine, which he at once took measures to rectify in that & future ones of the same kind. I was somewhat frightened, but not so much so but I was able to go on hay-making with my fork whilst B was away, & at the same time thanking God for my escape from what might have been suffering or even sudden death; as Papa says I might have broken my neck.

*July 14th*

One of my letters to-day was written to Ted in reply to his to me for my birth-day, which reached me on Tuesday. I was more glad to have it on that day than the 10th since he did not let the occasion make him break his rule of not posting letters for Sunday delivery & as he said 'rob the Postman'. If all would be as mindful of their individual responsibility in this matter, many a poor country postman would have a

---

[111] A small separatist Christian sect, fundamentalist in character, with a strong emphasis on prophecy.
[112] Granville Waldegrave, 3rd Lord Radstock was a remarkable man, described as 'a wealthy man who, like Jesus, walked among the poor as a servant'. He died in 1913.

rest day where now they never have such. London can do without its letters on the Sabbath but the country folk & even villagers must have theirs.

I have to-day heard from Papa that the Show is likely to be very successful & he says if it could have been, he should have liked myself & the girls to have visited it.[113] I have written to tell him that in my case the thing is not impossible &, as I have nothing to keep me at home, to-morrow I shall take a first class return ticket & come to him for the day at least, leaving Bedford at 7–15 in the morning.

*July 25th*

I went to Derby on Friday 15th & found the journey there not unpleasant although the heat was very great. Finding out Messrs H's Stand, I at once saw Papa & John together. The former went with me to two or three of the other Stands in which he thought I should feel most interested & then left me for a time to John. We went together to see our old friend Mr Morton & whilst with him Mr Coleman & his daughter came.[114] I had not seen Miss Coleman since the time of John's illness at Chelmsford. I proposed that we should bear each other company for a time, which we did, until John took her off to see the Prince of Wales, leaving me at the Aylesbury Dairy's Stand to see the operations that were about to begin there.

After standing much longer than I intended in such a crowd as I had not expected either for character or number on the half-crown day,[115] & seeing nothing that was particularly new or interesting, I again went to the Howard's Stand, had a little talk with Mr Sidney Farrar & his brother, congratulated Mr FH's son on his safe return from his year's travels almost round the world, & then with Papa & Miss Coleman, who returned to us, had another walk; after which with the latter went to the Grand Stand & sat looking at the horses that were brought out & paraded before the Prince.

Then wishing Miss C good bye & meeting John at the entrance as arranged, returned with him to the Midland Hotel where with great difficulty & by waiting on me himself, he got me refreshment & then accompanied me to the Station. After waiting a long time for the train, I insisted on his leaving me & returning to dinner. It was more difficult than I imagined to find a seat, even in a 1st class carriage, & I was not sorry to see Papa, who came to me from the Hotel when he found the train had not left. The heat seemed greater at night in travelling than in the day, & I felt thoroughly wearied before reaching Bedford a little before 11 o'clock, quite cured I believe of special trains. Papa returned home Saturday afternoon, John not until Tuesday.

I have had a very busy but pleasant time the past week, having two of the small houses prepared for tenants who have taken them; collecting my half-year's subscriptions to Foreign Missions, & last but not least watering the parched garden. To-morrow I go to Cricklewood, hope to meet Hattie Wednesday.

---

113   The Royal Show this year was held in Derby.
114   The Mortons had moved in the 1860s from Bedford to Chelmsford to join the Coleman brothers in their agricultural machinery business, Coleman and Morton.
115   The opening day, when entrance was more expensive, so normally excluding the large crowds and working-class visitors.

*Tuesday, August 23rd*

The journey to Derby was neither a pleasure nor success to Papa. The continual rain made the trials of Binders a very unpleasant business & the more so as he was disappointed in the working of his which did not do nearly so well as it did here. Will's work was to give a report of the Derby trials for 'Engineering' for which Paper he now frequently writes. He returned here before Papa & went on after early breakfast next morning to London & to Shanklin the same day. A Post-card dated thence, for further information about the trials, was the only intimation we had of his arrival there. Since he has had a wife to write for him he never troubles to write except on business matters, so that it is now a rare occurrence for me to have a letter from him &, considering we have more instead of less anxiety on his account than in the days when his letters were frequent & have so much more to do for him, it grieves me that he will not take the trouble to give us pleasure at so small a cost to himself. It is so pleasant to us to have any proof that our children appreciate the sacrifices we often make for them, even though they may not know them to be as great as they often are. I did not intend to write all this when I took my pen, but what I felt flowed from it.

My time is now very much occupied with the duties of Circuit Steward's wife; those are preparing the house Mr Cornforth has left for his successor Mr Sargeant, who will arrive next week. The former took his departure a week yesterday, & each day since I have been to the house once & often twice in the day. Paper hangers, painters etc having nearly finished, a great deal must be done in the little time remaining, since the whole of the carpets must be new or renovated & many things beside to a much greater extent than is usual at such changes.

When all is in order the money must be found to pay for it. The Sale of work etc by which we hope to get part of it is to be held the beginning of next month. I have been tolerably successful in obtaining articles for it, & my friends promise more. Lottie spends all her spare time now she is at home in working for it. Hattie is doing some Terra Cotta painting also, & John making some ingenious puzzles that are, he reckons, to bring a guinea. If others will help to the same extent as we are doing, & we can get customers, our financial difficulty will be overcome, but if we get only £50 it will be worth the effort, even with the opposition & annoyance I have had. I want to do what I have to do as unto the Lord, & for His cause, & if so shall neither be vain-glorious at success, nor depressed at failure.

*Saturday, Sept$^r$ 3rd*

A week of hard work & continual coming & going is over. The four first days of it were passed almost from rising to going to bed at the minister's house, having to meet work people every morning there & returning at night so tired as to rest in bed until I had to go again. All is, I am thankful to say, done & this afternoon I have with Mr Elton met our new Superintendent Minister at the Station, made tea for him in his new home, with which he expresses satisfaction. A letter from him a few days ago told us he would have to come alone; Mrs Sargeant's health has so suffered in the West Indies (whence they came after twelve years only a few weeks since) that she remains in London until better able to travel this last stage. Mr Sargeant seems an intelligent, pleasant man & his residence amongst us will, I believe, be a change very beneficial to the Circuit in which matters have been very depressed during the past year.

Papa went to London on Wednesday, to Banbury to meet Mr Samuelson on Thursday & on Friday at noon left for Hanover. The journey thither had been talked of for days before it was decided, & at first Papa talked of my accompanying him & I thought of doing so, but proposed that John should be his companion instead, & he has gone, taking a holiday trip instead of a fortnight later. He has been rubbing up his German, which had been rusting ever since he left School, & seems to find sufficient to make himself I should think tolerably understood. This morning's post brought a few lines from him enclosing two insurance tickets for himself & Papa & expressing the hope that they may be watched over & brought back again in safety.

*Wednesday, Sept' 21st*

Papa & John returned from their short tour on the Continent last Monday week. John especially made the most of the time, which he could better do as his journey was for pleasure. After going with Papa twice to the Steam cultivating trials at a small town a dozen miles from Hanover, he left him for a trip to Berlin, travelling at night & spending the daylight in looking about. Another night was spent in going from Berlin to Cologne, which Papa reached from Hanover by a night's journey also, & met John at the Station there. They spent the day together. The Cathedral was of course the chief object of interest. A magnificent pile of buildings just completed & still dedicated, as it was when begun in darker ages 700 years ago, to the mummery of image worship of which they saw something.

Eau de Cologne, Papa wrote to me, was most plentiful during the day, not as I could have wished intended as a present for me, but coming from the clouds in such torrents that they had frequently to find shelter. Another night of travel brought them to Paris which Papa wished to visit principally on account of the great Electrical Exhibition which was being held there.[116] He intended to have stayed over Monday, but weary of the night work, left early in the day & a telegram from Newhaven after tea told me that they had arrived there in safety & desired that the carriage might be sent to meet them at 9–42 pm.

Both looked better for the 10 days' change they had had notwithstanding the extra strain, John especially feeling fully repaid & very much pleased at having been able to see & do so much, I most thankful that the insurance tickets were worthless.

*Nov' 24th*

The first event to be recorded since my last entry is one of importance to Will & Florence, the arrival of another Son, Novr 21st. Fresh responsibility for them & for us too, for their cares are ours until the time that financial matters do not form part

---

[116] This exhibition was remarkable, amongst other features, for its demonstration of the use of the telephone. Clément Ader's experiments with distant telephone listening used dual lines connected to microphones placed on both sides of the stage, with the then remarkable result that the sounds were heard in stereo, including the novelty that 'aural impressions change with the relative positions of the singers, and their movements can in this way be followed'. This early demonstration of stereophonic sound was known as 'binauricular audition', and was compared to the use of stereoscopic images. In order to enjoy this phenomenon listeners had to join long queues and then to hold a small circular speaker to each ear.

of them; may the boy grow up a blessing to his Parents & the world, as he will do if they have faith & wisdom to train him 'in the way he should go'.

On Saturday Papa & I rambled into the field & on through the fence into the gravel pits & cuttings on the other side & almost fancied ourselves on a beach amidst the regular layers of pebbles & sand that looked as if they might have been washed into their position but yesterday instead of ages ago.

### Dec$^r$ 1$^{st}$

It scarcely seems possible that this can be the last month of another year, but so it is. I have this evening had a letter in pencil from dear Florence, not telling me much about herself, but saying 'We have a great deal to be thankful for just now' & going on to relate that her Husband had undertaken to edit 'an American law book' for Mr Sweet,[117] which would bring about £30; that Mr Lake had sent him a cheque for £16, & that he had just returned from the Albert Hall where he had been for 'Engineering' to report on an exhibition of appliances for smoke abatement being held there, which article he had to write at once. As their cares are, as I said before, ours, so are their joys too, & that in addition to all F is so far recovered as to be able to write such a list of mercies should fill us too with gratitude. Papa thinks that the editorship of a work may be a great means of Will's becoming known, if he does it satisfactorily. In a postscript to F's letter he says 'Very busy from morn till night'.

### Dec$^r$ 28$^{th}$

As I write, recollections of the past almost crowd out the present, & I wonder that I, the eldest of six all spared to manhood and womanhood, should in such health & strength be the only one of them left.

## 1882

### Jan$^y$ 18$^{th}$

Lottie has seemed to enjoy her stay at home & has several times expressed her pleasure at being with us. Her companionship is often a great pleasure to me & would be always so if we could see more alike as to what becomes us as professors & disciples of Christ; we have had arguments which have caused me regret, & not tended I fear to convince her. Am 'I', as I am sure my children think me, narrow-minded, strait laced & puritanical? Or do I so love my Lord & Master as to desire in all I do to serve & please Him? I do trust the latter is the case.

### March 30$^{th}$

[From Will's house in Cricklewood, where Hattie was staying] Thursday was Hattie's seventeenth birthday; she remained at home to spend the day with me. In the morning Mrs Kelly came; Florence went with her to the florists for a little drive, they returned with some nice plants which Mrs K bought & which I was pleased to find places for in the Conservatory, which I spent a good part of the day in setting

---

[117] Henry Sweet was in business as a law publisher with his two sons. He was Florence's uncle.

in order. When it was finished Hattie took me for a walk to the Cemetery. The afternoon was very fine, so much so that we sat down on a bank sheltered from the wind & ate oranges on our way, enjoying both that & our ramble homeward by the Church exceedingly. After dinner left Cricklewood & arrived at the Station about 10 o'clock; John met me & we called at the Chapel for Papa who with J had been attending a meeting about building new schools & re-pewing the Chapel; the first badly needed, the last certainly not until the means of doing it are more likely to be found than they now seem.

A letter from Lottie which Papa forwarded to me in London made us decide, as soon as I got home, that we would telegraph for Ted to come home for rest & talk. She said that she thought he much needed a change, so I was very glad when in reply to our message he walked in early Saturday morning, having taken the journey at night, to gain the day. In the afternoon we went to Kempston for Clara who came back to stay here with him. On Monday morning they drove to Wootton to dine with Clara's sister, stopping at Kempston Church in returning to hear Revd M Haslam preach at one of the Mission services being held there.

That same morning, whilst having breakfast in bed & thinking about our Son, it occurred to me that it might be both to his happiness & benefit if he could be married instead of waiting until later when his practice & income would seem to have better warranted it. When Papa came up for his after-breakfast dressing, we had a few minutes quiet talk &, with the probability there appears to be that he will get on more rapidly as a married man, we calculated that with the same amount of success this year as he had last added to this probability & what we could afford to add to his income for a couple of years, as we had done for Will, it would not be imprudent for him to take the step, & the sooner the better. He was entirely taken by surprise & highly delighted at our proposal that it should be in May, & was not long in communicating it to Clara & obtaining her acquiescence also. So the matter was soon settled so far &, before he took Clara home again the next evening, the day was named which according to present arrangement is to be Saturday May 27th.

*April 8th*

I had a most enjoyable day with Papa & John yesterday. Although we have lived so many years within 11 miles of Olney, we have never made a pilgrimage to the spot where my favorite poet Cowper lived & wrote.[118] This we determined to do. Starting about 11 o'clock Papa & myself in the chaise, John on his new tricycle, we drove very gently in brilliant sun shine tempered by easterly breeze through Bromham & so on towards Turvey. The only event that interfered with our pleasure happened just as we passed the Station near there. Papa wished to change places with John & try his tricycle; he got on so well & so far before us that he took it into his head to return & meet us. We were watching him & wondering what he was going to do in suddenly making a circuit, but instead of turning completely round, the machine darted across the road, & he & it disappeared in a deep ditch under the hedge. We were dreadfully frightened; I gave a great scream which nearly set the horse

---

118   William Cowper (1731–1800) suffered from severe depression, from which he found refuge in his fervent evangelical Christianity and his literary work, particularly his poetry and his hymns, numbering among them some of the best loved we have: for example, 'God moves in a mysterious way' and 'Oh for a closer walk with God'. *John Gilpin* is perhaps his best known poem.

off; John flung me the reins & the whip into [the] road, & rushed to see what had befallen Papa. Fortunately the fall was broken by the bushes & the ditch so deep that he was below the tricycle whilst it rested across it; a few scratches & the seat bent was fortunately all the damage done, but it was a most providential escape. Not understanding the steerage was, Papa said, the cause of the accident; his little frolic might have been a sad termination to our pleasure.

Recovering from our alarm all round, we continued our journey, John remounting his tricycle & Papa driving as before until we came to Olney where we left the horse at an Inn & walked on to Cowper's village, Weston Underwood, saw the outside of his house, went into the Church, & returning looked over a house belonging to the family of his friends the Throckmortons, & through the garden that belonged to their mansion which was pulled down some fifty years ago. The garden of more than two acres surrounded by high walls has an opening into 'the Wilderness', in both of which the Poet had doubtless often walked & composed some of those poems which seem as full of wisdom as of poetry. We set out to drive home again as soon as possible & arrived soon after 7 o'clock.

*Monday May 29th*

To-day has been Bank holiday[119] & after spending the morning writing letters & from after early dinner until 9 o'clock in accompanying Papa, Fanny Cato & Charles Barns to & from Turvey where we have taken tea, I sit down at the first opportunity to begin to chronicle the events of the last fortnight which will include the important one of my Son Edward's marriage on the 27th instant.

A week ago to-day I went down to Weston super Mare with Aunt Collins & secured lodgings for Ted & Clara as they determined on not taking a more distant wedding trip, both as a matter of economy & that he might be able to visit patients thence, should any particular need arise. He has a steady increase in their number although the total is not yet great. On Friday morning, after a much earlier breakfast than usual & alone, he started off to Lawrence Hill to see a patient, returned & put together what he wished packed, then went a couple of miles in an opposite direction to visit another & also to perform an operation on a poor babe who had an abscess in its neck. This he did successfully whilst Lottie was packing his portmanteau, & returned to set out with me at 1 o'clock for Islip, where Clara's eldest brother lives at the Manor House, from which she was to be married.[120] Beds had been taken for E & myself at the village Inn. After visiting Clara & Mr & Mrs A Henman, we went to it for the night.

Saturday morning was bright as we could desire; after breakfast we set out for the Station to meet the wedding guests, none of whom beside myself arrived the previous night. John had engaged a Saloon carriage for the wedding party which consisted of Mrs Henman, Mr A Henman, Mr & Mrs Hunter, Mr & Mrs Foster & their two little girls, Papa & John, who all left the NW Station together at 7.30 am. Will & Hattie met them at Bletchley & got into their carriage & all reached Islip in

---

[119] The Bank Holidays Act of 1871 had guaranteed modest annual holidays for bank workers, and this spread to other groups as time went on.

[120] According to the 1881 census, he lived at Manor Farm and farmed some 390 acres of land: a substantial property.

good time for the wedding which was fixed for a quarter before 11 o'clock. I walked to the Church (which is very near to the Inn) with Papa & our three sons.

The Manor House is not more than three or four minutes ride from it, & as only one carriage was needed, the bridesmaids, 5 in number, were brought first & waited for the Bride in the porch. On her arrival, leaning on the arm of her eldest Brother, Hattie as chief Bridesmaid followed them alone, then two of Mr Albert Henman's daughters - younger than H, & after them the two little Fosters. The clergyman's daughter presided at the organ. Clara & Ted responded & followed in the service very distinctly, but there was nothing in it beyond the ordinary ceremony, nor did the clergyman at the breakfast give any idea that could be said to be for the especial guidance or benefit of the young people, as was the case with Canon Duckworth at Will's wedding.

After the chief actors in the day's excitement had gone, we returned to the table for a little time, then wandered in the large garden & took a walk through the village which was shortened by the showers that fell soon after the breakfast; the after part of the day was fine as the former & the whole of it passed very pleasantly. About 7 o'clock all returned to the Station where I took John's place in the carriage & he went on to Bristol to spend a day or two with Lottie. Will & Hattie left us again at Bletchley; Papa & I returned to our almost empty home with subdued thankfulness. So ended another important day in our family history.

*June 2nd*

In the month that has elapsed since I went to London a great change has come to John's prospects in more than one respect. When I was with Will he told me that Mr Lake had asked him whether he knew a good man for a position they had to fill in their Office, & laughingly added that they offered him £500 a year if he would take it. I asked W whether it was one John could in time fill, with some assistance & training & a proportionate salary at the present. He said he had not thought of John but would mention the subject to Mr Lake, which he did. After some conversation & correspondence, the request was made that he would go to London to see Mr L. He did so whilst I was at Bristol, & the result is that he has been engaged at a salary of £150 per annum to begin with. His mechanical knowledge is his chief present qualification for the work which he will have to do in a Patent Agent's office, but to make himself valuable he will have to read up a good many subjects which are connected with the many things for which patents are taken out; Electricity, Chemistry, etc. This will be an incentive to study, which he had nothing at the Britannia Works to call forth.

Both Papa & John have expressed their dissatisfaction at the position in which the latter has so long been kept at the Works (& which it was only intended he should fill for months instead of years) both to Mr J[ohn] & Mr J[ames] H[oward], but as no steps were taken by either to alter or improve it, I am very thankful that an opening has been found for the business tact & ability, which I am sure he possesses, in another direction, & one which will tend to enlarge his mind also. But I am very sorry for him to go away from Bedford, which he need never have done if those, whose chief fame has been built on his Father's inventive skill, had felt as they ought to have done, what they owe to him, & given John position & pay in accordance with it, which they have not done although we have patiently waited four years. However, he is not going away from his country & will be near enough to frequently spend Sunday or a holiday with us.

*June 21st (Wednesday)*
On Thursday I went to Pavenham with Fanny Cato to comply with a request that I would lay one of the memorial stones in the new school-room that is being built adjoining the Wesleyan Chapel there. I found a small stone placed on one side of a doorway with my initials cut upon it which, under Mr Sargeant's direction, I 'truly laid'.

*Saturday, July 1st*
To-day another has flown from our home nest. John left this afternoon for Cricklewood to be ready on Monday morning to enter upon his new duties in London. The only advantage conceded to him on quitting the Britannia Works was a single day before the end of the month which he asked for in order to see Mr Lake & Florence before going, to remain. On Thursday evening he came from the Works looking very jubilant at having taken his farewell of all connected with them, & without a single regret at having left a place on which he entered with expectations & hopes which have never been fulfilled. I had hoped we might have had one Son living in Bedford who could have been a comfort near to us, & a convenience in years to come if we should be spared to be able to leave home for lengthened periods, as we often talk of doing. But whilst we have proposed, the Great Disposer of all events has otherwise ordered his future. He is to live with Will until he can meet with lodgings near Westbury Villa, so that he may have the advantage of his Brother's help & direction in his work & reading for a time.

*July 10th*
'What shall I render' for the benefits that have surrounded & followed me through another year? Truly I marvel at their number. My anxiety as to my children's temporal circumstances greatly relieved; Will's prosperity beyond anything I could have hoped for, Ted settled with a good wife & hopeful prospects, John's way made for him in a direction I could not have thought of! The latter came home on Saturday night after a week's trial of his new life in London & the result is satisfactory beyond my hopes & expectations, which were greater than his Papa's.

Mr Lake, & his brother also, have given him work to do which has been rather a severe test of his capabilities in more than one respect, & they expressed satisfaction, & the importance of that which they have entrusted to him shew that he has made a good impression & won their confidence to a greater extent than could have been anticipated after so short a trial. He will be engaged, he says, for the next fortnight searching in all likely directions (the British Museum Library as one) for information required in reference to patent rights in a great trial between the manufacturers of a certain Gun, in which his Brother is retained as Counsel.

*August 15th*
A month has elapsed since the events entered last in my Diary. In that time Hattie has returned for her holiday; John has been home twice to see us, the last time with his Office colleague Mr Young; they came on Saturday & stayed over Monday the

7th (Bank Holiday). Although it was a holiday Papa had arranged work for himself, trying a Binder at Brick Hill Farm. After early dinner he drove Mr Y & Charles Barns to the field & I followed shortly after in the Chaise with the girls. John went on his tricycle.

Taking all necessary for tea with us, we were supplied with hot water from a cottage & obtained permission to pic-nic on the lawn of an unoccupied house belonging to the Farm. We spread our meal under a tree; after we had looked at the Binder at work in the cornfield a few minutes, Papa dismissed the men, had tea with us, & a walk afterwards, he with Lottie & Hattie over the fields, I with John & Mr Y to the Cemetery. The next morning the two latter returned to London, apparently pleased with their visit. John seems perfectly satisfied with the change he has made, likes his work, & Mr Young is, I am thankful to find, a steady sober man, some years older, & in many respects a very suitable companion for him.

That same day Papa & I paid the last tribute of deserved respect to our faithful friend Howcutt,[121] and followed him to the grave at the Cemetery. He was only ill three or four days, I was with him the greater part of the last & when he passed away. We do, & shall, miss him continually; anything that was needed to be done at any of our houses, he was always at hand to do, & it always seemed a delight to him to do us any service. His mind wandered very much & he never knew the end of life was near, but he so lived that for him to depart was 'to be with Christ'. The prayer & praise which he loved so much on earth are but exchanged for higher communion & praises before the Throne.

*August 23rd*

A week yesterday Florence came bringing with her the two boys. Will was not able to accompany her, having a very important Arbitration case to see finished before being able to leave.

On Saturday Papa drove Lottie, Hattie & myself to Ampthill after dinner. Florence stayed at home to receive her Husband, the time of whose arrival in the evening was uncertain. Our drive was partly to try a new horse. A fortnight ago, whilst driving Mrs A Morton & her little girl, I forgot to exercise my usual care in driving our old one whilst coming down the bridge near home, & met with my first misfortune with him in the four years I have driven poor Charley. He fell & cut both knees most sadly, fortunately nothing worse happened to us than a great fright, as he recovered his legs again instantly & I got him on without further stoppage, but he is getting better & I have ordered knee caps, & much prefer keeping him to having another.

*Septr 28th*

Of late I have not felt much inclined for writing in my Diary. Amidst much to be thankful for as ever, many of the circumstances surrounding the daily routine have not been joyous & I have often a feeling of depression amounting to sadness, the cause doubtless partly in myself. I need to exercise much more the Christian graces, charity towards others, & faith & hope for myself, to make life what it might be to me, but 'every heart knoweth its own bitterness' & a single drop can destroy sweetness & a single cloud obscure the sun; it is only above & beyond it that the clouds

---

[121] Billingham's predecessor.

of earth can never come. I think I am learning to live more in anticipation of that blessed place & longing for preparedness for it.

### Saturday Oct<sup>r</sup> 7<sup>th</sup>

I do not remember that I have written of the fact that some weeks since I allowed my name to be put on the Committee of the Mission of the 'Blue Ribbon Army' which has as yet been little more than talked about in Bedford.[122] Having attended two or three committee meetings in St Cuthbert's School room & got the proposition carried that as neither Major Poole (who was first asked), nor any other notable man connected with the Army, could promise to conduct the mission in the Corn Exchange at the earliest time at which it is available, next February, Mr Hull (a clergyman of Northampton who has been most earnest & successful in the work there) should be invited to begin it there; & he having consented to do so by coming for three days during the 10 days mission which it is proposed to hold, I felt some anxiety lest the remaining ones should not be filled by other influential speakers & lest their co-operation should not be asked until too late to secure it. To know more of what was being done (not being able to attend the last committee meeting), I called on Mrs Saunders, one of the first promoters of the movement in Bedford, went with her the next day to a prayer-meeting which Dr Goldsmith has in his house every Thursday, hoping also to see & hear from him what he could or would do, as he is on the committee. I was again disappointed in not finding him at home.

On Friday I accepted Mrs Hobson's invitation to visit her in the pretty new Chalet which Mr H has built as a summer residence at Woburn Sands. There I spent a very pleasant day, although the weather was not fine. Mr Hobson's sister, Mrs Rust, met me at the Station in the chaise & we had a drive through the woods together, returning to dinner at 1 o'clock. Mrs R seems a devoted Christian, full of faith. From her I got a great deal of information of the work of the 'Blue Ribbon Army' in Leicester where she resides, & an invitation & offer of help, if we make the efforts which we ought, to secure some of the earnest men who have carried on the work most successfully there.

I called again on Dr Goldsmith on Sunday & obtained his promise to see the Secretary & stir him up to timely endeavours to obtain promises of assistance from those who have contributed to the extraordinary success which has attended the movement in so many places.

### Novr 10<sup>th</sup>

On Saturday night John came home also very pleased with that[123] & everything else. He is very comfortable in every way in his apartments at Cricklewood but seems to think there is 'no place like home' more than in the days when he was always in it. He appears quite contented with his work & the progress he is making in Messrs Lake's confidence, which they have given him several proofs, is increasing.

---

[122] See the Introduction for a summary of the development of the temperance movement at this time.
[123] CEB is referring here to improvements made by her husband in the conservatory.

*Novr 14ᵗʰ*

The Blue Ribbon Army Movement had made some further progress during the time I was away. Mrs Saunders has enlisted the help of a gentleman who has not much to occupy his time (Mr Cockburn living in the Crescent);[124] he has been to Northampton, seen Mr Hull & become so interested in the work that he consented to become Chairman of the Executive committee which was to be formed. He called whilst I was from home. A letter from Mrs Saunders the day after my return told me what had been done & that it was proposed I should be on it as Treasurer. To this I replied that I must know more of what my responsibility would be before acceding, when she called to tell me from Mr Cockburn that he would take all beyond the caretaking of the funds as they came in, which is therefore all my business.

I went to the Committee meeting at which the Executive was to be formed, which was held in St Cuthbert's School-room on Thursday evening. Mr Cockburn was in the Chair. The Vicar, Dr Goldsmith, Colonel Guise & several influential gentlemen, many of whom were not total abstainers, were present, but the majority was composed of men who were more zealous as such, but lacked both means & influence to carry out alone the proposed Mission &, but for a rescinding of a resolution they had got passed at a former meeting that none but tee-totallers should be on the Executive committee (which was not done without a very stormy debate in which the Vicar took part & in which I had the temerity to ask to be allowed to speak, which I did from my seat to a few of the most headstrong in their opposition, telling them I thought they could not be aware of what they were doing in rejecting the co-operation of those without whom they must bear the whole responsibility of paying over £40 for the Corn Exchange, beside all other expenses of Speakers etc for a fortnight), they would have swamped all that had before been done if it had not been reversed, which was at length done, & after a good deal more discussion & opposition from the same individuals, a Committee of 9 was formed to carry out all the arrangements necessary to hold the Mission next February.

The meeting was so exciting that I came home past 10 o'clock with so much color in my face that when I told Papa about it, & how nearly the whole thing had collapsed, he said I was too excitable to attend such meetings & was rather vexed with me; but I am so thankful that half a dozen business men are willing to use their time & influence to endeavour to stem the tide of intemperance which is doing so much to ruin the bodies & souls of men & women here as elsewhere, that it matters little whether they profess to be more than temperance men or not to me, if the work can only be carried out successfully.

Papa & I were abstainers from the time we were married until rather more than 12 years ago when I had an illness which occasioned my going to a Physician in London under whose orders I took a little stimulant, but it has been always so little & I feel so anxious to throw the whole of my influence into the cause I have lately espoused, that I have done what I never did before, signed a pledge, and adopted the Blue Ribbon. I am thankful that I was able to bring up all my children without

---

[124] Francis Cockburn was a retired Bengal civil servant, an Anglo-Indian (see Introduction), living at 17 The Crescent. Five of his six children had been born in India, the sixth in Germany. There were in-laws from Scotland and Australia to add to the geographical diversity present in the household.

ever allowing them a drop except as medicine & they were taught to regard what I took in the same light. I trust they will so train theirs.

*Saturday Novr 25th*
We have been without any of our children from John's return until last Saturday when Will came soon after 1 o'clock to spend Sunday with us. Mrs Booth called to see me in the afternoon & whilst we were talking he went with Papa to the Works, after expressing his approbation of the Conservatory which he had not before seen. On Sunday, after going together to the Wesleyan Chapel in the morning, we thoroughly enjoyed the brightness of the beautiful sunshine amongst the flowers. Will so much so that he sat there a great part of the afternoon, reading & smoking, I fear more of the latter than the former for certainly the habit has increased, & will I often fear eventually tell upon his health. Home training in this respect has not influenced him now, for he never saw his Father touch a pipe to smoke nor acquired the habit himself until his College days were over, & he went to Manchester for his six months completion of his engineering training at Sir J Whitworth's, after he took the Whitworth scholarship.[125] But I am running off into matters of which I had not the least intention to write when I began this page. I do wish however Will did not smoke so much.

*Decr 8th*
Monday Decr 4th was the day appointed for the Queen to go to open the new Law Courts, [126] & I quite expected Will would make efforts to be present & take his wife; neither however cared to go, but the former accompanied Hattie & myself to the Strand & returned at once leaving us to wait for the passing of Her Majesty, which we were invited to witness from Mr Slack's window. The morning was as bright as the proverbial Queen's weather which so generally attends her public appearances, & not so cold but that we stood outside without discomfort, watching the dense crowd beneath, & the carriages that for nearly two hours continually followed each other bearing Judges, QCs, & grandees of all degrees to the Courts before she came. For the first time I saw Mr Gladstone, who was the only individual beside the Queen that got a continued & hearty cheer as he passed on, seated in an open carriage with his wife & daughter & wearing cocked hat & court dress. The procession passed too quickly for more than a glimpse of Royalty & I was almost more interested in watching the marvellous crowd, so closely packed that they swayed together almost like a field of corn, & often turned aside the police both on horse & foot, & even a line of Dragoons drawn across the street, & surged from the pavements until the roadway seemed as completely filled. How they were driven back from time to time by the mounted police & soldiers without being trampled to death by the horses or each other was the greatest wonder.

After we at length got clear of the crowd, we did some shopping after which,

---

[125]  Will enjoyed academic success at Cambridge, graduating as sixteenth Wrangler in the Mathematics Tripos. After this, he won a scholarship to work at the eminent engineer Joseph Whitworth's factory in Manchester. Will was indeed a polymath, not just a fine mathematician.
[126]  CEB refers to the Royal Courts of Justice in the Strand.

leaving Mrs A & her daughters[127] in Cheapside, I returned to Cricklewood alone; Hattie left with John who met us at Mr Slack's & returned to School for the afternoon, then back for dinner, after which Florence & myself accompanied her back to the H & I High School[128] for the concert at night in which she took part playing one of Chopin's Nocturnes very nicely. I had a little conversation with Miss Whyte before leaving; she spoke very well of Hattie as 'good all round' & said rather significantly when I alluded to her feeling rather disappointed that she had just missed a prize (as Hattie supposed by 1 mark) that the prizes were not yet named.

### Dec^r 30^th (Saturday)

Hattie's return home a week last Thursday is the first event in order that has transpired since I last wrote. After 4 terms at the Highbury & Islington High School she has finally left having gained two prizes, one for languages (Latin & French), the other for English generally, & in addition a certificate from the School. These however do not at all compensate for the mortification she feels that she completely lost her head over the Arithmetic Paper in the Cambridge Exam, & was so dreadfully nervous that she is quite sure she did not do a sufficient number of the sums right to pass in that, & however well all else was done there is scarcely a chance that she will obtain a certificate in the Senior Exam, after working for it so long & honestly as she has I am sure been[129] doing. She seems to have got on very well with all her other subjects including Latin, & it certainly is hard that all should count for nothing through a misadventure which would not have happened if she could have had more time & more collectedness.[130]

Lottie's case was just the same for she has told me that she could have done what she failed to do in the Examination room under ordinary circumstances.[131] I was more disappointed & sorry than I let Hattie know, but I shall not regard the result, if she has failed, as a test of her capability or attainments, for both her teachers who have been most successful in passing girls in the exams tell me she has good ability & she must have the advantage of having worked as industriously as she has done at School. We have not yet decided whether she shall pursue Painting only in future, or take some of the classes at the new High School for Girls here.[132]

After further debating the journey to Southport, Papa decided that we should all accompany him thither to spend Xmas with Grandmama Bousfield at Aunt Jenny's. To avoid the crush of Xmas travellers, he got the Station-master of the L&NW to send to Euston & engage a compartment for us from Bletchley. Leaving home on Saturday morning at 11 o'clock we arrived there to find the train with a through carriage to Southport & an engaged compartment with Papa's name on it waiting in the Station. In this we travelled very comfortably alone, notwithstanding the efforts

---

[127]  This refers to Mrs Harriet Akerman, CEB's mother's sister, so the daughters were CEB's first cousins.
[128]  CEB refers to the Highbury and Islington High School, a Girls' Public Day School Company foundation.
[129]  CEB writes 'being'.
[130]  Hattie had problems with the arithmetic paper she sat in the Cambridge Junior Local Examinations three years earlier, when she failed to hand in one of the sheets (see entry for 17 December 1879).
[131]  Lottie is referring to her Senior Cambridge arithmetic paper, which she also failed – see 17 December 1878. The sisters did not share their eldest brother's mathematical ability.
[132]  CEB here refers to the Bedford High School, which opened in May 1882.

which were made at one or two of the largest towns at which we stopped by some of the crowds on the platform to get into our carriage.

Arriving at Southport at 5 o'clock Aunt Jenny welcomed us very warmly & Grandma with mingled tears & smiles, the pleasure seemed almost too much for her. After tea Aunts Polly & H Maria came to see us, stayed & had coffee when Papa & I left with them for a walk in the bright moon-light which succeeded the sun-shine with which the day closed, although we had several very heavy storms during our journey.

The first sounds we heard on Xmas morning were voices on the landing on to which all our bed-rooms opened singing 'Christians awake', the singers Lottie & Hattie who had, in accordance with a promise which I did not expect they would carry out, saluted us with a carol at daybreak, & then came into our room in their dressing gowns to know whether we enjoyed it, to which Papa responded at the breakfast table by passing each of the carol-singers an envelope, each containing a reward for their singing. We found Xmas-cards & a smelling bottle for me & thermometer for Papa from [them][133] opposite our places at the table, & a little joint present from them also for Aunt Jenny, all helping to make a happy beginning to our day.

We reached home after a journey not so pleasant as our outward one, but thankful for the pleasure we had been able to give & receive, but best of all that Papa had been unusually well all the time we had been away & returned appearing much better for the rest & change.


## 1883

*Jan^y 7^th 1883*
With the last page of my Diary comes the end of the first week of a new year. I might fill it by simply making it an index for all the mercies recorded in the preceding ones. I have sometimes looked on the blank sheets & wondered with what they would have to be filled. In the nearly five years that have passed since the first was written 'no evil has befallen us, neither has any plague come nigh our dwelling'. I & my dear Husband have truly realized the blessing of them 'that fear the Lord' yea even to the extent of 'seeing our children's children'.

---

[133]  CEB writes 'Papa' but must mean 'them'.

# Volume 2

## February 1883 to August 1887

**1883**

*Feb[y] 26th 1883*
With the last days of the past year I finished the last page of the volume with which Will furnished me when I began to keep a diary nearly five years ago. I have had some disinclination to continuing to do so, but my children seem to wish it & to be so much interested in listening to some of the records of the past with which I occasionally amuse them that for their sakes more than by my own wish in the matter I will continue a remembrance of the chief events of our family life.

Hattie has begun to make her painting her chief occupation after the few household duties that fall to her are performed; it is a new thing for us to have her at home & for her to be here without school duties that must be performed to keep pace with others, so that she does not readily fit into the new groove in which she finds herself, & is not so enthusiastic in the profession[1] she has chosen as I wish her to be. She does not yet feel the responsibilities of life, & so is impatient at being frequently reminded of duty & the necessity of having regular times for it.

Lottie has lately more than ever given me great comfort & satisfaction; she has exercised great self-control over her temper, & strives very much to restrain herself when I find fault with her, or Hattie vexes her, which however annoys the latter more than an angry reply, but is at the same time an influence which may I hope show its effects as years & wisdom increase.

The chief occupation of some weeks past has been connected with the Blue Ribbon Mission. As soon as the girls were able to go out, they joined the choir which was formed for it & went with me to the practices at St Peter's School-room. Thursday Jan[y] 25th there was a General Committee meeting to receive a report of the proceedings of the Executive committee which I did not attend, but Friday Feb[y] 2nd the Secretary Revd AH Jones gave an address at the Working Men's Institute to all who had promised to help in singing, visiting to distribute hand bills & notices etc. The following Monday a week of evening prayer-meetings was begun in the same place conducted each night by a different Clergyman or Minister.

Monday the 12th the great meetings in the Corn Exchange were begun by Revd Hull of Northampton, the Clergyman I first heard of when I went there to see about a servant in the summer, & proposed to the Committee. Not only were we satisfied but entirely surprised at the crowds that gathered from the first night. Mr Hull made an admirable speech for the opening one & those who followed him each night to the 24th kept up the interest to the last. Amongst these were Barristers, Clergymen & Ministers of various denominations. One of the former, Mark Knowles esqr, was

---

[1]  The profession to which CEB alludes is that of an artist.

our guest. He was to have come to us just in time for the meeting Saturday 17th but at Mr F Howard's request arrived at the Works at noon to address the men, & here, after luncheon with Mr H; I invited Mr Stephens, Mr & Mrs Donkin & Miss Saunders to meet him, the three latter are new friends whom I met for the first time in connection with this work, & who have thrown all their energies into it. Mr Donkin is Mrs Saunders' brother & has only just come to the town from America where he has, by his own exertion, raised & left a flourishing Young Men's Xtian Association; he is an unexpected & most valuable addition to our list of workers.

Mr Knowles is a most remarkable man, & kept us willing listeners both in private & public. Originally the child of poor parents, he had to enter a workhouse with his Mother after she became a widow; but although crippled on one side from his birth, he managed to raise himself to a position of affluence & influence in his native town, Blackburn, as an inventor & manufacturer of machinery for weaving, then losing £20000 by a great failure of a Russian house, had to begin life again & did so by reading for the Bar at the age of 43. Succeeded so soon at this that the third year of being called he made £700 at it, out of 100 cases which he had, only losing 14. He seems also a most earnest Xtian man & is a powerful speaker.

After his lecture he returned for supper, leaving by last train near midnight to return to London for his Sunday work, part of which was preaching in the Victoria Theatre in the afternoon. He had been engaged for two of the meetings in the Exchange & before the second came in time to hold a Drawing-room meeting here at 4-30 p m to which I invited Mr Kempson, Mr Donkin, Colonel Elliott, & several other gentlemen and ladies, to listen to his suggestions as to the best means of continuing the work after the end of the Mission. The two latter were appointed, together with those present, to form a Committee & call a meeting. After another speech in the Exchange the following Wednesday, Mr Knowles returned here for the night but we did not retire to bed until 1 o'clock so much were we interested in his histories of himself, which he gave us in the frankest possible manner.

Next morning the Brougham was at the door to take him to the Barracks at 9 o'clock that he might address the soldiers. About 150 mustered with the Colonel's permission to listen to him, beside about a dozen wives & children of the men. Lottie, Hattie & myself were also present & much delighted when 35 came forward at the conclusion of his address & signed the pledge. I promised to go again the next afternoon & pin the Blue Ribbon on, which I did with Mr Rae (the Speaker for that night in the Exchange). Over fifty men mustered again in the same Barrack room when we drove up. To these Mr Rae spoke a few minutes & at the conclusion of his speech I had the satisfaction of fastening the ribbon on 51 red coats, much to the delight of Sergeant Bell who is now forming a Temperance Society amongst the soldiers.

The results of the Mission have in every respect been most satis[factory]. The afternoon meetings for women have been larger each time from the first; at the last there must have been between 700 & 800 women present. Many of them signed & took the Blue Ribbon. The total number of individuals that did so during the Mission was considerably over 2000.

The work of assisting in the choir, & especially that of furnishing the 8 tables at which the pledges & Ribbon were taken, with ladies to take the names & addresses of all applicants & pin the blue (four for each table), brought me into contact with many more Christian men & women of all denominations than I had ever an opportunity of meeting before in Bedford, & in every instance has the introduction been pleasant & the utmost good feeling has prevailed in all the labors which we undertook together.

At Mr Knowles's first visit he suggested a Drawing-room meeting in reply to the query what must be done in the future for those we succeeded in reclaiming during the Mission. He consented to address any who could be got together. I wrote this fact I see in a former page last night, & only ought to have related the results. First a committee meeting of gentlemen at the Exchange, when Colonel Elliott was chosen Secretary with Mr Donkin to assist Mr F Howard President & Mr Cockburn Treasurer to carry out Mr Knowles's suggestions to provide as speedily as possible one or more places of resort & amusement for those who, having been accustomed to the public-house, would without such probably soon return to their old haunts & habits. I want Papa very much to let me have a very simple one of wood & iron erected on our own ground but cannot yet succeed in getting his consent. Perhaps this may be ultimately included in the general scheme.

Many of the inhabitants of Southend have donned the Blue, some of them just such as will be greatly benefited by so doing if they can only be kept. On Saturday night John came home bringing with him Mr Young. Both attended our last meeting in the Corn Exchange, & although John has always been a Teetotaller, I was very pleased that he signed a card & allowed a young lady in the room to fasten the ribbon on his coat, not however in a very visible place, but I hope he will in time wear it more boldly.

*Friday March 2nd*
On Wednesday afternoon I drove into the town with Lottie & Hattie, & intending to call on Mr Donkin. We met him just before reaching his house & found that without waiting for permission from any Committee to begin the work for which the one I mentioned in the Exchange met, he had fitted up a loft over his Stables for the immediate reception of any who wanted to keep away from the public house. This I promised to return to see after the Drawing-room address at 3-30 at Gen Swinhoe's,[2] to which I had an invitation, to listen to Gen Field, who gave an account of some of the working of the Evangelical Alliance, & desired to form an association in connection with it at Bedford. At the end of the meeting I returned to Mr Donkin's & was surprised to find what a comfortable Refuge he had managed to prepare in little more than a day. A little white-wash, a stove, tables & about 3 dozen chairs had converted the loft into a comfortable warm apartment.

After tea with Mrs D (who fully enters into her Husband's work) I called on Colonel Elliott, & after a little talk as to where, & how quickly, the same on a larger scale could be carried on, he very kindly took me to the Building in Thurlow St which is available & could be fitted up at comparatively small cost in very little time. I promised to try to get Papa to meet Colonel E at the place the next morning, which he consented to do, & we went together. Captn Glubb was there also, &

[2] Swinhoe was a retired Indian Army officer, who had served in the Punjab and on the North-West frontier.

all agreed that the situation was just what was required & the place in all respects desirable. Papa was invited to attend a Committee meeting at night in the Mayor's parlour at the Exchange; two other spots were to be mentioned. Mr F Howard was in the Chair. He was very much in favor of putting up an Iron Building at the back of the Coffee Tavern, but nothing was settled further than that enquiries should be made as to the cost of one & another meeting held next Thursday to receive the report, so with all the talk little is done & time wasted.

I was the only lady elected on this committee & might have attended but refused to so do unless with another. I mentioned Miss Cockburn in speaking of it to Revd Mr Kempson, & she was proposed last night Papa told me, so that I shall go next Thursday & try to influence them to do something at once. Thurlow St is the right place.

I met Papa in the town after he left the Exchange & we went on together to see Mr Donkin's 'workmen's hall' we may call it. We found the loft occupied by from twenty to thirty men, some singing the temperance hymns & tunes to which they have become accustomed during the Mission, others playing draughts, dominoes, etc & drinking coffee & all looking pleased & thankful. To make sure that they were such men as we want to get in, I took advantage of an interval in the singing to ask whether many of those who were present had been accustomed to go to public houses, & the amused laugh that went round was a sufficient answer to my question.

Colonel Elliott & Mr Kinsey came also to see the place & men whilst we were there, the former is very much in earnest to do something & will not fail if he is not hampered & obstructed. I am very thankful Papa has joined the committee; I have tried hard to get him to wear the Blue, but failed in this, so far.

Lottie & Hattie have been busy painting some texts & mottoes to place along the beams in Mr Donkin's 'Hall'; we have already taken him a lot of pictures to enliven the walls, & papers & old periodicals for the tables. A coffee urn is kept hot by a lamp on one of them, which the men patronized to the extent of 22 cups the first night it was opened.

This morning Lottie walked with me into the town; she went to the Class-meeting, whilst I went on to a meeting of Collectors of London City Missions at Mrs Pigott's.[3] I had arranged to go to Cricklewood to-morrow & after Sunday to Norwood, but wrote to Florence this morning that I could not leave until the end of next week. My last letter to Florence before this was written on Monday when I took the opportunity of telling her when the new servant I have just sent her would arrive, to beg her to make an earnest effort to overcome late hours on Sunday mornings & then being kept from God's house, as I experienced when I was last with them was the case. Florence's reply was so sweet & full of desire to do what was right that I can only love her for it, especially if she has firmness & strength to carry out the intentions she expresses. I feel as anxious to know my children are doing right & living to prepare for the never ending life as I did in the days when their actions & conduct were under my control. To see either of them careless of the Sabbath serv-

---

[3]   The London City Mission was an important evangelical and philanthropic organisation founded by David Nasmith in Hoxton in 1835. Also known as the Hoxton Gospel Temperance Mission, it developed into one of the largest and most successful missions in the UK – by 1885 it had some 460 staff.

ices, & indifferent to God's worship & house, would take away all the brightness of the pleasure we feel in seeing their temporal success. May the Psalmist's words 'I was glad when they said unto me Let us go into the House of the Lord'[4] be theirs and their children's experience.

*Tuesday March 20th*

[In London] I went on to the Albert Hall where Florence was to meet me to see Hattie receive her prize with her former school-fellows, at the hands of the Princess of Wales. Arriving at the Hall an hour before the time of opening the doors, I crossed to the Albert Memorial & spent some time looking at the sculptures; then returned to wait in the crowd that gradually gathered until 2-30 when I was very glad to get inside the building out of the bitterly cold wind, & also to get some refreshment. Mrs Kelly was amongst those waiting for admission, Florence came soon after & in order that her mother might have a stall ticket exchanged hers next to mine with her & went into the balcony.

The sight of the 2500 school-girls that filled the orchestra & arena was very pretty. All wore white muslin fichus[5] (no bonnets or hats), & a rosette of different color for each of the 10 schools present. Hattie's school was distinguished by cerise. About 300 girls took prizes. The prize takers were assembled in the arena directly under the raised seats prepared for those who were the principal personages in the proceedings. The Prince of Wales accompanied the Princess & three young Princesses their daughters.[6] The girls ascended two or three steps & in a continual stream passed before the table at which the Princess of Wales stood, handing to each her book, which was received with as graceful a curtsey as the recipient knew how to make. Hattie has for some time been fearing because she had not learnt dancing she should be specially awkward in her movement, which however was certainly much more gracefully performed, first to the Princess, & then to the Prince, than many others, & she carried off her prize with becoming dignity. This consists of two volumes, one for Latin, the other French & English. The girls sang several pieces both before & after the ceremonial. Speeches from Lord Aberdare,[7] Lord Lansdowne & the Prince concluded the proceedings.

At the close Florence met me & with Hattie we went together in a cab to the Station. Then F took train for home, Hattie & I for Westminster, hoping Will had been able to get us a Member's Order for the House of Commons. Arriving at King St on our way to Mr Kelly's Office[8] we found ourselves in the midst of a crowd

---

4    Psalm 122.

5    A three-cornered cape, worn over the shoulders.

6    The Prince of Wales ascended the throne in 1901 as Edward VII. His wife was Alexandra of Denmark, his three daughters the Princesses Louise, Victoria Alexandra and Maud, who became Queen of Norway.

7    CEB does not comment that as H.A. Bruce, Home Secretary in Gladstone's first ministry, Lord Aberdare had attempted to introduce in 1871 a drastic Licensing Bill which contributed to the fall of Gladstone's first ministry in 1874. She would have approved of the former, though not the latter (see entry for 26 April 1880).

8    Mr Kelly was an advertising agent (including for the *London Gazette*) and parliamentary printer, in business as George Kelly & Co. at 23–25 King Street, Westminster. King Street now no longer exists but in the 1880s it ran from Great George Street (at its meeting with Bridge Street) to the junction of Downing Street and Whitehall. The premises were well placed for CEB to call on him on her way to the House of Commons and also to be the target of 'outrages'. CEB's chance meeting with Mr Kelly in the

gathered to look at a scene of devastation such as we had never before witnessed. The public buildings, shops & houses of all descriptions as far as we could see in every direction had the windows so smashed that scarcely a whole one was to be seen, in some cases every pane of glass entirely gone, in others the thick plate glass fronts were shivered in strips from top to bottom. The whole caused by a single explosion it is supposed of a canister of dynamite placed in the stone balcony of one of the windows of the Government Office facing King St by some Fenian, or other wicked wretch, with the design of blowing it up.[9] Mr Kelly had had the whole of his window sashes from the first floor upward carried away to be re-glazed, & the large plate glass window on the ground floor was entirely gone & boarded up. Mr K went with us through the crowd back again & showed us the very spot whence all this mischief originated.

As Will had not been able to get an order for the House of Commons, we were turning towards Cricklewood when a Baker St omnibus came up & Hattie thought she should like to finish her day by another visit to a place to which she last went as quite a little girl, so we turned into Mme Tussaud's Collection of Waxworks, & after an hour there got back again to Westbury Villa where we found John had been some time awaiting our arrival.[10] The next evening we had tea with him, Will & Florence coming later for coffee. John's rooms are quite a specimen of order & cleanliness, the former due to himself, the latter to his landlady who seems to delight in doing anything that is for his comfort or convenience.

### March 24th

This evening we have met for the first time in our new Blue Ribbon Coffee & Reading-room about a dozen men. We invited Mr Donkin to take tea with us & afterwards to meet them to explain the basis on which his own was being worked. Accompanied by Papa & myself he did this & it was agreed to adopt his rules & carry out the same plans which he has found successful in keeping the men who joined the BR Army after the Mission, most of whom have remained true to their pledge. Our gathering to-night had in it some who are not yet total abstainers, & these have taken until next Saturday night to decide whether they will join those who are & have to-night enrolled their names as the first members of 'The Southend Blue Ribbon Coffee Room'.[11] This is the third that has now been opened since the Mission only a month ago, & the only cause for regret is that each is depending on single, instead of united, effort.[12]

The Committee which was formed has come to an end through the resignation of Colonel Elliott, the Secretary, because he & a few other gentlemen saw Thurlow St

---

Isle of Wight had led not only to Will finding a wife in the person of Florence Kelly, but also to useful family connections with parliamentary and legal publishing and printing in the form of Mr Kelly and Mr Sweet.

[9]   The Fenians belonged to a political and national movement, established in 1858, which aimed at bringing about an independent republic in Ireland. Predecessors of Sinn Fein and the IRA, they adopted violent methods, usually described as 'outrages', which brought the Irish problem to the forefront of British politics.

[10]   John's lodgings at 8 Claremont Road were a matter of a few yards round the corner from Will's house.

[11]   The Blue Ribbon room was situated at the bottom of CEB's garden with public access from Offa Road. Access was by an external wooden staircase.

[12]   CEB writes 'each is a depending ...': the word 'a' is redundant, and has been omitted.

to be the right place in opposition to the majority of the other members, & in order to do at once, he took the premises that were offered & could be speedily & cheaply got ready for those who, whilst a place of resort was being only talked of, would soon in all probability have returned to that to which they had been accustomed, the Public House.

I drove down to Thurlow St last Tuesday night with Lottie & was delighted to see the upper room there crowded with men, in their right mind, sitting playing games of draughts etc drinking coffee & reading. Before we left, the chairman (who a month ago was one of the greatest drunkards in Bedford) told me he had for years until then been accustomed to spend between two & three £s weekly on drink & betting, asked the company to sing three hymns out of the Gospel Temperance Hymn Books, the last being a hymn of praise concluding with 'Praise God from whom all blessings flow', & to hear the voices which had been so accustomed to the song of the drunkard turned to His praise brought tears to Lottie's eyes as well as mine, & made us feel full of thankfulness for the work which we had been permitted to help forward.

*March 30th*
On Wednesday afternoon before Easter Hattie returned from Cricklewood having seen Will's family off for Shanklin where they will spend his holiday with Florence's Parents. Hattie's success in the Cambridge Exam, in which she has passed in all the subjects for which she went in (English, Latin, French, German & Drawing) has led us to think that it will be a more useful occupation of her time to go on with her education for another year, with some help from Mrs Brown, & matriculate, instead of giving up the greater part of it to painting as was at first thought of after she had done with the High School in London. That in Bedford is not sufficiently advanced for a sixth form, or we should have liked her to have gone to it. At first she did not like the idea of again taking up school work, but Mrs B has made special arrangements for her, & she seems to have begun in earnest from last Tuesday. She is to go on with German & Mathematics only until next Term when all the subjects necessary must be taken up.[13]

John came home for his Easter holiday but it was broken up by his having to return to Town for some hours both on Saturday & Monday. Whilst I felt sorry for this it certainly was cause for pleasure to think that in so short a time he has made himself so valuable. He spent some hours on Easter Monday with Mr Waddy QC MP, as also on Saturday. Mr W, in conjunction with an inventor of a flying-machine, is taking out a patent for it. John evidently does not think it will ever mount into the air although he has had to do so much in connection with it.

All being ready for the opening of Southend BR Room on Saturday, I invited Mr Donkin to take tea with us, & afterwards to go with us to it to meet a few of the men who have been foremost in helping to prepare it, read his rules to them & tell how they had worked at his own room. About a dozen came, several of them not abstainers by any means. Papa did not wish any opening further than permission to

---

[13] Hattie's examination was the Senior Cambridge Local Examination, the equivalent of today's A level exams.

all who chose to come, but Monday being a holiday[14] made a favorable opportunity for getting a few together who either had already been, or we hoped might be, influenced to join. In the morning one man who a short time ago was a great drunkard got tables that would seat more than sixty persons ready before I got to the room, & with help from others, with Lottie & Hattie we soon made it look pretty for above that number of guests, whom I invited to tea & a social evening.

Amongst them were most of those in our neighbourhood who were known to drink to excess. All did not come but several whom we were specially desirous to see were there, together with those who had already taken the Ribbon. To one notorious tippler who only had changed his course a month before, during the Mission, & is now made 'Chairman' of the Thurlow St Room,[15] I gave a special invitation to come; his confessions & experiences I believe helped to lead some to begin a new course also.

After tea Papa took the conduct of the meeting in a very informal manner, getting many of the men to make little speeches, between which were songs & solos in which John, Lottie & Hattie took part as also Mr Greenhill, a gentleman who has lately come to Bedford & being very musical we asked to help us. Some of the men made very light work of fetching the Piano from the Drawing-room & carrying it up into our former hay-loft, so that we had a very lively evening. Papa's was the speech of the evening & he made it without our ever knowing his intention to do so. At the conclusion of the meeting the names of those who wished to become members were taken. They are to pay 6d entrance fee, & the same amount monthly, for the privilege of using the room any night from 6.30 until 10 o'clock, for reading the papers, playing draughts & drinking coffee, as much as they like at 1d per cup. Smoking is allowed & the singing of the Gospel Temperance Songs learnt during the Mission is a very favorite amusement.

At present all seems jovial & innocently free & easy, but I do not feel satisfied with this only or even that some have given up or are kept from drink. I cannot yet find any one who is willing to take a Sunday afternoon Bible class for any who may be willing to come to one, so until I can do so, although not in accordance with my own feelings, I have offered to meet any who will attend from 3 to 4 o'clock. This is a much greater task than any I have before undertaken, & one which I shall be glad to relinquish if I can get a gentleman to take it.

### April 9th

There is no necessity for endeavouring to get help for a Bible Class at our BR Room; I went to it at 3 o'clock last Sunday afternoon & no one came. Personally I feel relieved, but should have been thankful if some of the youths around us could have been interested & instructed. I have been to see Mr Donkin & begged him to visit our men when he can spare an hour from his own work which he is prosecuting most successfully & carrying into some of the neighbouring villages.

This wave of Temperance which is gradually sweeping over the country (as proved by the Publicans' complaints, & the decrease in the revenue from Excise Duties) has only swept away a small portion of the intemperance of Bedford, but the

---

[14] Easter Monday.
[15] The Blue Ribbon Room was at no. 7 Thurlow Street, not far from the town centre.

teetotallers of the town have not been wise & after some expressions of jealousy or dissatisfaction from them it has been thought best to dissolve the committee formed to carry out the mission, which was done last Thursday evening, when all the executive committee tendered their resignation at the last committee meeting which was held in St Cuthbert's School-room.[16]

The visitation of this District (south of the river) devolves on me but I have not yet been able to organize such a staff of visitors as will be necessary to look after it properly. Lottie continues very anxious to do all she can & takes opportunities to visit & get the pledge taken when ever she finds them. She has been to the Bedford Laundry to read to the women, & between twenty & thirty gathered & listened to her for half an hour, after their work was done, last Tuesday evening.

### Wednesday May 9th

Within a week Hattie has painted an original picture for an exhibition at the Bedford rooms of which she had notice on one Saturday & had finished it by the next. From Lottie sitting on the ground leaning against the raffia basket as a bank, she has contrived a very pretty, & as Papa & I think, very clever picture of a girl seated under a tree, with surroundings of foliage etc of which she could not get any model from nature at this season. We had no idea she could have done so well. Monday morning we left it at the Room where the Exhibition, which is open to-morrow, is held.

### May 21st

On Whit-Monday morning Will went with his Papa for a long walk, whilst John drove Florence, the two boys, Lottie & Hattie in the chaise round by Clapham & Bromham in spite of the rain which threatened the whole morning, but only came on heavily for a short time soon after 1 o'clock whilst the members of our Blue Ribbon Club were on the lawn with their new banner & a band of music. Mr Donkin had arranged for our men & his own to meet in the Market Place, but as the former did not gather in as large a number as he expected, he sent to the Clapham Rd Room to tell them to come to Southend, & start on their intended walk round the town from ours. Whilst waiting the band played several pieces until (as rain was falling) I begged them to go to the room & sent Baylis to regale them with bread & cheese & ginger-beer. Mr Donkin was evidently annoyed that we had not a larger muster, but the whole made a very respectable procession when his men arrived with their Banner also, & marched off together towards the town. I did not understand either his wishes or intentions in the matter, nor what end was answered by this. About 3 o'clock I walked into the town expecting to find all in the field near Mr D's house, calling at Bunyan Room (which had been lent for the tea) on the way thither. I met Mrs Donkin & found they were still on the march, so returned with her to the school-room.

Mrs Kirwan asked me to take 4 o'clock tea with her which I did with Mrs Glubb; whilst at her house, which is very near the room, the procession & band appeared before Captn Kirwan's, he being himself in it with Mr Donkin. Then after singing

---

[16] The reason for the resignation of the entire committee is unclear. The following entries (21 May and 7 June) indicate an element of friction between CEB and some of her colleagues.

etc all adjourned for tea when nearly 300 sat down, & about 200 more after the first party had done. Mr Kempson the Vicar of St Cuthbert's was present. After tea Captn Kirwan presided over the meeting which was addressed by himself, our late BR Secretary Mr Jones, Colonel Elliott & several gentlemen from the Thurlow St Club who just came to show friendly feeling. Between the speeches were songs & readings. Amongst others Lottie sang & was encored. Florence came after tea & helped by singing a duet with Lottie.

As far as the entertainment of some 700 people (at a time when many of them might have been tempted to do wrong) went the whole affair was a success, but I felt considerable disappointment that advantage was not taken of the opportunity of so large a gathering to do something more to amuse them, or rather to bring the whole to a more practical result by giving any who were influenced by Captn Kirwan's & Mr Jones' speeches an opportunity to join the ranks of the BR Army.

During the evening Mr Donkin came to me & proposed that some one should go to Thurlow St (where they had a similar gathering to ours on a smaller scale) & give them a friendly greeting in return for theirs. Papa acceded to his request & accompanied by Mr Stinson [Stimson] went & gave them a little speech, much to the satisfaction of some of the Thurlow St men.

Tuesday morning Will intended to have returned to Town but as the morning was delightfully fine he consented to remain until night, & we determined to go for a picnic. A hamper of provisions was quickly packed. Papa, Will & John started together to walk to Brick Hill Farm.[17] I drove Florence & the girls with the Babies. The good-natured Farmer Mr Ford took in the horse & gave us full permission to pitch our camp where we would. Will's greatest idea of enjoyment seemed to be to light a fire to boil our eggs etc. He spent a long time building an arched fire place & then got so fierce a fire that he boiled not only the water but the handle off a new tin saucepan which, at his request, I got on our way through the town.

After the mid-day meal the male part of our party went for a wander in Clapham wood. I took Baby down to the Chaise & amused him at the Farm looking at the Poultry etc whilst Florence & the girls cleared away & prepared for the second meal. Will returned in time to carry out his favorite occupation, boiling the water, & we sat down again for tea, after which he walked to the Station with Papa & John, & we returned as we came, only lengthening our drive by turning through Goldington, as the evening was still beautifully bright. Florence stayed the night with us & left with her little ones by early train next morning.

### June 8th

A fortnight ago yesterday (Thursday) I went with Hattie to the prayer meeting which is held fortnightly in the lower room in Thurlow St Blue R premises. Mrs Sampson (a lady who has taken interest in the work & is one of the District Temperance visitors in Trinity Parish) asked me to help by saying a few words at a women's meeting which was to be held the following week in Trinity Schoolroom. Thinking it was a sort of Mothers-meeting I did not object, & went last Friday night. Mrs S offered me the conducting of the meeting but this I declined & she led it herself. It was of a much more mixed character than I expected. Half a dozen young ladies

---

[17]  This rural area is now a northern suburb of Bedford.

who help[ed] during the Mission came to assist the singing. A Mrs De Witt whom I had not before known spoke first, & then after a hymn my turn came. I was surprised that I did not feel more nervous before some fifty people, but felt little more perturbed than in speaking to the women at my own Mothers' meeting.

*Thursday June 28th*

Father & Grandma Collins's visit came to an end on Tuesday morning when they left us for Newark where they have gone to spend a week. With the exception of an attack of indigestion which made Father very poorly for a day, he has had nothing to interrupt the enjoyment of his stay with us which has I believe been a real pleasure both to him & Grandma. They have walked into the town every day I have not driven them thither, when the weather would allow. We have had our little Saturday afternoon excursions, the first with them, to Turvey, where after a walk in the Park we had tea. Returning home afterwards we were overtaken by a severe thunder-storm accompanied by drenching rain, but fortunately just as it came pouring down managed to find shelter for ourselves, the horse & chaise under a shed in a farm yard at Kempston, where we remained more than half an hour. The following Saturday we drove to Warden & returned in charming weather.

Last Saturday Grandpapa proposed we should stay & look after the hay which was being made in the very small piece of the field which remains to us, now that Papa has re-sold it to Mr Pearse.[18] After dinner I walked with Papa about a mile on the London Rd to see a piece of clover which he had bought & had cut, leaving G-papa & G-ma together making hay in the field opposite.

*July 7th*

A letter from Colonel Elliott last week asked me to attend a meeting to be held in Thurlow St (before the fortnightly prayer-meeting) to which Mr Donkin, Mr Jones, Drs Goldsmith & Kinsey & a few others came, to hear from the two first some details of a scheme which they had themselves begun for a grand 'Temperance Demonstration' for next Bank Holiday: this meeting was followed by another in which Mr D more fully disclosed his plans which Captn [Glubb] (who attended on behalf of Thurlow St) did not approve of & nothing was decided except again to adjourn the meeting. Captn Kirwan sent me a notice that it would be held last night in Mill St, as before, at Mr Stinson's [Stimson] office, & I went for a little while after the women's meeting in Moise St, at which at Miss Bevill's earnest request I said a few words to the very small number of Mothers who came. The Committee meeting seemed unlikely to come to a decision or an end near 10 o'clock, so I left promising 1 guinea's responsibility & no more. Mr Donkin altered & contracted his first ideas very much in the matter of giving prizes for races & some of the other proposed amusements which are to fill up the intervals between meetings at which Mr Hull, Mr Knowles & Mr Rae are to speak. But for this I should not have had anything to do with the fete.

To keep from drink & amuse some hundreds or thousands of people on a day which is a greater evil than a boon to many working men is worth attempting, if the

---

18  Theed Pearse, town clerk of Bedford, and clerk of the peace for the county, like his father and grand-father before him.

latter can be done in a manner in character with the Gospel Temperance Mission, which now seems more likely to be the case than at first. Mrs Donkin & Mrs Kirwan have called this afternoon to say that Captn Glubb has withdrawn from any share in the responsibility, & to ask whether I would go to another meeting to-night, which I have declined to do, as I could not be of use.

Grandma Bousfield & Aunt Jenny arrived from Southport two days after the departure of our last visitors. Grandmama bore the journey very well.[19] She stitches away at her fancy or wool work as much & as well as ever; but she moves with more difficulty, & is very soon wearied when she walks. Her great pleasure is in the drives which we take, especially when Papa is the Driver. This afternoon we have had a picnic on the road side in a charming spot not far from Southill Station. Lottie & Hattie we left to follow by train but they arrived before us. After tea they rambled on the railway embankment, gathered a quantity of wild strawberries, & so much honeysuckle & fern etc as they could carry. Our Saturday afternoons are a great delight to them.

### July 20th

When I read over what I have written I sometimes feel as if that part of it which relates to myself were egotistical, & yet I do not know how to make a diary of the occupations & events I wish to recall otherwise. Pronouns of the first person, nominative, possessive or objective, are continually needed, and those for whom they stand are so intimately connected with my daily thoughts, hopes & desires that I have little to tell in my small world that does not require I, me or mine to express it.[20]

To continue, 10 days ago I passed another milestone in life's journey, with step as light & heart as thankful as at any former stage.[21] With more reason than ever for the latter. Letters from Will, Florence & John, & a present of a pretty pair of terracotta statuettes from Lottie & Hattie were the proofs which I value of my children's recollection of the day. Father, Grandma Bousfield & Aunt Jenny also did not forget it & gave me a birthday present. Papa asked me what his was to be & I told him 'a bit more field', for the piece he has reserved after re-selling Mr Pearse all but the strip containing the trees is so narrow at the far end that to be able to walk through it, as I am very desirous to be able to do, he must get sufficient for a pathway, the which would be a very pretty private walk under the trees I value so much.

As the time for Papa's annual visit to the Royal Show drew near, I felt disposed to accompany him to York, finding he would have a little time to spare before real business would keep him there, & that we might have parts of several days together at Scarboro' which is only an hour distant. A chat at the tea table on Thursday evening ended in its being decided that we should leave for York by early train next morning which we did arriving there before 11 o'clock. After taking some refreshment at the Station Papa left me, to go to the Show Yard, with the understanding that I should go on by next train to Scarboro' & telegraph to him where to find me there.

The hour which I had to wait I spent in going into the Minster, & into a Roman

---

[19] Grandmama Frances Bousfield was then 85 years of age. She died in the following year.

[20] Does CEB's soul-searching reflect her concerns over the recent disputes related to the mission?

[21] CEB seems relieved to return to less contentious events: she had celebrated her 55th birthday on 10 July 1883.

Catholic Chapel close under its walls. The bare lofty building is almost devoid of anything like ornament except where through a screen I could see in the first the high table surmounted by crucifix & candlesticks etc. The latter (the Catholic Chapel) scarcely less in accordance with my ideas of worship.

*Tuesday July 31ˢᵗ*
Papa remained in York until the following Friday, reaching Sandy to find the Bedford train had gone. A telegram from the Station Master directed that he should be met on the road as he was walking homeward. Baylis accordingly drove on in pouring rain, fortunately with the Brougham, & met him before he had got as far as Willington.

In a letter which I had from Papa whilst he was at York he said 'You will be delighted to hear from Will that he has won his case'. This was the first intimation of the fact that I had, & even then was not sure what 'case' was meant, as in Will's letter to me on my birthday he had told me he was very busy having 'three cases on at once to-day, including Hotchkiss v Gardner Gun Co, which is however postponed again for a few days'. As I was driving into the town the morning I got Papa's letter, I called at the news-room to look at 'The Times' & was indeed delighted to find it was the latter that had been decided in his favor for his former clients, & against his old opponents Webster & Aston QCs, who were together again on the other side with a junior also. Again he has had to fight them, & this time (as he told me after the Nordenfelt trial he should have an opportunity of doing) has 'won back his laurels' entirely single-handed. The prize was ...[22] Whilst proud of his courage in undertaking such an important case, & against such powerful antagonists alone, I thankfully attribute his success to the Giver of all Wisdom through whom & in whom is all which has helped him in this & every time of need, & given him discretion & favor in the sight of those even in whose cause he was before defeated. John tells me that Aston went out of Court whilst judgment was being given, & that Will won his verdict by his cross examinations, & his speech, without calling a single witness on his own side, although Dr Hopkinson & others were ready.

John came home on Saturday week, & returned on Monday morning after going to the Works with the Specification of a new Patent which Papa is taking out with Mr JH (one of many).

*Thursday, August 9ᵗʰ*
The first thing after breakfast on Monday morning was a drive with John into the town to get some shrubs for the Corn Exchange Platform, at Mr Greenhill's request, in readiness for the Concert at night. Then we drove to & round the field in which the Temperance Fete was held. The morning was fine, & the swings, round-a-bouts & stalls which were erected gave the place a fair like appearance & added to the attraction of the programme of Sports & Speeches to which during the day 3000 people must have flocked. Mr Hull of Northampton was the first Speaker advertized to give an address at noon, at which time the number of hearers was small; after waiting half an hour they increased, but it was a pity he had to speak so early.

I left the field during the address to go to the Station to meet Mr Mark Knowles

[22] A space was left in the text but unfilled.

& bring him here for early dinner, after which we all accompanied him to hear his Speech at 4 o'clock, when much larger numbers were present. Walking round the field afterwards we met Dr Goldsmith & I & Hattie took tea with him in a Booth, leaving Mr Knowles to return with Papa, John & Lottie. At 6 o'clock Mr Rae of Reading arrived, just as a heavy shower of rain came on. I had a few minutes' talk with him, listened to part of his address & then came home to see Mr K before his departure, & accompany the others to the Exchange for the Concert. Lottie's name was on the Programme for a Song, but she had yielded very unwillingly to Mr Greenhill's request to sing, & decided not to do so until just before starting, when she was persuaded to alter her mind. She sang 'Home sweet Home' very sweetly, & so carried out her part of the day's performance.

### Friday August 17th

On Saturday Papa drove Lottie & myself to Pavenham. Whilst they were sketching the Church I obtained permission from Mrs Tucker's gardener to go through the grounds of the House; the churchyard immediately adjoins these which with the Park beyond are very pretty.[23] Lottie was delighted with the old trees. We had tea at the Coffee-room in the village.

### Wednesday Sept' 12th

Will's time was much occupied the first week of his visit with writing some kind of treatise on the New Patent Law which he intends to publish. Since then however he has been spending most of his time in Photography, & has taken some very successful pictures of Papa & myself amongst others. The photographic apparatus which he has got is expressly made for travelling & taking landscapes & he has been so using it in the Isle of Wight where, in company with Mr Malden the Curate of Cricklewood (& part of the time with Mr Thunder),[24] he has had a walking excursion. Taking with them a tent which they removed from place to place with a donkey & cart, they camped out by day & night for a week; starting from St Lawrence (where Mr M's Father is Vicar) & going to Freshwater, Carisbrook, & other places of interest of which they took Photos; finishing by a Picnic in the Landslip, in which Florence & all at Clarendon Lodge met Mr Malden's family. Will brought a very good picture of the party, as well as others he took, with him. His last attempts at Photography were as a boy some fifteen years ago; some small pictures done then I have still.

How marvellously the years have flown! Twenty years ago this very month this house was finished, & we took possession of it as our own, calling it 'Alpha Villa', because [it was] the very first house built in a neighbourhood newly divided into building sites, most of which are now covered by streets of houses, inhabited probably by more than 800 people.

Twenty five years ago this very month too, Papa accepted the Managership of the Britannia Works, then just built. A quarter of a century of service not altogether congenial to his natural disposition, but I believe the way in which God saw he

[23] Mrs Tucker was the widow of Joseph Tucker of Pavenham JP and High Sheriff of Bedfordshire in 1861. He died in 1877.

[24] Mr and Mrs Thunder were friends and next door neighbours of Will and Flo in Cricklewood – he was a solicitor, and they had a son almost the same age as Will and Flo's eldest son George.

could serve his generation & himself best, & therefore the right way, & certainly a good one for 'the Britannia' for which his inventive brain has been faithfully at Work (whilst others have reaped the honors) from that day until now. A pile of Blue Books[25] is the only record, & 'Royalties'[26] the proof, or only reward, but with bare justice he is content.

*Oct^r 2^nd*

During the last two months I have had much to make me thankful & to encourage us in our Temperance work. I am thankful to say us, for Lottie has been more than ever before willing & able to co-operate in whatever has fallen to us. In addition to her weekly visits to the women at the 'Steam Laundry' she has begun a Sunday afternoon Bible class for girls in our BR Room, which has increased in three Sundays from two to ten. She has also prevailed upon the most drunken woman in our neighbourhood to sign the pledge &, by occasional visits & lending her books, has continued to show interest in her. For more than a month she has kept from the degrading drink & has regularly attended my Mothers-meeting & Sunday evening service. The most notorious & noisy drunken man near us, after keeping a Pledge-card which I gave him un-signed three weeks previously, came to show me his signature on it the day after Bank Holiday, & he too up to the present has remained true, & regularly attends our little Chapel. Both are such known characters that their reformation has been as public as their former sin.

Some time ago I felt almost a want of satisfactory occupation & am glad that some of a pleasurable kind has been thrown in to fill up time that I had to spare without neglecting home duties. A question which I put to Mrs Windsor (the woman who attends to Thurlow St BR Room) as to whether there was a Mothers' meeting in the neighbourhood led her to mention the subject to me a fortnight later & tell me she believed there were several women who would come if I would begin one. I promised to be at Thurlow St the following Friday at 3 o'clock to meet any who chose to come, & found about a dozen women assembled; the following week the number increased & last Friday 23 had given their names. So with the permission of the gentlemen who manage the Rooms a BR Mothers-meeting is begun, & judging from the smallness of their weekly payments towards the clothing Club in connection with it (mostly only 2d), they are of a class more needing benefit in this way than the Mothers of my own meeting here. A kind hearted needle-woman Mrs Westrop came to the first meeting & offered her services to cut out & help in this way & this she continues to do, last week even fitting a dress bodice on one of the women.

I left that meeting in Lottie's charge as soon as she came to it, bringing Mrs Sampson, with whom I left, to call with her on several ladies whom we are desirous to influence & interest in forming a Bedford Branch of the 'The British Women's Temperance Association'.[27] I have been corresponding with Mrs Bradley the Secre-

---

[25] A blue book is a report or other paper printed by Parliament: CEB is using it here to refer specifically to patent specifications.

[26] Some employers of inventors did not pay royalties to their employees. CEB makes it sound as if Edward was being harshly treated, but this does not appear to be the case.

[27] This is the first mention of the British Women's Temperance Association (BWTA) which was to become an important part of CEB's life.

tary as to the desirability of having one here as a help to Blue Ribbon & Temperance Work & find that country Branches are doing a great deal in that way in other places. Mrs Aukland, who gave one of the afternoon addresses to women at the time of our Mission, volunteered to come down & help, & as Mrs Sampson has cordially entered into the idea, we are going to see whether we can get a sufficient number of Ladies to co-operate before inviting Mrs Aukland down.

### Friday Nov' 23rd

The effort made to form a Branch of the BWTA has been successful beyond my most sanguine hopes. Many of the choicest women in connection with the different religious bodies in the Town, both Church & Dissenting, have entered so heartily into it that it is an accomplished fact, & not only organized but to some extent in working order, promising to draw together & give both pleasure & profit not only to the Ladies who have formed the General and Executive Committees, but to their poorer sisters. To benefit working-women by associating them more with those whom they would not otherwise meet, & showing them sympathy, is one great object we have in view, & many of these have given in their names as Members of the Association which now numbers altogether ...[28]

On Oct' 2nd in response to my invitation Mrs Aukland came down & addressed a meeting of between thirty & forty ladies in Thurlow St BR Room, from these a Committee was formed, on Oct' 8th this met for the first time; then a tea-meeting was arranged for an opportunity of explaining the objects of the Association to as many women (abstainers or otherwise) as we could get together. Mrs Alexander of Pavenham, who has consented to become our President, came to the tea, presided at one of the tables, & afterwards at a meeting that completely filled Thurlow St BR Room, the men turning out that night for our accommodation. Mrs Alexander, a friend she brought with her (Miss Hamilton) & Mrs Sampson addressed those present, most appropriately, & I came in at the end with a few words of explanation & exhortation. At the close 14 women signed the pledge & more than double that number joined as members of the BWTA. Others have since joined. At the last Committee meeting Mrs Lewis & myself were deputed to map the town out into districts for re-visitation which we are now doing. A Women's Prayer-meeting is arranged for the first Monday afternoon in each month, in Thurlow St BR Room. A cheap cookery class is proposed; we want in things temporal as well as spiritual to make the women feel the benefit of the Association. The new Mothers' Meeting has weekly increased & now numbers about 50. Last Friday 41 were present. One or two ladies have shown an interest in it. Mrs Goldsmith has consented to take it when I have been absent from home and is now willing to continue regularly to do so once a month.

The decision to have a Richmond Student every alternate Sunday has been productive of results that have been a matter for much satisfaction and thankfulness.[29] The very first Sabbath (the one before we left home for Barmouth) Mr Roe, a very earnest young man & a wearer of a Blue Ribbon, was sent. After the night

---

[28]  A space is left for the figure, but unfilled. CEB's comments about her 'poorer sisters' may sound patronising, but reflect the nature of the class structure of the period and are kindly in intention.
[29]  The Wesleyan Theological College at Richmond on Thames, founded in 1843, was a training college for Methodist ministers and missionaries.

service more than a dozen men & women came out into the vestry as seekers of salvation; amongst them Abrahams, the man who a few weeks before had turned from drunkenness & signed the pledge, & this is not the only instance of sobriety leading to higher aspirations. The poor woman whom Lottie induced to take the first step was also deeply moved last Sunday night, after the same Preacher had been speaking, & at his invitation to all who felt their need of Christ as a Saviour to hold up their hand, held up hers in the Chapel, & came out into the vestry where I had the satisfaction of pointing her to Him who is ready as ever to say 'Daughter thy sins are forgiven thee' to this penitent one. These are all great causes for thankfulness, but we have also failures to deplore. Some of the men who were the most earnest in their request for the BR Room here, & most interested in it, have gone back to drink & in ceasing to abstain themselves have led others away from both the Room & sobriety. Lottie is very anxious about several of the men in our neighbourhood & has surprised me lately by going to their houses when they have been at home at night & endeavouring to influence them to join us & give up drink. Truly thankful am I to see the readiness with which she enters into any work that she can undertake to help forward that to which we have been called amidst our neighbours.[30] Without self-conceit I trust, I cannot but believe that God placed us amongst them to be an influence for their good & His glory, & ours only should be that in any measure He has made use of us to these ends.


## 1884


*Monday Feb^y 4^th 1884*

When I arrived in Bedford a week ago last Thursday, I found Papa at the Station. Thankful indeed was I to reach home again after my long absence.[31] After tea together in the Dining-room (which I was rather surprised to find him occupying) he left me to go to his class-meeting, & it was not until I began to look into the different rooms that I found out how much he had been doing both useful & ornamental whilst alone in our home, to make a pleasant surprise for me.

Papa likes his own way & time for doing, & had carried out far beyond my requests some things for which I had been for some time asking. I was delighted to see the kitchen range, which was as old as the house, re-placed by a beautiful new one, the white marble chimney piece in the Breakfast-room cased over with a carved oak one which he had himself designed, to match the old carved oak of the book-case & employed a clever old carver who lives near, to carry out. The book-case was made from part of the screen of Northill church which was removed from it when it was restored by the man who built our house for us, from whom we had it, & is probably some hundreds of years old. With the imitation of it Papa has contrived

---

[30] CEB expresses some surprise but no concern that Lottie, a young woman of 22, should venture alone and at night into a house occupied by several men who are alcoholics. This comment, like the subject of the last but one footnote, reflects the different attitudes of the time: in this case, for the better.

[31] CEB had been away from Bedford for some six weeks, first visiting Ted and Clara, then to Ventnor where the family spent Christmas and the New Year, then on to London where she and Hattie stayed with the Kellys.

most tastefully to place my monogram on one side of the fire place & his own on the other, as he did on the top & bottom of the stair case of our house with the date 1863 when we built it. There will be much of interest for our children in the old home (which will last in all probability long after their Parents have passed away).[32] But I have gone off into moralizing instead of finishing the list of my Husband's doings which I can however scarcely enumerate. The gas laid on for fires in both our girls' bed-rooms, & the Drawing-room, amongst them.

I seem to have got home again just at the time needed, finding notices of meetings, Committees etc, for the following week awaiting me. A letter from old Nurse East (whom I visited in the Workhouse where she has been more than three months just before leaving) reached me Friday morning entreating I would carry out my promise to try to get her out of it. After the Mothers' meeting in Thurlow St on Friday, Mrs Sampson told me of an old lady, bedridden, who wanted a nurse, & after a good deal of running about I managed to get her away, & saw her on Monday morning with Mrs Emmoney in one of the Alms Houses, & as comfortably placed as she will ever be, but looking scarcely more contented than when in the Union.[33] She wants the real & only sweetener of life for the old & poor, love of Christ in her heart, & hope beyond this world, but she has been my nurse[34] with each of my three girls, & I could not bear to let her remain where she was so miserable at her loss of liberty that I really believed she would die if she did not regain it.

### Feb^y 13^th

The last entry I made was incomplete for want of time to conclude the recital of events after Friday. Since that day others more important have made those much less so than they then seemed. The BWTA tea & after meeting in Grey Friars Walk BR Room[35] on Wednesday followed a Band of Hope[36] Soirée on Tuesday. At the last Hattie had been invited & consented to help, by giving a piece on the Piano, & (although Edward came in from Bristol just before we had to go to accompany Papa to London next morning & we only intended to stay a short time) got so far interested in the Dissolving views etc that concluded the entertainment that we were induced to stay to the end & so walked home late.[37] Wednesday morning at her Drawing, the Ambulance Class in the afternoon & accompanying me to the tea in the evening made a long laborious day at the end of which Hattie looked tired & pale (the latter I had noticed for some days previously). Whether from over exertion, & walking home in the night-air combined or from some other unknown cause, on Thursday morning at breakfast she complained of pain which she attributed to

[32] Alpha Villa lasts still, indeed, but has been converted into flats.
[33] i.e. the workhouse. The name Union refers to the scheme initiated by the Poor Law Amendment Act of 1834, by which parish workhouses were amalgamated to form the feared and hated Union Workhouses. The Bedford Union Workhouse is now part of Bedford North Wing Hospital.
[34] Nurse East may have suckled the girls as babies as well as performing the functions of a nanny as they grew older.
[35] The Blue Ribbon Room was at no. 20 Grey Friars Walk, within a short distance of the Thurlow Street Blue Ribbon Room.
[36] The Band of Hope was a non-denominational organisation dedicated to spread the message of temperance among children of both sexes between six and twelve years of age.
[37] Dissolving views were a popular form of entertainment, a feature of a magic lantern show. They used two slides which ingeniously 'dissolved' from one to the other. Temperance themes were frequently featured.

disordered liver & thought the walk to her Drawing Class would remove. Instead of this she only walked to the top of the railway bridge when the pain so increased that she was obliged to return & came in looking ill & distressed.

*March 11ᵗʰ*
Will's book is out & he has this evening sent Papa a copy of it. Florence's cousin Mr Sweet is the Publisher. Will does not expect to reap much profit from it beyond becoming more known.[38] His great Case is just coming on in the Court of Appeal. The Solicitor-General is with him this time, for Gardner. He expected it would have begun on Monday, but the Belt Libel case has been dragging its weary length through this Court as it has done in the others before, & unless it has finished to-day is not yet over.

*Monday March 17ᵗʰ*
John's head is rather full of a new attraction at Cricklewood, & he thinks himself tolerably sure of a young lady's favorable regard. I tell him not to make too sure. He seems quite sure that I should approve. He left this morning in his usual good spirits, perhaps slightly more elated than usual that this evening he is to be one of a musical gathering at the house of the Parents of the aforesaid damsel. May he be 'prevented' in this & all his doings by Him who sees the end from the beginning.

*Wednesday April 16ᵗʰ*
To take in order the occurrences of the last fortnight. The BWTA occupied for a week much of my time & thoughts, from one day previous to the 1st when I met Mrs Sampson in the street when we were driving & heard from her for the first time of a Committee meeting to be held the following Saturday at Mrs Goldsmith's of which she said I should receive notice. I expressed my surprise that such should be called without my knowing anything of it, & begged she would ride a short distance with us in the Chaise & explain, which she did, & I then found that she had requested the Secretary to call it with the object of carrying out an idea on which she had written to me three months ago & I hoped at my earnest entreaty abandoned, that being to reduce our minimum subscription of 1/- per annum for Members of our Association, to 2d annually because we had money in hand for which she thought we had no present use!

The next day I made a point of calling on a few of the Committee on whose judgment I could rely, & in no instance found any who did not think that to propose & carry such a resolution would not be most suicidal policy for the Association which is working on lines that seem to be entirely successful. The working-women, when I put the question to them publicly after the tea in Grey Friars Walk Room as to whether they would prefer to give or not give their penny per month, seemed almost ready to shout their readiness & willingness to help others, as well as themselves,

---

[38] Will's book was entitled *The Patents Designs and Trade Marks Act 1883: the rules and forms thereunder with notes and introductory chapters*. Sweet's was an important law publisher during the 19th and 20th centuries. The book was a substantial one of 250 pages, but sold for 2s 6d, a fraction of the cost of major law textbooks at the time, so it is not surprising that Will did not anticipate much profit of a financial nature from it.

as I told them to such a small extent. I did this to satisfy Mrs S but it had not the desired effect.

I went to the meeting at Mrs G's which was attended by all the ladies on whom I called & several others. Mrs S was not present until the time we had to spare was half gone, but before she came in I explained all I knew incidentally as to its being called, begged the members of the Committee would express their views as to the course suggested, but declined to put any resolution to a meeting altogether informally called, as both Papa & Captn Glubb whose opinions I asked advised. The discussion had nearly ended when Mrs S entered (almost all the ladies being entirely opposed to her views) but was revived by her, only ending however in our all feeling we had been got together at inconvenience to many on Saturday morning, for no purpose.

I took the opportunity however of saying that Miss Beville would allow herself to be proposed as Treasurer at the next ordinary Committee meeting, & also of distributing the tickets for the tea in St Cuthbert's School-room on April 3rd. As I had undertaken the tea entirely, promised to hand over gains, or bear losses in connection with it, I invited the Visitors to ask every member to bring another woman with her at the same charge of 4d as a recruiting ground; those who could afford 6d to give it. To both these arrangements Mrs S took exception, but 'nothing succeeds like success' & as we had over 200 women present at the tea, gained 25 new members for the BWTA, took nearly half that number of new pledges, & gained also 10/6 profit on the tea, no-one has found the fault that a few seemed ready to do. The last tea got by a committee being at a loss of over £1, there was some talk of dis-continuing the quarterly teas, which would have been almost as bad as giving up the subscriptions.

The weather has been as cold the last week as it was before warm, so that we had no inclination for driving against the bitter easterly winds & spent the morning in the house. After dinner with John & Hattie, I walked to the Cemetery & sat down for a quarter of an hour under the shelter of the Chapel close to my dear Babe's grave, whilst they wandered amongst the tombstones. Returning we struck off at the first opening out of the Cemetery Road into the new Park which is being made immediately adjoining, & were astonished to find roads or drives in all directions extending to the Kimbolton Rd from which we turned to the Goldington Rd, thence through one of the newly laid out streets down to the river. All this was new ground to John. After resting again on one of the seats of the Embankment, we returned from our long & pleasant walk to a quiet tea & evening together.[39]

The Wesleyan Chapel St Paul's is being renovated & the services in the school-room are not very attractive especially to the young folk. On Sunday morning therefore I proposed we should go together to the new Iron Church which good Mr Kempson has got built as a Chapel of Ease to St Cuthbert's, & not far from it, but in the new town which is springing up close to the Embankment with no other place of worship nearer.[40] We were pleased at the service which was short & simple, like

[39] CEB refers earlier to the expansion of Bedford south of the river in the later Victorian period: a similar development was taking place in the north of the town.

[40] The 'new iron church' was of the type known as a tin tabernacle, quite common in towns all over the country at this time of rapid urban population growth. It was situated first in Castle Road, which CEB

St Cuthbert's, & without any of the ritualistic tendencies which are reported in most of the other churches of Bedford.

John went back to his work Tuesday morning & the same day we received a letter not altogether a surprise after what he communicated to Papa & myself, with his usual frankness, the first evening he came home. He had made proposals in writing to the young lady who has for some time been a special object of attraction & attention at the choral meetings which he has attended & of whom I have before made mention. She like a dutiful daughter has shown the letter to the Parents, but with such marks of favor towards the writer as has led to an invitation from the Papa to call at their house to see him. This John did at once, & he related to us a good part of a conversation, business-like but pleasant, with relation to 'Miss Mattie', which concluded so far satisfactorily to John, that he was quite willing to comply with the request that matters should remain in abeyance until Mr & Mrs Southwell's return from a long journey & stay from home which they were just about to make, during which time he would not in any case be able to visit at their house.

This has been followed by an equally business-like letter to Papa in which our views, John's prospects, etc etc are enquired into, but with these proper & wise questions, a vein of anything but disapprobation runs through the whole. Papa's reply will be an expression of his desire to do for his youngest Son as he has done for his elder sons, add his help to their own efforts to provide themselves a home in accordance with what we consider right for beginners in their position; & of satisfaction that John has evidently formed the conviction that he is asking for the Daughter of a family whose Christian principles & predilections are in accordance with the ones to which he seeks to introduce her. I trust she is herself a true Christian, as well as a Sunday-school teacher & 'Blue Ribboner' as John tells us is the case. My prayer is that he may be helped in this, or prevented in it, as may be best for his highest good, as well as his temporal happiness.

*Friday May 2nd*

Papa was in London on Patent business last week & saw John at the Office. He found opportunity to communicate the intelligence that he had received another communication from Mr Southwell containing an invitation to his house on the previous Saturday, & that he had availed himself of it.[41] This is an unexpected concession, since Papa's letter was received, & of course very gratifying to John, but he is so absorbed in business, or love, or both that we have fewer letters than ever, & I hear of more frequently than from him. He visited Ted & Clara at the OKR.[42]

Hattie has given me much more pleasure of late. She has been making great effort to conquer her natural irritability & more than once within the last few weeks has come down from her room to me, after she had retired for the night, to express regret for, or acknowledge some word or act during the day for which conscience reproved her in the quiet of her chamber. We have been together two or three evenings to some special services for the young people of families above the working classes,

---

refers to as 'the new town', and opened on 18 March 1884. It was later moved to the junction of Denmark Street and Goldington Road and eventually consecrated as Christ Church, Goldington in 1958.

[41] Mr Southwell was a fruit importer with a factory and wharf near the docks. He lived at Gurrey Lodge, Child's Hill, Kilburn.

[42] The Old Kent Road, no. 363. Ted and Clara had moved in two months earlier, in March.

which have been held in the Bedford Rooms by a Mr Arrowsmith who has been a very successful worker amongst such, & the direct appeals he made not only to the thoughtless but to those who professed to be Christians have I believe been influence for good both to her & many others of both classes. Colonel Elliott furnished me with a number of cards of notices of the meetings (which have extended over more than a fortnight) for distribution on this side of the town, & I imagine he has been the chief mover in having them here. I have heard that especially amongst the boys in the Schools they have been greatly blessed.

### Wednesday May 7th

Last Monday our BWTA monthly prayer-meeting was held at Thurlow St BR Room, conducted by Mrs Goldsmith. A good number of working women were present; for myself I found it good to be there. After the meeting the usual committee meeting was held. At the last it was proposed by Mrs Sampson that I should be sent as a Delegate to the Annual Meetings of the BWTA in Exeter Hall[43] from the Bedford Branch, in accordance with an invitation given. I have undertaken to go for the Public & Council meetings on the 15th & 16th instant & have received an invitation from the President of the Association Mrs Lucas (the Sister of John Bright[44]) to a reception of Delegates at her house from 6-30 to 8-30 on the evening of the 14th.

### Wednesday May 21st

The past fortnight has been a time of much enjoyment. I left home by 8 a m o'clock train on the 8th in bright sunshine, & after a pleasant journey reached Cricklewood Station to find Lottie ready to accompany me, & with her on the platform Will, Florence & John. I had only time to exchange a few words with the first, & hand out a little hamper of cauliflowers & eggs. The latter I was surprised to find an hour later than his regular time of leaving in the morning, but this was explained by Lottie's laughingly giving me the intelligence 'He's been waiting to come with you on purpose to show you a photograph' which was presently produced in a leather pocket case. It was that of a very pleasant girl's face, & such an one as at once favorably impressed me.

John left us at Farringdon St, & we went on to Ludgate Hill where we left our luggage & walked on at once to Exeter Hall, arriving in time to secure good seats for the Annual meeting of the London City Mission. All the speeches were excellent & stirring. At its close we went to Will's Chambers where John again met us & accompanied Lottie & myself to some Dining-rooms where we had dinner together.

[The next day CEB arranged to meet Lottie in the Ladies' Waiting Room at South Kensington station, in order to go on to visit the International Health Exhibition at South Kensington Museum.[45] Lottie did not arrive, so CEB went on to the Exhibi-

---

43 Exeter Hall, opened in 1831, was well known as the venue for evangelical meetings. It could hold 3,000 people, and was sited in London where the Strand Palace Hotel now stands.
44 John Bright (1811–1889) was one of the leading radical Liberal politicians from his leadership with Cobden of the Anti-Corn Law legislation of the 1840s to his support for a wide democratic franchise in the 1867 and 1884 elections and his attempts to restrain the powers of the Lords. He held the office of Chancellor of the Duchy of Lancaster in Gladstone's second ministry until he resigned in 1882.
45 The South Kensington Museum was renamed the Victoria and Albert Museum in 1899.

tion without her, having a vegetarian lunch which she did not enjoy while waiting for her.]

Returning several times to the entrance Hall to look for Lottie, I at length sat down on one of the many comfortable seats ranged round it to rest & even nap for a few moments whilst alone in the crowd of comers & goers. I had almost forgotten where I was when Lottie at length found me, & explained that she had reached the Station by mistake much earlier than the time I named, & leaving word with the woman in the waiting-room when she would meet me had left. As I did not get her message we had both been several times very near each other without knowing it, but had managed to enjoy ourselves, although very glad to meet. When we did so Lottie said 'Who do you think I have met & been with? John's lady-love!' & very shortly after as we were walking through the 'restored Old London Street' (which is one of the sights of the Exhibition) we met 'Miss Mattie' in company with her sister & several friends. As Lottie had told her I was somewhere in the Exhibition she knew who I was, but in a crowd & under the circumstances, I thought it best not to be introduced & we passed each other with only a mutual look of recognition, but the impression I received from the glance I had of her face was very favorable.[46]

Arriving at Cricklewood Tuesday night, I was glad to find Will & Florence with their little ones all well. Will seems to have more to do than he can get done at Chambers, & was busy with books & papers & looking over a Brief. Wednesday morning (the 14th) I spent quietly with Florence; after luncheon, with Lottie, we took the Omnibus to Sutherland [Avenue], found Mrs Kelly just about to go out in the Brougham, & as we had intended going on to Westbourne Grove, she very kindly offered to drive thither with us. Some time was spent at Whiteleys[47] shopping, & then I left them & made my way alone to Mrs Lucas's house in Charlotte St, Bedford Square.

This was the day for her Reception. Arriving about 6-30 I found many Ladies connected with the BWTA there before me, all of them except those residing in Town Delegates from the various Branches of our Association. Mrs Lucas welcomed many of us in the Hall. She is a tall fine dignified elderly lady, of much the same type of feature as the portraits I have seen of John Bright, & the same kind expression on her face. Tea was spread on a large table in the Dining-room from which we were served as we sat around the room. Arrivals continued until many of us had finished & thence adjourned to the Drawing-room up-stairs, which I was surprised to find occupied already by many ladies. Mrs Aukland (who came down to Bedford to begin our Branch last Oct[r]) introduced to some [sic] but all were strangers to me except Mrs Stewart the Treasurer & one or two that I had accidentally seen when I called at the Memorial Hall[48] when the Committee happened to be sitting.

---

[46] An interesting insight into the formality of social behaviour at the time. Lottie had already met Mattie, and CEB and Mattie both recognised each other, but CEB would not speak to her until she had been properly introduced.

[47] Whiteleys was the first department store in Britain. It opened on Queensway, Bayswater in 1863. By the 1880s it had 17 departments and by 1906 it employed six thousand people there and in its farms and factories.

[48] The Congregational Memorial Hall, in Fleet Lane, Farringdon Street, on the site of the old Fleet Prison. Opened in 1875, it became the administrative centre of Congregationalism, and would have resonated well with CEB who was a member of that church until her marriage.

I forgot to say that whilst we were holding our meeting in the Lower Hall Thursday night, the 'Salvation Army' were having a grand demonstration over our heads in the larger one. I slipped out of our meeting before the end to see for myself of what I had before only heard. 'General Booth' was in the Chair with his wife at his side looking very sweet & simple in her close bonnet, & behind them entirely filling the Orchestra were some hundreds of their soldiers male & female. Many of both these were allowed to relate their experience from the depths of drunkenness & crime until they were found by & joined 'the Army'. When their story seemed likely to be too long 'General' cut it short, by telling them to 'get saved' & then starting a song of thanksgiving which was taken up with voice, drums, tambourines, fiddles, etc in a triumphant shout, amidst waving of flags & arms.

At the close of our meeting below I accompanied Mrs K, Florence & Lottie & returned to the Upper Hall where we heard Mrs Booth give her address on 'Drink'. I like her much better than her Husband; she is doubtless a great power for good amidst the masses amongst whom the S Army is working, & the testimony that the reclaimed (if not renewed) gave must be believed to a large extent, but I cannot sympathize to the extent that many do in the means they use, not to the modes of speech & action which, if calculated to attract, have also the tendency to bring sacred things into disrepute. That there is a large amount of faith in General Booth & his work however was proved by the fact that before the conclusion of the meeting he read out the names of contributors to the amount nearly £10000, which it was intended we should understand was all promised by papers handed up to him in the meeting, but on telling Dr Goldsmith of hearing his promise of £5 read out, & supposing he was present, I found his was in response to an appeal by circular some days previously & that he was not there. Was this right? Time will show whether the immense amount of money entrusted to one individual for a public good is wisely placed.

*Tuesday June 10th* [Alpha Villa]
Our happy gathering was well nigh clouded over almost as soon as we were together. Whilst on the lawn, & about the gate to meet Papa who was coming towards us across the road from a short walk in the opposite field with Ted & Clara, we saw our horse galloping in the cart without a driver & the reins broken & dragging, towards us & the town. In an instant John rushed after it as it passed, & succeeded in overtaking & stopping it before it got very far, whilst I stood in an agony of fear lest the animal should drag him under the wheels when he overtook him. But a few moments before, Hills, who had been to the Station for the luggage which could not be put on the Brougham, deposited it safely, & left to put Charley in the stable. Finding he did not come to take him after John had secured him, I ran to the Farm & found Hills in the road seated on a stone near the gate, surrounded by a crowd & bleeding from his head. Shouting for Ted, attention was at once turned to him. Ted got him into the house, & after the first examination hoped he was not seriously injured. After going to the Infirmary for strapping etc he returned to dress a wound which he found under the poor fellow's left arm, & then discovered that it was much larger & deeper than he at first thought, & that he must take him to the Infirmary to get it properly attended to; so putting the horse into the chaise he was lifted in with Will & Ted on each side of him & John leading the horse. Fortunately

it was found that nothing was broken or injured vitally but so seriously that he will probably be there for weeks.

Monday morning was just the morning for carrying out my pet idea of a family group being taken & accordingly the Photographer appeared early as arranged & before we had scarcely finished breakfast. The group of 11 consisting of 5 children, their parents & 2 grandchildren were placed in due position on the front lawn, in the same corner in which I was taken with Hattie on my knees & John & Lottie at my feet more than 16 years ago. When the Photographer had taken us twice, Will, who had brought his photographic apparatus with him, got him to remove the slide from his own Camera which he had put into position, & so made his own picture of us also.

After early dinner, tea was packed in a hamper, & John drove Clara, Lottie & myself to Ampthill Park; Papa accompanied Will, Ted, Hattie & Georgie by train, the former taking his Camera for some pictures of the fine old Oaks. We met just as tea was ready & Will photographed us as we sat around, on the sheltered side of a mill, waiting to begin. A happy merry party we were, but like all earthly delights, the pleasure no sooner came than it had passed, & we had only time for tea & to pack up before we had again to disperse, the party by train for the 2 mile walk to the Station to catch it, & we for our drive homeward.

After our arrival John & Will drove to the Midland Station to meet Mr Maulden who had promised to join them in a day's boating on the morrow. After breakfast John & Mr M went to secure a boat, whilst Lottie & Hattie prepared for the picnic on the river bank in which we all intended to join except Papa who had to leave by early train in the morning to attend the B&W of England Show at Maidstone.[49] As some of us had not been on the sea-ward side of the river further than the lock,[50] we prevailed on Will to go that way, but found the course much more uninteresting than the one we were accustomed to take, & much more difficult as to pass the next lock at Cardington Mills we had to have the boat unloaded & pulled over land to the other side as it could not be opened. At the lock at Castle Mills, we fastened our boat &, carrying our luncheon ashore, found the best place for taking it to be the sheltered side of a steep old Roman Mound, thrown up in the midst of the surrounding flat, & so sloping that we could with difficulty retain either our seats or our dishes.[51] This however only added to the general amusement. Returning after about an hour's rest, we went on to Kempston where Will carried out his usual chief picnic diversion of lighting a fire on one side of the river bank whilst we laid the cloth for tea under the trees on the other. Mr Maulden & John had to punt across the stream many times before the fire had finished its duties, whilst they were boiling water & the eggs. Will once more got ready for a Photo of us & our spread on the grass, after which we had tea, then a wander in the woods, & home.

Next morning John left us after early breakfast. Will & Mr M went to the Works. After dinner the former & Papa drove to Sandy to see his new Binder work & the

---

[49] Either the show or the venue is wrong. The Bath and West of England Agricultural Show would not be held in Kent.

[50] This refers to the Bedford lock, on the Embankment just below the Town Bridge.

[51] CEB is a thousand years out: the 'Roman' mound is an eleventh- to twelfth-century motte, i.e. the earthen mound which would have been topped by a wooden structure (the castle), both set within a bailey or courtyard. It is known as Risinghoe Castle or Goldington Castle.

latter with Ted left to return to town. Will remained until Thursday morning when he also departed leaving Flo & the boys until Saturday at noon. After dinner Papa drove Clara & the girls to Warden where they had tea. I remained at home very busy in the Conservatory & garden in poor Hills' absence; he is however progressing very favorably, although weak, having been laid aside one week & probably will be many more before able to resume his work.

I must not close my record of family events for the week without mentioning the fact of John's disappointment which however I am thankful to say has not spoiled his or our pleasure. After a month of suspense Mr S has again invited him to his house on his return home. Very direct questions as to John's probable income in two years' time revealed the fact that his ideas for his daughter are so much beyond what either he or we should think either necessary or right to attempt to meet, that further debate was useless. We would not desire that John should have a wife who wanted to begin where his Parents are content to leave off. 'Miss Mattie's' views seem to coincide with her Father's, & as £.s.d. form so important an element in winning her further affections I can only be thankful that our Son's do not appear to have been so far engaged as make him very unhappy. My prayer was 'May he be prevented or helped, as best for him', the former part of my petition has been answered & the latter will be in the future if he 'Seeks first etc'.[52]

### June 13th (Friday)

After alternate decisions, first to go & then to stay for months past, Hattie is at length gone for her long talked of entrance at Caldron's School of Art [sic].[53] She left us this afternoon for Mrs Kelly's, where she will remain to do a little work for a Bazaar which is to be held at her house, & visit the Royal Academy etc several times before she settles to the serious business of continuing her study of Painting. Her Master here has given her so much encouragement to prosecute it that I believe we are doing right in sparing her for at least a year from home which, now that the time of departing has really come, she does not like the thought of leaving. She has taken with her a painting on which she has been engaged for some time (for which I had to sit as her model of a stern Mama); she has an introduction from Mrs Anthony to her Brother, the celebrated Caldecott, to whom she intends to show it for his criticism be it adverse or otherwise. A letter from John this morning begs that I will let her go direct to him; she cannot do this but is very anxious to take up her abode with John as soon as possible & I shall be very glad for them to be together.

I was obliged to leave directly after dinner for Thurlow St M Meeting & to say good bye to Hattie then; since the meeting I have had tea & a very pleasant hour with Mrs Sampson, whom I had not seen since the birth of her baby, before I went to London. Since leaving her I have been to the Station, & arranged with the Station-Master for a special train to take the members of the BWTA to Oakley next Thursday week, as arranged at our last committee-meeting. Mrs Alexander has

---

[52] 'Seek ye first the kingdom of God and his righteousness; and all these things shall be added unto you.' (St Matthew vi 33)

[53] Philip Hermonegese Calderon RA (1833–1898) is described as looking 'like a Spanish hidalgo and ... nicknamed the fiend'. Hattie's actual art teacher, a Mr Ridley, 'may have been Matthew Ridley, one of a group of artists who powerfully influenced Van Gogh', as John Hamilton expresses it in *Glad for God* (p. 155).

kindly offered to receive us at The Bury for the women to have the afternoon in the Park, & to see to the providing of the tea for us. Mrs Donkin announced at the same meeting that the Church of ET Society intended to begin a Women's Union in the town which will I hope be useful in finding fresh ground on which to work & will not I think much interfere with our Association.[54]

*July 31st*

On Saturday John came down early in the afternoon. I met him at the Station with Aunt Jenny & Bessie, when he drove us to Warden where we were to meet Papa & Lottie who started before us with the tricycle expecting we should overtake them. As we did not do so John drove back, whilst I took Aunty & Bessie into the woods. On our return to the Inn we found they had arrived, but the tricycle had hindered instead of helped their journey, the rubber band[55] having come off one wheel almost directly after starting so that Papa was glad to send it back by a man, & then walking on to Cardington they were just in time for the train to Southill. Tea in the arbour is one great attraction to Warden, but a nest of wasps having found it a pleasant spot also we were obliged to adjourn to a seat in the garden, there Papa & John complained of too much wind, & rain coming on we sheltered in the arbour where the wasps seemed at rest. I very boldly led the way but paid for my temerity by bringing one away in my dress & getting a sting. As there is no evening train from Southill, two of our party were obliged to walk homeward, so I started with Papa again, in a heavy shower, which ceased before we had got far. When John overtook us driving, I took his place & drove some distance beyond Cardington when Aunt Jenny & Bessie walked, & I returned for Papa & John who had reached the Green. Lottie was too foot-sore to walk again, but we all reached home nearly at the same time not much the worse for our small adventures.[56]

Sunday morning the rain again fell heavily just at time to leave for St Paul's, waterproofs & umbrellas enabled us to brave the weather however & we all went to Chapel in the town. In the afternoon I had the Bible class for the boys, & as there was a good number I sent to ask John, Lottie & Bessie to come & sing to them before they separated, which they did.

Of late I have felt very discouraged in trying to work here. The boys with few exceptions seem so utterly unimpressible [*sic*] & careless, & more, wicked that when they choose to come on a wet Sunday, or when they do not prefer (as very frequently) to wander in the fields, what I can say to them seems like casting seed on the stoniest of ground. Some of the men too who have for months run well as abstainers have returned to their wallowing in the mire of intemperance, deeper than before. Must we give up?

*August 7th*

So many visitors & events as have occupied my time & attention for two months past have to a great extent prevented any record of those circumstances which preceded

---

[54] The Church of England Temperance Society was established in 1872. It included in its ranks both total abstainers and also those who were not teetotallers but believed in the necessity of working against intemperance.

[55] i.e. the rubber tyre. Pneumatic tyres for bicycles were invented by John Dunlop in 1888.

[56] A walk of about ten miles.

that time. Most of these are in connection with our Temperance work, principally the BWTA. Our President Mrs Alexander's invitation to Pavenham was accepted, a special train starting from the Midland Station at 2-30 p m for our accommodation to Oakley Station, where we found as many vehicles as she could possibly send waiting to take the Mothers with babes, or those who could not walk the distance of nearly two miles to the Park. Lottie drove the chaise to Oakley where she met me, & we were also able to give a lift to a few for part of the distance. About 200 women took tickets, & the appearance of so many in their holiday attire at Bedford Station was very gay.

The day was delightfully fine. Mrs Alexander with her Mother & Husband received us on the lawn in front of the house. Seats were placed under the spreading trees, & on these the women rested some time before tea was served, listening to & joining in the singing which Mrs A led with an Harmonium, & also to an address volunteered by a lady who was a stranger to most of us. The women were easily waited on as they sat, by the ladies of the committee, & appeared thoroughly to enjoy their meal amidst such delightful surroundings. After they had finished Mr Alexander addressed them very appropriately, & they were then given permission to wander as they pleased around the flower-beds & grounds & into the church adjoining them, which is a very ancient one & was open for their inspection.

Whilst they were thus engaged those who had been waiting on them were invited by Mrs Tucker to enter the house where a sumptuous tea was provided of which from forty to fifty ladies must have partaken; this was laid out in the dining-room, which large as it is could not accommodate all at once. Whilst the first part was there, I sat with some other ladies in the Drawing-room, & was glad that my being late gave me an opportunity of a very friendly chat with Mrs Tucker, who entered as fully as her daughter in our entertainment, in which her great age only prevented her being less active. Mr Tucker was for many years the leading Temperance man in the County, but died just before the recent movement in the direction for which he long labored without such results as we have been permitted to see.

The women were helped back to the Station as in coming & returned without accident or weather to mar in any way their enjoyment, the train reaching Bedford about 9 o'clock. I drove home with Lottie, thankful for the share we had had in helping to the enjoyment to which so many were little accustomed.

### Saturday August 9th

A week ago John came home again to remain over Monday Bank Holiday. The same day Papa had to leave again for Shrewsbury where the Binder trials are being held, & where he now is, & probably will remain until Tuesday or Wednesday. Before 12 o'clock a hamper of fruit was picked which I packed & then drove to the Station with John to meet the new maid that was leaving for Cricklewood that day & despatch[ed] her & the hamper thither.

Returning John drove me to Thurlow St where I had promised to meet any women of the BWTA who chose to join the grand Temperance Demonstration which had been organized for that day. We found those who had met there just starting & so joining them in the Midland Road where John left me, I walked to the Cattle Market where some 2000 children of the Bands of Hope of the town & neighbourhood & the various Temperance Societies also met, & marched in procession to the field through

Potter St in which a grand Fete was held. Mrs Ransom[57] promised to accompany me with other representatives of our Association, but we missed each other, & my companions on the march were two mothers with their babes in perambulators, one on either side, four more with perambulators & babes behind & after these a dozen or two of the women! These I accompanied to the field, returning at 2-30 to find John had driven Papa to the Station, whence he came back almost as soon as I had taken a little dinner, after which he drove Lottie & myself on to Kempston where a flower Show was being held, & in the adjoining field the Cricket Club belonging to Southend Blue Ribbon Room were playing a match against the Village Club. We arrived in time to watch the game & see our men win, then took a cup of tea in the tent on the ground & drove back to the Fete in time for the meeting that was part of the day's programme, at 6-30.

The sports formed such an attractive feature that little attention seemed to have been paid to what ought to have been the most important one of the day. Mr Rae of Reading was engaged to address the meeting, but on reaching the ground I found him with Mr Weston standing & seemingly wondering when & where they should begin. We managed to get the Secretary to attract an audience by sending the Band to occupy the railway trolley, which was the only platform, procured some seats from the 'free & easy concert' tent for the Speakers & Chairman, ranged a few others round the trolley & so got a tolerable gathering, considering the counter attraction of the distribution of prizes for the races going on within earshot of the speakers, but with 10,000 people around a grand opportunity was missed. No pledge cards were provided, & although any who were influenced by Mr Rae's animated appeal were invited to give in their name to become total abstainers, only one man came forward after the addresses & did so. I promised to call on him with a card. The chairman was a JP whose name I had not before heard, Mr Gibbard of Sharn-brook.[58] I had a talk with him afterward, & he promised to come to take the chair should we ask his services on some future occasion. John & Lottie remained in the field with me until dark; we left it amidst a great crush of outgoers through the entrance for the public which we ought to have avoided. The day was grandly fine & the concourse of people beyond this most orderly.

Lottie & I have had what by comparison with several weeks past has been a most leisurely & quiet one since Monday. John left us on Tuesday morning. The quiet of Wednesday was somewhat disturbed by an incident at night on our return from Kempston where we drove to take the promised card & see also the husband of our laundress who came to me in great trouble the previous morning on account of his drunkenness. I was told immediately on returning of a great hubbub in a street near & at Lottie's solicitation went to see what was being done, hearing a poor woman was extremely ill in the house from whence the commotion arose. I found another sick person in one close by also, & after talking awhile with her, I went into the outside crowd which I found surrounding a row of chairs, a bedstead & other arti-

[57] Mrs Ransom was the wife of Edwin Ransom, proprietor of the *Bedfordshire Times and Independent*. He was elected Mayor of Bedford in 1885 (see entry for 19 November 1885).

[58] Mr Gibbard, or Stileman-Gibbard as CEB refers to him later in the diary, was born Leonard Stileman, the younger son of Major-General Stileman of the Indian Army and Frances Gibbard. He inherited the Sharnbrook estate from his uncle John Gibbard in 1871 and adopted the surname Stileman-Gibbard. CEB also refers to him as Mr Stillman-Gibbard.

cles ranged in the street & guarded by a bailiff until a conveyance was brought for their removal. The owner of these I found intoxicated standing by & his miserable wife with a babe in her arms. A paper bag of flour was aimed at the bailiff just as I appeared on the scene, & on the arrival of the other man with the hand barrow, the mob of youths principally & men became more unruly, hooted & ran off with it, & so increased the noise & pelting of the men employed, that for the sake of the poor invalids, & to stop further uproar as no police or others that had the least control appeared, I offered them £1 (of the 38/- for which they told me the seizure was made) if they would take it & go, which they, seeing they were powerless to enforce their warrant, thankfully accepted, & so walking off between them, I was a sort of protection from further violence, for which they were also thankful; a few stray shots of gravel & a tin canister at our heels being all that was attempted until they lost sight of us in the dusk, when one turned into the garden with me & the other was glad to slip off alone. The man & his wife who were the cause of all this came & signed the pledge the next night as also did Jane's Husband this morning.

I have never seen more of the sorrow & sin caused by intemperance than this week. Two habitual drunkards of our neighbourhood who for months have been lifted from their degradation to respectability outwardly have gone back again 'like the sow that was washed to her wallowing in the mire'. Both met & saluted me with staggering civility, within a few yards of each other on that same Wednesday night as they were reeling home, one of them coming up towards the horse & quite frightening Lottie who, notwithstanding her willingness to help to reclaim drunkards, is terribly afraid of them. On Saturday poor Johnson the publican in the next Street was carried from the neighbourhood where he has so long been exerting an evil influence to his long home. I saw him a day or two before he died & prayed at his side, but heard little from him that give me hope in his end, which has doubtless been much hastened by the same terrible curse. My hope is more for the future men who are now being trained as abstainers, than for those of the present whose reclamation can be so little depended on. Abstaining Mothers will conduce to this more than any other influence.

Letters from Papa speak of the intense heat which he has felt a good deal from being exposed to it so much in the fields during the Binder trials but he seems better for his change. We have not had such a hot summer for 10 years, but Lottie & I have enjoyed the last week very much in spite of the heat; we have had meals in the garden (supper twice by moon-light), doors & windows all open day, & almost night. Several drives in the evening together with our neighbours Mrs Bradshaw & Mrs Booth (the former has been ill & as she is not allowed to walk at present has greatly appreciated the change of air & scene) have concluded our quiet days & been the only recreation we needed.

### August 22nd (Friday)

On Wednesday I drove to the Union with Lottie to see our poor discontented old Nurse who was as miserable out of the Workhouse, as in it; after various efforts to get a home for her I had to take her back again. She was in her usual mood but slightly relaxed when I promised to come & fetch her for the day, with a poor blind woman who is in the same ward, where she has been over twenty years, & is as bright & cheerful as Nurse is the opposite. On Friday morning I carried out my

**Plate 1.** Portrait miniature of Charlotte Bousfield, painted on ivory, by Hattie Bousfield, undated

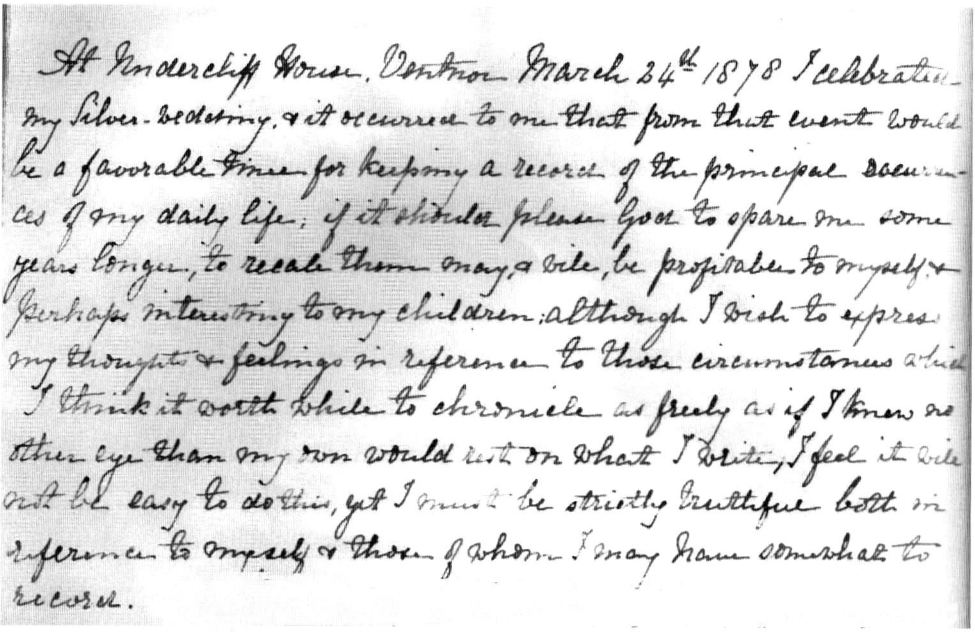

At Undercliff House, Ventnor March 24th 1878 I celebrated my Silver-Wedding, & it occurred to me that from that event would be a favourable time for keeping a record of the principal occurrences of my daily life; if it should please God to spare me some years longer, to recall them may, a while, be profitable to myself & perhaps interesting to my children: although I wish to express my thoughts & feelings in reference to those circumstances which I think it worth while to chronicle as freely as if I knew no other eye than my own would rest on what I write, I feel it will not be easy to do this, yet I must be strictly truthful both in reference to myself & those of whom I may have somewhat to record.

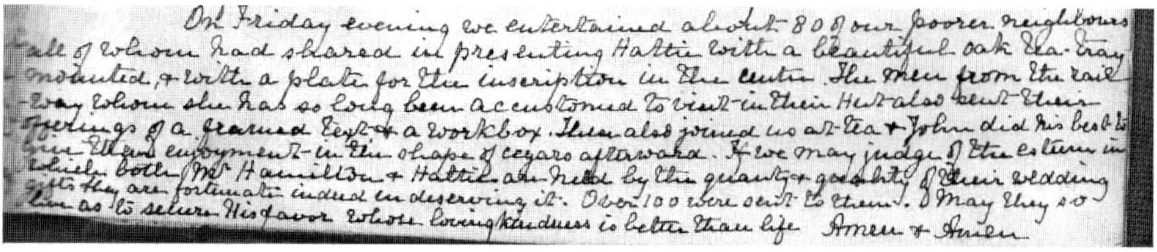

On Friday evening we entertained about 80 of our poorer neighbours all of whom had shared in presenting Hattie with a beautiful oak tea-tray mounted & with a plate for the inscription in the centre. The men from the rail-way whom she has so long been accustomed to visit in their Hut also sent their offerings of a framed text & a workbox. These also joined us at tea & John did his best to give them enjoyment in the shape of cigars afterward. If we may judge of the esteem in which both Mr Hamilton & Hattie are held by the quantity & quality of their wedding gifts they are fortunate indeed in deserving it. Over 100 were sent to them. O may they so live as to secure His favour whose lovingkindness is better than life. Amen & Amen

**Plate 2.** The first entry in volume 1 (24 March 1878) and the last entry in volume 3 of the diaries (12 June 1896) in Charlotte's hand

**Plate 3.** Alpha Villa, Ampthill Road, Bedford: 'the very first house built in a neighbourhood ... now covered by streets of houses'

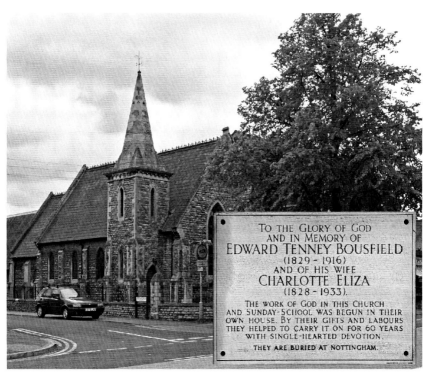

**Plate 4.** Southend Methodist Church, Ampthill Road, Bedford ('our little chapel'), with commemorative wall plaque inset

**Plate 5.** Wesleyan Methodist Chapel with Minister's House, and the Bedfordshire General Library, c. 1840
The Wesleyan Methodist chapel, known at St Paul's, is the large building on the left behind the horseman, with the Minister's house to the left of it. The only feature still visible is the porticoed façade of the building to the right, known at various times as the Library and the Assembly Rooms, and now as the Harpur Suite. The spire of the Anglican church of St Paul's is just visible. (Lithograph, Bradford Rudge, Cecil Higgins Art Gallery, Bedford)

**Plate 6.** Bedford New Schools, mid-1830s
This fine façade designed by Edward Blore in the Gothic style is familiar to Bedfordians today as the front of the Harpur Centre. It was completed in 1837 and housed the Commercial School, now Bedford Modern School. It was favoured by dissenting families as staff were not restricted to Anglicans. Will was a pupil here from 1864 to 1870. (Coloured lithograph, George Moore, Cecil Higgins Art Gallery, Bedford)

**Plate 7.** The Bedford Grammar School house, built in 1756, is seen here in 1858, with the statue of its founder, Sir William Harpur, visible in a niche over the door. It is situated on the west side of St Paul's Square – the church's railings can be seen on the right of the picture. Ted and John were educated here. (Engraving, Rock & Co, Cecil Higgins Art Gallery, Bedford)

**Plate 8.** High Street from the bridge looking north, c. 1906

The Town Bridge over the River Ouse was built by John Wing and completed in 1813. In the inter-war years congestion became a problem here and the width of the bridge was doubled (1938–40). The buildings on the left and the George Hotel are now demolished. (Coloured postcard, BLARS, ref Z1130/16)

**Plate 9.** Skaters on the frozen River Ouse (undated, but possibly 1890 or 1892)
This photograph is taken from the Town Bridge looking downstream. The stone balustraded new embankment is on the left, and further down is the Town and County Club, built in 1885 and demolished in 1971. The Bousfields frequently enjoyed the opportunity of skating here. (Postcard, BLARS, ref BP 28/10)

**Plate 10.** The unveiling of the John Howard statue by the Duke of Bedford, 28 March 1894, and the Floral Hall
The statue commemorating the centenary of the death of John Howard, philanthropist and prison reformer, stands to the east of St Paul's Square. He is no relation of the Howards of the iron works. To the right is the Floral Hall, opened in 1849, the predecessor of the new Corn Exchange. The new building, larger and better equipped, made the first one redundant, and it was demolished in 1904.
(Photograph, BLARS, ref X466/1)

**Plate 11.** Britannia Iron Works, from the north side, early 1860s

The complexity and size of the Britannia Works are both evident in this fine lithograph. The River Ouse is flowing east from left to right, down to King's Lynn and Wisbech, with boats carrying goods to and from the wharves. Locomotives are busy transporting finished goods and the necessary raw materials both internally and in and out of the factory to St John's station (see Plate 18) and the national network. Top left is the despatch bay, and opposite is the administrative building where Edward and the Howard brothers had their offices. Two statues, of Britannia and Ceres, can be discerned, crowning the building and symbolising patriotism and the indebtedness of all those employed there to the goddess of corn and the fruitfulness of the land. The main part of the foundry is the five rows of buildings parallel to the river. (Coloured lithograph, Cecil Higgins Art Gallery, Bedford)

**Plate 12.** Britannia Iron Works, entrance gateway, built 1859, photographed in 2006. 'Nothing beside remains.' *Ozymandias*, Shelley

**Plate 13.** Hattie and William Hamilton and bicycles, c. 1890 Hattie and William are pictured here in a rural setting contrived in the Southport studio of one of her uncles, Benjamin Wyles, the husband of Edward's sister Mary Ann. The bicycles which they are preparing to mount are known as 'safety bicycles' and were invented in 1885. They are similar in design to modern bicycles, and made cycling safer and much more popular, particularly among young middle-class ladies who found in them a socially acceptable way to independence as well as an agreeable pastime.

**Plate 14.** Aspley, painted by Hattie Bousfield, undated

In 1887 the Bousfields leased a house in Aspley Heath, a village some 12 miles south of Bedford, as a retreat for Edward who was suffering from stress and depression. It assisted his recovery and proved a popular holiday haven with the children. Hattie's painting conveys well the peace and beauty of this rural setting.

**Plate 15.** Charlotte and Edward's Golden Wedding, 1903

The senior members of the Bousfield family outside Alpha Villa in March 1903, just before Charlotte and Edward left to join their daughters in Nottingham. Left to right: Flo, Will, Hattie, Edward, William Hamilton, Charlotte, Ted, Clara, Lottie, Alex Morton, Mattie, John.

**Plate 16.** Edris' gravestone in Bedford Cemetery

Charlotte's last child died six years before the diaries began, but is still very much in Charlotte's heart. She is referred to as Edris, but her registered Christian names are as they appear on the stone. The motto across the top reads poignantly 'It is well.' The cemetery was opened in 1855 (see map, Plate 22).

**Plate 17.** Charlotte's presentation to George V and Queen Mary, Nottingham, 1928

King George V and Queen Mary visited what was then University College Nottingham on the occasion of its move from a cramped city centre site to its present campus to the south-west of the city. Charlotte's hundredth birthday was celebrated on 10 July in the same year.

**Plate 18.** St John's Station, London and North Western Railway, c. 1870
St John's was the first of Bedford's two railway stations. Situated south of the river, it opened in 1846, with the line to Bletchley, connecting to London Euston and Birmingham. In 1862 the line was extended eastwards to Cambridge (see map, Plate 20). (BLARS ref Z50/11/16)

**Plate 19.** Midland Road Station, Midland Railway, with Kirtley engine c. 1870
In 1857 the Midland Railway's line was opened from Bedford to Hitchin, where trains joined the Great Northern line to London. Bedford's Midland Station was opened in 1859, and from 1868 a direct line to London St Pancras via Luton was available, reducing journey time to 80 minutes (see map, Plate 20). The Kirtley engine was a typical MR 0–6-0 locomotive. (BLARS ref Z50/13/207)

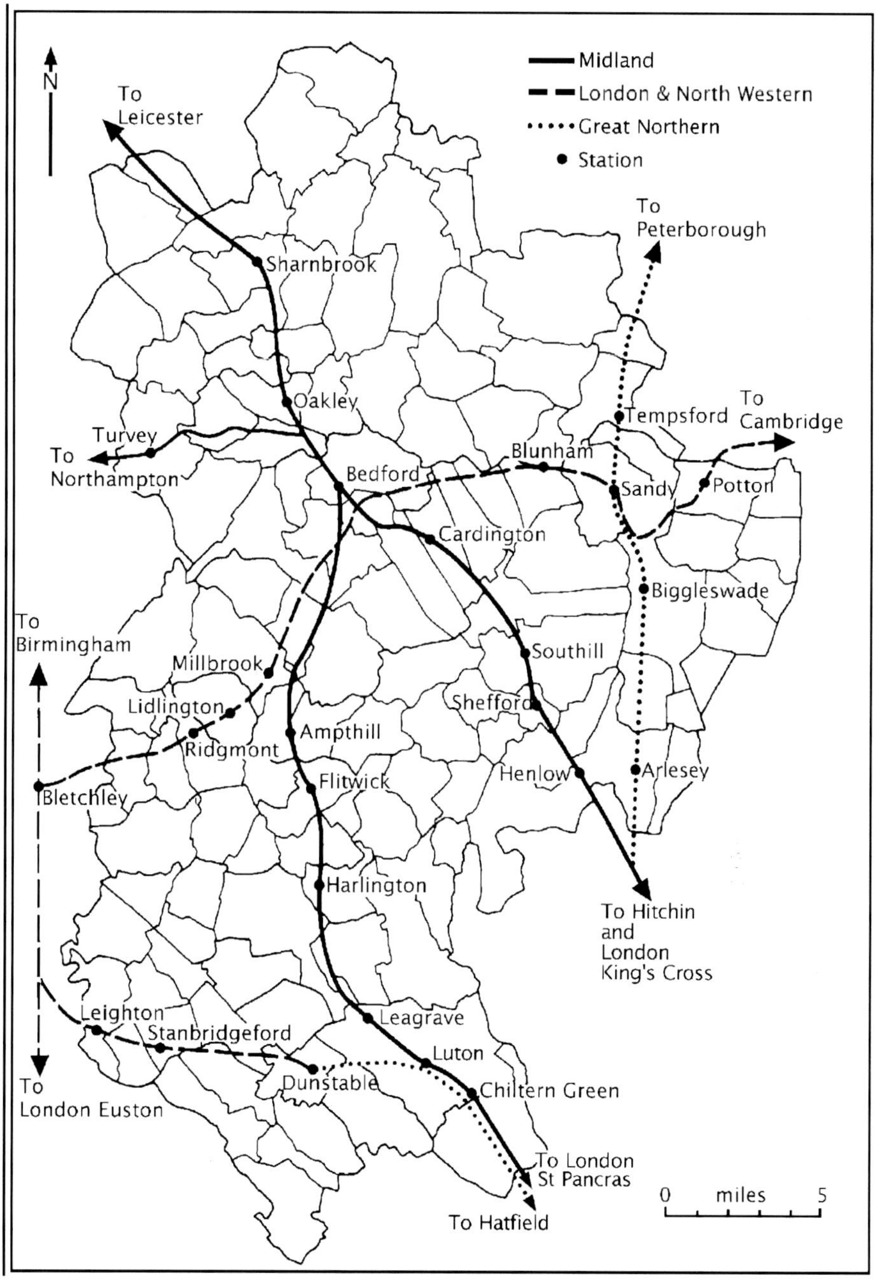

**Plate 20.** Map of railway lines and names of parishes in Bedfordshire, up to 1868
(BLARS)

**Plate 21.** Reynold's map of Bedford, 1841
This delightful map, almost like an aerial photograph, shows Bedford as a small market town. (BLARS)

**Plate 22.** Ordnance Survey map of Bedford in 1901

This map can be compared with the Reynolds'map opposite to show the expansion of Bedford in the Victorian period. The scale of the original is 6 inches to 1 mile. (BLARS)

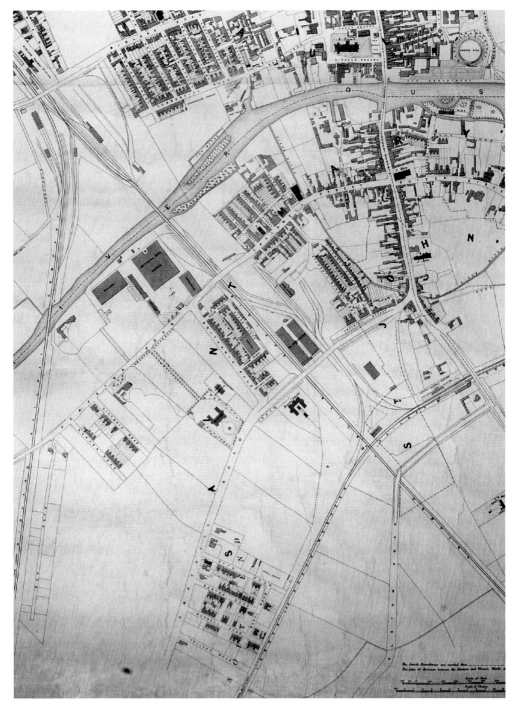

**Plate 23.** Mercer's map of 1876 to 1878

A detailed map of Southend and the town centre, in the year the diaries begin. The scale of the original is 25 inches to 1 mile. (BLARS)

promise & took both for a little drive before bringing them here; they were very delighted, & I felt as happy in giving them the pleasure. Lottie very much admired the appearance of the two old ladies in their white frilled caps & spotless aprons, & was very pleased to entertain them whilst I was at[59] Thurlow St M Meeting all the afternoon & to drive them back at night.

On Tuesday morning Mrs Ransom came & had a long talk over the business of our Association in which she seems more than ever interested. I have lately felt more than ever the need of a good Gospel Temperance Missionary who could be entirely set apart for such work in the town & neighbourhood, & mentioned the subject to Mrs R who encouraged me by a promise of £2 towards a stipend for him, if we could carry out the idea. Our small house will be at liberty Sept^r 29^th & Papa would be willing to let it be occupied by a good man & his family if we can raise the £80 or £90 which is the least we could offer. On Thursday I had afternoon tea with Mrs Sampson, & again met Mrs R. Whilst there Dr Goldsmith came in. I talked the matter over with him & was still further encouraged by a promise of help to the amount of £5 per an[num] & a hint that his neighbour Mr Kinsey might do the same. I have written to Mrs Tucker, & am awaiting her reply before proceeding further.

*Monday Sept^r 8^th*
The time is drawing near when we hope to leave home but we have not yet been able to decide exactly in what direction. I have written to M^rs Barns about a lodging for a week at Moreton-hampstead to which place I proposed to Papa to go both to see my old friend, & also with the hope that it would be an easy distance from Cornwall which I have a great desire to see, & which I hoped we might get a peep at if only as far as Bude about which place I wrote to Mrs Thompson of Bideford to make enquiry. Papa does not however seem at all willing to over step the boundary of Devon; I have this evening been trying to coax him to go direct to Penzance but fear I shall not succeed.

Last Wednesday we had a very pleasant guest, the Revd Forbes Winslow MA, Vicar of St Paul's, St Leonards. He visited Bedford at the invitation of the Good Templars[60] who asked me to entertain him which I was pleased to do. I went into the town early in the afternoon & turned into the Assembly Rooms to the Public Tea instead of returning home, made tea for Mr Winslow & the other speakers (of whom there were more than were needed) & then took a short walk & went into St Paul's Church with Mr W. His speech at the evening meeting was scarcely as convincing as amusing, but he is a charming man & very unusual type of clergyman; did not hesitate to declare himself a thorough Radical, believes in 'Women's Rights' & that the Church of England would be better for, instead of injured by, being dis-established, but withal he is a truly Christian man, & indefatigable temperance advocate. He left us after early breakfast Thursday morning, feeling his visit & cheerful conversation quite a refreshing episode.

---

[59] CEB writes 'as' but must mean 'at'.
[60] The International Order of Good Templars, claiming to be the largest temperance organisation in the world, was founded in Sweden in 1850, and brought to England in 1868 by Joseph Malins. It rapidly spread despite, or because of, the secrecy of its ceremonies and elaborate rituals, somewhat similar to those of the Freemasons.

*Monday Sept[r] [61] (Moretonhampstead)*

[The Bousfields are staying in Devon to visit some old family friends, and embark on a walk across Dartmoor.]

Arriving at Okehampton Station an hour earlier than expected, we found there was time to get out at Lydford Station to visit the Falls there, which we managed to do, & get back in time for the next train on to Tavistock, which we took & arrived about 5 o'clock, & after refreshment & rest at the Temperance Hotel were able to walk round the town & visit several places of interest, then to bed early, & before 9 o'clock next morning we were on foot for the walk for which the girls were so ambitious.

The main road across the Moor is from Tavistock to Moretonhampstead 21 miles. The first three are an ascent to, rather than on it. Reaching the wilder part, we found the breeze which had before been stiff, rather stronger than we could face with ease, but in spite of this & the bright sun-shine with which we were favored (but which made us glad to walk under the shade of our umbrellas), we marched on our up & down-hill course until the turning to Princetown, at which (instead of carrying out our first plan of walking direct to Two Bridges for the night), we determined to make the circuit of about 2 more miles to pass the Prison.

A short mile brought us to the granite quarries in which many of the Convicts work, & on some blocks on the road outside we sat down for our luncheon. Just as we had finished & were wandering round the spot, we found we were not alone as we thought, but that a number of tourists had assembled at a point in the road overlooking the Prison below it, & these we soon saw were waiting to see the poor prisoners employed outside the walls, marched back to their labor after their dinner hour. Joining the crowd of about 30 or 40 persons (excursionists we found, from Plymouth), we saw first one gang, & then another & another emerge from their gloomy confinement by different routes, & guarded by warders armed with rifles & fixed bayonets, walk in pairs up the paths leading to the highway which they had to cross to get to the Quarries, & their work, on the fields above them. The warders ordered all the lookers-on to one side or the other of the road, the opposite to that in which the gang in their charge had to turn, but I was able to get near enough to see nearly every countenance in passing, & was rather surprised to see less of either vice or misery depicted in them than I expected. The extreme pallor of the face of one poor fellow was most noticeable amidst the brown & burnt visages of most of the others, & just as he was cross the road trying to keep pace with his comrade, he stumbled forward, & would have fallen but that those in front & behind instantly caught him, & without stopping the gang managed to carry him along, where we did not see, but the hearts that we could only suppose to be hardened by crime were evidently not dead to human kindness. Some were grey-haired men, some mere boys. I remarked as they were passing 'I wonder how many of them would have been where they are but for drink.' 'Probably about 1 per cent' said a gentleman at my side. I tried to discover faces more refined than the majority amidst them, but cropped, & dressed alike in their coarse caps & clothing, it was not so easy to see this as the reverse, which however struck me in only a few instances.

---

[61] No date is given here.

After all had passed we resumed our walk through the town meeting smaller gangs harnessed by ropes to long trolleys, we supposed for removing the stone. Some were making a barley rick in a farm yard, others at work building new parts of the Prison, some sweeping & making the roads good, but all under the watchful eyes of the warders standing armed near, & around; when we got further off we could still see these at the very top of the surrounding hills posted at regular distances, their bayonets raised & ready for any emergency, such as too frequently takes place. One of those standing told Lottie there were about 180 warders for the 1100 convicts but that 500 would not be too many!

*Oct 1st*

To visit my dear brother Robert's grave was my chief reason for the journey to Torquay. Twenty three years ago[62] I left home with Lottie a babe of six weeks old, & travelled with her in my arms over one thousand miles, first to Newark where Robert[63] then was living with his young wife to whom he had been married six months, then after seeing him (strength & health gone) set out with some remaining hope for Matlock. I went on to Stockbridge where my youngest sister was dying,[64] staying until the end with her, then on to Bristol to meet my poor Brother again at my Sister Hattie's home as he rested there on his way to Torquay whither the D[r] at once ordered him. In a few more days the tidings came that he was much worse & wished me to come, dear Hattie's delicate health making it dangerous for her to leave.[65] So once more with my baby I went to him, left him at the end of a week in the hands of a Christian physician D[r] Tetley who ministered to him body & soul, & then at his earnest request went back to Newark to sell his furniture & settle his affairs there which was scarcely done before he passed away. Last Saturday was the first time I had visited the spot where as the inscription on the headstone reads 'He sleeps in Jesus'. Before the journey from Newark back to Bedford was made, a brother & a sister had both been taken from earth, to heaven, & I reached home again with Lottie three months old, thankful for the mercy which had kept us both in health, amidst the trial of strength that I experienced, when I seemed to have less than now.[66]

*Monday Oct 6th*
[Back in Bedford.]
On the night of Wednesday Oct[r] 1st a special Trustee meeting was called at St Paul's Chapel by the Chapel Steward to decide the important question whether I might be permitted to use the boards & trestles of the adjoining School-room for the BWTA Tea in the Assembly Rooms! This seems almost too ridiculous to be true, & I could not accept a concession so ingraciously [sic] given when it came next morning. I should be sorry to show a resentful or unchristian spirit, but I do so strongly feel

---

62  In 1861, when CEB was living in Cauldwell Street, Bedford. Two of her sisters had already died: Mary Jane in 1855, aged 22, and Frances Catherine in 1839, aged 18 months.
63  Robert Luther, born 1829, died in 1861, aged 32.
64  Maria Louisa, the remaining twin sister, born 1837, died in 1861, aged 24.
65  Hattie died two years later in 1863.
66  After 1861 only one of CEB's siblings remained alive, Alfred William, who lived abroad, and he had died by 1881.

that the same individuals who endeavoured to thwart the efforts made to get the Circuit funds supplemented during my Husband's Stewardship have never forgiven our success, & have now taken another opportunity to cause me annoyance, that I cannot continue to put myself in their way, or attempt to worship when I look around on the faces of those from whom I have had so much that has been painful. Papa has been a large contributor to the new School-rooms just completed, & we have both endeavoured to show the opposite spirit to that which was manifested towards ourselves by going to the Bazaars which have been held, & spending as much as we could afford, & helping in other ways; but in spite of all that we could do the same spirit that has prompted this last act has shown itself in many ways, & I have expressed to Papa my decided wish to entirely withdraw from the place of worship to which we first went 27 years ago next Jan$^y$, & concentrate all our influence & means on that where it is most needed, the little Chapel which we were the means of getting for our neighbours, & where we know many of them feel pleasure in meeting with us.[67]

Mrs Lucas arrived at the Institute with Mrs Alexander in time for the afternoon meeting last Thursday. It was well attended, but much disappointment was felt at Mrs L's address which was not nearly so good as when I before heard her speak. Most of the 60 or 70 ladies present remained for the afternoon tea which was provided, & whilst this was being taken about 7 of them became members of our Association. The tea in the Assembly Rooms was attended by more than 200 women who filled every table, & sat in double rows in some parts of the Room. Many more came in for the Public meeting, for women only. Mrs Alexander presided & spoke well, Mrs Lucas again, not with her best manner or matter, but she got the attention of the meeting. Then I was asked to address the women, which as I am so accustomed to talking to many of them in the MMs I did not find it difficult to do, although less than two years ago I should have thought it a most formidable matter to stand up in the Bedford Rooms filled to speak even to women; the power has come with the work which I believe God has given me to do. I am striving to do it for His glory, & to put down those weak thoughts of self which will arise sometimes. Mrs Sampson followed the practical remarks which I endeavoured to make with the more spiritual, & so concluded our first Anniversary of the Bedford Branch of the British Women's Temperance Association.

Little did I anticipate such an amount of success as we have been permitted to see, when we had our first little meeting in Thurlow St the 2nd Oct$^r$ last year. The Secretary Miss Cockburn reported 240 members & 22 were added to our number as the result of that meeting. May the work go on until every Mother shall be influenced to train, both by example & precept, those who, in the generation to come, shall be men & women who have neither tasted, nor handled, the accursed drink.

The following morning after the Meeting I had a long chat with Mrs Lucas which I greatly enjoyed although we thought very differently on some subjects, chiefly political. Mr Bradlaugh's character & conduct she vindicated the former more successfully than I thought possible from the latter. But whilst she called his being kept out of the House of Commons 'religious persecution' I only expressed satisfac-

---

[67] CEB sees the St Paul's Chapel Trustees as deliberately obstructive, petty and vengeful in their attitude.

tion at the spectacle exhibited to the world, & in particular to the nation the nearest to us & the deepest sunk in infidelity,[68] of a body of British Legislators shutting out as unfit & unworthy to take part in the legislature, the man who would ostentatiously flaunt his atheism in its face. I agreed with her that there were probably men amongst them equally atheistic, & rejectors of the Great Fountain of all human law, but of those who did not avow these sentiments, we could not be judge.

The Chaise was brought round at 11 o'clock & Mrs Lucas was very pleased to accompany Lottie & myself for a drive. She was much pleased with the town, the Bunyan Statue & Memorials which last we took her to Mr Brown's to see. They are kept at the house of the Pastor of Bunyan Meeting, & consist of the Church book, containing the names of the Members of the church at the time when Bunyan occupied that position, & many articles that once belonged to him. After dinner I had to attend the Thurlow St MM, there I bid Mrs Lucas adieu, & Lottie drove her on to the Station on her return to Town.

*Monday 20th [October]*

Last Saturday was a glorious autumn day, & at breakfast we planned a very early dinner & long afternoon drive. A Post Card from John came soon after accepting my invitation a few days previous to come home for Sunday, & saying he hoped to reach by the 3-45 train. Lottie proposed to meet her Brother, & that we should do as we before intended as far as Papa & I were concerned. We agreed to her proposal & started for Turvey.

On the way Papa said he was glad of the opportunity for a little quiet talk alone. Of late he has been more than ever decided in his intention to make next year his last at the Works. With his last effort, the Sheaf Binder, which obtained the 2nd Prize at the last Royal Show (but which from the judgment of the Public & the Press ought to have had the 1st) he seems to feel there is little in the way of invention & work in his line to be accomplished further by him for the Britannia, & his position there has become so irksome that I shall be thankful when it can come to an end. We are not rich, but God has given us enough to place us beyond anxiety & enable to continue some work for him. So as we drove along Papa disclosed to me more than he had ever before done his half formed plans for the time when he should have done with what has been the work of his life, at least so far as the Works are concerned.[69] I was thankful to find that amongst these was the idea that we should go on more than ever & together with Temperance work, which he now speaks of as 'our work'. Whether he will succeed in some other plans in addition remains for time to prove, but I did not discourage although I do not think them as practicable as he considered them. To be more useful than we have hitherto been for others, now that our cares for our own are I trust decreasing is I believe the great desire which God has given us, & He will I hope & believe enable us to carry it out as work for Him & His Glory.

Our sphere of labor is to some extent changing even in present circumstances. I

---

68 CEB refers to the reforms of Jules Ferry, Prime Minister of France between 1883 and 1885. The Ferry laws made public education free, compulsory, and secular. A political opponent at the time (de Broglie) declared that it was the beginning of '*écoles sans Dieu*'. It is interesting to note that CEB's dislike of atheism prevailed over her antipathy towards Catholicism.

69 Edward must be referring to his decision to qualify as a barrister, which he achieved in 1887 (see diary entries for 24 October and 5 November in that year).

have this evening penned a letter to Revd C Sargasson who is the Leader of the Class in which Lottie & I have met telling him that it is my wish after the last of a series of painful annoyances from those in authority in the St Paul's Circuit to cease my connexion with it. I do this to prevent any recurrence of them, feeling at the same time that my power of usefulness is not at all curtailed by the step I have taken with Papa's consent. He intends to withdraw after a little time & concentrate more of our means & efforts at the little Chapel & amongst our neighbours.

### Oct<sup>r</sup> 29<sup>th</sup>

After winding up home work & pleasure, the latter by seeing the new Bridge over the Ouse[70] opened in Bedford on Tuesday Oct<sup>r</sup> 21<sup>st</sup> & driving over it with Lottie as soon as the Lord Lieutenant of the County Earl Cowper, the Mayor & other town Magnates & all who composed the long procession formed to celebrate the event, had fairly passed between 1 & 2 o'clock, we returned by the new route to Alpha Villa & dined alone, Papa having taken advantage of the general holiday to go to London.

### Friday Nov<sup>r</sup> 14<sup>th</sup>

The chief last week was the re-opening of our Blue Ribbon Room. I invited the Members of the Southend Cricket Club to tea last Friday, & with them as many of the men of the neighbourhood as we could seat comfortably. About sixty took tea together at 6 o'clock, after which with Papa in the Chair we had a very successful meeting. Dr Goldsmith came up & gave the men a stirring address. Papa's also was very good, & these & others interspersed with songs by Mr Greenhill & Lottie, & temperance hymns, filled a very pleasant evening which was well concluded by 8 signing the pledge, & 10 putting on the bit of blue. During the past few weeks several men addicted to drink have become total abstainers, & one who had sunk very low has again joined. These are beginning to frequent the Room instead of the Public House.

### Nov<sup>r</sup> 20<sup>th</sup>

On the last page I almost complain of the very ordinary round of events of apparently small importance which make up my diary, but on this I must chronicle one that is altogether new in our own family record, the birth of a grand-daughter, which happy event took place on Monday Nov<sup>r</sup> 17<sup>th</sup> at 11-20 a m, as Mrs Kelly's letter announcing it to me testifies. Will also wrote from Crown Office Row as soon as the intelligence was telegraphed to him there; he does not express any special gratification, but I know that both he & Florence will be delighted to have a little girl.

### Tuesday Nov<sup>r</sup> 25<sup>th</sup>

Papa went to London on Friday & again to-day, & on both days called on Will & John; the account the former gives of Florence & our little grand-daughter are very satisfactory. Will is not busy, but the number of his Clients increases although their cases have not been of so much importance as those of last year. Webster & Aston QCs are of course at the head of the list of Patent Cases, after them Will told Papa he

---

[70] The bridge is situated just upstream of County Hall.

came, as far as number of cases go. He & we have got reason to be thankful, but he will not probably earn as much this year as last. Mr Wheeler told me when I was at Crown Office Row last, that the general depression in agriculture & trade would be felt at the Bar as much as anywhere & that 'people had not money to go to law'. If this were the greatest evil arising from it, it would scarcely be greatly deplored, but throughout the country the distress is very great although bread may now be bought for 4d the 4lb loaf & potatoes at from 1/- to 1/6 per bushel. Farming was never so un-remunerative, & the free trade which has over stocked the corn market seems not an unmitigated blessing since with cheapness of many articles of food there is great scarcity of work both in fields & Factories.[71] At the Britannia the number of men employed on short time or discharged is greater than I ever remember hearing of before. Many who have been earning high wages in the early part of the year through improvidence & drink are reduced to straits which they never need have experienced; this last more than any other is the enemy which is still bringing want & misery into ten thousand, aye, ten times ten thousand homes.

*Tuesday Dec[r] 2nd*
I cannot help contrasting the light clouds that have been passing over me, with the deep darkness that for a time seems to shut out sunshine from the life of our nearest neighbours. Little more than a month ago Mr Bowick's eldest daughter, a healthy looking girl of 17, was taken ill & buried, in less than a week. In the next house to ours on that side, Hattie's old school fellow Katie Halahan, just her age,[72] is to all appearance rapidly weakening in consumption, & on the other side of us is the long afflicted sufferer Miss Risley,[73] who has been in bed weeks, after a most painful operation. On Friday evening she sent for me to sit a little while with her whilst her nurse went out. The previous day I followed to the grave Mrs Donkin who was found dead in her bed the previous Sunday morning, from heart disease. A touching spectacle was the grief of her Husband & four motherless children around her grave. Mrs Sampson & Miss Cockburn accompanied me to the funeral, which was largely attended.

*Wednesday Dec[r] 31st 1884*
On Friday we gave the harmoniumist [sic], singers & a few of our neighbours who attend the little Chapel tea in the BR Room, & presented Mr Watters & his wife with a little table which Lottie painted very prettily for them as a small recognition of his services. Music, guessing games, a little speech making on the presentation, & then reading & prayer filled a very enjoyable evening from 5 until 9 o'clock. All seemed very happy & pleased at our entertaining them & John, Lottie & Hattie I believe felt more satisfaction in helping Papa & myself than they have often done in more aristocratic gatherings. About 24 were present.

---

[71] The depression in agriculture was caused by the importation of cheap wheat from the USA which caused widespread unemployment in both rural and industrial areas, as CEB explains. A minor cause of the increasing cheapness of corn from the States was the invention of the self-binder which when attached to the reaping machines enabled one man to do the work previously done by two. This, somewhat bizarrely, was of course the development to which Edward's work had contributed!
[72] Catherine Halahan was 18, and lived at no. 46. Alpha Villa was no. 44.
[73] Mr Risley, a widower, lived at no. 42 with his unmarried daughter aged 44.

**1885**

*Jan^y 14^th*

We have had to part with Hattie again to-day. She returned to Cricklewood by the noon train. She has not been at all well the last few days, & thinks her health is better there than at home but I feel very uneasy at her being away during the very cold weather we are now having fearing a recurrence of last year's ailment. Her school-fellow & friend Katie Halahan who lives close to us has for some months been laid aside from the effects of what began as a cold, & has now developed into rapid consumption. Hattie has been to see her once or twice since she has been at home, but was much shocked this morning when she called to wish her good bye at the great change within the last few days. Poor Katie only seems to have lately realized how ill she is & with tears said 'it may be good bye for ever'.

*Saturday Jan^y 24^th*

Last week I yielded to a request from Miss Cockburn to go to Harrold, a village 10 miles from Bedford, to assist at a meeting of a Branch of BWTA which has been formed there since & through the formation of our Branch. An elderly maiden lady of means who is a resident in the village of Harrold, & very interested in evangelistic & temperance work amongst her neighbours, heard of the object & working of the Association & invited Mrs Alexander to visit them & begin a Branch which she did about a year ago, but of which I knew nothing more than the fact. Miss St Quintin asked one or two of our members to go over to speak at an afternoon meeting; neither of those invited were able to do so. A note from Miss Cockburn stating the case induced me to accede to the request made to her to find help for them, although I did not know Miss St Quintin or any of the people. The distance too was much greater than I at first thought & the weather very severe with some snow, but by starting early with a foot warmer in the Brougham, difficulties which seemed so great that I almost repented my promise were overcome & I arrived at Harrold at the appointed time 2-30 pm. The meeting was in a very pretty Mission Hall which Miss St Q has built adjoining her own residence in the middle of the village & for which she entirely employs an Evangelist, a gentlemanly well educated young man, who with his wife lives in a delightfully pretty cottage close to the Hall on the other side; she played the Harmonium & prayed at our meeting, Miss St Q presiding. About 40 women were present, but I was delighted to find that out of a population of 1000 there were 70 in the Association. I spoke to them with some pleasure to myself, & thankfulness that our influence had spread to this extent. After tea a Band of Hope meeting was held in the same Hall, conducted by the Evangelist (whose name I forget), a good number of children were present to whom I was asked to say a few words which I did & then at a quarter to 6 o'clock started homeward arriving safely at about 8 o'clock; although snow fell the journey was much more pleasant than I expected & except for poor Charley's being rather tired, none were the worse for it.

*Friday Jan^y 30^th*

The shortness of work at the Britannia is more talked of than ever before during the long time we have been here, & is the ostensible reason of a great deal of distress, which however on being traced to its true source in most cases arises from the improvidence of men who in the time when work was plentiful spent on drink the money which would now have kept them above poverty. This is the real cause of the depression of trade. The nation spending annually £136 millions on alcohol, & only £140 millions on bread & house-rent together![74] When will the common sense of Government and Christianity seek to cope with this national source of misery! Our poor little Association can only touch the fringe of the gigantic evil but we must work on if by any means we may save some.

### Tuesday Feb^y 17^th

Nearly three weeks have elapsed since I recalled passing events to write them & I could imagine the time even longer; the reason I suppose that I have been twice to London within that period. The first visit, this day fortnight, was principally to be present at Exeter Hall the following day, or rather night, to hear the farewell addresses of 7 young men, BAs of Cambridge who, having completed their College course, determined to devote themselves, their learning & their means, to spreading the truths of the Gospel in that most densely populated & darkest region, China. Of the 7, one Stanley Smith was stroke of the Cambridge 8; another, Studd, Captain of the Cambridge 11, & two others the sons of the late Conservative Member for Bedford, Captain Polhill-Turner.[75] Of the eldest of these it was said some two or three years ago at the time of his Father's death that his wild conduct was the cause of it. (His younger brother was an officer in the Dragoons.) These with about 40 other Under-graduates became convinced of the folly & guilt of sin, under, I believe, the influence of Mr Moody,[76] became truly Christian men, & most of them intend to devote their lives to missionary work believing it to be their duty to obey the command of Christ 'Go ye into all the world & preach the Gospel to every creature'. That young men of position & learning should so resolve & act has raised quite a commotion both in the Church & the world. The newspapers comment upon it & wonder.

### Feb^y 22^nd Monday

On Saturday night John came home to tea bringing with him Mr Hailes, a gentleman Papa has long known in business & with whom John frequently meets. He is a great Microscopist, & has proposed Ted for membership of the Queckett Club,[77] at which they were to meet the day, or rather night of the day I left London. Soon after John's arrival he showed me a letter he had that morning received from Mr Southwell inviting him to call upon him at his house next Wednesday. This I soon found was brought about by his having written to Miss M S to ascertain the real state of her feelings towards him. He has had continual reason to believe both from her manner, when they accidentally met, & from frequent intelligence which he has

---

74  The economics of unemployment are perhaps not as simple as CEB suggests.
75  Captain Frederick Polhill-Turner of Howbury Hall, Renhold (a village a few miles east of Bedford) was High Sheriff in 1854 and MP for Bedford from 1874 to 1880. He died in 1881. The two sons, Cecil and Arthur, were both active workers for the China Inland Mission.
76  Dwight L. Moody, the American evangelist, visited Britain for the second time in 1881 with his colleague Ira Sankey. The Moody and Sankey hymn books are archetypes of evangelical hymnody.
77  The Queckett Microscopical Club: its purpose was to further the use of the microscope in research.

had of her from Mrs Clay (who has sympathized a good deal with John) whom she has visited a good deal, that her apparent indifference nearly a year ago was not so real, nor brought about by such mercenary considerations as then seemed to influence her, but was entirely owing to her attempt to coincide with her Father's views & wishes. This has kept alive the flame which John has sometimes endeavoured to extinguish, & which for his peace & comfort I have often hoped might be the case. I have however often admired the manly way in which he has met the annoyances which have again & again arisen, & the dignity which has characterized all his action in the matter of his disappointment. I think Mr Southwell must have also thought even better of him than before, for his letter is couched in terms anything but discouraging, & he would scarcely renew the invitation to bring about the same issue as before.

### Feb^y 28^th

The end of another week & month, which has brought with it what I cannot but consider an important event in our family history. A letter from Hattie yesterday says the result of John's visit 'to his damsel yesterday evening was entirely to his satisfaction. He is going this evening to take the ring to her, it is a most lovely one, three big diamonds', so now my youngest boy has probably made, & been accepted in making, his choice for life. I trust it may be for their mutual happiness both in the present & future. Hattie says 'I am glad for John, for I hope that he will not be so mopish as he has been especially lately'. Only little more than a fortnight ago I was writing of his low spirits because of those things which he thought against him. In trying to comfort him I said 'mark my words, when you can look back upon these things you will say, they were all wisely ordered for, not against, me' but I little thought that he would so soon have so much light thrown on the path that seemed so obscure to him that evening; now it is easy to see how all has been arranged just in the very best order & time.

### March 2^nd

This afternoon our BWTA Prayer & Committee meetings have been held as usual. At the first Mrs Goldsmith presided, at the last myself, the duty being allotted to me in the absence of our President at the annual re-election of Officers in Jan^y , as it was last year. Last Wednesday another Branch of our Association was formed at Pavenham at the wish of Mrs Tucker. She invited Miss Cockburn & myself to assist at the meeting which she convened in the village Reading-room. I wrote proposing that it should be deferred until Mrs Alexander could be present, but as Mrs T's reply said she was 'far too busy in her work in London' (whither she had lately gone to reside) I again yielded, to give what help I could, but after my experience of the journey to Harrold (which lamed Charley for some days), Papa was not willing that I should drive to Pavenham.

Miss C accompanied me by train to Oakley Station to which Mrs T sent to meet us. The meeting was held in the village Reading-room, about forty being present, amongst them the Clergyman's wife. Miss Cockburn first spoke relating what we had done at Bedford, in a way that I thought rather too independent of the Parent Association, to which I consider we owe every thing as far as first ideas & organization are concerned. I followed with an attempt to influence the Total Abstainers present to join the Association, & those who were not to become such. At the close some 12 to 15 women signified their willingness. Mrs Tucker & the Clergyman's wife Mrs Linnell promised to become Vice Presidents & a lady present accepted the office of Secretary.

The visit to the old mansion called the Bury, Mrs T's residence, was very enjoyable. We had luncheon before the meeting & afterwards Mrs Linnell, Miss C, Miss Cook (the daughter of the Vicar of Goldington) & myself took tea in the room of Miss Peacock, an invalided sister of Mrs Tucker's who, although confined to her couch & joining in the conversation by means of an ear-trumpet, was much interested in the work we had been beginning. Her room is a combination of sitting & bed-room on the second floor, in size & comfort everything to make as pleasant as possible her long seclusion. The house is altogether worth a visit; the fine old oak panelling & carving with which the walls are covered were very much to my liking & gave an air of grandeur which no gilding or paint however elaborate could impart, & the views from the windows on to the Park & fine old trees were quite in keeping with the interior.

*March 10ᵗʰ (Tuesday)*

On Saturday afternoon Edward & Clara came together from Town to pay us their last visit before the former[78] takes upon himself all the responsibility & work of the Practice which he will do from Saturday March 21st on which day Dr Palmer leaves him in possession of 363 OKR. He appeared to be in excellent spirits at the prospect, & in good health except for a morning cough from the effects of a cold; this always gives me concern in either of my children. I met Ted & C at the Midland Station with the Brougham, & left it in St John's St to look for a dying old woman, of whose case I had been told at the M Meeting the previous day. Edward hoped to have been able to remain at home over Monday but was obliged to return that morning to be present at an operation on one of his patients whom he had sent to a Hospital. Clara remained until the afternoon when she went to Sutton Cottage.[79]

Papa has to-day been in London to meet Mr J Howard & Professor Gamgee at Will's Chamber.[80] The Professor has some new motive power which he is very anxious to get Mr JH to assist him in carrying out & of which he is most sanguine. The former desired Papa's opinion which was not very sanguine, but he proposed submitting it to Will's, that he might bring his mathematical powers to bear on it. The four have been nearly two hours together at 4 Crown Office Row this afternoon.

*Wednesday April 8ᵗʰ*

John having expressed a wish to bring Mattie to see us, I wrote to her that I should be very glad to see her with him. Mrs Southwell wrote to me expressing her willingness for Mattie to visit us, & it was therefore arranged that John should bring her during his Easter holiday. Last Thursday evening Lottie & Hattie went to meet

---

78  CEB writes 'latter' by mistake.
79  Her mother's residence in Kempston.
80  Arthur Gamgee (1841–1909) was a physician and researcher. Is the 'new motive power' diesel oil or petrol? Edward was to become interested in 'explosion engines', as described in the patent books, in the 1890s.

them, but returned saying they had not arrived, & we had just concluded to wait tea until after the next train when they walked in, John looking very much discomposed that they had not been met. It was soon explained that on account of the number of holiday passengers, the train was obliged to be divided, & they being in the last half of it arrived just at the moment Lottie drove off from the Station without thought of their being able to reach [Bedford] until an hour later.

Mattie was I think rather pleased than otherwise at the rather unceremonious introduction which their sudden appearance occasioned & the apologies & explanations which followed served to set us all at ease with each other at once, so that the ordeal of meeting us was not so formidable as she seemed to have imagined it would be. We soon felt very much at home with her, & very happy to see the satisfaction which she & John have in each other's society. Our impressions are very favorable, & when I say I think we shall love her quite as well as either of our other daughters-in-law, that is saying very much.

Good Friday morning John walked to Elstow Church with Mattie & his Sisters, after dinner he had the Chaise & the former accompanied him for a drive, whilst Papa walked with the girls & myself. The weather was fine but wind very cold; on Saturday morning however notwithstanding it so continued, John took Mattie for a row on the river. After dinner we all started for Warden, Papa, Lottie & Hattie walking forward. We overtook them the other side of Cardington when John walked with Papa, & the girls got into the Chaise. I drove them nearer to Warden & then returned for Papa. Whilst tea was being prepared the young folk walked to see the Church & after tea John drove them home, whilst we returned by train from Southill.

Sunday morning Papa, John, Mattie & myself went to Bromham Rd Chapel & heard Mr Prescott preach an excellent Easter Sunday sermon. At night they went to St Mary's Wesleyan Chapel, praising the singing on their return with Hattie but more amused than impressed by the accompaniments of the worship in its imitation of Church forms beyond even those to which they are accustomed. Flowers on the Communion Table, intoning, Mr Clough leaving the pulpit & coming to the front of the communion rail to receive 'the offertory' & then pronouncing the Benediction at the foot of the pulpit stairs, all most unusual proceedings in a Wesleyan Chapel in these days, but whether there will gradually become High & Low Wesleyanism, as Churchism, remains for the next generation to see. To me it appears more likely that the first will be speedily absorbed in the last.

Monday was an uninviting day out of doors, in the afternoon pouring rain. The morning though cold was fine enough for us to have the Brougham & drive to the Cemetery which Mattie thought very pretty. Hattie visited the grave of her old school-fellow Katie Halahan.

*April 10th*

Mattie has been quite poorly from a swelling in the roof of her mouth, which was really an abscess proceeding from a stopped tooth. I drove to the Dentist's with her on Thursday afternoon & he at once said the tooth must come out, & the sooner the better. As she had before taken gas, & had no fear of its being given again, I was very glad that she at once decided to have it extracted. She certainly was the most brave little woman I ever saw under the circumstances. She settled herself in the chair without the least fuss, folded her hands & sat perfectly still whilst the Dentist with one hand on her pulse, & the other holding the apparatus for administering the gas, over her nose & mouth for a little over a minute, produced unconsciousness, of so short duration, that he had scarcely & most dextrously got the tooth out before she opened her eyes with a smile that betokened pleasure rather than pain, & but for the bleeding, scarcely seemed to show or know that any thing had happened. She did not experience the least effect from the inhalation of the gas, but was much relieved & brighter than she had been for a day or two the rest of the evening.

*April 16th*
On Saturday John came home again to spend Sunday with Mattie who had recovered from the effects of her trouble from her tooth, but looks more delicate than I like to see, & perhaps a little more so than before it. The continued wet & cold prevented the Saturday afternoon drive which we should have had with Papa had the weather been propitious. Mattie drove to the Station to meet John, & highly delighted they seemed, to be with each other again. I think their visit has done very much to strengthen their mutual attachment. John returned on Monday morning, Mattie by noon train yesterday, expressing the pleasure it had given her to be with us, & her willingness to come again. I have promised to visit her at her home when I go to London as I hope to do for some of the May meetings to some of which she will probably go with me.

*Wednesday April 22nd*
The probability of seeing Will had scarcely been thought of, but I was not in the least surprised when he arrived a little before 9 o'clock. It was so long since we had seen him here without his family that it carried us back to his bachelor days much to his Sisters' satisfaction. Sunday morning he went to the little Chapel with Lottie whilst Hattie walked with Papa & myself to Bromham Rd to hear Mr Prescott. After dinner I took the Bible-class which I have recommenced for some weeks past in our BR Room, the number has increased to over a dozen, the most troublesome boys & girls of the neighbourhood it seems to me, but for that very reason those who most need (if possible amidst their levity & thoughtless[ness] which is sometimes almost more than I can bear) to be restrained, & impressed.

    In contrast to this I have had amongst them at his own request a man who has spent the greater part of his life in prison & is now out on ticket of leave after a third conviction. He has had enough to endure in three terms of penal servitude of 5 years each to sober him, & as far as I can judge seems a reformed man. Mr Hammond sent him to our tea on Easter Monday & he came to see me the following morning, showed me his papers & told me all I wished to know of his past course. He had received help in clothes & money from the Prisoners' Aid Society, & only wanted character & work. This latter Heywood has found him for some weeks as a house painter, & has promised to help him to procure the former if he only goes on as he has been doing since he began. To keep him out of the way of temptation of drink which has been the cause of much of his misery I have got Hills to let him lodge in his cottage instead of at the Public House to which he was recommended by the Police. He has put on the Blue Ribbon & shows some signs of change of heart as well as life.

On Sunday evening Papa walked with Will to Kempston to the evening services at 'St John's'. After every one else had gone upstairs but Will & myself, our talk led to one of those fruitless discussions which I have so determined to avoid, & yet find it so difficult to keep from when our conversation turns on religious subjects.[81] All his views & feelings on these seem now in a state of transition, influenced by his latest reading, but only I pray & believe to return to the simplicity of his early faith as he becomes more illumined by the light from above which he assures me he is seeking, & which none shall fail in finding who, distrusting their own unaided reason (which is but groping in darkness) go for it to the only Source of light & life.

*Friday May 29th*

[Meeting of BWTA in the Memorial Hall, London]. Being rather late in rising & breakfast, I did not reach the Hall until after the Council meeting had begun. It was to me anything but a profitable one. The same lady, who last year so pertinaciously endeavoured to alter the constitution of the Association & to introduce voting by proxy according to the number of members which each Delegate represented, carried her point so far as to get it settled that a 3 years' trial of her system should be adopted, & looked very satisfied at the achievement when we broke up for luncheon. But the first proposition that was carried in the afternoon was that a Delegate might be sent for every 100 members instead of for 50 as before, & so her morning's work, which caused a great deal of unpleasant argument, was half undone. I said a few words about 'the settlement of this vexed question' & was requested by the Vice-President Miss Docwra (who conducted the business for Mrs Lucas on account of her deafness) to withdraw the expression, which of course I did, at the same time feeling, with many of the ladies around me, that the term was a correct one, the general feeling being that the discussion was very unprofitable. One matter-of-fact north country lady whispered to me 'all law, & no gospel'.[82]

At the close of the afternoon Council, tea was provided in the Library, after which the annual Public meeting was held in the Great Hall, Dr Richardson occupying the chair. All other speakers were Ladies, & I never felt so proud of my sex as in listening to the speeches of three of them, whose eloquence I have seldom heard surpassed by any male speaker & Dr R predicted that not only would women of such power soon have a right to vote but would stand shoulder to shoulder with men in the House of Commons & exert it as representatives there![83]

After the meeting I returned to S[utherland] Avenue & the following morning Mrs Kelly accompanied me to the Conference which was a public meeting. Many

---

[81] Will disagreed with his mother's fundamental views. He would have met (from his Cambridge days, through his time tutoring the children of Captain Alcock in 1878, to his work as a barrister) a large number of people who would not have shared his mother's staunch evangelicalism nor her disapproval of even moderate drinking. More recently, he had become associated with the Conservative party, and indeed was about to become adopted as a Conservative candidate (see entry for 29 June, below). The Conservative party was associated with the Anglican church, and was supported by the brewing industry, and *vice versa*.

[82] Miss M.E. Docwra was a neighbour of the Bousfields in Bedford, and a prominent member of the BWTA. She was the author of several papers, e.g. 'Women's Work for Temperance during the Victorian Era', a paper read at a WTAU meeting and published as a tract by them in 1897.

[83] The subject of incorporating the wider issues relating to women's role in society was to cause a split in the movement some years later – see entry for Saturday 14 May 1895.

strangers were present, some gentlemen, chiefly American, from their manner of speech. Two Papers were read by two Ladies, the last by Mrs Atherton on 'Homes for Inebriates' a question which was raised at our Autumnal meeting, the question being whether one for women should be supported by our Association. The discussion which followed Mrs A's paper related to the mode, rather than the means of carrying out this idea, & after several had given their suggestions (amongst them Lady Elizabeth Biddulph, the President of the Ledbury Branch), I said it appeared to me useless to propose how a Home should be carried on until we could find the funds, & enquired whether any one was prepared to suggest a scheme by which they might be obtained which we could present to our respective Branches. This led to my being requested by the presiding Lady to draw up a motion to put to the meeting which I did, which was however thought to comprehend too much & as I was not prepared with any other, the proposal to postpone the matter until another year was made, when one earnest woman rose up & begged this might not be done & offered £20 towards a beginning at once. I guaranteed £5, Lady Biddulph the same, Mrs Sutton of Southport £10, & so offer after offer was made & £120 promised. Then Mrs Atherton proposed a Committee should be formed & named Lady B, myself & one or two others as members of it. This was done & we arranged to meet at the BW[TA] Office at 10-30 next morning. Mrs Kelly was among those who volunteered £5.

The afternoon was occupied by a clever paper which Dr Alfred Carpenter read on 'Alcohol as a medicine' at the close of which questions were permitted, which were so many & so varied as to try the patience of the Dr, although he took great trouble to answer them.[84] I left before the close of the meeting to return to Winchmore Hill where Hattie had promised to meet me for tea.[85] Willie Moore & his wife came to supper.

The next morning I left with Hattie, who had to go to her Drawing. I had promised to meet the other members of 'the Home Committee' at 10-30. Lady E Biddulph arrived whilst I was standing at the entrance to the Hall, & we had some talk before going up to the Committee-room. There we found Mrs Lucas & four other ladies, so we were only 7 who met, out of the 14 named. After some discussion Lady B was proposed as Chairwoman of the Committee, an office which she willingly accepted, & then drew up a circular to be sent to each Branch, begging for a reply before the end of first week in July, saying what help might be look[ed] for from each, after receiving which we are to meet again in the same place to see what further steps can be taken. Lady Biddulph is a most charming woman, & from her conversation & manner, I should believe her to be a humble & devoted Christian. Leaving the Memorial Hall, I once more took train & after my day's varied peregrinations reached Bedford at 8.30.

Hattie's & Mattie's visit is sooner than they expected when they were here together at Easter; they are both Exhibitors, as also Lottie, in the Art Exhibition which is now

84 Many doctors, then as now, considered a moderate consumption of alcohol to be beneficial.
85 Winchmore Hill was where Aunt Fanny lived, in Stonard Road. Aunt Fanny was one of Edward's sisters who first married Revd John Moore by whom she had three children, Fanny, Charley and Willie, who, with his wife, joined his mother, sister-in-law and first cousin for supper. Aunt Fanny's second marriage was to Revd Clulow, after whose death she moved to North London. She is sometimes known as Aunt Clulow.

being held in the Assembly Rooms, & were naturally anxious to see it, especially as Hattie has taken the First Prize for Amateur Oil painting for one of three heads from life which she has sent to it. The Judge wished to have given it to the smallest, that of a child, which she marked 'not for competition', because her master had put a few touches in it, & her honesty was rewarded by another of her own taking it, with a most complimentary comparison between her work & the Professional class in the Exhibition. Lottie sent a fire-screen & two prettily painted table tops. Mattie a 'Study of eggs' very nicely done & for which she had taken a prize in a Home Study Society to which she belongs. John was of course glad of any reason or excuse for Mattie's spending the Whitsuntide holiday with him. Monday was a pouring wet day & we could only get to the Exhibition by going in the Brougham just before tea, but I do not think this much interfered with their enjoyment. Lottie was very disappointed we could not have a Picnic, for which she prepared just before the rain began. Papa had to go to London on Tuesday, John also to return, so all went back together by the 8-10 a m train.

*Monday, June 8th*

New work in connection with our BWTA is arising. I had more than once thought we might be able to begin some Temperance work at Elstow, but was surprised to find that our Secretaries & some other Ladies had decided to begin at once, & that at the Committee meeting held whilst I was in London, it was decided to visit from house to house there to invite the women to a tea; about 60 accepted, & half that number joined our Association. At our Committee meeting in Thurlow St last Monday I was asked whether I would begin a Mothers' meeting (for which some of the women seemed anxious) in connection with the Elstow Branch, which held its first Prayer meeting last Wednesday in the School-house on the Green which is granted for our use. About 16 women came to it, Mrs Goldsmith led the meeting. I was asked to attend & speak to them about the M Meeting which all present promised to join. Instead of taking the responsibility of this M meeting I proposed that three others should share it with me; Mrs Goldsmith, Mrs Scott, & our Treasurer Mrs Hutchinson at once consented to do so. The latter had afternoon tea with me to-day, when we made our plans for the first meeting to which we are to go together next Wednesday. I trust we may be made a means of some good to our poorer sisters. Elstow has not the benefit of the residence of a single godly family of influence as far as I know. The Clergyman lives in Bedford, & no other minister of any denomination visits it. The 'Green House', which with the except[ion] of the new roof which was put on it a year ago is as when Bunyan used to play at 'Cat' close to it, is used as a school-room & place of worship on Sundays by members of the Church of which he was the former Pastor, in Bedford, Teachers & Lay Preachers being supplied from it, so that there is room for doing good in a village so large with so few on the spot to care for it.

*June 11th*

To-day I have received another invitation to begin another Branch of BWTA at Goldington. Miss Cook the daughter of the Vicar writes to beg I will go over to-morrow evening for a meeting at 7 o'clock for which she has arranged in the School-room adjoining the Vicarage. I am rather surprised at her request & wish to form another branch of our Association, instead of the CEWU which has just been formed in Bedford & will I fear do harm, not so much to our Association as to the cause of Total Abstinence.[86] One of the Lady Visitors called on a working woman, a member of it & a well known Abstainer, with an invitation to a free tea, & to join 'the Moderate Drinking Society', this invitation has been given to many of our members, to whom the new society seems to be directing its efforts, rather than to those who need them. A Society that would under the garb of Temperance undo the work which has already been accomplished is surely a device of the Adversary, & the consequences hardly realized by those who are promoting it. From whence do all the 'Immoderate' drinkers come if not from amongst those who were once moderate, & never intended to be otherwise?

*Monday June 15ᵗʰ*
The meeting at Goldington was not as far as we could judge by results, a success. I asked our Treasurer Mrs Hutchinson who is a clergyman's widow to accompany me, called for her, & [arrived] together in time for the meeting [at] 7 o'clock. Some thirty women of the village, two or three farmers' wives with the Vicar's wife & daughter, were assembled in the School-room adjoining the Vicarage. After singing, reading & prayer, I told them the object of our visit, & endeavoured to persuade them to assist Miss Cook in carrying out her desire. Mrs H very much pleased & surprised me by giving an address that was truly 'gospel temperance'. I did not think she would have been able or willing to do as she did, & was truly glad she consented to accompany me. The ground on which we strove to sow the seed seemed however very stony, & very little prepared in any way to receive it. Scarcely a single Mother present was an Abstainer, only one signified willingness to become such; a few promised to think about it, but the greater number were evidently unwilling either for their own sakes or their children's to give up what they liked, some of them I was told, too well.

Our poor neighbour Hulett who has been a great sufferer for months died on Saturday. I visited him a day or two before I went to London the beginning of May when he received me very ungraciously telling me I had sought the interview, & not he. I thought him very near his end then, but finding he was still living when I returned at the end of a week, I went again with great reluctance feeling my visit would be unwelcome. It was scarcely more pleasant to me than the former one. I felt both speaking to, & prayer with him a great difficulty, & met with no response that in the least encouraged me except 'amen' after the latter. He spoke of himself as 'a thinking man' & there was evidently a pride of intellect that was unsubdued & I feared uninfluenced by anything I could say to show him his need of forgiveness for the past & his only hope for the future.

A few days after, the door bell was rung between 4 & 5 o'clock in the morning by a woman who had been sitting up with him, who came to beg that Papa would go to see him. This he did at once & found that he had during the night been wishing to see him, it seemed to be to tell him of his unbelief, & disquietude of mind, & to use his own words, that he had 'been looking too much to God the Father' apart from

[86] The Church of England Women's Union is perhaps connected with the CETS (Church of England Temperance Society) – see entry for 13 June 1884.

Him who said 'I am the Way' 'No man cometh unto the Father but by me'. I felt very thankful when Papa told me this, feeling it was the first token of the humbling of the proud self-sufficiency which had prevented his acceptance of Christ. When I went to enquire after him during the day I was told he wished to see me if I called. I said to him 'I think Hulett we can understand now why God has permitted you to live on in suffering so long', at once he assented, & when I had repeated through to him 'Just as I am without one plea, But that Thy blood was shed for me' & asked him whether his heart followed those words as I repeated them, he replied 'I can follow them in every word'. Then I thanked God for His great mercy, & was going to leave when he kept me to say with great difficulty that he wanted to tell me 'honestly' that if I had not persisted in coming to see him, he should never in all probability have been led to see as then [he] was able to do, & that he could only wonder at the great change he felt in such a short time.

My heart was full of thankfulness that I had been enabled to point out the way of Salvation to one who seemed so unwilling & unlikely to receive the message which I do not doubt I was sent to offer, by Him who 'came to seek & to save that which is lost'. The last night of his life his mind frequently wandered, but even amidst this seemed to be fixed on the 'Lord Jesus' on whom he called for help & release; during the two hours I was with him his sufferings were very great, but subsided before I left, about 1 am, he passed away quietly at 2 pm.

*June 20th*

Father & Grandma's visit came to a close yesterday, soon after dinner Lottie & I drove with them to Warden on Thursday, Papa coming by train to Southill Station where I met him & walk[ed] with him through the fields whilst Lottie drove on & ordered tea in the Arbour, which all greatly enjoyed. Father's visit is much shorter than usual as he quite made up his mind to return for the Handel Festival at the Crystal Palace, but it has been merry if short, he & Lottie have joked & laughed with as much glee as if they had both been the same age. His spirits & strength are surprising. A slight bilious attack made him poorly & very quiet for a day, but soon passed off.

He has taken a keen interest in the political changes of the last few days. Mr Gladstone's ministry has resigned, the Marquis of Salisbury is forming what he believes will be a very short-lived Cabinet![87] When he went into the town to the Prayer-meeting at Bunyan Chapel on Monday night, he came back with the intelligence given him by Mr Brown of having seen in that day's 'Daily News' that Mr WR Bousfield, Barrister-at-Law, was to be the Conservative Candidate for Falmouth at the next Election. This is all we know, not having heard a word on the subject from Will. Papa has to-day gone to London to stay over Sunday & will most likely spend to-night at Cricklewood & hear how far the rumour is true. Hattie is to meet him this afternoon at the Academy.

---

[87] CEB was right: Lord Salisbury's first government took office in June 1885, but was defeated at the General Election which returned Gladstone to power in February 1886 with a programme of Home Rule for Ireland. She was right also about the unpopularity of Gladstone's foreign policy, and about the strength of Liberalism, then as now, in the Celtic fringe areas – the West country and Wales. CEB is disappointed that her eldest son is linked with the Conservatives rather than with the Liberals, where the interests and concerns of non-conformity are strongly represented and supported.

Mrs Goldsmith went with me to see a poor woman in her District of whom I was told yesterday at Thurlow St M Meeting & went to see afterward to take to her the voluntary contributions of the women present. She had been a member of the Meeting. One of the Mothers passed up a letter which she wrote herself stating the poor sick woman's need, which I read aloud just as they were dispersing, & instantly pence were passed up the table until there was a little heap of 23 to which I added 1/- & so had 3/- to carry to her. I found her much worse than I expected, scarcely able to speak or move, & yet on a couch downstairs with two little children & two boys, the only ones near to give her any help. The usual tale, a drunken Husband, void of love or sympathy; I did not see him, but fearing she would die in this state I sent a woman to her whose services he would not let her accept, but this morning I was thankful to find a daughter had returned from service in London & was with her. Truly 'the tender mercies of the wicked are cruel' but the spontaneous help so readily given by the Mothers was truly gratifying.

*June 23rd*
Will's name has been mentioned in political circles in connection with Falmouth, as I imagined through the influence of his friend Mr Kelland of Kelland Hall, which is I know somewhere down West. He tells Papa that he has little expectation of getting into the next Parliament, but thinks it well to allow his name to become known, also that he has received a communication from the Carlton Club intimating that it would be better to allow himself to be nominated for a London constituency than one so distant, & I think they might have added, unlikely, for Liberal interest seems to be strongest there. Will's Conservative notions are not I believe very pronounced & he says his political views have not changed, but in common with many others who admire much in Mr Gladstone, he does not agree with his foreign policy. From the Zulu war, to the occupation of the Soudan, it seems to me the Liberal Government has committed a series of blunders, & spent an immense amount without gain or glory to this Country, & little benefit to those they went to succour; but to identify himself with the Conservatives, instead of going in as an independent man, is I think a mistake on Will's part. In this as in all beside I trust his own honor or advancement may not be the first consideration. The great want of our Government is God-fearing Legislators be they Whig or Tory.

*Tuesday July 7th*
Political events have not much to do with those recorded here but I cannot (after the last sentence written) help expressing my gratification at those which took place in the House of Commons last night. Mr Bradlaugh, the notorious atheistic would-be member for Northampton, presented himself for the third time at the table of the House to be sworn in, & for the third time was sent back. Sir M Hicks-Beach the new Leader of the Government taking the same ground the Conservatives have always acted on, that a man who had no belief in a Supreme Being was not competent to take the Oath or to be a member of the House if he so declared himself. I am thankful that amidst so much that is evil in this country of ours, the spectacle is presented to the almost infidel government of France & the world of the rejection by the majority of our own of the man whose shameless flaunting of his infidelity has brought on himself its own punishment.

*Saturday July 10th*

I have not had leisure this week to chronicle my own occupations. It has been a busy one when I have been out of my home although still so quiet in it. A committee meeting, M Meeting or some other has taken me out each day until to-day; this afternoon I have been with Papa to L&NW Station to see him off for Southport on his way to the Royal Show which he is once more going to attend, this time at Preston, I almost hope for the last time in his present capacity. He is growing more & more weary of the annoyances rather than occupations of the B Works, & I shall be thankful for him to have done with them. I believe wear rather than work has a good deal to do with his frequent complaining of want of elasticity & power, & his health generally. I am glad for him to have his evenings near the sea as he will have this next week, intending as he does to spend his nights at Aunt Jenny's.

On Wednesday our BWTA picnic was held at Sharnbrook. The women complained so much of the distance to Pavenham last year that we asked Mr Stillman-Gibbard to allow us to meet in his Park which he did most cordially. I engaged the Special-train more than a week ago & nearly 200 members availed themselves of it; in addition the Harrold Branch asked to be allowed to join us, & I undertook to provide their tea with ours at a fixed charge per head. The day was a very uncertain looking one, & the rain came down sharply for a few minutes after I left home with one of the maids to go forward & see that all was right, which I did by driving within two miles of the village & then walking. Everything was to be obtained on the spot & I found all arranged in a great empty Barn, which was to be our refuge in case of rain. This was not needed fortunately for anything but our preparations & in it piles of cake & bread & butter were soon ready.

The train arrived in bright sunshine which made all glad to take advantage of the forms & seats which they carried whither they would into the shade, & rested after their walk of less than a mile. I asked Mrs Gibbard to let us have her harmonium on the lawn that we might keep them in good time until tea was ready, with singing. They heartily joined until the business of tea drinking was to begin when each produced the cup & saucer they were requested to bring with them, & as soon as we could get them into rows the piles of cake & gallons of tea were served & vanished with marvellous rapidity. Then those who had taken tea were requested to wander as they would, whilst we who had been waiting on them refreshed ourselves in like manner; after which at Mrs Gibbard's special request we went into the house to partake of strawberries.

All assembled again in an hour, when after singing & prayer first Mr S-Gibbard & then his Father General Stillman, gave most earnest Gospel Temperance addresses. After the latter Mr G asked me whether they had not had enough, without anything more from another gentleman from Harrold who was present & ready to speak to them; I told him he had better put it to the women for them to decide, which he did, & all hands were held up; so after another short address more singing & thanks to Mr & Mrs Gibbard, all dispersed for another ramble, & then finally assembled & started for the Station, after what seemed to have been a time of great delight to every one. I heard nothing but approbation & expressions of pleasure on all sides, & felt very happy to have assisted in giving so many who have so little opportunity of pleasure, enjoyment, & I hope profit also.

*Friday July 17th*

After seeing Papa off for Southport last Saturday I drove through the town to settle sundry matters relating to our BWTA fête, as well as those which I thought necessary before leaving home, then returned to tea alone after which I had letters to write ready for Monday morning post. One to Harrold to decline an invitation to meet some of the BWTA members, who could not join us at Sharnbrook, the following Thursday at Miss St Quintin's. The evening was so warm that I was glad to sit in the garden to write. Whilst so doing the Student who was appointed to preach here on Sunday arrived. Just before the evening closed I asked him to accompany me to Elstow to take some articles ordered by the women of the new Mothers' meeting, the previous Thursday. This he willingly consented to do & after calling on Mrs Smith (a very respectable woman who is very much interested in our meeting & takes charge of the work) & hearing from her the character of a new member at the last meeting, who she told me was a dram-drinker, we walked across Elstow Green to call on the woman & look at her garden of which I had heard she was very proud. Her Husband is under-gardener to the chief man in the village. We found both at home, & after a little chat about the garden & buying a few plants I managed to say a few words of encouragement which the poor woman much needed both on account of the craving which she at times felt, & from the opposition she was meeting from her Husband & his Mother for having signed the pledge. The former I believe was so far conciliated by our visit that he will not continue this. She has been to see me this evening & tells me that 'no one knows what she has been suffering' since she gave up the drink, but that she is just getting over it, & has induced two or three other women to become members of the M Meeting, of which all must be Total Abstainers as they know. These were present last week when Lottie took the meeting in my absence as Mrs Goldsmith was unable to attend & requested I would take her place. She did not know whose influence had induced them to attend & until this evening I had little thought that so soon a worker would be raised up, herself only just rescued from the snare. May she have strength given to continue faithful.

I reached home to-day just before dinner, & afterwards went to the Thurlow St meeting as usual. I found a number of women there before me, & a conversation going on about a woman of the neighbourhood who, with a babe a fortnight old, had been drinking for days past, & her Husband formerly a Teetotaller, doing the same out of spite. I stopped further remark, but was told the man wished I would call. When the meeting was over I took a couple of pledge cards, & with Lottie who came to me, went to No 10 Greenhill St. Such a scene of squalor & misery I scarcely before ever met with. A tall man, wandering with his arms folded, amidst a crowd of 5 tiny miserable looking children. The wife in the midst looking as miserable as her Husband, or worse, for she had a black eye; a poor babe covered up in the corner; dirt & disorder reigning. The utter degradation & starvation to which they were reduced seem to have aroused some desire to escape from the awful cause in both Husband & wife & after talking with them I had the satisfaction of getting them to sign the pledge, with evident desire to keep it.

*Tuesday July 21ˢᵗ*

[CEB is staying with her step-mother in London to visit the Grand Annual Temperance Fete. 'Grandmama Collins' lives at Penrith House, close to the Crystal Palace, where the Fete is being held.]

Next morning we all had a walk together passing, & going into a Church, very High in a two fold sense. So tall that it is cracking down the side wall & only kept secure by props outside (Grandpa says it will soon be dis-established!) within, crucifix, altars & candles. A side altar in a corner especially provoked some remarks as to the efforts that were being made to bring back the very things for which our forefathers suffered martyrdom, which were overheard by one of two individuals, walking about & I suppose admiring, & led to a small controversy, from her choosing to make a reply. My anger is kindled when I see these imitations of Rome & I wonder whether the time will come that we shall need another Reformation. I did not intend to write a word of this, but it is written.

After early dinner Hattie & I left Penrith House going together as far as Farringdon St where I left her to proceed to Cricklewood alone, whilst I went to the Memorial Hall to attend the Committee meeting with reference to the proposed BWTA Home for Inebriates. Lady Elizabeth Biddulph presided, Mrs Lucas, & four others beside myself being present. The promises of support from the Branches were not so large as we had hoped they would have been, but were considered sufficient to warrant a beginning. I left before the end of the Committee meeting which lasted more than two hours, & was adjourned.

John left the City by an earlier train than usual & I with him, to dinner after which, it being Wednesday, the night on which he always goes to see Mattie, he left, & Hattie accompanied me to Will's; we found him in the garden, & sat down in the arbour with him whilst he smoked. Presently he fetched rugs & wraps & brought candles & we spent the whole evening there talking a good deal about his new position & intentions in coming out as a politician. He has been invited by Mr Houldsworth,[88] one of the present MPs for Manchester, under the cover of advocating Lord F Hamilton's candidature of one of the Divisions, to let himself be heard & seen in that city, in which as a Whitworth Scholar & as such, having been for a time in Sir Joseph Whitworth's Works there after he left College, he is supposed to have some interest. He has consented to address a meeting in moving a resolution, but would not be the one Speaker of the evening as was requested. He seemed to know what he was going to say to the people. I tried to make him see the Temperance question was one which ought to be legislated on, but he says both drunkards & teetotallers are in the minority, that the majority is made up of moderate drinkers, considers Local Option does not deal with the vested interest of the Publican![89] & evidently he must

[88] Sir William Houldsworth (1834–1917) was a Manchester cotton industrialist. His development of mills in Stockport included houses and amenities for his workers. He was Conservative MP for Manchester, and involved in the Church of England Temperance Society.
[89] Many areas were over supplied with liquor licences, and there was support for their reduction, as one way of reducing drunkenness. The local option was one way of achieving this: a licence would be granted to the inhabitants of a district to undertake it. CEB would dearly like to be able to persuade Will to exercise the influence he will be able to exert as an MP.

be further educated before he sees & feels the necessity of throwing the weight of his influence in public & private against our country's deadliest foe.

After our political chat which lasted until 11 o'clock, I just spoke to Florence (who had been spending the evening at her Mother's) & returned with Hattie & John who joined us an hour earlier. It is very pleasant to be able to move about amongst my children, & know more of their movements than I could do but for my frequent visits to them.

### Wednesday August 5th

Bank Holiday was a very pleasant day with us. Since last Wednesday Lottie has had a Swiss girl whom Mrs Carter introduced to us staying with her, & as Mlle speaks very little English she has been very glad to rub up her French & was therefore quite sorry that Mrs C was not willing to spare her longer than Monday morning when we drove her to St Peter's Green after breakfast, & thence ourselves to the L&NW Station where Papa met us, & accompanied us by train to Woburn Station. A notice in the Bedford Paper that Woburn Abbey & Grounds would be open to Visitors induced us to take the journey. At the Station we [joined a] crowd attracted like ourselves [to visit the Abbey], & by the fine day also. By keeping behind these on leaving the train, & turning out of the high road into the woods at the first possible entrance, we managed to keep almost as clear of the stream of excursionists as if we had not come with them, & were charmed beyond all expectation to find ourselves all at once in the midst of splendid woods intersected by wide footpaths (under canopies & avenues of trees) so numerous that but for slight barriers of branches placed across some of them, we should easily have lost our way.

After luncheon near Shepherd's Cottage, where we could procure water, we walked onwards in the direction of the town, where we were glad to hire a dog-cart, the distance thence to the Abbey being greater than we expected. Lottie was very much impressed with the grandeur of the grounds, the Sculpture Gallery (which being under repairs we could only see through the windows), & the exterior of the Mansion, & thought to be a Duke & owner of so much magnificence was almost overwhelming!

After wandering in the lovely gardens some time we made our way back by a shorter path across the Park, & were fortunate in meeting with the same driver & conveyance just as we reached the outer part of it called 'The Evergreens' as it truly is; a broad stretch of grass on each side of the roadway planted entirely with all kinds of evergreen trees, & reaching almost into the town. We drove as far as the end of this & then again left the high way for the woods & the cottage where we had left our baskets. Here we procured more milk, & a bottle of water, & wandered on until we came to a lovely secluded spot where I lay down on the bank whilst Lottie & Papa got the little spirit kettle at work again, & after a very refreshing rest & tea, we were quite ready to walk on to the Station & reached Bedford about 7 o'clock.

### Monday August 10th

On Saturday morning Mrs Ransom called to see me, & to tell me that Mr Brown the Pastor of Bunyan Meeting had suggested to her that she should, with some others who might be interested in the work, hold a series of meetings in the town & neighbouring villages for the wives of working-men to enlighten them as to the great danger of being tempted, by offers of high wages in advertisements, to send their daughters to London & other large places without further knowledge of those to whom they entrusted them. Recent revelations in the 'Pall Mall Gazette' have stirred the whole community to care for the young girls who in ignorance & innocence leave their country homes, often to become the prey of infamous men & women.[90] The extent to which their hideous business is carried on, & startling details connected with it, have been brought to light by a 'Secret Commission' instituted by the 'Pall Mall' & the facts that have been elicited, & verified by such men as the Archbishop of Canterbury,[91] Samuel Morley MP,[92] & others of equal integrity & influence can neither be doubted nor denied. Mrs R's visit was to ask my co-operation in carrying out the meetings, this I could only readily promise. In the afternoon we called together on Mrs Walters, a lady who has just come to the town & is said to be greatly interested in all social matters. We found her to be more fully informed than ourselves on the subject we had under consideration & a friend of Mrs Josephine Butler,[93] who has for years been working for the better protection of young girls. Mrs W appeared to be very glad to make our acquaintance & readily gave her consent to assist in any way she could in holding a meeting.

*Monday August 24th*

Arriving at the Station by the noon train from St Pancras on Saturday I called on Mrs Ransom before returning home, & finally arranged with her about our first Women's meeting which we held the following Monday at the Grey Friars BR Room. As we had not sufficiently published it the attendance was not so large as it would have been if it had been more widely known. About 80 were present & these Mrs Ransom & Mrs Walters addressed, the latter reading her address & giving an account of the political events which had led to the 'Secret Commission' which has resulted in a Bill 'for the Protection of Young Girls' (which had been thrice during the past two years blocked or rejected by the Commons, after being sent down to them by the Lords) being passed by the Parliament which has just closed, at the very end of the session, & which would certainly not have become law but for the excitement & outcry caused by 'the Pall Mall Revelations'. I said a few words before & after Mrs R's address. Many of the women were entirely ignorant of the systematic efforts which are being made to entrap their daughters, & I believe the effort to enlighten & warn them will prove a great benefit to many. This is the first of a series of meetings which we have undertaken to hold in the town & neighbouring

---

[90]  The journalist W.T. Stead ran a campaign in his journal, the *Pall Mall Gazette*, against vice in London, in which he highlighted the prevalence of child prostitution and the ease with which young girls could be procured. He did this by buying a 13-year-old girl for £5, with whom he showed he could have had intercourse, and published the whole story. Stead's brand of sensational journalism had the effect of raising the age of consent from 13 to 16, as it is today, by the Criminal Law Amendment Act of 1885.

[91]  Edward Benson held this office from 1882 until his death in 1896. He is best remembered for initiating the Service of Nine Lessons and Carols which was first held in Truro where he was Bishop in 1880.

[92]  Samuel Morley was a wealthy textile manufacturer from Nottingham. He was a Liberal and a nonconformist, a munificent philanthropist and an enthusiastic promoter of the temperance movement. He died in 1886.

[93]  Josephine Butler was an active feminist and a passionate Christian, concerned particularly with the welfare of prostitutes, and led the campaign for the repeal of the Contagious Diseases Acts which was successful in 1886. She died in 1906.

villages, all as preliminary to a larger one in the Corn Exchange, when a Committee can be formed.

Whilst I was in London last week Lottie took the M Meetings at Elstow & Thurlow St; the women always seem very pleased to have her, & from all I hear she conducts them very nicely. At the M Meeting here last week the women told me a sad tale of the disorder & annoyance caused by two or three families in our neighbourhood, much of it occasioned by the dreadful drink traffic especially at Southend Hotel, & on Sunday mornings. I called on the Landlady as I returned from Elstow on Thursday, & told her what I heard of the sale of drink in her house in prohibited hours. On the whole she was as civil as I expected & although denying the reports will I think take heed to my warning of the consequences she might expect if she continued to break the law. To make her see the sin & misery her wretched trade brought on many families around was more than I expected, or succeeded in doing, or at least to acknowledge it.

A second visit to Town only five days after the last I did not in the least contemplate until receiving a letter from Mrs Ransom in which she enclosed a cutting from the 'Pall Mall Gazette' in reference to what is now called 'the New Crusade' containing also notices respecting Conferences to be held in St James's Hall, & a great Demonstration in Hyde Park, on the following Friday & Saturday. When I thought the matter over I felt that to be really useful in the cause in which I had promised to co-operate, I must know more of it, & so determined with Papa's consent to go to London for these meetings which I did after tea Thursday night arriving in time to have a chat with Will & Florence before going to John's lodgings for the night.

The previous day I had written to the Secretary of the Ladies National Association[94] for two tickets of admission to St James's Hall,[95] & to engage two seats in a Brake in Saturday's procession. The former I found awaiting me in a letter at Westbury Villa with an intimation that seats would be reserved for me in a carriage starting from Endsleigh Gardens Euston Square at 3 o'clock on Saturday. Florence was quite willing to be my companion the following morning, & we left Cricklewood by the Omnibus to Brondesbury, thence by train to Baker St, & by taking a Hansom managed to reach the Hall a quarter of an hour before the time of meeting 11 o'clock. Mrs Lucas's was the first face that I saw & knew, & she made room for us next to herself in a very good position near the front of the platform or rather Orchestra, which was soon occupied by men & women whose names are known & reverenced as Social Benefactors. Mr Stansfeld MP,[96] who we heard had sacrificed a seat in the Cabinet for his determined opposition to the Government legalization

94  The Ladies National Association for the Repeal of the Contagious Diseases Acts. This legislation was intended to control prostitution and the venereal diseases that accompanied it. Any woman suspected of being a prostitute could be stopped and forced to undergo a genital examination to discover if she had such a disease. If she was found to be infected she could be effectively imprisoned.

95  St James's Hall was a large concert hall, seating 2500, fronting Regent Street and Piccadilly. It was demolished in 1905.

96  Rt Hon. Sir James Stansfeld (1820–1898) was a barrister, and Radical MP for Halifax from 1859 to 1895. He was selected by Giuseppe Garibaldi as his adviser when the Italian patriot visited England in 1862, inspecting the Britannia Iron Works. In 1871, Stansfeld became the first president of the local government board. The remainder of his life was mainly spent in endeavouring to secure the repeal of the Contagious Diseases Acts, and in 1886 this object was attained.

of Vice in the Contagious Diseases Act, Miss Ellice Hopkins who has for years written & worked in other ways for the prevention of & rescue from vice of her poorer Sisters, Dr Butler, now Dean of somewhere, late Head Master of Rugby School,[97] Revd Webb-Peploe, Hugh Price Hughes,[98] & many others, not forgetting the Chairman Mr George Russell MP,[99] a truly noble man physically & mentally.

But I might write on & on of all that was said & done on that memorable day. The chief work was to form a 'National Vigilance Committee' to see that the newly passed Law was not a dead letter, & that its provisions should be as strenuously enforced as possible. The speeches of Mr Stead the Editor of the 'Pall Mall', a short one in the morning & a longer at the Public meeting at night, were the greatest excitements of the day. The amount of abuse that has been heaped upon him on one side, & of praise on the other, has perhaps scarcely been bestowed on any living individual in this country, but the enthusiastic reception his rising to speak (most [of] the audience standing up & waving handkerchiefs) proclaimed the feeling of those present. He was the last Speaker at night, & it was only by leaving before the end of his speech, about half past 10 o'clock, that I managed by taking a Hansom outside the Hall & driving to the top [of] Regent St to catch the last Omnibus to Cricklewood which I reached just at midnight.

About 2 o'clock I left Westbury Villa & made my way to No 11 Endsleigh Gardens, Euston Square & found this to be the house of Mr Percy Bunting. Here assembled many ladies & gentlemen, chiefly the former, who from this point intended to take part in the Demonstration & Procession to Hyde Park. How many brakes & carriages started from this point I cannot say, but a large number, & these joined a long train of others awaiting the assembling of the various contingents from all parts of London on the Thames Embankment. I was seated in a Brake I should suppose near the centre of the Procession; it was only when turning some corner at which I could look backwards as well as forwards at the long line of carriages, banners & foot passengers stretching in both directions as far as I could see that I could get an idea of its length; & a better one far can be formed from the fact that it took more than an hour to pass through the Park Gates. A dozen Brakes formed as many platforms, placed at sufficient distances from the various Speakers at each, not to interrupt the other; & around these were assembled crowds of for the most part decently dressed working men, marvellously enthusiastic & orderly. The numbers in the Park were variously computed at 70-000, 100-000 [sic], & even double that number. Such a sight I had never witnessed & if the sympathy of the people with those who had organized this mighty Demonstration against the social crime of our great cities might be judged of by the ringing cheers from platform after platform as far away in the sea of humanity as I could see & hear as I stood on the seat of the carriage in which I rode, it was indeed a grand protest against it.

I question whether Mr Stead the Editor of the 'Pall Mall Gazette' has been entirely

---

[97] CEB is probably referring to Josephine Butler's husband, who was Headmaster of Liverpool College and Canon of Winchester Cathedral.
[98] Hugh Price Hughes (1847–1902) was Superintendent of the West London Methodist Mission, founder of the *Methodist Times*, and first President of the National Free Church Council.
[99] Sir George Russell (he had inherited a Baronetcy in 1883) was Conservative MP for Wokingham in 1885.

wise in some of the means he has used to discover the depths of the iniquity which he has revealed; but that the country has been so stirred, & a 'New Crusade' set on foot is proof that good men & women are not so scarce as abounding iniquity would lead one to fear; & that evil-doers will not sin unnoticed & unpunished.

The great Gathering dispersed at the end of about an hour & half without the least disorder or mobbing of any kind. The faces that betokened derision were those we saw looking out of the windows of the great Club Houses in Pall Mall & the streets through which we passed where these chiefly are.

*Tuesday Sept' 8th*

The time is now drawing very near for Papa's holiday & rest, of which lately I have also felt need. Sundays as well as week days have been more than usually occupied. With the help of Charles Barns, & Mr Smith (a good man who has for years past been accustomed to go into the Lodging-houses in All Hallows Lane), I have invited the Tramps who resort to these to come to the Thurlow St BR Room for a cup of tea & a cake that we might take the opportunity of talking with & to them. The last three Sundays we have had from twenty to thirty, men & women, chiefly the former, assembled soon after 4 o'clock, thankfully accept what we could give them to eat & drink & listen (some of them with tears) whilst they were told of His love who 'not having where to lay His head' on earth could sympathize with them in their wanderings. Continually is the same story told 'drink brought us to this'.

Last Sunday we had a most sad confirmation of this. Almost immediately after I went into the room a shabby gentleman about fifty years of age put into my hand a piece of paper on which was written the name of a celebrated Wesleyan minister, an MA of Cambridge (who was the Super of that Circuit when Will was at Caius College) & underneath his own; he told me the first name was that of his Brother; that having had misfortune in business he had given way to drink, lost one situation after another, until, entirely destitute, he was making his way by walking & almost barefooted from Birmingham to London where his Brother then lived. He seemed truly penitent, signed the pledge, & with many promises of reformation, & thanks for advice, a little help & a coat & pair of old boots of Papa's, went on his way after calling Monday morning for these. I wrote to his Brother (who deeply feels the disgrace of having such an one) found his tale was a true one, & having sent him with a note to Mr Rae the Secretary of the Gospel Temperance Mission at Hoxton Hall, am hoping that he may be able, if his penitence be sincere, to give him further help towards leading a new life. In his reply to my letter, Mr S told me of another brother also who was a trial to him. I wonder whether the Mother of those men trained them in the 'moderation' with which all drunkenness begins? If one escaped, it is a rock upon which thousands make shipwreck, & I mean to continue to call (louder if I can) to those who advocate it 'Breakers ahead'.

Every body nearly has been away from Bedford for some weeks past with their children during holidays, so the M Meetings have almost entirely fallen on me. The country meetings for Women which Mrs Ransom has asked me to assist her in, one at Kempston & another at Wotton, were very interesting meetings to us both. Mrs Sampson has lately returned to Bedford after a long absence, & willingly accompanied me to speak to the women of Elstow last Thursday; at each of the village gatherings about 40 have been present, & appear fully to appreciate our efforts to point out to them some of their children's dangers, & the way to prevent falling into these. We hope to hold a much larger meeting in Bedford after a few weeks.

Yesterday was my Southend Mothers' tea, last year I did not give them one, & to save trouble took them with the Women of Thurlow St to the BWTA picnic, but they have for so many years been accustomed to come to the house that nothing else satisfies them. So this year by removing the middle vase in the Conservatory & putting tables the entire length of that & the Breakfast-room, we managed to seat 44 beside a lot of babies. Kate Gedye, who has been staying with us, helped Lottie & Hattie to entertain them with music & singing after it became too dark for them to play tennis, croquet etc in the garden & field; one of them made quite a nice little speech of thanks to me before they left, & said some things which gave me both encouragement and pleasure. These records of teas are not very interesting, but it is only possible in some cases to be useful to others by mixing a good deal of sympathy & pleasure of this mild kind with efforts for their spiritual good. I know that is the chief aim I have in view, & thank God that now & then He permits me to have proof that that end is answered.

*Thursday Sept<sup>r</sup> 17<sup>th</sup>*

The District meeting being held in Bedford this quarter, two of the ministers came here to dine on Tuesday. One of them a Mr Ward strangely enough told us he had a Brother in practice as a medical man in the Old Kent Rd. As soon as the ministers were gone I drove with Aunt Jenny to Kempston. Mrs Ransom wrote asking me 'to keep her in countenance' by accompanying her to the laying of a foundation stone of a new Temperance Hall which she laid at 2-30 p m. I was not able to go so early, but met her at Kempston where we had tea with her & other Temperance friends in the village School-room. The people there imagine they are building a place in which they will continue to work un-denominationally, but now under the auspices of the Church of England Temperance Society! I fancy the dissenters who have contributed with this idea, & who are in the majority, will find their mistake before long. Mrs R gave £10, I promised a subscription if they could assure me that all the Temperance Societies would have equal right to use it, this they have not yet done.

*Friday Oct<sup>r</sup> 16<sup>th</sup>*

Lottie & Hattie reached home Tuesday night after a very pleasant visit to Bessie & Kate Gedye. On Monday they managed to call on most of Lottie's former friends & seem to have enjoyed it immensely. Lottie had complained of not feeling well when I saw her at Cotham Chapel on the Sunday night, & of soreness in her mouth as soon as she returned on Tuesday, & this so increased, with feverishness the next two days, that instead of having her help, I had to leave her in Hattie's charge whilst I was as busy as I could be Friday morning, first at the Bedford Rooms where men were fixing the tables, & then to the Station to meet Mrs Pearson, our chief Speaker, who I was very glad to find was willing to be left quiet here whilst I went back to the B Rooms where I found a number of principally young ladies busily preparing for afternoon tea after the Drawing-room meeting. Mrs Goldsmith, Mrs Scott & some others helped me to lay the Women's tables. Plants were sent from several Conservatories, & the inner room made quite pretty with these, which were brought out for the tables & platform after the first meeting.

Mrs Pearson spoke very well as far as what she intended to say went, but she had a critical audience, & I was rather mortified at some slight provincialisms & inaccuracies in speaking which I saw were sufficient to raise a titter where she intended to be impressive. The women trooped in capitally for the tea & evening meeting. It was a sight worth seeing, that gathering of chiefly wives & mothers, in whose hands was the training for good or evil of little less than a thousand of the children of this town. Considerably over 200 sat down to tea & many others & some men came to the after meeting, at which Mrs Pearson again spoke, much to their delight as their clapping, & approving countenances showed. Dr Goldsmith spoke as I hope he will act, but we have had so much to contend with from Dr's orders, that even in his presence when it came to my turn to say a few words, I entreated the women to be brave 'British women' & tell the Drs if they would insist on their 'taking a little' to insist on having it sent in doses that would neither bring back their longing, nor give them uncertain quantities, & to resist as far [as] possible the use of alcohol. I was surprised when the report was read to find that our number of members had increased to about 340. Surely an influence for present & future good must be silently working in the homes represented.

*Friday Oct*^r *23*^rd
A new friend, Mrs Clark, with whom I have become acquainted in our BW[TA] work, came here yesterday to go to the Elstow M Meeting with me, to become acquainted with the women. She has undertaken to be the Elstow visitor. After calling together at several houses in the village she returned with me to tea, & afterwards walked with me to the meeting at GF Walk, on the way telling me a sad history of the sorrows of her domestic life; but she seems determined to live to & work for God, although she has little but opposition in her home. She has undertaken to go to talk with the tramps next Sunday when I am away. Charles Barns delights in helping & the new Missionary also, but the words of a woman seem specially to touch the hearts & cases of many of them. Oh how I wish I could afford to build a night refuge for some of these poor wanderers, their tale of what they have to undergo if they ask for shelter at the Casual Ward is such that I do not wonder they prefer to sleep night after night out of doors rather than endure it.[100]

*Thursday Nov*^r *19*^th
Politics is now the engrossing topic.[101] Last week I went with Mrs Ransom to hear

---

[100] The casual ward was the part of the workhouse used for temporary accommodation for one or two nights for vagrants. By the 1870s most able-bodied men and women vagrants who were capable of work used the casual ward system. They lived in crowded cells, slept often on the bare floor and were given tasks to do to pay for their keep, including picking oakum (often using a spike as a tool) and stone breaking.

[101] This is not surprising, as the contentious issue of Home Rule for Ireland was in the balance, and both parties were angling for the support of the Irish MPs, whose votes in the Commons in June had led to Gladstone's defeat and resignation. On 21 November, two days before polling for the General Election was to start, Parnell the Irish leader, issued a manifesto urging the Irish to support the Conservatives. Nonetheless, other reasons led to a Liberal victory with a majority of 86 seats over the Conservatives, exactly the same as the number of seats gained by the Irish Home Rule MPs. But, behind the scenes, Gladstone had in August become convinced of the rightness of giving Home Rule to the Irish, and it was not until the middle of December that his conversion became known, and the Irish MPs turned to the Liberals. Not only this, but Joseph Chamberlain, President of the Board of Trade, had campaigned in

Mr Whitbread address the Electors in the Corn Exchange. Mr Ransom had the previous day been chosen as Mayor. He accompanied us in the carriage as far as the door, where after showing us the way to the Ladies Platform he left us.[102] Here Mrs Walters joined us. We listened for Mr Whitbread's reply to the questions in which we were chiefly interested.[103] He referred to the BWTA letter, but if what we could not hear, from the continual disturbance, was as unsatisfactory as that which reached us, we can have as little hope from him as might be expected from one so closely connected with the brewing interest. The Liberals seem satisfied with every thing Mr Whitbread says, Teetotallers, & Liberationists alike,[104] although he avowed himself entirely opposed to Disestablishment,[105] & thought the closing of Public Houses would lead to 'greater evils'.

The Conservative Candidate on the other hand seems willing to promise anything to get in. Mrs Walters went with me to hear him speak & answer the questions proposed to him, on Tuesday night; but from first to last the meeting was most disorderly. Neither the Chairman nor the principal speakers seemed to have any idea of putting the rough element in it into good temper, & took advantage of the lucid intervals rather to declaim against the other party than to set forth the views of their own, & the subjects on which they declared themselves were those very little affecting, or interesting, to the working classes. No reply was or could be given to any question. The breaking down of seats under the weight of humanity piled on the backs of many of them, or an imitation cock-crowing, or ridiculous rejoinder seemed far more entertaining to the enlightened enfranchised electors than any replies or subject that could be brought before them. The last sight we saw just before escaping from the uproar about 9-30 was the Chairman Mr Green standing on one Chair, & the Candidate Mr De Ricci on another, making what looked like dumb motions, & below them a free fight going on, & the chairs flying about, as we found after, thrown into a heap in the centre of the Exchange to keep them away from the mischief makers. Our Platform at the end was soon nearly in as much confusion, all the occupants of the chairs on it rising, & tossing them as far back as possible, out of reach. We thought ourselves fortunate in getting safely from the door, from which a rush was made just as the horse's head was turned from it.

Our Son Will has been advocating the cause of several Conservative Candidates since his visit to Manchester. The last (we find from a Norwich Paper which we received this morning) in that City last Tuesday. His speech, which seems pretty fully reported, was 'in the spirit of a sentence' which he said he had read in one of Lord Beaconsfield's [pamphlets -] 'I am a Conservative to preserve all that is good

October on a list of wide-ranging social reforms known as the Unauthorised Programme, bringing into the open a split between the traditional Liberals and the Radicals (see the last paragraph of this entry and the footnote).

102  Women were not enfranchised until 1918, and so not entitled to speak at an electors' meeting.

103  Samuel Whitbread III was MP for the Borough of Bedford from 1852 to 1895, and the head of the Whitbread brewery, founded by his grandfather in 1742. Whitbreads had represented the town as Liberals almost continuously since 1768, though the brewing interest was more closely associated with the Conservative party.

104  Presumably, CEB uses this word in the sense of women's liberation, in particular the right to the franchise, which was physically evident in the separation of women from male electors in the hall.

105  The disestablishment of the Welsh and Scottish churches was a cause which many Liberals supported, though Gladstone, as a fervent Anglican, did not.

in our Constitution, & I am a Radical to remove all that is bad'.[106] I thought when I had read it there was a good deal of common sense in his remarks about 'Fair Trade' rather than 'Free Trade' & the improbability of Mr Chamberlain's idea of three acre plots of land for the agricultural labourer being a sufficient means of livelihood for him, when the English Farmer with all the appliances of steam machinery & engineering had not been able to make a living.[107] But when I find the man he is recommending the electors of Norwich to return to Parliament advertising in the same Paper as that which contains his speech 'Bullard & Sons, Anchor Brewery', I mourn that he should use his influence in a direction which tends to prevent legislation which would do more to raise the working-man than any of the imaginary boons that are promised him. Close the Public House on God's day, decrease the temptations to drunkenness on all others, & thus help him to help himself: this is what his best friends desire, but which Brewing Members of Parliament are scarcely likely to help forward.

*Thursday Dec' 3rd*
Papa went to London last Saturday week morning, & I followed as far as Cricklewood at 2-30. Hattie had returned also, & was staying with Florence to bear her company. Will had taken another political journey, this time on his own account, as Conservative Candidate for Mid-Lanarkshire. To quote from the 'Glasgow News's' report of one of his meetings 'The Chairman in opening the proceedings remarked that Mr Bousfield at very great personal inconvenience, and owing to their inability to secure a local gentleman as candidate, had come forward at the last moment to champion the Conservative cause for that district'. This he has done by addressing 8 meetings in the division the last three days before the election, & I do not know how many before these. Every where he has been listened to patiently, & well received, & in a letter which I had from him Monday morning said he thought he had 'a fair chance'. That he should have so far succeeded on such short acquaintance with the electors, & in such a stronghold of Liberalism, shows that he managed to secure a good deal of respect & influence as 'a fit & proper person to represent them' but the result is as I expected, the L[iberal] candidate is returned by 2875 votes, against 2579 for Will. I only hope he is as little disappointed as his Father & myself are. We are not sorry that he has had all the opportunity for speaking in public, & intercourse with the canny Scotch, but relieved to think that for the present he will not have the mental & physical strain which such an addition to his work must have entailed. His friends say that it will be to his advantage professionally to become an MP, & as his wishes are in that direction his Conservative allies will probably think of him again when an opening occurs, but I hope it may be after he has had for awhile longer the ordinary burden of his profession which seems gradually & surely increasing. He has of late been having a great deal of work, & had to give up some to go to Scotland, & to be in Court this morning.

---

[106] The Conservative leader Disraeli had been created Earl of Beaconsfield in 1876.
[107] Chamberlain's proposal, part of his Unauthorised Programme, was that local councils should have compulsory powers to purchase land to provide smallholdings and allotments for farm labourers who were struggling to make a living during this period, when the depression in agriculture was at its worst. It resembles the plans of the Chartist Land Scheme devised by Feargus O'Connor, in order to enable workers in crowded and unhealthy towns to move to the country.

*Thursday Dec* 17th*

The time I have had to spare since I got back has been chiefly spent in the field. The Midland Railway Co whose land adjoins it has consented to take a piece of our length & give us the width of the widest part, so that we may have a straight fence & I have quite enjoyed being out directing & watching the levelling of the high bank.

*Tuesday Dec* 29th*

Xmas day was a very pleasant one with us. As last year the breakfast table was piled with a good many packages & parcels which almost hid the plates & dishes. The various little presents contained in them occasioned many noisy expressions of amusement & pleasure, & the mirth of my up-grown children is more pleasant to me than more decorous expressions would be with less of the juvenile spirit in them. After early dinner, that the maids may have the afternoon out, we all had a walk by the river to the end of the Embankment, in returning John & Lottie turned aside with me into the Thurlow St room, to see the Tramps who were gathered there from all the Lodging Houses for a meat tea which Mr Fitzpatrick (a Cambridge Undergraduate & Brother of one of our BWTA Committee) had been the means of getting up, & called to ask me to attend. Some of the 'Promoters' who had objected to my teas were present, & one of them after Mr F had addressed them spoke also. I left before the end & returned home to tea after which talk & varied reading, & occupation finished the day.

Monday morning John returned to Town leaving Mattie to spend the week with us, promising to return if possible on New Year's day, to stay over Sunday with us & take her back with him. Mattie is quite willing to sit for Hattie, & she is very pleased to have an opportunity of beginning to work at her painting again, the first she has done since her cough compelled her to give up going to the Studio in London. The light in her Studio at home she does not find sufficient, so after some argument I have induced her to try the Conservatory, & she finds both the light & the temperature all that she could wish. Her beginning is remarkably successful; I was quite surprised to find what she could do towards making a likeness with even the first rough strokes of her brush.

## 1886

*Monday Jan*y 4th*

The days of the old year & the new have so entwined with each other in the past week that it is difficult to realize that the one has ended, & the other begun, yet so it is. 'What shall I render unto the Lord for all His benefits towards me?' I cannot tell, but will trust Him both to point out & to give strength for whatever He may require of me.

*Friday Jan*y 29th*

M*r* Smith came to ask me what could be done for a little girl who was tramping the country with her Father, an Irish man who had had no settled dwelling since the death of his wife 5 years before. She was at our tea on Sunday with her little brother, & he met her again in the lodging house at night with her Father, who seemed as careful as he could be to shield his children from the influence of the terrible surroundings into which he was forced to take them. I told M^r S to bring them here & after a little conversation with the Father (who seemed a very decent man & got a scanty living by selling small articles), finding he was willing to allow her to be placed in more favorable circumstances, & that the child herself wished it, I called on M^rs Goldsmith who is one of a Committee for a 'Home' for young girls in the town, & she at once warmly took up the case. We found a very decent old lady in Grey Friars Walk who was willing to take her in until we could see what arrangements can be made for her. Lottie & Hattie have been mending up some of their old linen & doing what they could to make her clean & comfortable, & have had her here several times to learn a little in helping our maids, & also to sit for Hattie to paint. She finds her a capital little model. M^rs Goldsmith thought she had found a situation for her which would have been much better than sending her to the Home, but she came to me at Thurlow St to-day to tell me that in this she was disappointed. We went together to the house of the old lady with whom we have placed her, & she has consented to keep her longer if we wish it, & is in the mean time doing all she can for the poor child in mending & washing the few articles that she had on when we found her, that were worth it. M^rs G wishes me to go before the 'Home' Committee on Tuesday & state her case for admission to it.

*Friday Feb^y 5^th*
The week that has passed since returning home seems a long one. My mind has been a good deal occupied, first with correspondence about the 'Home' in reference to which I may say that M^rs Lucas has accepted all my proposals, & requested me to engage M^rs Northcott & her Daughter, & to make an offer for the Penge House, both of which I have done, & if the latter should be accepted we shall soon be able to report progress.

The next cause of satisfaction is that a home has been found for our little mother-less waif than which it would be impossible to find one more suitable for her. M^rs C Hutchinson, a Clergyman's widow, & a gentlewoman in the best sense of the word, has taken her to be trained as a housemaid by her only servant, a staid woman who seems well pleased to have such a nice little helper. M^rs H told me when she asked her if she had any message she replied that she was 'very happy, & very thankful'.

Sunday at the tramps' tea there was present a maimed miner who also came to the previous one a fortnight earlier, he was minus a leg & had with him two companions who had met with similar misfortunes. He looked almost too respectable to join us, & almost too proud to accept the tea. A hardheaded north countryman of about fifty, good looking, & in spite of his crutch quite a man of mark amongst the others, I was drawn towards him, & into a conversation. With the greatest self-possession he gave his opinion of the gathering which was decidedly favorable, but in conclusion said 'but if you Blue Ribbon people want to do us real good, you should provide a sleeping place for us away from the drink'; he went on to tell me what had to be endured in the Lodging Houses which he said was worse in Bedford than most other places. I was much impressed by the strong common sense of what the man suggested & told me, so much so that I have been looking round to see whether any suitable place could be found & asked M^r Carter who is the chief member of Thurlow St to look out & make enquiries for me before I went to London. Yesterday when I called on him, to my astonishment, he told me that it was intended to give up the Thurlow St Rooms as recreation rooms & to make use of Grey Friars only for that purpose. I had not the least idea of this when I was thinking at our BWTA Prayer-meeting the very last Monday that no place would answer the purpose better than that. I have mentioned it to my Husband & at first he began to talk of 'too many irons in the fire etc' and I feared would set his foot firmly on the scheme, but since he has been saying that if I really did anything, the best way would be to use corrugated iron divisions between the bedsteads for cleanliness! That means that he will help me!

### Saturday Feb^y 20^th

Thursday morning I met two of our most drunken neighbours walking together, & stopped the one who I thought had the most influence with the other (& who until a few months ago had been an Abstainer more than 4 years) to beg him to strive to help his companion up instead of letting his company drag him down still lower. He took of[f] his hat & just with a word or two passed on. The afternoon I spent collecting what I could towards the £5 I have undertaken to get for the 'Home' calling on M^rs Ransom, M^rs Seabohm, with Lottie, & then we had afternoon tea with M^rs Sampson after which Lottie returned home, putting me down at Bunyan Chapel where was to be held a Zanana tea, before listening to an account of Mission work in India from a Missionary's wife. About 60 ladies were present together with M^r Brown & M^r Murgatroyd & I intended to have remained to the meeting, but a message from Lottie begged I would return home at once as the man to whom I spoke in the morning wanted to sign the Pledge in my presence. I went to his house & found him with his friend of the morning & another whom I had not before seen waiting for me. The last a Commercial Traveller, a young Scotchman, but with the same sad propensity. After kneeling with them & making the act as solemn as possible, they each signed a card which I dated & witnessed. Three Fathers of families in the prime of life! What happiness or misery for them & theirs for this world & it may be the next will depend probably on the keeping or breaking of that Pledge. Moderation is an utter impossibility for either of them. I hope & rejoice with trembling.

### Friday March 5^th

I had promised M^rs Ransom to be at our BWTA Prayer & Committee meeting in the afternoon, which I managed by leaving Cricklewood at 2 o'clock. After the meetings M^rs R returned with me to tea with Miss Wilkinson. I had engaged to take them afterwards to Elstow to a meeting in the Green House, at which the latter was to speak on Women's Suffrage, one of a series of meetings she has been holding in the neighbourhood of Bedford. These meetings were preliminary to a large meeting on the same subject held in the Corn Exchange at which the widow of the last Post-master Gen with two other ladies were present as Speakers supported by M^r J Howard & several other gentlemen. M^rs Fawcett was not eloquent but seemed to convince the large audience that women whose means contributed equally with men to the upholding of the Government of the Country ought to have a voice in the representation.[108] Miss Biggs another Speaker mentioned the fitness of Women to be elected as Poor Law Guardians, & a call I made on M^rs Walters & conversation with her induced me to write a letter to our local Paper to help to stir the matter before the annual election of Guardians which is just at hand, the letter was published in the 'Beds Standard' with some Editorial remarks. M^rs Ransom is very earnest in the matter & I have engaged to accompany her to call on several ladies we think suitable & ask them if they will allow themselves to be nominated. Of all places where a good woman's influence can be beneficially exerted, as a Guardian of the Poor seems one of the most fit, especially on behalf of her own sex & the children.[109]

### Thursday April 8^th 1886

Visiting a few sick neighbours, & the ordinary round of weekly meetings Tramps', Mothers' etc was the principal out of door work; whilst within a large amount of correspondence on account of Home matters filled a great deal of time. After the numerous failures in finding suitable premises, I determined to advertise in two or three London Papers for what I knew to be necessary, & the replies are perfectly bewildering. Agents sent long lists of Properties to let, Landlords' descriptions of houses, in many cases not at all answering to our means or purposes, so from all I was obliged to choose, & write for further information of the most likely.

I left home about 11 o'clock to fulfil my promise to call for M^rs Ransom & with her, on several ladies whom we wanted to influence to be willing to allow themselves to be nominated as Poor Law Guardians. From one house to another we went from that hour until near 5 o'clock, & in that time only succeeded in finding two legally eligible women who would allow themselves to be nominated. Some were too modest, others too busy, & I began to fear our effort would be entirely useless. I intended to have gone to London that night but was too tired to leave until the next morning, & glad also to have a little time with Florence who remained with the children until the following Saturday.

The time fixed for the 'Home' Committee meeting was close at hand & I was not even prepared to say I had found a suitable place for it. So leaving on Thursday morning with no other guide where such could be found than my bundle of answers to the adv^t, I got to the first place on my list at which I could stop, Kentish Town, & thence went on to South Tottenham, another nice neighbourhood but the houses I went to see as unsuitable as others have been.

After a little refreshment I at once continued the search for a house by going to the second set of places at Forest Hill. Here, one Landlord whose 'To let' board attracted my attention in passing, refused to let for our purpose. To another who had answered my advertisement I went, again unsuitable, & so on until near dark until

---

108  Mrs Fawcett, the wife of Henry Fawcett, a Radical Liberal MP, Postmaster-General from 1880 to 1884 in Gladstone's government, is best known for her support for women's political enfranchisement, as member, and from 1890 President, of the NUWSS (the National Union of Women's Suffrage Societies). This organisation, like Fawcett herself, was committed to the use of constitutional methods in their cause, rather than the militant actions of the WSPU (the Women's Social and Political Union). She died in 1929, having seen the success of her work in the previous year when the vote was finally awarded to women on the same terms as men.
109  The office of Poor Law Guardian was one of only two areas of public life at this time to which women could contribute on the same terms as men, the other being that of membership of a School Board. Though there was a property qualification at this time, it was removed in the early 1890s.

the last & most distant of the other replies. Fortunately the Landlord lived close to his house, & was quite willing to show it to me although a candle was needed to do so. I could see that the garden was very suitable, prettily laid out & well enclosed & with the house I was not less pleased. Three sitting rooms, kitchens & offices on ground floor & six bed-rooms all on one floor above, were as conveniently arranged as the house I liked at Beckenham Rd, with the additional advantage of being on an eminence instead of in a hollow. 'The Mount' is the name inscribed on the front of the house. I was on the whole so well satisfied with this that I determined on getting Mrs Lucas to look at it before searching further, & returned to OKR for the night in a much more cheerful frame of mind than before during the day, for I had felt very depressed & weary.

Next morning I went to Charlotte St by arrangement, found Mrs Lucas expecting me, had a talk & early dinner with her after which we left together to visit 'The Mount', Perry Rise, Forest Hill. The old Landlord seemed very pleased to see us & most willing to do anything to make the place suited to our convenience. Mrs L coincided with my opinion that it more nearly answered our requirements & means than any other we had seen, & we left determining to recommend the Committee to take it when we met at her house the following day. Our President Lady E Biddulph was present, & all expressed themselves very thankful for the trouble I had taken & quite willing to adopt Mrs L's & my recommendation that the house should be taken as the 'Home' for the BWTA.

So much to my relief this matter is settled much more quickly & easily than I imagined when I started with my bundle of papers & letters, & I cannot help thinking that I was directed by the same Helping Hand that has so often cleared & pointed the way. I asked the Committee to name a sum which they thought I might expend on furnishing but they gave me carte blanche to do what I thought necessary.

Wednesday, Thursday & Friday were very busy days. Lottie came up to help me put the last finishing touches & it was well she did so for without her arrangement of curtains etc we could not possibly have presented the aspect we did on Saturday. Mrs Northcott & her Daughter worked well also, the latter especially & with a woman one day, to bind stair-carpet ends etc, in the three days we were ready for the visit of inspection to which we invited Lady B & Mrs Lucas on Saturday. I asked Edward to meet them to luncheon. The appearance of the whole is most cheerful & Home like, & I should have been disappointed if our visitors had been less satisfied than they seemed to be. Lady B in particular pronounced everything 'charming'. She prognosticates great success, & will be Visitor for the month of May. Edward has consented to act as Hon Physician this first year.

### Wednesday April 28th

Before leaving [Bedford] Mr Ransom gave me a donation of £1 for our 'Home' of which I told him, & at about 8-30 a Cab was at Mrs Reid's door to take me to the Station from whence I took ticket to Kings X, & on arriving at once took Cab for London Bridge to get to Forest Hill as early as possible, to see that all was ready at The Mount for the Committee meeting & opening service for which I had issued notices and invitations. I found that Lottie had attended to some unfinished matters I had left to her. She had spent an afternoon in planning some carpets which Mrs

Kelly brought us for two bed-rooms, & on the same Grandpapa & Granmama had met her & seen the Home for the first time, staying to tea, after which they left together. Mrs Northcott & her Daughter had done their best to have everything ready for our expected visitors.

Arriving at the Home I found the Matron engaged with a lady, to whom she introduced me as one who had seen our advt in the 'Lancet' & who desired to place herself under our care. Conversing with her she told me her besetment was Chloral,[110] which she had first taken to procure sleep, & had at length been entirely overcome by the habit, & from its depressing effects had resorted to stimulants also. In spite of all she seemed a true gentlewoman & I encouraged her all I could to carry out her brave determination. She left promising to return [at] the end of the week which she did.

*Thursday May 6th*
I find I have forgotten that I spent Monday night the 19th April at the Home, which I left about noon the following day, after calling the previous evening on Mr Chancellor, & a lady living very near to him (Mrs Powell) who promised to co-operate in any way she could at 'the Mount' & has since called. It seems beyond anything we could have expected that from date to the present we have five Inmates in 'the Home', four of them Ladies & I have applications for two other 1st class Patients. How does this show the need of such a place, & the terrible extent of the Drink curse. Mrs Northcott writes of her charge almost as a happy family; they certainly appear much more contented than I expected them to be.

On Saturday afternoon John drove us to Turvey, stopping at Bromham wood for Lottie & Mattie to fill their baskets with primroses & wood anemones. Papa followed by train & joined us for tea, after John had taken Mattie to see the pretty Church etc with which she was much pleased. Leaving them to return by train, Papa drove us home afterward.

A quiet Sunday, with a smaller tramps' tea than usual, preceded a very busy Easter Monday. Our Association united with the Thurlow St Committee to take the Corn Exchange, & keep it open for refreshment & amusement the whole day. This was done by arranging with a confectioner to supply cheap food with tea coffee etc & with ladies who undertook to give half hour concerts at intervals throughout the day. In addition to which I undertook to supply a Magic Lantern attraction in the lower-room, with the loan of that used by the St Mary's Circuit, Mr Clough kindly undertaking to manipulate it for us. The day was very fine, & out of doors most attractive, but we found rational amusements for more than 800 people who paid 1d for admission, & concluded the day by a capital Temperance meeting when the Exchange was filled, Mr Hull & Mr Myers being the Speakers. I remained in the Exchange from morning to night. John & Mattie came & had luncheon with me, & after returning went with Papa by the 3 o'clock train to Woburn Sands. They had a long afternoon wandering as far as the Abbey, & did not get back until near 10 o'clock. Lottie came to me at the Exchange, & sang two or three songs very well,

---

110 Chloral is a liquid prepared from chlorine and alcohol, hence its name. It is otherwise known as knockout drops and is a depressant inducing sleep. It was used extensively by alcoholics whose sleep patterns had been disturbed by heavy drinking. It was highly addictive and the effects can be imagined. It substituted two cravings for one craving. Today we would use the word addiction.

filling up several gaps between the half hour entertainments which no one seemed to think their business, nor to make any provision for.

## May 27th

The record of some weeks past if I could recount all that has transpired would be a little history of battles lost & won. I have not had time to write of the various interviews, meetings, encouragements & disappointments all in reference to a Blue Ribbon Lodging House for Tramps. The Mayor entered into the matter very warmly & at my request convened a meeting of the Gentlemen who had promised to become guarantors, in his Parlour at the Corn Exchange. Drs Goldsmith, Carter & Kinsey came, & in spite of a lawyer's letter from the Brewers, & a petition signed by a number of inhabitants of the neighbourhood of Thurlow St, determined on accepting the remainder of the lease of which I had been promised the refusal, & turning the BR Room into sleeping apartments for travellers, & I came away from the meeting quite jubilant. But the next day came a letter from one gentleman saying he was not prepared for any other than the share in the <u>financial responsibility</u> & another soon after from the Committee begging I would relieve them of their promise, & as it was from the most influential of these that my chief help was to have come, I felt I could do nothing but act in accordance with their wish & abandon the idea. So the publicans & sinners are triumphant, & I am defeated. The lease of the Rooms is to be given up to the Landlord, & the whole work carried on in Grey Friars Walk, whither I found the women of the Mothers' meeting also had migrated when I went to meet them a fortnight ago. The use of GF Rooms for this purpose is kindly permitted instead of the others.

## Saturday May 29th

Yesterday afternoon we received a Telegram from our Son Edward 'Twins, son & daughter, doubtful if they will live. Mother doing well.' This followed by a letter this morning tells us of the birth of their first-born<u>s</u>, I must so call this latest addition to our family. I hardly know whether to hope or fear that the little ones may be spared. Edward says 'they are mere dolls'. It will be a great disappointment to their Parent if they do not live, but a much greater anxiety to bring up two little weaklings that may lack the chief element of pleasure in living, health, but in this as in every event of their course may they be enabled to <u>pray</u> as well as <u>say</u> 'Thy will be done on earth, as it is in Heaven'. The little boy is the most weakly. Edward writes that he is going to stay up a good part of the night with his 'son', to do his best to save him. He is a great lover of children & I can imagine the new experiences & interest with which he will watch this baby life.[111]

## The Mount, Wednesday June 9th

How little I thought when I last wrote that my next entry in my Diary would be from this place. Before I have time to recall my first visit here the second has come. On the former occasion I made the acquaintance of our first five Patients (that is what we call them). The very first the maiden lady before referred to, then a Dr's wife;

---

[111]   Edward's expert and loving care bore fruit: the twins not only survived but lived to a ripe old age: Alex died in 1975, aged 89, and Evelyn in 1986, aged 100.

a magistrate's widow (whose Husband took his own life through drink), the young wife of a Wine Importer (who wrote to me 'if the step I am taking should be the means of curing my wife I shall never forget the day I saw your advertisement in the Lancet') & last, a married woman, in the Kitchen. Since these came, another has been added in the kitchen, a good cook, these six make up the family.

Tuesday morning June 1st the postman brought two letters. One from the Matron saying my presence was desirable as there was a 'concoction' amongst the Patients, & another from one of the Ladies, telling me that she was most indignant with the Matron who had been telegraphing to her best friend 'very restive please advise' because of some disagreement & that 'she could not remain'. I at once telegraphed to her 'Be patient until I come by next train' & with my Husband's concurrence & begging G-pa & G-ma to excuse my leaving them, came off by 10-40 a m train, having first also telegraphed to Lady Biddulph to ask her to meet me.

Arriving I found all just finishing dinner at which I was told there was a most uncomfortable scene just before I entered. The whole household was disorganized, & Mrs N is certainly not suitable for her position. I can only wonder that I could have been so completely mistaken in her character, & feelings toward myself. My coming was a great relief to the Ladies whose welcome made some amends for the annoyance of having to leave home to come to them. Their explanation of the circumstances which led to the irritation between themselves & Mrs N convinced me that she was very much the cause of it, apart from her direct opposition to my directions to send to me in case of any difficulty.

Lady B arrived very soon after myself, & we were both spared further trouble in reference to Mrs N by finding a note on the Drawing-room table from her, giving in her resignation. This we gladly accepted, but it did not prevent Lady B from telling her most plainly how we blamed her, & how entirely she had proved her unfitness for her position. After seeing & hearing what the Patients had further to tell us, Lady Biddulph had all together in the Drawing-room where she played for us to join in singing a hymn, then addressed them as only a truly Christian lady could, & prayed. After some further talk with her, I expressed my readiness to stay & take Mrs N's position in the house which she neither could, nor desired to fill any longer. In this she willingly concurred, & from that afternoon I have been in charge.

*Monday June 30th*
Still at 'The Mount' & with a very heavy heart. During [the week before Whitsuntide] I received a call from a middle-aged maiden lady, a Miss Stephens, whom I had before met at the BWTA meetings as the Delegate from Bridport. She called thinking it was Lady B's visitation day, bringing with her a Portfolio of water-color drawings to show the ladies. I thought her a very companionable & intelligent person, & in answer to her enquiries whether she could do anything to help me suggested as she wished to stay in London longer that perhaps she could do so by taking my place whilst I went home to spend Whitsuntide. This she appeared capable & willing to undertake & after mentioning the proposal to Lady Elizabeth & having her concurrence, I was very thankful to go on the Friday, calling at Cricklewood on my way home, & arriving by the 8-30 p m train. Papa was at the Station & glad to see me but not quite sure that I had done a safe thing to leave.

Saturday afternoon John brought down Mattie, & Hattie also came; these with

Grandpa & Grandma, whose visit was to terminate the following Tuesday, made quite a family party & I thought myself very happy in being able to join them, & Miss Stephens's visit most fortunate as allowing me to do so. Sunday was a very restful day. Monday, in spite of cool winds & a little rain, the young people much desired to go on to the river. A boat was engaged in which they took with them a substantial luncheon which they arranged to spread on the river bank in the Kempston woods where we older folk promised to join them by land which we did much to their delight, & still more when we had finished[112] at our all being persuaded to have a row in the boat with them, which we quite enjoyed & were landed at the Works about 4 o'clock.

The next morning brought a bundle of letters amongst them one from M^rs N (the D^r's wife) telling me how comfortably they were doing & another from Miss Stephens, begun in the same strain, but concluding by telling of the sudden determination of Laura (one of the women in the kitchen) to leave. So at once making up my mind to return, I did so with Grandpa & G-ma by the 10-40 am train, leaving them at Kings X station.

[Three of the inmates had persuaded Miss Stephens to take them on a visit to the Zoo]. The visit had given them the opportunity of evading her & of obtaining drink. M^rs T-S by parting with an article of clothing she wore, to the woman in the lavatory at the Gardens got sufficient to bring on a mad fit of craving in which she kept poor Miss S following her from place to place until late at night, & every one awake the night through when she got back, & at early morning demanded to go out again. This being refused she had jumped over the drawing-room window (the bottom part of which I had taken the precaution to have securely fastened before any Inmates arrived) & being followed by Miss S into the road as quickly as possible, again kept her going from one Public House to another for several hours, & it was not until just before I arrived that she had been got back again, & I found her lying on the sofa in M^rs Northcott's room inflamed with the drink she had been taking but perfectly conscious of all she had been doing.

This terrible episode I soon discovered was but the climax of a series of deceptions which had been carried on during my absence by three out of the four dining-room Patients. Patients indeed, diseased past all sense of right by their terrible craving. Voluntarily giving themselves up to be cured & at every possible opportunity doing their utmost to carry out the means of perpetuating the malady!

Mrs T-S in her ravings told all, either with or without questioning. Her wedding ring I discovered was replaced by a brass one, & each had, by means of a ring each, pawned by slipping out of the Drapers into the Pawnbrokers, of one of the three when Miss S was not watching, got a few shillings & managed to secure a supply of spirits which only had an apparent effect in one case but was partaken of by all. The cunning & degradation of these poor victims is beyond anything I could have imagined.

But my trouble was not over with the unhappy woman who had caused Miss S such terrible anxiety. I found the latter in bed resting after her night & morning of fatigue that I only wonder did not occasion her serious injury. The former seemed recovered from the effects of her folly by the afternoon & as Lady Elizabeth, Mrs

---

[112]  i.e. when lunch was finished the older folk were persuaded to risk being rowed back to the Works.

Lucas & some other ladies were coming to see an applicant for Mrs N's late position, & I could not give her special attention, I very unwisely yielded to the suggestion that to allay her restlessness she should accompany Mrs Northcott & her Daughter where they wished to take her with them, & as she promised to keep with them I thought protected by two she must be safe. Returning with them she had insisted on visiting a Chemist's shop for a bottle of Eau de Cologne, drank this, & then at the last Spirit shop she passed refused to go a step further unless permitted to go in & purchase a bottle of brandy. To get her home this was allowed, & she came back carrying it under her mantle, & a few minutes after daringly told me she was going to her room to drink it. Without replying to this I watched my opportunity & suddenly wresting the bottle from her dashed it against the door post, & had the satisfaction of seeing the accursed liquor stream down the passage. A slight cut on my hand, & a not very severe cuff on my head were the only consequences to me, but fearing the excitement would increase during the night & that she would become unmanageable, I sent off for Edward, & he arrived soon after mid-night, & remained until 3 o'clock in the morning not until which time could he persuade her to go to bed, & even then she would only lie outside dressed. I lay down on another bed at her side not knowing what would happen before the morning, & truly thankful was I when I heard she was sleeping.

I was not disturbed until nearly breakfast time & left her in bed, hoping after the rest she would be sane at least. But to my astonishment we had scarcely breakfasted before she appeared dressed for going out which she demanded to do. Then began a struggle which lasted the whole day during which she walked round the fences in the garden & remained in it, with her bonnet on declaring her determination to go out. This I as stoutly declared she should not do, telling her that two strong wills were opposed to each other, but that mine had the key on its side which nothing should induce me to use to permit her to repeat the sin & folly of which she had been guilty the previous days.

At tea time Edward came & found her in the same state of mind. He offered to accompany her, but this for a long time she would not accept. At length finding it useless to endeavour further to get out alone, she consented to taking a walk with him, which he requested me also to have with them, & we set off together to the Recreation Ground where after watching the cricketers, & sitting & walking for a time, she appeared more like herself, & on asking her to return quietly with me, she promised to do so, & I begged him to go on to the Station for his Saturday evening work at home which is generally more than other evenings. I was indeed glad when I found she was once more reasonable, & we talked & walked homeward almost as usual. Edward's kindness & patience were most praiseworthy, & I never felt more thankful & proud of him than in hearing him talk to that poor degraded woman, trying to lead her to see her conduct & its consequences in their true light.

Yesterday (Sunday) was a very anxious day. M$^{rs}$ N's extreme annoyance at my deciding not to go to Church that morning aroused a suspicion which was confirmed by observation at night, & ended in discovering an endeavour to communicate with an individual sitting in the choir on the opposite side of the Church. This I had to bring before her most plainly the following morning & of course to bear the anger caused by my plain speaking which ended by her declaring her intention of leaving in a month.

Scarcely had I left M<sup>rs</sup> N's room when Fanny our one Kitchen Inmate came to me & expressed her desire to go, because of some altercation with the young girl who had come to help. After reasoning with her for a long time & pointing out the probable consequences of her going out into the world without home or character, I told her I should neither give her permission to go, nor hinder her if she persisted, when she returned to her room as I supposed to pack, remained there until 4 o'clock, & then came to ask me if she 'was to go'. Another half-hour's talk, & she went back to the kitchen, & resumed her duties there which are very valuable to us as she is an excellent cook.

In the mean time M<sup>rs</sup> N came to me & expressed her sorrow for what had passed, & her willingness to stay at The Mount for the year for which she came. M<sup>rs</sup> T-Smith has also shown contrition, so I have great reason to acknowledge with a grateful heart the help which has been given me in these days of need & anxiety such as I never before experienced. But whilst feeling this I am thoroughly dis-heartened by the proofs from almost each one of these poor women of the entire deterioration of character I discover in them. Virtue, honor, truthfulness seem well-nigh [sic] dead, & it is only to show how the vice of drunkenness fosters every other, & produces moral deformity, where every womanly grace might be seen, that I think it worth while to recount the sad occurrences of these last days.

### July 26<sup>th</sup>

One remarkable episode in my sojourn at The Mount was a visit from a stranger who presented a summons to me for the attendance of 'Bousfield, Widow, Lodging House-keeper' at Greenwich County Court on July 21st for the non-payment of a bill for a Bottle of Brandy! (the one I smashed). This summons I sent on to Will who was engaged himself for that day, but sent the young Barrister who has taken one of his Chambers, Mr Gill, to defend me. The Judge seemed to think it a good joke that the man should sell to, he knew not who, & then come upon me for payment, & in reply to his query 'who must he sue' told him he must find out. He left muttering revenge which he carried out by a scurrilous PC addressed to The Mount.

### Thursday August 19th [Bedford]

Aunts Fanny & Jenny arrived before Papa's return. The day before they came was Bedford Flower Show & having tickets & no one at home to accompany me I asked M<sup>rs</sup> Tyler, the wife of our Superintendent minister to do so to which she consented & I drove her. In the field I was glad to meet M<sup>rs</sup> Ransom, & to hear from her how our BWTA work had been going on. Her Husband also was there & told me of a meeting of which as Mayor he was to be Chairman to be held in his 'Parlour' which he invited me to attend. The object was the formation of a Vigilance Committee. One other lady M<sup>rs</sup> Edwards (one of the two Lady Poor Law Guardians whom we have succeeded in getting) was present, with the Head Masters of the Grammar & Modern Schools, & two other gentlemen beside the Mayor. A committee was formed after a second meeting, at which Mrs Sampson also was present. She was deputed to invite several ladies whose names were mentioned to meet those already elected the following Saturday morning & form a separate ladies' committee to work in connection with the gentlemen. We met & after talking a good deal & doing little more than propose the names of those who should be asked to join it, deputed

Mrs Ransom to act in any cases of which she might, through her Husband or otherwise, obtain knowledge, she being almost the only lady of those present who would be remaining in Bedford during the vacation time. I have heard from her that she is very anxious for me to return & talk about 'our new work'.

### August 23rd (Monday)

[CEB returns to 'The Mount' where things are still unsettled.]

Sunday morning we went to a Church near where bowings & turnings & various kneelings before the table & a small box placed on it made up what I suppose would be called 'High Church' so that I felt our wanderings in search of a congenial place of worship were not over. I asked Miss B to walk with me to Norwood in the afternoon to have tea with Father, intending to worship with him at night, but rain came on just as we were starting & instead of accompanying him & Grandma we turned homeward & went into the Congregational church in 'Jew's Walk' half way home. The Ladies had been to another Church at night & were much pleased with the Clergyman who they said spoke with a foreign accent.

The following morning I took the first opportunity of calling the Dr's wife into my room, & questioned her as to a Visitor she had asked to be allowed to receive the day before I came, as her brother-in-law, of whose relationship however I heard doubts expressed. She flatly refused to give me any information as to who the stranger was or to answer any questions, & at once declared her intention to leave the following day. This was sufficient proof of what I had been told that the individual who came to see her had followed her when she had managed to attract his attention, that she had thrown her name & address out of the window, inviting him (after correspondence) to call. Such a flagrantly immoral act could not be passed over, & I did not attempt to induce her to remain longer than I could communicate with her friends, her Husband being as I knew away from home. She determined on not waiting for any one, & as a last effort to save her from what she had declared her intention of doing, I told her I would give her the option of remaining until she was fetched or if she insisted on leaving should retain her luggage & call all the Inmates to witness her expulsion as a woman of immoral character. As she still insisted I assembled all in the Hall, to witness what I intended as a warning to others, & told them she was then expelled. She administered a parting blow with her umbrella which frightened others more than it hurt me. A telegram from the Husband asked where she had gone, to this I was not able to reply, but a subsequent letter said she had returned home & begged me to keep her luggage until further action was decided on; it remained three weeks when I begged it might be removed; direction was given to send it to her Husband's, since which I have not heard a word of the unhappy woman, so our first case of complete failure has come to pass. It is mortifying to chronicle the fact, but as I have before said the demoralization of drink knows no bounds.

A few days later a new Patient arrived, a Lady who had been a month at West Holme[113] & had been brought through a serious illness caused by drinking over a bottle of Brandy daily as the gentleman who brought her (a young Barrister) told

---

[113] West Holme is a district in Bexley, Kent – perhaps the location of a convalescent home?

me. They did not wish to keep her owing to the 'preferential attention' she received, their class of Patients being lower than ours. She is a splendid woman, physically, & mentally whose manner & conversation must have made her very attractive in the circle of high society in which she had been accustomed to move, & to this is added great musical talent, but once more all womanly graces are drowned in accursed drink, & she gives up her liberty seemingly determined to make another effort to free herself from a greater bondage. I had a great deal of conversation with her & but for the caution of the subsequent letter of the friend who brought her should scarcely have thought it possible that there was in her case the same fear of deception & intrigue as we have before met with.

The day she came was that of the departure of a young married woman who was sent for a short time & whose husband, anxious to have her home again, came the previous day & consented to her remaining a week or two longer for my convenience as well as her benefit & without further payment. Allowing her to accompany him to the Station where he was unwise enough to give her money, she returned with gin secreted, drank it during the night, & under pretence of excruciating neuralgia the next morning at first so deceived me that I sent her to the Chemist for relief, & only after she had gone discovered her real condition from my suspicions being confirmed by what others knew; she only returned to pack up & depart immediately she found her duplicity discovered, so I must record failure number two, but her being received for a month was a mistake which led to this, as our power over her after the end of that time ceased. She was such a clever woman in the house that I should have most gladly retained her services if I could have done so, but her craving & deceit destroyed every quality that made her valuable & I was thankful to be rid of her, although from the day she left domestic matters became entirely disorganized, & it was only by great personal effort that I managed to keep the least appearance of order or comfort.

*Saturday Sept$^r$ 4$^{th}$*
The fortnight since my return home has been one of a great deal of enjoyment. The charming weather we have had has enabled us almost to live out of doors & picnics and meals in the garden have been very frequent. Thursday morning Lottie had invited a young lady staying with Mrs Walters to go with her on the river, & I proposed that they should take luncheon with them, & with their Brothers, Florence & the boys have a long day on the water returning to tea if they felt inclined to do so. To this all willingly agreed, so packing various baskets with provisions, & these into a wheel-barrow with Will's photographic apparatus, Bowler wheeled all to the river side at the Works where Florence & the children also embarked.

My day was occupied first with the Elstow M Meeting, then as there was no return home for tea, with Lottie's children's working meeting in the BR Room, & lastly the prayer meeting in the School-room, but this I left before the end being very anxious to know whether our children had got back. When I found they had not, & the shades of evening drew on, I became very uneasy, & begged Papa to accompany me to the ferry where we crossed & soon obtained the intelligence that our party (the only distinguishing feature of which I could give being that one wore a crimson cricket cap) was still up the river. This however was a mistake for after waiting nearly an hour & watching the return of one boat load after another until we could not distinguish faces, they calmly paddled up from the opposite direction having been past the Embankment to listen to the Band. The two little ones were both asleep but with this exception all seemed as fresh as when they left in the morning & to have had a day of unalloyed pleasure.

Monday afternoon to give all pleasure we shut up the house taking the three maids & all the children with us for a final picnic in Kempston woods. Bowler drove them with baby Hilda, & the provisions as near as possible to the river whilst we went in a boat. Papa accompanied us but so many were tempted to the same spot by the fine weather that he did not enjoy the excursion as much as if we had been more alone. He & I walked back over the fields a good part of the way in returning which he said was 'real enjoyment'.

On Friday Mrs Ransom came to me at the GF Blue R Room after the M Meeting to talk with me about what steps we could take to stop the Sunday traffic at one of the two Public Houses in this neighbourhood which has become notorious for this as well as general immorality. We have been to see a lawyer together, & he tells us that we must have very strong evidence to have the least chance of putting any check on the evil by summonsing the landlord. The Police are known to connive & cannot be depended on for the least assistance either for this or to put down some immoral houses near that are ruining the reputation of this once quiet locality. Mrs R most nobly gave up her time on Sunday morning to obtaining ocular demonstration of the facts of which we had been told. She went to a house immediately opposite the Southend Hotel & from the window saw men & women enter & come out of it in the prohibited hours, some with jars or jugs which they concealed in various ways. I was to have obtained confirmatory evidence in the afternoon, but as Papa was preaching at Turvey & wished his girls to accompany him, I was obliged to stay in for the Bible Class which Lottie now generally takes.

*Tuesday Sept' 7th*
After the BWTA Prayer & Committee meetings yesterday Mrs Ransom told me what she had seen the previous day & that her Husband, the Mayor, had been to the Owner of the Public House & told him that he had sufficient evidence of the practices which had long been carried on there, & that a summons would be taken out unless he took it out of the hands of the present disreputable occupiers, the same that I went to & warned a year ago. Mrs R will not rest until these & the other haunts of iniquity are removed from our midst. I feel ashamed that she should do so much, whilst we have done so little in these matters beyond complaining of them.

*Thursday Sept' 16th*
A monthly journey to Forest Hill now seems the least I can repeat as long as I retain my present responsibility, & from another of these I returned on Tuesday evening, having had a visit on the whole more free from anxiety than any previous one. This is accounted for by the absence of the disturbing element of the unhappy woman's influence who last left us.

The three ladies left welcomed me warmly. A telegram soon after announced that one of the Patients I expected to receive utterly refused to come. The next morning a sorrowful Mother (the wife of a respectable Farmer) came to bring her eldest daughter, a young ladylike woman of 27 who she left in our charge. I said all that I could to encourage the poor girl, & gave her Mother some comfort & hope in leaving her. Although so young, she confessed that drinking was not merely a habit but a 'passion' & told Mrs A of the artifices to which she resorted to get it from her Father's cellar, & she is not the only one of her family addicted to the vice, her eldest brother the Mother herself told me being also, & yet I could not persuade her that to banish it from their home was their first duty, & the girl herself thought it such a necessity for her Parents, that she declared she would rather never go home again than keep them from that to which they had always been accustomed. What a price are they paying for it!

Another fresh inmate in the Kitchen is the Mother of 10 children all under 15 years of age! The Husband seems a most intelligent man from his letters. She is an excellent cook, & a thoroughly clean industrious woman, with us. It seems passing strange that she should so readily render us service, of which she is depriving so many, simply because she is shut up from temptation. The utter loss of <u>will</u> power is to me the most striking feature of this fearful malady, for such it must be.

*Monday Oct^r 18^th*
The ten days since last writing have been eventful ones. The first week spent in visits to my children, Father, & The Mount, the last three in receiving & entertaining Mr & Mrs Southwell whose first & long promised visit has closed this evening. Nothing could have been more pleasant & satisfactory both to Papa & myself. Mr & Mrs S arrived by 4-50 train Saturday evening; I met them at the Station in rain which scarcely abated during their stay but did little to damp what I believe has been mutual enjoyment. After tea Mr Southwell & Papa remained in the Breakfast-room whilst the former smoked a cigar. After sitting some time & chatting pleasantly with Mrs S in the Drawing-room I left her with Lottie to see whether they were nearly ready to give us their company. I found them engaged in a conversation that so much interested me that remaining longer than I intended Mrs Southwell also came to us, & the Mothers as well as the Fathers were soon engaged in discussing the future of their children, John & Mattie, with very little difference of opinion.

The views of Mattie's Parents as to what they might prudently begin housekeeping upon have modified since the first days of John's conversation with Mr Southwell, & neither dissented much from my mention of £300 as an ample yearly income to begin on together, & expressed willingness to unite with us in any arrangement that we were willing to make to increase John's present income to that amount.

It is long since Papa has met with a more congenial acquaintance than Mr Southwell. Conversation flowed as easily between them on all subjects as if they had known each other for years, & whether business, science or religious views were discussed, they seemed to understand and agree with each other. With Mrs Southwell I felt equally at home which was less to be wondered at as we had before known each other, but that the two Fathers, who had never before met, should be so much so was a pleasant surprise to me especially in the case of Papa who is usually so slow to be at ease with new friends.

Sunday morning the rain compelled us to drive to Chapel & at the suggestion which a letter from John at breakfast time gave I took Mr & Mrs S with Lottie to Bunyan Meeting, to hear Mr Brown (whose life of Bunyan they had read), & after the service went into the vestry to show them Bunyan's chair, & the prison door of his gaol which is let into the wall of the vestry. At night we all went together to the little Chapel in which Mr & Mrs S seemed to enjoy the service. Family worship, singing & pleasant conversation finished a very pleasant Sabbath.

Monday morning was too wet for us to think of any out of door exercise for Mrs S beyond a drive. Mr S went over the Works with Papa, after which we met him at the Lodge with the Brougham & showed both as much of Bedford as we could in an hour & half. In the afternoon I had to take the M Meeting from which I had been absent a month. The weather allowed of Lottie's walking to Elstow with Mr S. When I returned soon after 4 o'clock I found Papa had come home & was having a cosy chat with Mrs S in which her Husband shortly joined us, & over a cup of afternoon tea in the Drawing-room. Two hours later their visit came to a close, Mr Southwell being obliged to leave for business the next morning. Thus ended what has been I believe a very pleasant & satisfactory interchange of views & feelings on both sides, the result of which I hope may be profitable to our children.

*Friday Oct<sup>r</sup> 29<sup>th</sup>*

I called at Mrs Ransom's & found she was at the Shire Hall, helping to complete the work she had nobly begun the previous Monday when, acting on my represen-tation of the disorderly Sunday doings at Southend Hotel, after on two Sundays coming to see for herself, she took out a summons against the Landlord for selling in prohibited hours, & thus did what the Police had persistently shirked & we who lived in the neighbourhood had done little but complain of. The man was convicted & fined £2, & then the courageous Chief-Constable issued a second summons for the next offence (two following Sundays) for which he was also fined a like sum & had his licence endorsed. This last has irritated the Brewer Owner of the house, & at the subsequent prosecution of those who entered it those days in prohibited hours (which I suppose was a sort of formal necessity), a Solicitor was engaged who did his best to falsify the testimony of the only witness who lives in the immediate neighbourhood & that a woman who was brave enough to give the evidence on which, with Mrs Ransom's confirmation, they were convicted. Half a dozen at least of the most sottish of our neighbours were summonsed, but for some unaccount-able reason the charges were withdrawn in more than half the cases, three being however fined. This Mrs R knows will have a most deterring effect not only on this locality, but [on] the Publicans generally, & so at all events check the evil, which is her praiseworthy object.

The wives & families of those who have suffered most by the drinking habits of the men, at night, after the Landlord's conviction, made a most noisy & riotous demonstration in his favour, & against poor Mrs Foskett threatening & hooting around her door, & some teetotal neighbours! I was told of the uproar, & went out to find the street filled with a noisy crowd, their chief instrument for this, beyond their lungs, a great sheet of corrugated sheet iron which they were dragging & battering. It was enough for me to go amongst them, look into the face of one or two as if to be sure of them, & set my foot on this for them to scatter to the side pavements like driven sheep, leaving me in possession. After a time, & some saucy speeches about 'lady detectives' (which I told them they need not fear if there were nothing to detect) a valiant Policeman appeared & was with difficulty persuaded to take charge of the principal means of the uproar, the piece of iron. I gave them to understand that I would take good care there was better protection from a repetition of such conduct, which had the desired effect & there has not been any disturbance since that night, owing to the appearance of a couple of Policemen together each night; in addition to which the Mayor sent one in plain clothes.

This neighbourhood is just far enough from the town to be considered safe for some evil doers who have come out of it, & formed a perfect nest of iniquity near the Public House. Mrs Ransom is helping us also to get rid of these. At her Husband's suggestion I have got a Petition drawn up & signed by 24 of the neighbouring Owners & Householders which he as Mayor promised to present to the Watch Committee which sat at the Shire Hall this morning, praying that these disorderly houses may be <u>watched</u> more effectually, & suggesting the residence of [a] Police officer in Southend.

### Monday Nov[r] 22nd

Experiences & events of a very new & varied nature have filled the three weeks that have elapsed since I last wrote here. On the previous day with more zeal than discretion I hastily wrote a letter to two of the Bedford Papers incited to do so by intelligence that the lawyer who had cross-examined Mrs Foskett had been looking around the back of her house, as was supposed for proof that she could not make the observations to which she had sworn from it, & the intelligence that it was intended to bring against her a charge of perjury. Thinking to make the lawyer (a Wesleyan & a prominent member) ashamed of taking further action; after eulogizing the work that the Mayoress with the corroboration of Mrs F had accomplished, questioned the creditableness of the work he had undertaken in opposition to hers & said the thanks not only of the neighbourhood, but of the town were due to two brave 'British women' & asked whether as a prominent member of a religious community that had just been spending its energies on revival services it was not passing strange that with the one hand he (the Solicitor for the Defendants) should be so serving God, & with the other – whom? This seemed to have touched him more deeply than I imagined it would, & on Monday morning I had an early visit from the Editor of 'Beds Times' bringing with him a letter from Mr Clare demanding the name of the writer of the letter signed 'an old Inhabitant' & declaring it to be 'libellous'. Rather alarmed at such a terrible charge I said I would at once communicate with a lawyer for his advice & opinion which I did by writing to Will by the noon post & begging an immediate reply.

In the afternoon I went to the monthly prayer & committee meetings of BWTA & afterward had a long talk over the matter with Mrs Ransom. This made me much later than usual in returning home & when I did so I found that the Editor had been twice to see me during my absence, being threatened with an action against himself if he did not give the name within 36 hours! Finding him so frightened, & Clare so determined, I should at once have avowed myself, but as I had put the matter into Will's hands (& as Papa said any time within the next six months would do to prosecute me in!) I thought it best to see him at once, & so left by next train for Cricklewood, & on arriving found him with Mr Thunder at Westbury Villa, having together been debating my difficulty & just posted a letter to me. I told them of Clare's extreme haste & indignation & proposed to write to him myself at once, & after Will had acquiesced (which he had not in the letter posted) at once dictated an epistle of avowal & explanation which Will, & then Mr Wheeler (whom he took me to consult next morning) altered & softened down, until there was little of mine left in it. Tuesday morning at 1 Temple Gardens I wrote what Mr W considered 'a handsome apology' for what both advised me was amiss in my epistle to the Papers which although <u>not</u> libellous might be so construed by a jury if allowed to go to a trial.

[CEB visited Great Yarmouth to attend a meeting of the BWTA] Leaving Yarmouth on Friday morning I returned to Bedford direct, in time to receive John & Mattie (who came that evening to stay with us over Sunday) & a lawyer's letter from a London Solicitor! Clare's wrath was unappeased by my letter to him. Papa also wrote to him without my knowledge, but nothing short of a threat of an action for libel would satisfy him. Once more I forwarded the letter to Will who put the case into his friend Mr Thunder's hands. Knowing how anxious Papa would be to avoid a trial they together decided that to assuage Clare's injured feelings (for in his reply to Papa he had declared himself 'unnerved' & too 'paralyzed' to do or say anything in the matter except through 'his legal friend') & to make amends for my temerity in 'venturing to criticise his action from a higher than a professional standpoint', it would be advisable for me to again write a letter which Will dictated making him an offer of £25 with a retraction of my criticisms. So far in spite of my own <u>deep aversion</u> to the course suggested had we got on Monday, when John & Mattie left after breakfast, & an hour or two after Dr & Mrs Grosart of Blackburn arrived, as had been previously arranged to spend a night here on their way to London.[114]

Their visit was a great pleasure to us, & I think also to them. In the afternoon I drove them to Bunyan Meeting, on our way thither fortunately meeting Mr Brown, who got into the Brougham with us & returned first to the Chapel & then to his own house, where he showed the Dr all the interesting Bunyan memorials of which he is the custodian, after which we drove to the spot that of all others he seemed most anxious to visit, Elstow Green. During the evening I told Dr Grosart my difficulty, & showed him my 'libellous letter' which he believed <u>not</u> to be so, also, & added with his strong Scotch weighty manner of speech 'I wouldn't have offered him twenty five farthings' adding a corroborative opinion of the sentiments I had rather too plainly expressed. Next morning our friends left us to take advantage of the very last day for visiting the Colonial Exhibition.[115]

Some weeks previously I had been asked & had accepted an invitation to Hoddesdon, to speak at a Gospel Temperance meeting on Thursday Nov[r] 11th. Leaving particular directions about my address in case of being needed for 'service of writ' I left home for London, taking [in] Cricklewood en route to The Mount, the next day. I found Will at Westbury Villa, just going to dine alone. I joined him, & we had a quiet talk together, but I had no further letter or intelligence to give him. About 11 o'clock to our great surprise Papa appeared bringing with him another lawyer's letter of acceptance of the money offer, accompanied by a document for my

---

[114] Dr Alexander Grosart, born in Stirling in 1827, was a Presbyterian minister in Blackburn. He was a prominent literary scholar, producing amongst other things an edition of Donne's poetry.

[115] The Colonial and Indian Exhibition was held at The South Kensington Museum, now the Victoria and Albert. It celebrated the achievements of Britain's overseas colonies at this time of the height of Empire.

signature, & for publication, as long as it was abject, & I had only to hear it partly read to express my determination <u>never</u> to sign it come what may. Neither Papa nor Will wished it. The former returned home by mid-night train, & I went to sleep with Hattie, leaving the precious document for Will & Mr Thunder to deal with.

When I got back from Church between 8 & 9 o'clock I found Will's Clerk had been waiting some time for me with a draft of the 'apology' which had been agreed on between the Solicitors, the which was to be forwarded to the Papers if I also consented to it. I felt myself completely in their hands in anything reasonable & not entirely opposed to my own convictions, & as there were but two words in this to which I could really take exception, I allowed it to be sent that night.

The next morning after having written cheques for the month's bills at The Mount, & a little talk & business generally, I left for my promised visit to Hoddesdon, calling at 1 Temple Gardens on my way to Liverpool St Station. Will had a Conference which took him away as soon as we had had a little luncheon together, but I waited until nearer my train time watching from the window a gathering of 'Welsh Bards' in the Gardens below, who assembled there to formally proclaim the National Eisteddfod which is to be held in London next year. The circle of unhewn stones which marked the site of the proceedings was surmounted by a most <u>un</u> Druidical circle of umbrellas, under which even the Harper with his flowing robes & beard was sheltered from the thick drizzling rain which was coming down. Whilst looking at this M<sup>r</sup> Thunder came in bringing with him a telegram from the Solicitor 'Clare accepts' so I hoped I had seen the worst of the worry consequent upon my 'libel' & on arriving at L-pool St telegraphed the same intelligence to Papa for his relief before taking train for Hoddesdon.

*Tuesday Dec<sup>r</sup> 7<sup>th</sup>*

I have been cogitating for some minutes where & how to begin to disentangle the work & events of the last weeks sufficiently to place them in anything like order here. The week following my return from Hoddesdon was the most physically inactive I have spent for some time, a tea meeting for the funds of the new American Organ in Southend Chapel, & a meeting after, & a couple of Mothers' meetings during the week was my chief work but mentally I was more busy. Nothing but yielding to the wishes & advice of Papa on whom I had brought some anxiety, & of Will who was supposed to know what was best to be done to appease Clare's wrath at my 'criticisms' & prevent his prosecuting me for the alleged 'libel' (whilst at the same time he (Will) did not believe there was any libel in the case) would have induced me to consent to the course which was adopted & I felt landed in a very slough of ignominy when in the next week's Papers close to my apology was a letter from Clare misrepresenting the money offer & amplifying it to such an extent as made it appear contemptible to myself. Incensed that my Solicitors would only consent to publish this under the same nom de plume as that in which the offending letter was written, he wrote that 'having received an offer of £20 & all legal expenses he had consented not to publish the name of the writer'!

I at once sent the Paper to Mr Thunder & his reply was that I 'need not regret the letter'. He prepared another in the name of the firm giving their account of the whole transactions, to which was appended a letter to the Editors of the Times

& Mercury[116] telling them they had rendered themselves liable to an action for publishing Clare's letter, & requesting them to insert theirs in their next issue as 'the least amends they could make'. A letter at night, the day before it should have appeared, from the Times Editor said that he had a 'distinct understanding' with Mr Clare when his appeared & refused to publish anything further 'unless I communicated with him'. This of course I declined. Then nothing would have pleased Mr T & Will better than to have been allowed to issue a writ on Clare for a much clearer libel than that with which he charged me, but I would not retaliate, & it is only to-day that I have written him a final epistle to tell him this, & what I thought of his unjustifiable action, concluding by reiterating my first question how, on reconsideration, he could make the Master's service compatible with that of the Brewer & Publican & that I should not regret all that had passed if he could be induced to throw the weight of his influence in the opposite direction to their interests.

So concludes one of the most painful & annoying incidents of my life. Those who have only seen the surface think I must have endeavoured to inflict injury commensurate with the compensation offered, & I cannot explain that the money offer was only made to place me in the position of having tendered what was ample, in case he pursued me to a trial, but I am only sorry that anything was done that could be interpreted as <u>shame</u> on my part. The only thing I have to be ashamed of is <u>seeming</u> so, & I thank God I can dismiss a subject that has cost me so much anxiety & annoyance without any sense of having been actuated by a wrong motive, & in the consciousness that I have endeavoured rather to benefit than injure the young man himself in it.

*Saturday Dec' 18th*

'The Mount' is my present work. I have at length found another Kitchen Matron in Mrs Lane's daughter who although younger than I wished is a reliable orderly woman. Poor Fanny after all we dare not trust. Lottie has been spending a few days with the Ladies there & at the same time Fanny also was there, the general opinion was one of distrust in her, although there was no proof. For the sake of others it would have been very unsafe to risk what might have involved some of them at least in suspicion. Now all seems once more peaceful in the Home & I hope may remain so until I can visit it again for the quarterly committee meeting which must be as early as possible in the near year.

The tramp's little girl that I found a place for in the summer has been in it until this week when the people with whom she lived left the town & in direct opposition to my request paid her her wages which at first she determined to use in going to her Mother who is in Ongar Union, & I hear both from the Master & a Guardian such a bad woman that to let the child come to her would probably be her ruin, & they begged me to keep her if possible. The girl's mistress had evidently encouraged her to leave & was quite insulting when I blamed her for putting it into her power to go. The Husband came to the house in so violent a manner that poor Rose who let him in was quite frightened & thought he was going to strike me, but when Papa came on to the scene he became more reasonable, & when he could be got to listen to the letters about the Mother (which I had before taken to read to his wife) he allowed

116    *The Bedfordshire Times* and the *Bedford Mercury*.

I was right in keeping her, & promised to bring her to me before leaving the next day. No excuse could be made for his rudeness but I was glad to get him to use his influence to get the girl to stay which as I expected there was little difficulty in doing with that. The Matron of the Girls Evening Club kindly took her in for 1/- a day until some place could be found for her & this was soon done by Mrs Goldsmith (whom I had consulted) in the little home of a former housemaid married & living near, but after a severe illness needing just such a little helper, so she is a great benefit & well cared for for a month at least.

### Dec*r* 21*st*
Yesterday & to-day have been spent chiefly amongst our neighbours before leaving home as I intend to do to-morrow. Poor Galpin has for months returned to his wallowing in drink, & got out of the room when I went in to see his wife this morning, but I got him to come back, & once more tried to show him the only proof he could give that he was not past all hope was to show that he had sufficient <u>will</u> power left to carry out his 'intentions' at once, & determine from that moment to stop & turn. He promised to come & see me before I leave to-morrow. The three next calls I made on Mothers all turning back to stimulant 'to do them good'. Then on a dying man who waked up from a deep sleep in which he had been lying most of the day, but seemed fully conscious, & when I told him of the One who was ever ready to save he became so affected as evidently showed how much he felt his need of salvation. Oh that men would be wise & 'consider their latter end' before they feel it near.

### Clarendon Lodge Shanklin Dec*r* 31*st*
In an hour or two longer the year 1886 will have passed away. It closes as it began, amidst circumstances & surroundings that call for continued thanksgiving. The last week of the year has been one of crowning enjoyment & mercies & has been spent here with all our children & grandchildren excepting Edward & his little ones, the absence of one branch being the only drawback to the pleasure we have had in our Xmas family gathering here in accordance with M*r* & M*rs* Kelly's kind invitation.

## 1887

### Feb*y* 16*th*
It is not easy to recall events in the order in which they occur even in looking back a fortnight, which accounts for their being so mixed & disconnected in reciting them. I must go back to the 1st of this month & the Committee meeting which was not I think a very satisfactory one either to myself or others. Mrs Atherton's letter was disposed of without blame being attached to any one but the writer, but Mrs Lucas was evidently disposed to find fault wherever she could, the real ground of her discontent being I believe that her funds from subscriptions are running short with another quarter's rent in prospect. My funds from Patients' payments had met all housekeeping expenses & some others, & left a balance of over £32 at the end of 1886. This I offered her, but it was somewhat haughtily rejected until Lady Elizabeth

expressed her desire that it should be accepted & I wrote a cheque for the amount, for which by the bye I have neither asked for nor received a receipt. The thanks which several ladies present, particularly Lady Biddulph, lavished upon me were no doubt intended to solace my feelings, although they were I believe sincere, but I almost determined to withdraw from the offer I had made Mrs Atkinson to continue what I could do in Bedford in correspondence etc if she would become co-Secretary with me. A few suggestions were made for changes to meet Mrs Lucas's ideas, but I said the conditions on which I undertook the work could not be altered until my term of office expired & to this all agreed. It was decided that an afternoon should be devoted to the 'Home' at the Annual meetings in May & that the 4th quarterly Committee meeting should be held the first Wednesday in April, but not a single question was mooted that affected the internal working, or could be called business referring to it, as I had on several points intended to bring forward.

*Saturday March 26th*
On Monday I was to have met Mr Hilton (of the United Kingdom Alliance)[117] at the Station & to have taken him to Mrs Ransom's, but after the MM, the new Tenant that has come to the next house but one called & what with helping her to char-woman, servant & such other information as a stranger needed, I was too late for the train, but found Mr H at Mrs Ransom's where Mrs Clark, Mr Murgatroyd, & Mr Watts the Baptist minister also came to meet him at tea before the preliminary meeting at the Coffee Tavern for which he had come. Our Secretary Mrs Clark had issued invitations to representatives of all the different Temperance societies in the town & of these about 20 assembled to listen to the information & advice which Mr Hilton came to give. Dr Goldsmith was present, & the meeting was as unanimous as that at his house had been divided, in deciding on some united action. What that will be another will be called to decide.

*Thursday May 12th*
Saturday night I attended an ordination service of two young ministers in the Cauldwell St Chapel, & on Sunday afternoon the Camp meeting held in a field on the Goldington Rd. The impression I got of their ministers was that they were men of far more power & ability than many who have greater social & educational advantages.

On Tuesday evening the women of the Elstow MM invited Mrs Ransom & several ladies who are accustomed to meet them, including myself, to take tea with them in the same room as that in which our meetings are held on the Green. Nearly all were assembled when I got there at 5-30. The long table prettily decorated with flowers & well laden with different kinds of cake, bread & butter with cresses & jam, all of which they had subscribed together to provide for us. One of their number made tea at either end, the sides being quite filled by the others & their guests, amongst whom also were the two daughters of the village Squire Mr Macan. The Parish Clerk's wife, who belongs to the meeting, gave the ladies an invitation to inspect the Church whilst the tables were being cleared & most of us went & spent some time looking at the painted windows in commemoration of Bunyan, both of scenes taken

---

[117]   This group aimed to introduce the local veto to prohibit the sale of alcohol (see Introduction).

from the Pilgrim's Progress, & the Holy War. The restoration of the Church a few
years since left nothing ancient to connect it with him excepting the tower which is
as when he rang the bells. Going back to the room we found the women expected
a meeting & some speaking. I did my part at the beginning, thanked them very
heartily for the pleasure they had given us, & then returned home with a handful of
the flowers that had adorned the tea table, & very pleasant thoughts of the grateful
expression of appreciation of our endeavours which the entertainment had been their
way of showing.

### Friday May 20th

The only other incident of interest this week was the 'united Temperance Conference' which after many disappointments & efforts was at length fixed to be held last
night in the Institute. There were representatives of 14 different societies present.
The Curate of St Peter's took the Chair. All seemed to promise well at first. It was
unanimously decided that an united Committee should be formed & that it should
be called the 'United Bedford Temperance Committee', but when the first proposal
came to be discussed, the desire expressed in a message from the Vicar of St Cuthbert's, & the Chairman's sympathy with him, induced him to propose an 'amendment' which limited the whole work to be done to 'legislative or legal action', so
that to the great annoyance of the majority of those present, but in order as Mr Watts
put it that the whole design might not be 'wrecked', it was agreed to secure the
union of the members of the CET societies by yielding to the simple formation of
a sort of Watch Committee, which will certainly be helpful to Temperance although
a very small part of the work that might have been, & I hope will ultimately be
undertaken.

### Wednesday June 1st

As arranged Mrs Clark left with me for our annual BWTA meetings on Monday
May 23rd. Tuesday morning I was off in good time & arrived at Memorial Hall for
the Prayer meeting held in the Board Room at 10 o'clock before the Council meetings in the Library at 10-30. I should have said that at the meeting at Mrs Lucas's the
previous night I obtained the consent of several ladies living in the neighbourhood
of the Home to be on the Committee next year, & also one more distant who, with
a friend of Lady B's the Honble Mrs Yorke-Elliott, have allowed themselves to be
nominated Vice-Presidents. Miss Docwra will also be Vice at the BWTA meetings
on account of Mrs L's deafness which prevents her carrying out the duties of her
position.

I had received a letter from the Secretary asking me to second the adoption of
the Financial Report, which was not satisfactory, the Association being some few
pounds in the Treasurer's debt. When I was called on to do this I expressed regret
as I was aware that the deficiency was attributed to the funds that had been supplied
for our Home, & I hoped that the Branches would not allow one department of the
work of the BWTA to interfere with its general stability. My remarks which had not
taken more than two or three minutes were cut short by Mrs Lucas's rising suddenly
& telling me that a long speech was not necessary in seconding the Report, & that
what I was saying would come at another time. Fortunately I had said all I wanted,
or had an opportunity of saying on the subject during the whole of the meetings, but

I felt considerably snubbed by the uncalled for interference, & received afterward a good many apologetic entreaties not to notice Mrs L's irritability, her age etc being urged in excuse.

In the afternoon I read my Report, & proposed the new names on the Committee, all of which was received with evident satisfaction & applause, spoken to by two ladies, supported by Lady Elizabeth (who spoke in very warm terms of the work that had been done) & unanimously adopted. An appeal for funds to continue the work was responded to by very many present, & promises of subscriptions of small amounts poured in for some minutes faster than I could write them. The Home business ended by a vote of thanks being accorded to the Dr which Lady Elizabeth seconded with a word of reference to 'his indefatigable Mother' at which words there was a sound of a cheer, but this was the only recognition of the Secretary's services for the year that the BWTA thought fit to offer. Truly my reward is not from them.

*June 13th*

After Lottie left I had a couple of very quiet days, & on Saturday drove with Papa to Aspley where he has found a lodging, & is going to make trial of going there each evening by the 5 o'clock train & returning after breakfast in the morning. We took tea together at the house, which is delightfully situated close to the pine woods & on the top of the hill, looked at a vacant house adjoining which we feel half inclined to take if the experiment of spending the nights & mornings at Aspley benefits Papa's health. It is now quite a place of resort, & wonders are said to be worked by the pure air. He began the following Monday, & seems already much better. When we reached home Saturday night we found a telegram which Edward had promised when he could send down his wife & little ones for the country change for which he was very anxious, not only the telegram, but Clara the two babies & the maid. But for the little boy's cough & the damp days earlier in the week they would have come there, & the beautiful change on Saturday enabled them to leave. On Sunday Papa had an appointment at Turvey. Clara accompanied him whilst I took charge of her boy & girl. They are dear little happy creatures, but very delicate, over a year old, & no sign of a tooth nor the least idea of using their legs.

Since the date last entered various events have transpired which I have not had time to write of. The chief the commemoration of the Jubilee of our Queen whose Coronation on the same day of the month 50 years ago was, I can just remember, celebrated in much the same manner as on the 21st of this present June. Then I was a little one living with my Parents in the little town of Newnham on the banks of the Severn, & my recollections of a dinner for the inhabitants laid out in the street. At Bedford the same sort of thing was decided on for about 6000. The one present good outcome of the united Temperance Committee was a request from it that the special tables should be provided for Abstainers who chose to keep away from the drink temptation which was offered in all directions. This was conceded, & Dame Alice St with accommodation for about 600 was apportioned to us. I undertook to have the supervision of two tables of 25 each to supply waiters, carvers & all etcs. The weather continued all that could be desired, the proverbial 'Queen's weather'. There was both room & provision for a larger number than came to our tables, so seeing many crowding around the Barriers at either end of the street I took it upon myself to invite all who had no tickets, but the requisite knife & fork with them, to come & dine. A few went off hastily home to get these so that about 50 more were supplied.

Clara was with me, & George Hodson who has been spending a week of the Long Vacation with us, & returned to Cambridge [the] following Monday. After a rest at home & tea Clara accompanied me to the Committee field of the River Fête from which we watched the procession of illuminated boats which with a display of fire works concluded the day's festivities. Papa went to London from Aspley in the morning, & returned in time for the sight of the former which was exceedingly beautiful. Some 40 boats, headed by a sort of state barge containing the Mayor & Corporation, all lighted up by colored lamps in various devices. One in the shape of a large swan entirely in white lamps, the body holding some 8 or 10 people, we thought the most chaste of all. Papa had a very capital view of the Royal Procession after the grand Thanksgiving Service in Westminster Abbey. Standing on the very front of the pavement opposite Devonshire House he was as close to the Queen & the Royal Carriages as it was possible to be as also to the numerous grandees & guests from nearly every country in the world who had assembled to honor her Jubilee. Such a gathering of Princes & nobles from all quarters of the globe has never been, & such a display of loyalty on the part of the people no Monarch has ever before received.

### Monday August 8th

Coming to the last page of another record of mercies & blessings of more than 4 years I do not know how to condense into so small a space not only the many events which have transpired since I last wrote, but a summary of the special family causes of thankfulness.

First of these is Papa's restored health, which he attributes to his residence at Aspley Heath. We decided on taking the house there from June 21st, sent over what furniture we could well spare without changing the aspect of more than a couple of rooms of our Bedford home.

On Saturday Will came down to see us & our Aspley home with which he was as much pleased as all else who have visited us in it have been. When I made my first entry in this book Will was making the first struggles in his profession, now to use the words of the Attorney General in a case which has been going on for days past in which whilst on the opposite side he speaks of him as 'a Counsel whose opinion, it must be acknowledged, was rapidly becoming of weight scarcely second to any other' (or words to that effect). And the amount of work he has had to do especially the last three months shows it was not mere opinion. His fees in that time most young Barristers would be thankful to earn in a year or even two. Judge Bowen sent him a little note at the end of his speech a week or two since to congratulate him on 'a very able argument'. Compliments direct & indirect & general success seem to have been showered upon him. Edward's position is I believe becoming more assured. He does not seem likely to become rich, but in his profession he is having rather more success. As a Christian & a man of science he is taking a place in the Church & the world & in addition is now chosen as a representative of the Wesleyans on the School Board.

John's future is also assured beyond my most sanguine hopes for him. He too is living to benefit others & will continue to have a helpmeet [*sic*] in Mattie who seems to delight in helping him. All my boys around me with bright earthly prospects, instead of scattered in distant lands! & our girls left to brighten & cheer our home! What more could we have asked or expected if our Heavenly Father had permitted us to choose for all. To Him be all the praise & glory for all.

Amen & amen

# Volume 3

# August 1887 to June 1896

**1887**

*Aspley Heath, August 24th 1887*

It is now nearly six weeks since we took up our residence in our second home here. It seems likely to prove as we hoped it would a place of increased health & strength not only to Papa but to myself & our girls. Papa seldom complains. As for myself I have not felt the benefit of the change so quickly as he did, & having had to go to Bedford & stay over nights several times have not had quite the full proof of it having each time returned not so well as when I went; but on the whole am certainly better. Lottie & Hattie are in excellent health & spirits. The latter seems charmed with her new surroundings & (as we all do) sees new beauties in every direction we take in our wanderings in the woods. Papa has his walk in them each evening as soon as he has finished his tea, & returns for an hour & half's writing before prayers & supper.

I have had a good deal to do in Bedford & have been over for some time, at least one night each week. At a meeting of the United Temperance Committee to elect officers no one would fill the Secretaryship, & that the whole might not collapse for want of this I allowed myself to be nominated pro tem, & was unanimously elected. The first public work decided on was to oppose the extension of licenses at the Brewsters Sessions,[1] & for this purpose it was decided to send as influential a Deputation as possible to wait on the Licensing Bench. Invitations to gentlemen & ladies to join this, notices of Committee meetings & in addition the 'Home'[2] correspondence & notices for Sept$^r$ Committee have seemed to fill nearly every spare moment.

*Tuesday Sept$^r$ 13$^{th}$*

My first business at the Home was to tell poor unhappy Fanny that the conclusion of her holiday visit to me (when she returned the worse for drink) made it impossible for her to continue there longer, & that I had found another to take her place. She must leave as soon as possible & as she has no place to go to without being exposed to great temptation I put an adv$^t$ in 'the Christian' & offered her to come to Aspley Heath until a situation could be found where she would be received & shielded from her fearful besetment. I found our new Matron at the Home seeming quite capable & settled in her work, & well spoken of by every one in the house but Fanny.

---

[1]  These meetings review applications for new liquor licences and the renewal of existing ones.
[2]  CEB refers to the BWTA home for inebriate women, The Mount.

*Sept 21st*

The Deputation to the Magistrates on licensing day was a large & influential one (Monday Sept 5th). I was very sorry that being in London then prevented my joining it, & owing I imagine to my not having thought of the necessary introduction, it was not formally received,[3] but the presence of some 30 or 40 Total Abstainers watching the proceedings & applications in the Court (in which I believe they occupied the Grand Jury Box) seems to have been quite as satisfactory an influence as if they could have made themselves heard & all new licenses but one Grocer's were refused. One of the Solicitors who applied for a license began to talk of the opposition of 'those people with a craze called teetotallers' but being reminded by Mr Stimson of their presence there, no further disrespectful reference was made not even by my late opponent Mr Clare who was there both to oppose & apply, but both in the Brewer's or Publican's interest![4]

On Monday I returned home[5] leaving Lottie to visit our neighbours & members of the Association. Fanny came here from the Mount the previous Monday, strange to say the worse for drink. The temptation at the Railway Stations evidently too great for her to resist. After a day or two I told her once more of her sin & folly, & if her penitence is as sincere as are her efforts to please me, there is still hope for her. Her value as a servant is beyond any I have ever had, nothing comes amiss to her that has to be done in household matters. I sent one maid for her holiday, took the other to Bedford, leaving Hattie & Reita[6] with Papa, for Fanny to manage for. Everything has been done with the greatest order & punctuality & in addition she has done a quantity of needlework for me & seems as if nothing she can do is too much. To save such a woman is worth a great deal & I feel that I cannot give her up. She is going to a first rate situation in an Abstaining Clergyman's family on the 26th &, having signed the pledge again, promises me to do her utmost to keep it.

*Monday Sept 26th 87*

Our visitors have gone. Reita on Saturday, & Fanny also left for her situation after dinner. Neither the plainness of speech which I have used to make her feel her sin & folly, nor the continual opportunities of giving her warnings for the future which her stay here has given me seem to have made her glad to get away, for she has spent a good part of the day in tears, & left with the same. Her penitence is I believe sincere, but her power of will so weakened, that in spite of her determinations I almost tremble for her at the danger spot, Cambridge, where she must change, & wait half-an-hour. She promised me faithfully not to go into the refreshment room there. I knelt with her before she left & entreated that she might have strength given to resist.

Since we came here I have been away so many times that I have had no opportunity of engaging in any work (beyond helping a little at the Bazaar) & this will continue as until the middle of Novr I do not expect to be at Aspley Heath for more than a few days. On Wednesday I go to Bedford, on Saturday to London

---

3   i.e. the members of the deputation were not permitted to speak.
4   i.e. to oppose the removal of licences and apply for new ones.
5   CEB here refers to the house in Aspley Heath as home.
6   A Swiss friend of Hattie.

&, expecting that I shall not have much to do for John,[7] I have promised to go to Nottingham the following Saturday to stay until Thursday Oct[r] 13th.[8] On the 20th our Annual BWTA meeting at Bedford, & on the 24th the Autumnal meetings of the Association begin at Gloster.[9] After Gloster comes my promised visit to Yorkshire. This I feel to be a responsibility that would make me afraid of what I have undertaken only that I am (as I tell the friends who have invited me) but one of a band of workers whom I have promised to do my best to <u>assist</u>. May I receive the help without which I 'can do nothing'.

[The chronology of the next few entries is very muddling, because CEB was travelling a great deal, as she summarises above. In order to clarify this, the dates when the events described occurred have been added to the text and will be found in square brackets].

### *Alpha Villa Friday Oct[r] 7th*     *John's Marriage*[10]
The wedding is over. Another, & the last of the three who but a few years ago were 'our boys', has built his own nest, & Mattie Southwell is no more. John has waited a little longer than either of his brothers, but has begun married life with less of the element of uncertainty than in either of their cases as far as income is concerned & I consider the girl who has him for a Husband, with his <u>smallest</u> qualification, of so good prospects, a fortunate individual. I believe they love each other sincerely & nothing will be needed to make their home a happy one, if, amidst all God has given them, they continually live to serve & glorify the Giver. May they have wisdom & grace so to do.

I left Bedford by the 10-40 train last Saturday morning [1 October] coming in from Aspley with Papa. From Kentish Town I went on to the Elephant Station & thence to Edward's. After dinner he accompanied me to The Mount to visit his Patients there & for me to meet M[rs] Atkinson who came & seems as earnest as ever in the interests of the Home. We seem now more settled both with Matron & Sub Matron than ever before, both seem working comfortably with each other & the Patients. After conversation with a new one (the <u>Matron</u> of a Rescue Home who whilst engaged in saving others has to be rescued herself) & having tea, we returned to OKR, where I spent Sunday & heard an excellent stirring sermon at night from 'As for me & my house we will serve the Lord' preached by M[r] Stewart to the Parents of the Sunday scholars, it being the School anniversary.

[Monday's entry is not included. John's wedding took place on Tuesday 4 October]

---

[7]  John's wedding was to take place on Tuesday 4 October.
[8]  This may have been CEB's first visit to Nottingham; its purpose was to attend and speak at BWTA meetings. She visited the well-known Goose Fair, but found a lack of interest in the movement in the city, and yet much need for it. Her diary entry for 24 October 1887 (omitted in this edition) states that 'even the young girls were in the habit of spending their evenings in the Public Houses, for the sake of company rather than drink, but their immorality is proverbial'. CEB would not have imagined that she would spend the last 30 years of her life living in Nottingham, from 1903, when she and Edward moved out of Bedford, to her death and burial there in 1933.
[9]  CEB's idiosyncratic spelling of the west country cathedral city.
[10]  Several pages at this point in the diary have headings apparently added later by CEB. They have been inserted in this edition at appropriate places in the text.

The Church when we reached [it], nearly half an hour before the Bride, was rapidly filling & quite full by the time she came. John looked quite radiant amongst the flowers with which the pulpit & chancel were decorated, & very much at ease, chatted to his (2ⁿᵈ!) best man Mʳ Dixon & various other friends whilst waiting for her. Will & Florence came in Mʳˢ Kelly's Brougham with Georgie & Eric both of whom had baskets of flowers in their hands which they were to strew on the pathway of their Uncle & new Aunt as they left the Church.

Mʳ Everett an Uncle of Mattie's assisted at the ceremony with Mʳ Clay who concluded by giving an exhortation to the newly married pair as to those who had been & he evidently hoped would continue to be his friends & helpers. After the signings in the vestry John was leading off his Bride to the strains of the Wedding March when his steps were arrested by having left his hat behind, which pardonable forget [sic] was soon rectified & he marched off a married man!

After refreshments Papa & I had a walk in the garden with our two eldest Sons & their wives, & were fetched in by the announcement that the Bride & Bridegroom were departing. Mʳˢ Southwell was standing in the Hall with a supply of rice, which John guarded against by slipping into the Drawing-room & tying his handkerchief over his coat collar; a plentiful sprinkling was bestowed on them, & added to the hilarity of the guests, if not to their enjoyment in departing.

We left soon afterwards, & spent the remainder of the evening with Will & Florence with our girls. Edward was obliged to return at once with Clara. Papa slept with me at John's lodgings, & left by early train next morning. I went off soon after breakfast to the City to attend a united meeting of the BWTA Executive & 'Home' Committees at Memorial Hall, & at the end, instead of returning to Cricklewood, as I at first intended, went direct to Forest Hill that being I knew the only opportunity I should have of going there for a long time. I spent a very pleasant evening with the Patients, had family worship, & a little conversation with each of them & left after breakfast next morning. Made two or three calls returning through London & after dinner with Florence, went with Lottie to John's house.[11] All we could do was to put his books which were lying as brought from his lodgings, in order in the bookcases. The staircase required the last coat of paint, stair carpets had not arrived, so after seeing the landlord, & having his promise to send a painter next day, & then the gardener who had the contract for getting the garden in order, & finding that neither one nor the other were [sic] intending to do anything in front of the house (which was rough as the bricklayers had left it), to arrange for this being done & a few shrubs planted was all it seemed I could do. So leaving Lottie to make some curtains, & see that all was generally in order when John returned, I came away from Friday morning [7 October] or rather after early dinner at Westbury Villa, reaching Bedford in time to have a few minutes at GF Walk MM which Mʳˢ Forbes was kindly taking for me, & then waiting for the BWTA Committee meeting which was appointed for that afternoon to make final arrangements for the Annual meetings on the 21ˢᵗ, to which Mʳˢ Reaney was invited. As is so often the case Mʳˢ Sampson had views that I could not agree with about the collection etc, & it was only by being persistent that I managed to carry the point that there should be a hand to hand collection to defray the extraordinary expenses (7 guineas) we were

11 John's house was in Parsifal Road, South Hampstead.

incurring. This settled (but not until near 6 o'clock) I went to Alpha Villa where I found Papa, beginning to think I was not coming. He left for Aspley at 8 o'clock to meet Will & his Editor, who were to spend Sunday with him.

*Oct 24th /87*
On Friday [14 October] Papa came from Aspley at 2 o'clock having had a few days of partial absence from business, but coming to the Works for an hour or two each day. We returned here[12] together at night & had only been at home a very short time when Will came again, bringing with him Georgie to spend Saturday & Sunday with us. I found he had come at Papa's invitation to go over a little of his law reading with him before his final examination which began on Oct[r] 13th & lasted the two next days.[13] [This date must be later, in the week beginning Monday 17th October, as Papa must have had his tutorial with Will before the examination.] Papa was rather faint-hearted & half inclined to put off the ordeal to the end of the year as he might have done, but Will's opinion was that to make the trial would at any rate prove how he stood, & be a help to him for a future one if he did not succeed. However he has returned not very sanguine as he says the Exam papers might have been framed to miss the very subjects to which he has devoted most time. The result will be known about Nov[r] 3rd when the names of all who have passed will be posted up in the Temple.

*Penistone, Yorkshire, Saturday Nov[r] 5th*
*Yorkshire Tour                    My Husband's Exam success*
The events of my visit to Gloster & the week I have since spent in this county must be passed by to record the greater one which I received intelligence of at Hull on Thursday [3 November] in a letter from Papa which reads thus 'If you can refer to to-day's 'Times' you will see your Husband's name among others who have passed the Examination' which means the final one held at Lincoln's-inn-Hall for law Students. I am indeed proud & thankful. Proud that my Husband amidst all the worries & anxieties of business has accomplished as much as any young man with none of either could have done, & thankful as much that his mind is relieved of the extra strain it has had the last three years, as I am at his success.

*Alpha Villa Saturday Nov[r] 12th*
*Visit to Gloster*
[CEB describes her return from the BWTA meetings in Gloucestershire. She takes the Oxford-Cambridge line.]
Saturday morning [29 October] turning homeward, instead of taking my ticket for Woburn Sands as I intended to have done, I took it for Bedford. There was nothing to be done but come on to Bedford where the train first stopped, & wait at the station half an hour before returning by the next, which I was obliged to do, to

---

[12]  i.e. to Aspley.
[13]  John Hamilton, in *Glad for God* (chapter 10), suggests that it was Edward's dissatisfaction with the lack of recognition by the Howards that led him to take partial retirement, as indicated in the first sentence of this entry, in order to give him time to develop what he must have hoped would be a new career as a barrister in which he could work for himself, rather than as an employee, and utilise his great knowledge of patents and patent law.

meet the ladies who had promised to come to Aspley Heath that afternoon at 3
o'clock to confer about the formation of a Branch of the BWTA. To my surprise
& pleasure about 30 came. A detachment from Aspley Guise accompanied Miss
Courtney & Miss Laws, another from Woburn came with M^{rs} Blundell, & I had
invited a few at Woburn Sands who also came, with the exception of the Clergyman's wife who wrote a letter of thanks, but expressed her inability to unite with
those who considered or rather had said 'that moderate drinkers were a hinderance
to the cause of religion' I think that was the expression. After reading several other
letters of willingness to unite with us, I explained the objects of the Association. It
was unanimously resolved to form an united Branch of the three places represented.
Officers were named & an adjourned meeting to elect them arranged to be held at
M^{rs} Blundell's house. Lottie consented to become co-secretary with some other
lady, & promised to act as such at the meeting the following week. As I was leaving
again, for Yorkshire, on Monday all I could do further was to furnish an agenda of
the business to be done which Lottie seems to have well carried out. A committee
was formed & the first formal meeting was to be held at Aspley Guise on Wednesday
Nov^r 16^{th} to which she will have to go before I return to Aspley Heath as I stay in
Bedford for my M Meeting on Friday Nov^r 18^{th}.

[On Monday 31^{st} October, CEB departs for BWTA meetings in Yorkshire, travelling
to Hull, then to Penistone, to the north-east of Sheffield.]

Wednesday [9 November] was the day that stands out in my mind as the most
memorable one in my journeyings. Bidding my kind entertainers at Penistone 'Good
bye' at about 7-30 a m I took a ticket for Doncaster on my way to the next appointed
place Scarboro' where I understood I was expected to be at a Ladies' meeting in
the Town Hall at 3 o'clock, but was invited to arrive at 11 in time for dinner. Being
late in going to bed & early in rising, & getting pretty snugly wrapped up in my fur
cloak in a corner of the railway carriage from Sheffield (where I changed) I became
drowsy, & not aware I had reached Doncaster until the train was just moving. Here
I ought to have got out & have taken the train leaving almost immediately for York.
Finding the train stopped again at the next Station 5 miles distant I was not greatly
concerned thinking at that early hour, soon after 9 o'clock, I should be able to
accomplish the journey in time for the meeting, if not for dinner. I got out at the first
Station & found it would be about three quarters of an hour before I could get back
again to Doncaster. I made myself as comfortable as I could under the circumstances
before a good fire which I had all to myself in the little booking office.
Looking around amongst some parcels waiting for delivery, I saw close at my
side a large stone jar capable of holding some gallons, filled with, and labelled,

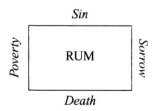

It may be that 'Satan found some mischief still, for idle hands to do' but after contemplating the label some time the temptation was too strong to be resisted not to appropriately border the broad white space around the three letters, which I did with my pencil as above, leaving it to carry at least a warning to its destination.

As soon as I could after getting back to Doncaster I made enquiry as to the time I could arrive at Scarboro' & to my dismay found there was no possibility of doing this until 3-40 & that I must remain where I was nearly three hours before getting a train for York. So going to the telegraph office at once I telegraphed. 'Missed my train cannot arrive until 3-40. Shall I come?' A reply came about a quarter of an hour before the time for the train 'You must certainly come, take Cab direct to Old Town Hall'. So after a very unhappy time of waiting I took my ticket for Scarboro', & my seat in a corner of a very comfortable third class carriage. The Porter placed my little dress basket in another, & the two others were filled by a lady opposite to me & a gentleman on the same side who looked quite an invalid.

Just before starting another Porter came up to the carriage his arms filled with the wraps etc of a gentlemanly looking man who as he looked around & saw every corner occupied said rather loudly, 'Helloa! Porter, I told you to find me a first class third'! I rose to move my basket, which he at once prevented, begged I would not disturb myself adding 'the age of chivalry was not quite passed'. A remark in answer to his politeness gave him the opportunity of saying that he had travelled a great deal that for twenty years he had been a Commercial traveller. Contrary to my usual inclination with fellow travellers who seem inclined to talk I replied, observing that his travels involved peculiar temptation, he readily acquiesced & I asked what he considered the greatest that commercial men had to meet, to which he replied he thought, lying. I suggested that a greater still was strong drink. To this he also assented & after a little further conversation asked me plainly whether I saw any indications of it in him to which I replied I thought I did. 'You have been influenced in what you are saying Madam,' he soberly remarked, to which I said I believed I had, but by God only.

Then he told me that he was born in the Highlands of Scotland, that the first drop put into his mouth was whiskey. That he had been a Student at the University of Aberdeen, was a good Greek & Latin scholar, had a good mother, & good wife & a family, but after all this acknowledged that that morning he had taken 7 glasses of spirits. 'My poor friend' I said 'Is it so? Then there is nothing for you but 'right about face'. Look at the title of this book, (I had Gustafson's 'Foundation of Death' in the carriage with me) it is a very terrible, but it is a true one, shall it be so with you?' He seemed struck with what I had been saying & I followed it on by asking him whether he would accept the book, & sign a pledge that he would from that moment give up what was so plainly dragging him down to destruction. A struggle seemed to be going on within him for a few moments, & then he said 'I will'. 'Then give me the book & lend me your pencil.' He crossed the carriage to my side, gave me his pencil & I wrote in bold characters on the fly leaf of the book 'I promise by God's help to abstain from all intoxicating drinks, & to discourage their use by others.' He almost eagerly took the pencil from my hand & placed his signature in a clear hand beneath it. Then I said 'let me add my witness, & the date which I hope may [be] that of a day you will thankfully remember as long as you live.' He held out his hand, I gave him mine which he grasped, & I signed my name under his as witness. 'My wife knows' he said 'that when I make a promise I can keep it, & I'll keep this to you.' 'Not to me' I replied, 'you have promised to God' (the thought seemed almost too much for him, & he closed his eyes & shook his head). 'He alone can give you strength to keep it.' 'But I'm under the influence of drink now' he said. 'Yes' I answered 'it may be so, & I only wonder you do not show it more & probably you will call yourself a fool for having been induced to make such a promise, but depend upon it you were never in your life such a wise fool, if you will only keep firm to it.' I told him what a miserable morning I had had through missing the earlier train & that I now thought what had caused me such uneasiness was God's way of sending him the message which was the proof of His willingness to help & save him. He said his wife had been praying for this & showed me a telegram he had that morning received from her to ask whether he was still at the Hotel from which he last wrote, her 'womanly instinct' inferring from the not too steady handwriting that he might not be going on with business.

Just as ours was completed the train reached York, & with another shake of the hand, a promise to write to me, & an invitation to call on me if he came to Bedford, we parted. The lady who sat opposite to me had listened with interest, & put in a few words saying he was a fellow countryman. On the Platform she came up to me & held out her hand with the remark 'You have done a good work, I am not a Total Abstainer but my sympathies are with you.' Thank you I said, but your <u>influence</u> is in the wrong direction, & so we parted, but I thought there was a softened rather than an angry look in her eyes at this remark.

*November 27th /87    Edward's birthday*
At the last Committee meeting of the Home, at which I was not present, a new house was decided on, & I am hoping to meet M^rs Atkinson at it & decide on what purchases we shall have to make, as soon as I get back to London from Ashford on Thursday, & between that & the following Wednesday if possible get the removal made. Applications for the Home have been coming in beyond our capability of entertaining them, & we must get into a larger place as soon as we can. We have now 11 Patients at The Mount, have sent some applicants to other Homes & deferred or refused others still. <u>Many</u> have also been applied for who either would not come, or for some reason apart from us did not do so, showing how much <u>female</u> drunkenness there is that we <u>know</u> of, but what a small part that is of what really exists! Of this we have heard some dismal tales to-night from M^r Garland who labours in the East of London & spoke in The Exchange.[14]

*Dec^r 13th*
Returning to London Thursday morning the whole of my time until the following Wednesday evening was occupied in 'Home' matters. M^rs Atkinson had written to me the previous week to say that a house suited to our need in removing had been visited & approved of by herself & some members of the Committee & I hoped to have been able to carry out my promise to undertake the removal that same week, but to my great disappointment when all negotiations <u>excepting</u> the signing of the agreement to take it had been completed, the Landlord altered his mind & refused to

[14]  Bedford Corn Exchange.

let it for <u>our</u> purpose. So all the work of house-hunting had to be begun again. I went into many alone; with M^rs Atkinson into many others, but nothing exactly what we required could be found until remembering a neighbourhood where I had seen some empty houses in my walks to Norwood. I returned thence after spending a night at Penrith House, took the same route to The Mount, & was fortunate in discovering a house containing 9 bedrooms & 4 sitting rooms, for which after M^rs Atkinson had seen & approved it with me, we offered £60 per annum, which as it had been vacant some time was gladly taken by the Insurance Co to whom it belongs, & as soon as a few necessary repairs are completed I must go to Town again & get the Patients into the new Home before Xmas. I should have said the Committee met as usual on Wednesday (the first in the month) & gave us full permission to take the house, purchase what more furniture was needed, & remove to it as soon as possible. M^rs Atkinson took me over the house that was thought to be so suitable, & I was only glad that it was refused to us. The position & number of rooms was not to be compared to the one we have at £20 less rent!

*Friday Dec^r 30^th*
The week which I spent at Aspley between the 7^th & 14^th was more pleasantly than usefully occupied. One very pleasant evening I spent with the girls at the house of M^r Blundell, whose acquaintance with that of his wife & daughter we have made since coming here. They live in a fine old Manor House near Woburn & having been previously for some years in Australia had so much of interest to tell in reference to their life in that country & so many objects of curiosity that they had brought from it, that the time we were with them was most enjoyable. M^r Blundell is as earnest in Temperance work as his wife & undertakes the arrangement of meetings at Woburn in connection with the Band of Hope etc. Lottie promised to sing for him at one of these, & he has promised to take the Chair for a meeting to be held next week in connection with the Woburn Sands Temperance Association of which Lottie has undertaken the office of Secretary as well as of the new BWTA Branch. I have promised to help by speaking at the meeting, which is to be held in the Institute.

On going to 'The Tor'[15] on Monday morning I was sorry to find the workmen had made very little progress with the work that was necessitated by finding the water pipes in a very bad condition, some of them being nearly furred up. Workmen were still about in all directions, but the first load of furniture from The Mount arrived in the afternoon, & with my three helpers this was soon placed in something like order in the available rooms, & these we occupied until Wednesday, whilst having the carpets altered, receiving the ordered goods etc. On that afternoon the remaining Patients & the last load of furniture arrived, & we had only to put chairs & tables in the dining-room to have it ready for the ladies to sit down in comfort for their first meal.

Saturday morning I left as early as possible to avoid the crush of the Xmas travellers, & arrived home to have dinner with Papa alone, & to go on with him in the afternoon to Aspley Heath. Here we arrived to find Lottie, Hattie, Katie Peace & George Hodson (who had come the previous day to spend Xmas with us) all busy decorating the dining-room with holly. Charles Barns arrived in time for tea & a

---

15   As the new Home was called.

merry noisy party the five young folk made! sometimes almost more than we older ones could endure, but it gave me pleasure to think that we were able to make three who had not the friends & enjoyments of their own homes happy, by partaking of that which our own dear ones have in theirs.

Monday, which was universally kept as a holiday, was a charming day, & we all started for a long walk in the bright sunshine going through the woods to Woburn & on as far as the sheet of water in the Park. Here we turned off the Drive to the water side, & were speedily followed & accosted by an old Keeper who found fault with us first of all for this, & then, finding we were not inhabitants of Woburn, told us very civilly we had no right there at all without an Order. In this case 'ignorance was bliss' we told the old man, truly, we had no idea of this but being there continued our walk as much further as we felt inclined, & in returning found our friend still hovering about, & willing to walk & talk with us of his encounters with former visitors. These sometimes certainly seem to take advantages of their privileges in plucking shrubs etc, & it is right to prevent this but his Grace of Bedford is by no means generous to the Public in the use of his vast Park & Woods. It is possible to walk miles in both without meeting a single individual, except on the high road through the Park which he cannot control, but beyond this, it is not allowed either to drive, or sit down for a pic-nic, without special orders which it is generally most inconvenient to get just as they are wanted. Getting back to Aspley Heath in time for dinner at 2 o'clock M$^r$ Rathmell the young Wesleyan Minister joined us. Afterwards the young folk went out for a little while to a Christmas Tree Sale, & returned to spend the remainder of the evening merrily together.

The record of 1887 is that of another year of abounding mercies. All the clouds have been those which distrust has gathered. Papa's improved health, his passing his legal ordeal, John's settlement in business & in a home of his own, are special matters for thankfulness. Will's has been a year of success, if of increased responsibility, of his own making. Edward is certainly the one of the family who has passed through the greatest trials & anxieties, & these we cannot help sharing with our children, when they come, may they prove 'more precious than gold which perisheth'.

## 1888

*Saturday Jan$^y$ 21$^{st}$ 1888*

Saturday was fine & we took a walk together in the afternoon going first to the Works where Papa showed me the new apparatus he has had put up within the last few months for the making of gas from mineral oil. The experiment is utilized for lighting one of the large Workshops, & also for supplying a Gas Engine & seems very successful. It is a very long time since I have been into the Works & I had no idea that with all else he had accomplished this to such an extent. The next few days were so restful that I can scarcely recall how they were occupied except that Monday was so bright & spring like that I was in the garden with James a good part of the morning. The following one was as great a contrast as possible, & the fog which came on then lasted three whole days.

*Thursday Jan^y 27^th 1888*

Thursday afternoon the Good Templars asked me 'to support' M^rs Ransom who was to preside at a Women's meeting for them in the Hall, which is now the only place of meeting we have that will hold 5 or 6 hundred people except the Corn Exchange. (We want a Temperance Hall more & more.) After the meeting which was not nearly as well attended as I should have been glad to have seen it, M^rs Ransom asked me to go to tea with her. I spent a couple of very pleasant hours with her. Five boys were at the tea table, the eldest son away, another little one in the nursery, with a baby girl; & the eldest of all the family, her daughter Annabel, a quiet sedate girl of sixteen. Truly M^rs Ransom is in the very thick of the battle of life, but with all her domestic duties (& her home & children show plainly she does not neglect these) she is full of public spirit & finds time to further most of the works of philanthropy in the Town. We feared she would not consent to continue President of our Association another year but the wish that she should do so was so earnestly expressed, that she would not refuse. We went together to the Good Templars' evening meeting at which D^r Carter was in the Chair. Excellent speeches by M^rs Meehan (who spoke in the afternoon), & particularly by a M^r Bingham, made one regret that they were addressed to a comparatively small audience, & most of those Abstainers. The same power under united auspices, & in the Corn Exchange, would have produced very different gatherings & results.

This afternoon was the time fixed for our Quarterly BWTA tea & meeting. I went into the Town about 4 o'clock, paid my MM bill & did a little other business before going to St Peter's School-room where it was to be held. Meeting M^rs Clark I accepted her invitation to go home with her for afternoon tea, after which we went together to receive the women for tea at 6 o'clock. Before that time they began to arrive, & continued to do so for nearly an hour. Not only were the tables filled but every available space in which a form could be put, & even then some rose as soon as they had finished to make room for those who were standing. There must have been considerably over 200 present, all members, (with a single exception) or who had come to join us. Truly it made my heart glad to think of even half the influence that is represented by that number twice over (more than 400) in this place, & to think of all the children who were being trained by these Mothers in paths of temperance, their prevention far better than any reformation, or moderation, which last, Sir Wilfred Lawson said in a speech last week, is 'the Mother of Drunkenness'.[16]

At the after meeting, at which M^rs Ransom presided & spoke with her usual dignity & force, I was asked to give some account of where & what I had been engaged in since I last met the women. I gave them some few facts about the Home, told them of 36 applications during the last 9 months, beside those who had actually been in it, & read three of them, that they might know the state to which so many were reduced before being willing to be saved from themselves, & then gave them some of my Yorkshire experiences, in all of which they appeared much interested.

---

[16] Sir Wilfred Lawson was a radical Liberal MP between 1868 and 1906 (with two short gaps) who promoted the right of ratepayers to veto the grant of licences for the sale of intoxicating liquors. Though this was never made law, Lawson was successful in passing resolutions to its effect in the House of Commons in the early 1880s. He was President of the United Kingdom Alliance, whose main platform was prohibition, on a local if not a national scale.

M$^{rs}$ Forbes, M$^{rs}$ Butler-Prior & Miss A Cockburn sang Solos at intervals, & M$^{rs}$ Sampson finished by an earnest Gospel address. I walked home with M$^{rs}$ Ransom, but passing her own door, she walked back with me quite over the new Bridge, where our pleasant converse ended.

*Monday Feb$^y$ 6$^{th}$ 1888*
Sunday morning was bright but very cold. We went together to the Wesleyan Chapel, & at night also staying to the sacramental service. In the afternoon Hattie went to fulfil her promise, whilst I made a first visit to some of our poorest neighbours. The first house I called at was that of a man of about forty five on whom consumption had evidently laid its hand. He seemed to have little hope or fear, & I could only endeavour to awaken both & pray with the family; the eldest son, a lad of sixteen being one of those who signed the pledge at our meeting. At the next lived the brother of a man whom I used to visit here who shortened his life by drink & died some years since. His son of about the same age as the other was another who promised to abstain which the Father would not; but I pointed him to Christ & when I asked the family of five to kneel together, he seemed as if it was an act to which he was totally unaccustomed. In another cottage more poverty stricken than either of the first, & close by, I found an elderly weakly looking man with an afflicted wife only able to move from the bed in the corner to the fire place by the help of a crutch. How they managed to sustain life together, with the very little he was able to earn with his poor wife to care for & attend to seemed marvellous. She was however uncomplaining & very intelligent, & when I made enquiry about her earlier life I discovered she had been a Wesleyan Sunday School Teacher. She was very pleased at my visit & I promised to go & see her again.

[CEB is visiting London]

From [William's Chambers in] the Temple I went direct to 'The Tor'. Several things which I had left to be finished were still waiting, or wanting, but on the whole the house looked comfortable, & the change a very great improvement on 'The Mount'. Matters with the Patients seemed tolerably smooth but the Matron & Sub-Matron had reached a point that made an understanding between them very necessary both for their own sakes & those around them. Both were in fault in irritability towards each other which however by talking with them both apart & together I hope was allayed. The Committee meeting was very pleasant & satisfactory to me. Having had nearly 40 applications for admission to the Home during the past ten months that had fallen through on account of either the length of time Inmates are required to remain, our terms, & other causes, I proposed that I should have increased power to deal with each case on its own merits rather than keep empty rooms & beds that might be occupied by those who had better have some help than be entirely rejected. This was granted. Two very hopeful cases have just left. The first the wife of a gentleman who told the Matron a sad story of his past life with her. She became a pledged Abstainer before leaving, & M$^{rs}$ Aukland told me she is now working as a member of the BWTA. The other is the Ipswich Matron. I told the ladies at our Committee meeting here of my anxiety to find a home for her as she was entirely friendless, & one of them came to me & most kindly offer[ed] to give her a month's trial if she would accept her situation which she very wisely resolved to do, & has come to Bedford. M^rs Gell tells me she is 'more than satisfied' with her, & I have been to see Charity. She is full of gratitude both to her Mistress & myself, accepts her position, & in cap & white apron looks simply a most superior servant.[17]

*Aspley Heath Feby 17^th*
The following day in company with M^rs Clark I went to Harrold at Miss St Quintin's invitation to have tea with the women of their Branch which now numbers some 120. Members & their friends to about that number sat down, & at the meeting after quite double the number of men & women were present. Both gatherings were held in the Mission Hall which Miss St Quintin has provided entirely at her own cost. I was told she bought a public house for £1000 pulled it down & at the cost of another £1000 erected the Hall, & adjoining premises for a keeper, & other convenient rooms. The clergyman of the village, who seems to have no sympathy with any work in his parish, refused her the use of the National School-room for Temperance meetings, & she told me she then politely told him what she should do if he persisted in refusing it, & he in reply simply made a polite bow. That bow has been a greater benefit to the poor parishioners than any words he has ever uttered, for not only has the Hall been built but any earnest work of evangelization carried on entirely at her cost, which fact however I believe I narrated after my first visit two or three years ago. M^rs Clark spoke first & I afterward. We spent the night at Miss St Q's & returned together next morning after a very pleasant visit.

The remainder of the week was spent in getting small bills settled, & various other matters which with Elstow M Meeting on Thursday & Grey Friars on Friday kept me almost entirely out of the house until Saturday when I came here, to find Lottie & Hattie glad to have me with them again. Papa left at the same time by train, that I did with one of the maids in the Chaise, in which we drove to the bottom of Brogboro' Hill, where I sent James back in spite of rain, which came on just as we were starting, & continued at intervals most of our drive, until just before we began to walk. Before we reached the top of the hill however it came on faster than ever, & before we met Papa, who promised to walk out to us, I began to regret the walk both for him & ourselves. To my astonishment Lottie was with him, at least two miles from home, when we met & we could only trudge along the now muddy roads with them until, regardless of getting more wet or dirty, we arrived here in a somewhat dripping condition. Fortunately however we did not take any harm but I found Hattie with a bad cold which has left a cough which is a cause of great anxiety to me.

*Saturday March 3^rd /88*
The continual snow & north easterly winds which have prevailed all through the past month have rendered it more inclement than for some years past. We came here [Bedford] from Aspley on account of this, Papa did not care to encounter such weather daily, & I was very glad to be able to attend to some of our home & outside work which we seem to be neglecting but of this last have done very little partly on account of the extreme cold.

On Thursday the weather changed for the better, & at Papa's wish I drove over to

---

[17]  There is no further record of 'the Ipswich matron'.

Aspley in the Chaise. Here most of the snow had disappeared, & as the sun shone & the journey was away from the north wind, it was by no means an unpleasant one. As we got on the road past Marston there was much more snow & nearer Woburn Sands the drifts nearly covered the hedges. At Aspley Heath everything was as winterly [*sic*] as when we came away. James managed very well in doing what was necessary after we arrived, about 3 o'clock, & by the time Papa came we had a bright fire & cosy tea table ready for him. After tea we walked up the hill to the wood which seemed still deep in untrodden snow. On Tuesday I went with M^rs Ransom to a meeting in the Corn Exchange in favor of 'Local Option' which many Teetotallers would not attend fearing it might injure the interest of our Brewing Liberal Member M^r Whitbread. Principle sacrificed to Politics![18]

*Friday March 16^th*
[CEB in London]
On reaching the Home I found there were three new arrivals, about which I had been corresponding. One the young widow of a D^r her Father one also, another the widow of a highly respectable Farmer who had died a fortnight previously since which time she had been continually under the influence of laudanum & brandy, & was then stupid & half dazed from the effects of it; & a third with memory so weakened that she could not remember the way into her own room after being days in the house. Drink! Drink! Drink! The Matron had been unwell & I offered to take charge for her until after Sunday if she would take a little change. I was very disappointed to find almost everything I had been obliged to leave in an unfinished state just as I left it. Very little interest shown in the appearance of the house. With the help of two or three of the most capable Patients I set to work trimming window blinds, putting down stair carpets, & various small matters that made both the inside & outside look very different. One poor woman, an Artist's wife, was greatly distressed that she could not get her Husband either to write or come to her. I telegraphed to him on Saturday without better success than a scrawl, without address, on Monday to say he could not come & without giving any reason. No doubt his wife thought but he was drinking heavily. How can she ever hope to be better?

*March 30^th (Good Friday) Aspley Heath*
I came back to Bedford on Wednesday to attend the United Temperance committee meeting at which the new Local government Bill as it related to the licensing question was, amongst other matters, to be considered.[19] After considerable discussion, we decided on drawing up a resolution to be forwarded to our MP disapproving of the proposed compensation to those engaged in the liquor traffic where a public house was closed by the local governing Boards, as creating a vested interest that had never before been acknowledged & did not exist.

The Salvation Army have just 'opened fire' at Bedford & no doubt the eccentricities of their methods will attract, until the novelty wears off. If they can only be the means of saving 'some' we will not grudge them those we lose, but I do not think

---

[18] Electors in Bedford who were Liberals and teetotallers had to make this choice.
[19] The Local Government Act of 1888 set up County Councils to consist of councillors elected by household suffrage for three years and aldermen elected by the councillors. It provided the framework for local government until modified by the Local Government Act of 1972.

their organization will long outlive 'General Booth' even if they are doing present good.

### April 17ᵗʰ

My Father's birthday, born in 1802 he is still hale & hearty & has written a long letter of thanks for our congratulations. Papa was at Cricklewood on Saturday. Finding Will & Flo were at Sutherland Gardens, went there, & returned for the night. Will going to Mid-Lanark Monday.[20]

### Thursday July 19ᵗʰ

After more than three months' silence my Diary must record another family event, the birth of our third grand-daughter which was announced by a telegram from John on Sunday morning as we were sitting at breakfast 'Mother & daughter doing well'. We rejoice in his happiness, & are very thankful that Mattie is still progressing favorably. John writes that it is so, & gives us some of the points of beauty which he discovers in his new treasure.

Another noteworthy fact is Papa's 'Call' to the Bar which took place at the end of last Term at the Middle Temple (13ᵗʰ June /88). Florence & Hattie were present in the Ladies Gallery.

### Aspley Heath Wednesday Octr 3ʳᵈ

I find it so convenient & pleasant to recall many things that I should not remember but for their record here, that I almost regret having given up a consecutive narration of the months that have passed without any, beyond those events above mentioned. The summer which has just gone has been the shortest & coldest that I ever remember. Glad to sit over fires on many dates that we used to consider the height of summer, little sun, & much rain, & easterly winds have prevailed until the early part of Septʳ when fine weather set in, only interrupted by occasional rainy days, so that the late harvest is nearly all gathered in; but yesterday morning <u>snow</u> fell, not much here, but much more we heard in other places, so that winter seems come again.

The constant journeyings to & fro between Bedford & Aspley Heath with occasional visits to the Home seem to have broken up the three months which we usually expect to be summer, into short periods that it is difficult to recall. In July after the Home Committee meeting I went to Chelmsford for a couple of meetings & spent from Wednesday to Saturday with Mʳ & Mʳˢ Morton, my only lengthened absence from home.

The immediate future too is now a very unsettled matter with us. Papa intends to sever his long connection with the Britannia Works at Xmas, at least in its present form, but in compliance with Mʳ F Howard's special request, has consented to continue as much supervision & advice as may be advantageous to the business, but leave his time pretty much at his own disposal.

---

[20] No doubt the purpose of his visit was to nurse his constituency.

**1889**

*March 6ᵗʰ*

Another three months' events I can only sketch. For Papa they have certainly brought relief from many annoyances, & complete freedom in the disposal of his time as far as the Works are concerned. He formally resigned all Managership at Xmas but places himself at the disposal of the Principals for advice or consultation. Since he consented to this the senior Partner has passed away. Mr James Howard died suddenly in London a few weeks since. In less than one year both Mr & Mrs Howard (who seemed likely for years of life) have departed, & left 4 Sons & daughters in a home desolate of Father & Mother. Papa generally goes to the Works for a few hours every other day & to London alternate days. Will has arranged for him to use one of his Chambers. He spends some time there looking at the papers of any cases that are interesting to him, or going into the Law Courts either with Will, or some other Court when he is not engaged there. His health is much better since Xmas. The journeys to London seem to suit him better than being so much in Bedford. I am glad to think living at Aspley Heath may not be necessary.

*May 6ᵗʰ*

Since my last return from London I have had nothing to call me from home excepting a short visit to Ampthill with Mrs Ransom for an evening meeting to which Hattie went with us. The only other public work has been the beginning of another Branch of the BWTA at Cardington, to which I went only last Friday with our new President Mrs Tyrer, Mrs Sampson, Mrs Ransom & Mrs Clark. We provided a 3ᵈ tea to which between 30 & 40 came & of this number 20 became Members of our Association. A few of them were previously Abstainers, but the greater number signed the Pledge for the first time. I brought all my co-workers back in the Brougham. Our short journey was a very merry one; full of thankfulness we were that so good a result had followed the breaking up of entirely fresh ground, for beyond a Band of Hope carried on by a good working man, there is no Temperance work in Cardington. When we parted at night Mrs Sampson said she believed there were not 5 happier women in Bedford!

*June 26ᵗʰ*

Two family events are first & foremost to be noted amidst those that have occurred since I last wrote. On May 28ᵗʰ (the same day of the month as that on which the twins were born 3 years earlier) another son was born to Edward & Clara, & on June 11ᵗʰ a fortnight later, Aunt Polly passed away. The first death in Papa's family, consisting of 7 brothers & sisters, & in nearly 68 years![21] He went to Southport to see his sister at Easter, & then felt sure that she would not recover although she

---

[21] CEB must mean that Aunt Polly (Mrs Mary Ann Wyles) was the first of Edward's siblings to die, but she has made an arithmetical mistake, as the oldest, William, was born in 1824, which is 65, not 68, years before 1889, when she is writing. Aunt Polly was born in 1835, so was 54 when she died. CEB is contrasting the longevity of Edward's siblings with the early deaths of her own, none of whom lived beyond 32, except possibly Alfred, whose date of death cannot be ascertained, but certainly occurred before 1881, when he would have been 50.

was herself still hopeful, & the suffering she has passed through the last few weeks makes us thankful that they have ended.

Instead of entirely giving up Aspley Heath house, we have let it for three months to a Clergyman, & intend for Papa's sake to use it as before for the remainder of another year.

### August 20th

[Under this date is a detailed description of CEB's visit to Switzerland, with Edward, Lottie and Hattie. They left Dover on 18th July, and spent three weeks abroad, travelling to Geneva, along the south shore of Lake Geneva to Vevey (where they climbed a peak which commanded a splendid view of a snow-clad Mont Blanc), further east to St Maurice and Sierre, and then back to Geneva along the north shore of the Lake.]

### Nov 26th

Winter has come upon us, but very gently, the first frost to do much harm being last night. Our three-months tenants at Aspley Heath left at the appointed time in Sept, & after a short stay at Bedford after our summer holiday I returned there to prepare for again making it our second home. Papa's trip had done him much good & every one told him how much better he was looking, but he seemed anxious as ever to get back again to the woods.

### Dec 23rd

The last entry for another year. Tomorrow I am to go with Papa to spend Xmas day with John & Mattie. It had been quite decided that all our children & grandchildren should meet us at our eldest Son's, in which case we should have made a family gathering of 18, but it cannot be. Will's children one after another have fallen ill with the measles. Eric first nearly a month ago, then George & Hilda, & just as we were hoping all danger was over for Bruce, he was taken, & only two days ago, so that there is no chance of his being well by Wednesday. John & Mattie are afraid to come to St Swithin's[22] on Baby's account, so we have settled to be with them for Xmas day & go to Will's on Thursday.

A poor Patient at the Home whom I received the previous night fell into the fire in a fit the following morning, & was sadly burnt about the face & neck, & in the alcoholized state of her blood, we feared what might result, but the danger of this case passed before I left, so that I came away with much cause for gratitude, after what had been a week of great anxiety.

Not the least reason for thankfulness was the fact that Edward determined to give up cigarette smoking, which he acknowledged to me he felt to be a growing evil both physically, & as a habit that was gaining a mastery over him. He was so unwell from an attack of the epidemic, the influenza, when I left, that that alone took away the desire for tobacco, which I do trust may not return so that he cannot resist it.

I have been staying in Bedford, with the exception of a few days at Aspley Heath. Work here which there is no one but ourselves to do seems to make it more & more necessary for us to be here much more than we have been of late. At the beginning

---

[22] Will and his family had moved to a large house in Hendon, St Swithins, in June.

of Nov$^r$ a 10 days' Mission was held in Southend Chapel by a good earnest Evangelist M$^r$ Gawthrop, who visited from house to house in this neighbourhood in the day & each night held services in the Chapel. The attendance at these was very good & lasting good was I believe done.

The following Monday I was also obliged to be absent when M$^{rs}$ Ransom kindly assisted Lottie. I had some time previously promised to assist at a meeting of the Wesleyan Temperance Society at Luton which I was invited to do by M$^r$ Scott, one of the ministers there who dined with us at the District Meeting. I asked for a Drawing-room meeting in the afternoon which was not, owing to bad weather, & not being properly made known, very largely attended, but I was not prepared for such an audience as I found before me at night. Nearly 1000 people must have been present. I did not feel as nervous as perhaps I ought to have done for I spoke about ¾ of an hour, & at the end felt I ought not to have been so long, & very vexed with myself, as there was another Speaker who came after me, & from what I heard of his speech before leaving to catch the train, might have used more time than was left to greater advantage than I did. However I managed to keep the attention of the people, & I trust left a few thoughts for the Christian & conscientious moderate drinkers behind me.

A new Iron Church (St Leonard's) has been built between this & the Kempston R$^d$ & the Clergyman & his brother who is his Curate seem to think Southend their special charge, & are constant in their visitations. They are reported to be 'High Church' & particularly anxious to baptize all the babies in their neighbourhood. I do not feel that their presence should either prevent our continuing the work begun here from the day the first service for Southend was held in our breakfast room & kitchen 20 years ago, nor that it in any way absolves us from responsibility to set before the people the simple gospel, apart from all forms & ceremonies.

Lottie has gone to Hendon to stay there with Hattie until the day after that on which we are to meet them at Will's & is then to go on to Chelmsford to spend the remainder of Alex Morton's Xmas holiday with him in his home. Papa goes with me on the same day to Upper Norwood where we have promised to stay with Grandpapa until Monday morning.

## 1890

*March 10$^{th}$*

I have had little opportunity of continuing the recital of the events of this year which I intended when I began this page, & pass them by for the moment to record the birth of another grand-child, 'a son & heir' as John styles him, on March 4$^{th}$. Mattie & baby are he says doing well. Our 10$^{th}$ grand-child!

The following week Hattie returned to help me to entertain a large party of our neighbours in our Blue Ribbon-room. The occasion was the presentation of a clock to our Southend organist on his marriage. All who had subscribed to this were invited. About 40 assembled, & with Hattie's singing, Papa's address in presenting the time-piece, & the bride & bridegroom's reply & thanks, we managed to fill an evening which all seemed greatly to enjoy. It gave us far more pleasure to make them so happy than it would have done to have had an equal number of the rich, or great, who have a surfeit of social enjoyments.

*Friday, April 25th*
Of course the Home was one of the objects of my visit to London, & I spent a night there, going to Penrith House for another. At the Home I found two of the 6 months Patients were out shopping together & the Matron showed considerable irritation that I complied with the wish of two others to take them for a little walk, & not pleased when I complained for the second time of Patients being out unaccompanied. Nothing like open displeasure was shown to me there but on reaching the OKR where I intended to spend Sunday I found letters, including one from Miss Herbert, who had sent a Patient to the Home from Bedford a month before & had sent for her back again on account of her Mother's illness. From this individual Miss H had such an account of the Matron's doings, & sayings in reference to myself & the Home as she said with M^rs Sampson's advice, she thought right to communicate to me. I talked the matter over with Edward & we thought it advisable I should see M^rs Atkinson before leaving London, & as there was time, that evening. To my surprise M^rs A (with whom I had afternoon tea & a friendly talk about the Home the previous day) received my annoyance in a very cool & unsympathetic manner, & to my mind confirmed the intelligence the letter contained that the Matron was seeking to lessen my influence with the Patients & also with the Members of the Committee. This has since been denied, but from some unaccountable reason, if this be not true, a sudden & entire change has taken place in the cordial relations that had hitherto existed between M^rs Atkinson & myself, which also extended to other members of the Committee, & finding they took part entirely with the Matron, in spite of positive proof of her wrong doing in reference to the Patients (who had I found been allowed to violate our first rule of never going out alone, to the extent of having permission to go to Kensington to ....[23] Show alone) I could only send in my resignation to the Committee. This I did, much to my relief as far as the responsibility & labour connected with the work were concerned, but I was greatly grieved that these should terminate in so painful a manner. I received a reply to my letter of resignation from Lady Elizabeth Biddulph expressing the regret of the Committee, or rather enclosing a resolution proposed by Miss Docwra & seconded by M^rs Ward-Poole expressing their regret, & begging my acceptance of the position of Vice-President in the place of the late M^rs Bright-Lucas. To this I consented & shall therefore have a place on the Committee of which I shall not often take advantage.[24]

I left early hoping to reach Hendon in good time, but in going from Kings X Station to St Pancras for the bag which we had left there in the morning, opened my little hand bag on the way & took from my purse the Cloak-room ticket, returning it immediately as I believed to its place; but getting back to the Metropolitan Station hastily, & in a great crowd & again needing my purse for the railway ticket, I found (in the short five minutes that had elapsed since using it) that it was gone. I turned

---

[23] Text unclear: it looks like 'Barning' but no sense has been made of this word.
[24] CEB seems to accept this situation philosophically, but she would be justified in feeling bitter about the way she was treated when she had not spared herself in her efforts for The Home over a period of five years.

back again hoping I might have dropped it when I took it out, in a dark part of the Station at St Pancras, but it had gone, & also the train by which I ought to have gone to Hendon which I did not reach until past 11 o'clock. Fortunately I took only a small sum with me, but beside the money there were little valuables which I was vexed to lose.

*Saturday June 21st*
The longest day seems to have come with a rush. I can scarcely realize that it is Midsummer. From the last date on which I jotted down a few passing events, succeeding ones have been very much mixed with extra duties at home both here (Bedford) & Aspley Heath. The removal from the larger house which we have occupied nearly 3 years, to the Cottage, keeping just sufficient furniture to make it a comfortable retreat, & finding places for the remainder here took more time & thought than might be imagined. However the work was pleasurable to me, as I had been looking forward to being once more settled in our old home as far as servants & general household arrangements were concerned. I made what appears to be a very satisfactory choice of a near neighbour without children, a very clean woman, who is to take charge of the Cottage to keep it aired when Papa does not use it but to have it always in readiness, & to wait upon him whenever he chooses to go to Aspley. Now that we have made it pretty I much prefer it for situation & size to the house we have left.

[CEB attends the Annual BWTA meetings in Memorial Hall, London.]

The chief event of interest in this year's meetings was the election of Lady Henry Somerset to the office of President of the Association in the place of the late M$^{rs}$ Lucas, whose death took place some months previously, not very long after that of her Brother John Bright. Lady Somerset cordially but very modestly accepted the position & her reception when she filled the Chair was most enthusiastic. The concluding Public meeting was an overflowing one in the large Upper Hall. Another was held in the Library beneath to which Lady Henry went for a short time & spoke.

Apart from the general business of these meetings intense interest was shown in opposing the Compensation Clauses of the new Government Bill for Local Taxation which proposed to Endow the Publicans & Brewers by paying them out at their own valuation for the suppression of such Public House Licences as may be deemed advisable in the interests of the surrounding neighbourhood, or rather the Public good. Canon Leigh put a resolution to the meeting strongly condemning the Government proposals which was cordially & unanimously carried, & telegraphed to several Members of Parliament engaged in the contest which, after the most determined effort on the part of the Government for weeks to carry their measure, they have been compelled to withdraw. Far better the present power of Magistrates to refuse to renew the annually applied for licence, than that a vested interest in them should be created which would greatly enhance Public House Property, & slightly advance Temperance by driving the drinkers from closed houses to those allowed to remain. The Compensation should be from these last to the first instead of taxing the whole community to prevent the <u>ruin</u> of the poor Brewers! Not of their Agents the Publicans, nor the poor victims of their ruinous traffic.

The General Temperance Committee here decided to hold an Anti-Compensation meeting in the Corn Exchange & having difficulty in arranging for Speakers asked me to go to London to endeavour to secure them. M$^{rs}$ Foster (the lady-Barrister from Iowa USA whom I met first at the Autumnal BWTA meetings at Gloster 2 years ago, & again in May at the meetings at M Hall) had promised to pay me a visit & was willing to address a meeting on the subject, so I consented to do my best to get a gentleman also.[25] After calling on Hugh Price Hughes & Mark Guy Pearse & failing with both I went to the Offices of the United Kingdom Alliance at Westminster, where I was most kindly helped in every possible way. A messenger was dispatched to see the Rev$^d$ Peter Thompson, & M$^r$ Hilton took me across to the House of Commons where we waited in the Lobby whilst he sent messages to several likely MPs who were specially interested in the matter. I was introduced to at least three, all of whom however were engaged so much in the fight that they did not feel it safe to leave. The last I saw, M$^r$ Theodore Fry[26] very kindly wrote me an order for the Ladies' Gallery & himself conducted me to it where for about an hour & half I listened to the 'Questions' which were going on until a Member moved the adjournment of the House to debate the matter of the vexatious regulations of the Commissioner of Police M$^r$ Munro, in insisting on a great Anti Compensation Demonstration arranged for the following Saturday, getting to Hyde Park by back streets! I had to leave before it closed, & felt well repaid for my trouble in London although not succeeding entirely. However M$^r$ Thompson consented to come the following week.

We had a grand meeting here [in Bedford]. M$^{rs}$ Foster's eloquence quite carried the people away. M$^r$ Thompson's experiences of the Drink Traffic in the East End told well also, & in a crowded meeting there were only 5 hands held up in opposition to the Resolution that meant 'no compensation'. M$^{rs}$ Foster's stay with us from Tuesday to Friday was very enjoyable. She was accompanied by her Son a very intelligent youth of nineteen. They move in the best American society, M$^r$ Foster being a Barrister & connected with the Government at Washington.[27] We were very much interested in their descriptions of social life in their own country, religious & class distinctions seeming to be very slightly regarded, & they in their turn appeared much to enjoy the freshness of the kind of domestic life which our home exemplified. The girls' conversation, industry, music, all seemed to have a charm for young Foster. They left home for a visit to M$^r$ & M$^{rs}$ Pass at Clifton, Thursday & he was certainly less buoyant after their departure. His Mother walked with me to Elstow after which I drove both to Cardington where we went over the Church & then into the old part of Cardington House which was once occupied by the great Philanthropist Howard,[28] then to D$^r$ Brown's to see the Bunyan Memorials. M$^{rs}$ Foster was not satisfied to leave the neighbourhood without seeing the home of Cowper so on Friday morning we went by train to Olney, visited his house, &

---

25  Mrs Foster was much involved with temperance movements in the USA, particularly the National Women's Christian Temperance Union. She travelled a great deal, and lectured and wrote prolifically.
26  Sir Theodore Fry was a member of the Quaker chocolate manufacturing family and Liberal MP for Darlington.
27  Elijah Foster had been recently appointed to a post in the US Justice Department in Washington, and from 1898 until his death in 1906 was Assistant Attorney.
28  John Howard (1726–1790), pioneer of prison reform. The Howard League for Penal Reform continues his work. He is not related to the Howards of the Britannia Iron Works.

the Summer House in a garden now detached from it, in which he wrote many of his poems; then walked to Weston Underwood, & returned in time for dinner at 3 o'clock after which M^rs Foster left for Banbury where she had engaged to speak at a meeting that night.

Now that we are really living in Bedford again, work seems to be awaiting us in all directions. We have begun a Bible Class in the Blue Ribbon Room Sunday mornings from 10 to 11 o'clock, & from 3 to 4 in the afternoons, in order to reach a few boys who go to no School & to keep the elder children who leave the school at the Chapel. Hattie is very pleased to help, & to take it once in the day, & Lottie helps also. The Sunday services at the Chapel we are told were attended much less numerously than they used to be, & on my expressing regret to the Superintendent minister that it was not made an undenominational Mission Room instead of a Wesleyan Chapel, he said he would be willing to meet our wishes to make the services less formal, & more attractive by singing, & planning such helpers as we could get to assist in Evangelistic Services. We have to some extent carried this out since May & the congregations have much improved. Lottie & Hattie have several times sung solos or duets & their voices never sound sweeter than when they are 'singing the Gospel'. Our only motive is to draw the people around us 'to hear words whereby they may be saved'.

I wish I knew this would be the case in the Iron Church erected in our neighbourhood by the young clergyman who has constituted himself 'Vicar of S Leonard the Confessor' (whoever that may be) with his Brother as his Curate. The latter has called, but I have not met him, nor heard him preach as I intend to do, but I am told that he is a Ritualist[29] & the former a Rationalist.

Just before leaving Aspley Heath I was invited to hold a Drawing-room meeting at Oxford on behalf of the Home. This I did at the house of D^r Murray, who is engaged with the help of younger University men in compiling an English Dictionary[30] which for size & scope is to surpass all others. The ladies present at the meeting appeared to feel much interest in the Home & gave me a collection of between £2 & £3. A little later I went to Cambridge at the request of M^rs Keynes[31] (Lottie's friend née Florence Brown) to address 'a Mothers' Union' of working women, not united on Total Abstinence lines, which however I did my best to inculcate, to the great satisfaction of many of the lady workers in connection with it. M^rs K is not of their number in this. She was however exceedingly kind in entertaining me. Drove me to Newnham & took me through the Ladies Colleges there (of one of which she was herself a Member before her marriage).[32] I fear I did not succeed in convincing her how much her influence would be strengthened amongst the Mothers by the example which she could not enforce in her present position.

---

[29] Earlier called tractarians, later Anglo-Catholics, the ritualists emphasised salvation through grace, grace received through sacraments, and sacraments only valid if administered by episcopally ordained clergy.

[30] CEB refers to what was to become the Oxford English Dictionary – the OED. Sir James Murray (1837–1915), a Scotsman, was its creator and first editor. The first part (or fascicle) was published in 1884, and it was not completed until 1928.

[31] She is the mother of John Maynard Keynes (1883–1946).

[32] Newnham College Cambridge opened in 1871, the first women's college at Cambridge. Girton College had opened two years earlier, but started its life at Benslow House, Hitchin, and did not move to Cambridge until 1873.

*August 28th*

The summers seem much colder & shorter than they did 25 years ago when I was glad to wear the thinnest of muslin dresses for weeks after Midsummer, & almost to live in the open air. A really warm day is now the exception rather than the rule for summer, & has been so for many that have passed. Hitherto since the longest day we have had a great many sunless days, without as well as with rain, & a great deal of wind, but on the whole I prefer this to hot dry weather, especially as we have not had a regular man since James left us to go to America in the Spring, & I have therefore had a great deal more to do in the garden to keep it in anything like order. Papa thought he should like to do more in the Kitchen garden himself, & I was very glad for him to take more interest & work at times in it for exercise. But between going to London, & <u>too much</u> to the works & sleeping often at Aspley Heath, he cannot even with a man's help keep his crops from being overgrown with the faster growing weeds, & does not thank me for my occasional remarks & proffered assistance in his domain. The flower garden is supposed to be mine & I sometimes think I spend too much time in it & the Conservatory.

*Oct<sup>r</sup> 3<sup>rd</sup>*

On looking back it seems more than a month ago that we left town for our holiday, Papa, Lottie, Hattie & myself, on Wednesday Sept<sup>r</sup> 3<sup>rd</sup>. After much consultation of railway Guides Papa determined on taking the L&NW route to Scotland in preference to either Midland or Gt Northern, the chief reason for thus deciding being that we could break our journey in returning at Preston & travel the short distance thence to Southport to spend a few days with Aunt Jenny. On Monday Papa was suddenly seized with an attack such as he had at Aspley Heath last year, & continued so unwell on Tuesday that I had great doubt whether he would be able to undertake the long journey next day. He had however recovered sufficiently next morning to be anxious to set off. I advised his taking breakfast before getting up, early enough as I thought to give him time to dress & be ready for the 9 o'clock train; but when we were all ready to depart, I found he was not so, so sending the girls & luggage on to the Station I remained to come with him, feeling almost sure we should be too late. At the Station Gate the Station Master met me, & I found quite a commotion amongst the Officials generally at our non-arrival, our tickets having been previously taken, & 4 seats reserved for us in the train from Euston which we were to join at Rugby, & travel in a through carriage to Edinburgh. With Lottie & Hattie on the spot & all arrangements made the Station Master positively kept the train 7 minutes for us, & was signalling it off just as we appeared. I was indeed thankful when we were once in the carriage safely off together. On arriving at Rugby we found the L&NW Company[33] had not only reserved seats, but placed an 'Engaged' carriage with Papa's name on it, at our disposal of which we should have entirely lost the benefit by a later train. We were able to let Papa lie down when & as he chose all the way.

[They return via Southport to visit Aunt Jenny, Edward's sister Sarah Jane Barker.]

---

[33]  L&NR Company is written.

We reached Southport some hours later than Aunt Jenny expected us & found her waiting at the Station & a sumptuous tea when we reached Saunders St. Letters there from home told me that Florence had carried out the arrangement which we had previously made to bring George to the Grammar School at the Michaelmas term.[34] As this would begin before our return, she brought him for the entrance exam as I suggested & was here awaiting our return. On Monday morning I prevailed on Aunt Jenny to excuse me, & returned home leaving Papa & the girls to follow a few days later. Alec left the afternoon of the same day as myself.[35] He had not much anticipated visiting Southport, but Aunt J's kindness made him feel quite at home & he expressed his enjoyment of the few days he passed there with us.

I reached home unannounced on Monday evening much to Florence's surprise, as well as that of the domestics, who did not expect me until the following Wednesday & were not as prepared for my advent as they ought to have been. Florence was very glad to see me, & we had some quiet time together until Friday when L & H returned. Will came on Saturday & left on Monday with Florence & the Baby (who by the bye from being called 'scrappy' has become quite a fine girl).[36] George was entirely engrossed with his new School, & made not the slightest trouble of being left behind, nor has he since. He trudges off most contentedly every morning with his satchel on his back, but is not quite so punctual in the time of returning for which however he has generally a very plausible excuse! Now that he is with us alone he is on the whole very manageable, & when there is no liquid temptation in his way, such as water, either from the garden hose, or the Bath-room, or a paint pot, seems not to delight so much in mischievous tricks as formerly.

Each time Will comes I determine I will not be drawn into argument, but the mention of a book, or an opinion, leads into it before we are aware, & often throws a cloud over the happiness of his visits, because our ideas seem to me to grow farther & farther apart, & I love him so much I cannot bear to feel this. If I cannot rest my faith on what a great Writer calls 'The Impregnable Rock of Holy Scripture' I have no other foundation on which to stand, or from which to reason concerning 'things which are unseen & eternal' & instead of yielding to the conflicting opinions & judgments of so many in the present as to the Inspiration of this or that part, accept where I cannot understand, as I am compelled to do each day in 'things which are seen & temporal'.

*Monday Novr 3rd*

A few days after my return home from Southport a letter from M^rs Morton expressed a wish that Papa & myself would visit Chelmsford, which after our holiday so recently we could not do, but I replied to M^rs Morton's letter begging that M^r Morton & herself would pay us a short visit to which they consented & we had a very enjoyable week together. After considerable pressure M^r Morton has consented to allow himself to be nominated Mayor of Chelmsford for the next year & from the very flattering way in which his name is mentioned by all parties in the town there is little doubt that he will be elected, & he is in every way highly fitted for the position.

---

[34] Now Bedford School.
[35] Alex Morton had joined them in Edinburgh for their holiday.
[36] She was named after Edris, CEB's last child, who died at the age of three. CEB refers to this in the diary entry for 16 January 1892. Sadly, Will's daughter also died as a child, aged thirteen.

We joked 'his Worship' a little on his prospective dignity. Always a most temperate man, he has for the last year or two, through silent home influence become a Total although unpledged Abstainer, & coming after two Mayors who have been most lavish in their expenditure on eating & drinking will find it more difficult to carry out his convictions, as I trust he may have courage to do.

Since we came home various vexations & disappointments seem to have hindered the work we would do amongst our neighbours. After consultation with Mʳ MᶜCullagh it was settled that after 17 years' wear our little Chapel should be renovated. An estimate for the work was given, which Papa offered to defray, apart from collections at the Opening Services, Peter Thompson & Charles Moore[37] arranged to come for these on Octʳ 16ᵗʰ & 19ᵗʰ, which would have given a fortnight to do the work after our return. As soon as I got back I called on Mʳ MᶜC to make final arrangement for beginning this, & accepting Mʳ Thompson's services with Charles's, found he wished to consult the Autocrat of the Circuit before concluding his consent, & in the afternoon received a letter saying that he had had an interview with him (Mʳ FH) that he was glad to hear of my Husband's intention to bear the expense, & that that being the case, such services & collections as were suggested would be unnecessary! Of course under such circumstances Papa declined to go further in the matter, & I subsequently called on Mʳ MᶜC & told him this. Our conversation however resulted in clearing up illusions & misapprehensions, in reference to an imaginary debt on the Chapel when Papa gave up his responsibility, of which his books & a memorandum dated Novʳ 1876 were indisputable proofs that only about £10 remained. It was afterwards proposed to begin the work forthwith but it is now by our desire postponed to the Spring.

Then one or two disagreeable men who can do nothing but find fault, are rude, complain of my beginning the Bible Class, of our new methods for a lively service Sunday evening, although they must see how the congregations have improved by this last. There is also the difficulty & discouragement of carrying on the Bible Class with often from twenty to thirty boys, many of whom are so ill-behaved that it seems almost impossible to do them good & poor Hattie when she has taken them has sometimes been quite over done.

These things with the ingratitude of some that we have been trying to help, & the going back into sin of others of whom we had hope, make up a chapter of discouragement that sometimes makes me feel weary of our surroundings here, & thankful if I could conscientiously be relieved of them & leave our neighbours (whose good God knows is our only motive) to care for themselves, or be cared for by others. I can only hope that these may be among the 'all things that work together for good' in an increase of patience & self-sacrifice. If we have been able to accomplish any good amongst them neither the praise of men, nor the 'Woe' of those of whom all 'speak well' will be ours.

*Thursday Decr 25ᵗʰ 1890*
The first Xmas for five years that we have spent in the old home, & with numbers diminished to Papa, Lottie, Hattie & myself of which there will probably be a further diminution should we be spared until next Xmas. We have had an unexciting but

---

[37] The son of Edward's sister Fanny and her first husband, Rev. John Moore.

very cheerful day, more so than we anticipated as Lottie after a week in her room, & under the D$^{rs}$ care, has been well enough to join us in the dining-room. She has been quite an invalid for that time & is still far from well, but sufficiently recovered to taste the turkey with us at our Xmas dinner.

Hattie's visit to her Club Exhibition has for various reasons been prolonged to a stay of two months in London & she only returned on Tuesday. On Monday our little circle was increased by another Swiss girl (the daughter of a Pasteur in the neighbourhood of Geneva) with whom we happened to meet in the summer. She is Governess with Lady Anson at Elstow Lodge, from which all the family is absent, except the very youngest children so that she would have had a very lonely time there as she has no friends near. She is a very pleasant girl & it has added to our enjoyment to see hers, to which she has in her turn contributed especially to Lottie & Hattie.

The day began as usual with a number of parcels & presents awaiting our arrival at the breakfast table. Florence & Mattie had contributed theirs by Hattie. After early dinner Papa went with Hattie to the river which has been frozen over for some days, to try the new pair of skates which he gave her as a Xmas present. Mademoiselle & I accompanied them, but finding it too cold to watch standing, walked away from them & amused ourselves by looking from the Embankment at the efforts of the many skaters whose awkwardness was on the whole more noticeable than their gracefulness. It must be more than ten years since the river has been entirely frozen over, so that very few amongst the many hundreds on the ice have had recent opportunities of practising.[38] Hattie got on pretty well considering she has not had any skating since she was quite a child, & enjoyed the afternoon with Papa very much. Poor Lottie very much lamented being unable to go out. I well remember how she & Will used to skate together, as I thought, very gracefully, when they were at home together, the last time the winter was so severe.

So much for Xmas day. The events of the last two months both public & private have been very varied. In reference to the former I have bought the book which has created quite a sensation amongst men of all & no religious persuasions written by the Chief of the Salvation Army 'General Booth' called 'Darkest England' in which he propounds a vast scheme for raising what he terms 'the submerged-tenth' the masses of pauper, criminal, & out of work population crowded together in misery or sin chiefly in London. He asks for £100,000 to make a start.[39]

On my way back from Maidenhead I spent Sunday & Monday with Edward. On the latter day I received a telegram from Will asking me whether I would come to the Temple at 6 o'clock for dinner & go with him thence to General Booth's meeting in Exeter Hall which he was going to hold that night. I immediately replied 'yes' & on reaching Crown Office Row found Will had three half-guinea tickets ready for himself, myself, & Florence. She came in soon after & Will with his usual mode of

---

[38] It was twelve years earlier, in 1878, that the Ouse had been sufficiently frozen to permit skating. Hattie was only thirteen years old when she John, and Lottie were skating together, as described in diary entry for 25 December 1878.

[39] William Booth's *In Darkest England and the Way Out* was published in 1890 and soon became a best-seller. The choice of the word 'darkest' in the title sets the theme, for it immediately brings to mind the phrase 'in darkest Africa'. Booth argues that missionary zeal is as much needed in England as it is in 'heathen' countries.

entertainment had a charming little dinner for three served in his Chambers, after which we adjourned to the Hall. The General gave the details of his scheme not so forcefully certainly as[40] he had done in his book, but sufficiently so to have promises amounting to several £1000 made that same night. Amongst them was one which I heard announced of '£3000 & a farm'. The meeting was very enthusiastic. The sight of the tall commanding figure of the Chief surrounded by the Salvation Army 'Soldiers' & 'Lasses' (which with the Brass Band filled the platform) created great interest in their favor. Will did not make any promise that night, but is disposed to help substantially if the work is carried out. It is a grand idea, but I fear far too great for private philanthropy to compass & seems to me to need nothing less than a Government measure to carry it out on the scale proposed, & more than the life & responsibility of a single individual. It must however be a means of great benefit to many but not until the wicked waste of the millions of pounds spent in drink is arrested will sin & misery be greatly diminished.

Another stirring event talked of in every circle is the great split in the Irish Home Rule Party brought about by the immorality & subsequent disclosures in the Divorce Court of the Leader of the party.[41] His great English friend & supporter M[r] Gladstone refuses further action with him as such, & the disorganization has followed. Believing as I do that Home Rule in Ireland would be Rome rule I can only hope that events in themselves sad may be over-ruled for a greater good & the first deferred until the poor priest-ridden peasantry are free to think & act for themselves. I have fastened in the beginning of this book a newspaper compendium of the chief events of the year which may be looked upon with interest in days to come.[42]

## 1891

*Jan[y] 23rd 1891*

Now I have to chronicle what I little imagined would be thus early inscribed on these pages. Our Son Will who 10½ years ago was called to the Bar was the day before yesterday 'approved by her Majesty' as QC. This just as he has completed his 37 year is an honor that comes to few so early in life. He is one of 9 on whom the dignity was at the same time conferred. Of these the first was 'called' to the Bar 30 years ago! The others, in 62, 65, 65, 66, 71, 72 & 73 respectively, so that he has come to his honors 7 years earlier than either [*sic*]. It is more a matter of wonder than of congratulation with Papa & myself that so it should be, as thus early in his career his responsibilities increase, whilst he will probably have to allow many lucrative small cases to pass by which would not be considered worthy of a QC. Oh that he may have the spiritual enlightenment which may keep him humble amidst all his prosperity, & make him increasingly useful in the service of Him from whom comes his powers of mind & who has conferred them for this end.

I have been to Hendon since writing so far accompanying Papa on Monday night,

---

[40] 'has' is written.
[41] Charles Parnell (1846–1891) had been cited as co-respondent in a divorce case, which ended his political career and set back the cause of Irish Home Rule.
[42] Unfortunately missing.

which we spent together there. On Tuesday morning (Jan[y] 27th) with Florence we went to the Law Courts to witness the function of the reception of the new QCs 'within the Bar'. After going to the House of Lords to be sworn in before the Lord Chancellor they returned to the Courts clad in full canonicals, all new for the occasion, from full bottom wig, to patent leather shoes ornamented with large steel buckles. These followed by black silk stockings, knee breeches, coat & vest of some peculiar cut, & the whole surmounted by the ample silk gown. The toute ensemble more imposing than becoming. The ceremony if such it can be called consisted in the 9 marching in single file through the great Hall & thence through the passages stopping at the several Courts as they came to them, & waiting in the door way until they attracted the attention of the Judge on the Bench, who then called the name of the senior, announced to him Her Majesty's pleasure to appoint him one of her Counsel as 'a man learned in the Law' & invited him to take a seat within the Bar. The new QC then bowed very low to the Judge, then to those already QCs, & then turning round to those he had left behind him, the 'Juniors'. The bows were returned by all, & then the seat was taken. Then the Judge asked 'M[r] So & so, do you move' to which question another bow was the reply & then M[r] – really moved on, & made way for the next to take his place, when the same performance was again gone through, & so on to the last, who was Will.

The Clerk of the junior is the individual who acts as Guide on such occasions, & Charles (Will's Clerk) looked quite handsome in his very best, tall hat, & white kid gloves. In one Court the Judge was summing up a case, & would not leave off to receive his Learned friends, so they would not wait but went on to another Court. Then at the end M[r] Justice Butt was attending to some business in Chambers, & would not come into his Court until he had finished & kept all waiting a long time much to M[r] Will's disgust as he had two cases going on & was most anxious to doff all his finery excepting his QC gown & at once go to them. M[r] Walter (whom I had not seen for several years, but who has now Chambers next to Will's) took us to the Courts in which we should see what was going on & was most attentive. John & Mattie also appeared on the scene & also M[r] Kelly & Madie.

I have had one other very pleasant meeting this year at Potton where Charles Moore got me to begin a Mothers' Meeting many years ago. I was invited to their annual meeting Jan[y] 2nd & after the tea told the Women how differently I felt on the question of Temperance to what I did when I first visited them, & begged them to consider the matter as I had done. About 30 women were present & of these about a dozen signed the pledge, & with a few already abstainers concluded to form a Branch at Potton. This, in a place where, as at Hendon, there is little Temperance work, is I hope & believe an influence that shall go on when I must cease to exert any. I called on the Clergyman's wife with M[rs] Blundell, the new Secretary, to ask her to be President as she had expressed interest in Temperance, but when she found it meant Total Abstinence she declined. The Vicar came into the room & we had quite a discussion, which really became theological, because I mentioned the word 'denomination' which he said 'you cannot apply to the Church of England' to which I replied, I considered it the favored denomination with which he did not agree, but we parted in a very friendly manner.

*April 3rd /91*

Whilst the girls were together with Will & Florence the subject of Lottie's wedding was of course discussed, & first as a joke, & then in real earnest they all together agreed that it would for several reasons be very fine to have it at Hendon. First there would not be the same formal leave taking of the old home, which Lottie dreads & I not less. Then all the guests who would be invited to be present would have to come from, or through London, the rooms at St Swithins are also much larger than ours & so altogether they made out such a good case & Florence seeming so really to wish it that Papa & I have consented, although I do not half like the idea of our Daughter not being married from her Father's house, & in the little Chapel so close to us. It is I suppose settled that the wedding is to be the middle of July, & we propose that Lottie & Alex shall come back to Bedford before going to their new home, so that our neighbours, especially the poorer ones, may see them & have some festal gathering without which they would be very much disappointed, as they will be however in any case, at not being able to see the wedding of one who has gone in & out amongst them so many years, & has done much to win their esteem & love.

*May 22nd*

It seems more than a month since my last entry, possibly because it has been a very busy one, the first fortnight with the proverbial 'Spring cleaning' which although later than usual with us seems almost premature for the weather continues so cold that the fires which are not supposed to be required after that process, for the summer, are still needful, & at this date we do not feel more willing to do without them than at Xmas.[43] On Whit-Monday in the early morning from my bed-room window, I saw the snow falling in large flakes! The dry north-easterly winds through the first part of this month are now succeeded by frozen showers & cold rain without the sunshine that tempered the former. This inclement weather is more noteworthy because it is supposed to contribute very much to the fatality of the fresh outbreak of 'Russian Influenza' which has been & is still making terrible havoc amongst all classes.[44] To-day's Paper speaks of the 'Ravages of the Epidemic' & states the total number of deaths from it in London alone during the last week to be not less than 318, & in some country towns the proportion has been much greater. Many MPs have been laid aside (amongst them Mr Gladstone) & several have died, principally men in the prime of life. Special care has been taken to fumigate the House of Commons during the Whitsuntide recess, even the Committee rooms & Library have undergone the same process.

Alex has been here from Saturday to Wednesday for his Whitsuntide holiday, but it was not until Tuesday Lottie could go out with him as she has had a bad cold on her chest which I feared might be the dreaded Influenza & so kept her in bed & sent for the Dr who did not confirm our fears. Tuesday was fine in the morning & L & A went to Aspley Heath together after breakfast, & had a delightful time in the woods, returning home, after dinner & tea in the Cottage. Papa consented to see the Dr when he came to Lottie, much to all our satisfaction, as he had continued to be

---

[43] Coal fires create dust, and thorough spring cleaning before they are shut down for the summer could be a waste of time.

[44] This was a pandemic of a severe strain of flu which lasted for five years from 1889 to 1894.

& to look very unwell. He (the D$^r$) could not discover any special cause of alarm, but gave him advice & not medicine, which former he is more likely to take than the latter. Papa went to Sydenham on Saturday to spend a very quiet holiday with Grandpapa & Grandma, & returned on Wednesday looking much better.

To go back to April 26$^{th}$ on that date Charles Moore came & preached re-opening sermons at our little Chapel after the renovation. It looks so pretty & bright with 'Ye shall keep My Sabbath & Reverence My Sanctuary' in illuminated letters round the arch over the Rostrum. My pet idea for a long time.

*June 16$^{th}$*

Two days after my return home Lottie had intelligence from Alex of his Mother's illness at Newport, Mon, whither she had gone to keep house for M$^r$ Gibson & her three grandchildren, whilst his Sister was away with the Babe & keeping away after an attack of Influenza. She returned home the beginning of that week & M$^{rs}$ Morton fell ill of the same complaint on the Thursday following & became so rapidly worse that M$^r$ Morton was telegraphed for on Friday. On Saturday Alex had the sorrowful news that there was little hope, was summoned by telegram on Sunday morning, & on Monday another told us that she had that morning passed away 'So swift trod sorrow on the heels of joy' for poor Alex! He is his Mother's only Son, & feels his loss bitterly. This sad event has cast a gloom over us all & altered everything for the wedding excepting the date which had been fixed for July 15$^{th}$ & which M$^r$ Morton wished should not be changed. Lottie will not now go away, but be married from our little Chapel in the presence of Parents & brothers & sisters only. Mournful changes have had to be made in the way of dress; but for those left only is the sadness 'Blessed are the dead which die in the Lord, they rest from their labours & their works do follow them.' Truly may this be said in relation to M$^{rs}$ Morton. Her work in the Church has been known & appreciated many years, & more recently in the cause of Temperance, her last effort in this direction being to use her position as Mayoress of Chelmsford to further the cause by inviting Lady Henry Somerset to address a Drawing-room Meeting which she gave at the Corn Exchange [Chelmsford] for which she issued about 300 invitations, & succeeded in getting about 200 together to listen, many of whom would not have condescended to do so under less inviting circumstances. M$^{rs}$ Morton was a little older than I am, but I know not how soon my poor efforts may no longer be needed by the Lord of the Vineyard. May I be found as faithful.

The funeral was a very large one both on account of M$^r$ Morton's official position & the great respect felt for him & his late wife. The mace draped in crape was carried before the wreath covered coffin, & attended by the Aldermen. Three carriages filled with ladies, members of the Chelmsford Branch of BWTA, & various others, testified to the general sympathy with the family & respect & love for the departed. Papa left home intending to have been present also, but unfortunately was detained in London by the commencement of a trial in which Will was engaged, & he himself was also engaged to take part, as a scientific witness, & which began rather unexpectedly at the very hour that the funeral took place.

Kate is now left alone with her Father, & will devote herself entirely to him. Hers is the saddest case of all. She was to have gone with her Mother to have put Alex's house in order for him. Now I shall have to go & do this with Hattie after the wedding is over. Lottie has been very sad both on her own account, as well as for Alex's sake, for she loved M^rs Morton more than ever since her last visit to Chelmsford, & both were so looking forward to seeing her in their home.

*July 19^th*

The month that has elapsed since recording the sad events of the previous weeks has been one of much discussion & re-arrangement, & of excitement for Lottie & now the crowning event is consummated, and more joyously than we could possibly have anticipated under the depression that the first brought with them.

This is the first moment of leisure I have had since Wednesday morning the 15^th to add the fourth, to the list of our children's marriages which my Diary contains. On that date my Lottie was united to the man of her choice & has bid adieu to the old home! May the blessing of the God of their Fathers rest upon them. The preparations which Lottie thought necessary to make for her wedding she had completed some days previously & so felt quite leisurely at the last & had time to wander in the garden, & especially in that part of it which she calls hers, & says is still to be so, & to regret that she was going just as some of the flowers were coming out. But very few regrets were expressed, she said she should like to think of home in all the brightness in which she left it, & call it home still. I thank God for the long happy girlhood she has had in it, & that she has so long been my Helper, & her Father's companion & comfort during the years that Hattie has been away from us so much. She now feels her new position as our only Daughter at home, & has at once risen nobly to it & although I know she keenly feels her Sister's loss, has gone through the parting without once giving way to any demonstration of it.

The day before the wedding Grandpapa & Grandma were the first arrivals about 3-30 p m. Lottie met them at the Station much to their delight. M^r Morton & Kate, with M^r & M^rs Alfred Morton I met later in the evening, when Alex also arrived from Nottingham. No other friends came for the night, but our kind neighbours Miss Risley & M^rs Iacchi both offered us beds so that we could accommodate all with comfort. Will & Florence with Hilda & Eric were the earliest to arrive next morning. Clara is staying with her children at her Sister's at Kempston & came in time to drive on to the Station to meet Edward, who came with John at 1 o'clock. Mattie was unable to come. Not altogether unexpectedly our kind friends M^r & M^rs Kelly came by the same train, sure of a welcome, to carry out the wish they long ago expressed to be present at Lottie's wedding. Luncheon was most prolonged. Lottie began hers early before many guests arrived, & had left to dress for the important function, before M^r & M^rs Henry Coleman, M^r Gibson, M^r & M^rs Kelly & her two youngest brothers came dropping in one after another. Alex with his friends M^r Robinson (his best man) & M^r Hamilton[45] lunched at M^rs Iacchi's.

At 2-15 p m all were ready to go to the Chapel to the door of which a strip of crimson cloth was laid from our gate. The little Communion Table & Rostrum we decorated with Ferns & flowers in the middle of which stood an Alabaster Vase that was one of my wedding presents filled with white lilies, the toute ensemble almost entirely Hattie's arrangement for her Sister & with rugs etc in front of the

---

[45] This seems to be the occasion on which he and Hattie met. He had been sharing lodgings with Alex in Nottingham.

Communion rail all looked very bright & pretty. I went in first with Grandpapa (who was to assist M^r Gibson in performing the ceremony) & showed him his place within the rail on the left of the table whilst to M^r Gibson was assigned the other. When I entered the Chapel it was nearly filled by our neighbours, nearly every one of whom had contributed to present Lottie with wedding presents. Over 50 women of my M Meeting & the BWTA at Southend sent her beautiful Fish Carvers, & nearly as many Members of the Congregation a pretty Epergne, so that, feeling they had a first claim to be present, I gave each one who asked permission, a ticket of admission. D^r Brown's two Daughters, & half a dozen other girl friends Lottie had invited to help the singing of two hymns which she particularly wished for during the ceremony, & a third was sung as a wedding march when she left the Chapel with her Husband. These with the two families & a few other friends quite filled the place. Edward kept one door to show into seats, John the other & everything was as quiet & orderly as possible. Lottie looked very sweet in her Bridal costume & veil, & went through the service with great composure. My dear Father concluded it by offering an earnest prayer for blessing on his Grand-daughter & her Husband, & pronouncing the Benediction. When the Bride came out of the Chapel half a dozen little girls (for whom their Mothers afterward told me they had obtained special leave of absence from School) scattered flowers in her path, as did also her little nieces Hilda & Evelyne. Hattie was the only Bridesmaid & looked very nice in her soft grey silk dress, with a big bouquet of pale yellow roses. Poor Kate relieved her mourning dress by a little scarlet & a bouquet of the same color, & both she & her Father did their best not to cast gloom over the day. It was a sad one for me, but excepting for a few minutes in the ceremony & when I said 'Good-bye' I did not yield to the feelings which were uppermost, it was fortunate that we had others to think of & entertain. The day following the wedding was almost as exciting for us. The card that gave entrance to the Chapel also gave an invitation to a friendly gathering & tea to all our neighbours who had contributed to Lottie's presents, & a few others, in all about 150. A tent was erected in the field & tables laid for that number. These were decorated with flowers, ferns etc, & a special wedding cake at the top one. This was cut up into strips & handed to each guest as the closing morsel of the entertainment, & was I was told by most carried away, as too precious to be eaten there at once. All seemed thoroughly to enjoy what else was provided. After the tables were cleared, all returned from the house (to which they went directly tea was over to look at Lottie's presents) when Papa made a kindly speech to them, then Grandpapa another, after which Hattie sang & accompanied herself on her Guitar. Then votes of thanks to us were carried with cheers, & a happy evening appropriately ended with thanksgiving & prayer by Papa.

*August 17^th*
To return to the week following the entertainment of our friends & neighbours on the 15^th & 16^th July; I had after these a much larger company to care for. The annual pic-nic of the BWTA took place on the 22^nd, & provision for between 300 & 400 had to be made. M^rs Goldsmith & myself as usual undertook this as far as ordering went; but as she was unable to leave home to go with me early in the day I arranged to take the two maids, the man, & the provisions, by the noon train to Cardington, the Special Train for Members following at 2-30. I found several willing helpers at

the Station, & a cart waiting at Cardington to take the 150 lbs of cake etc which needed to be transported to the Barn of the Farmer who kindly permitted us to take tea in his field. Before the arrival of the visitors, the cake & bread & butter was cut, & seats collected from the two little Chapels in the village & placed under the trees. The Clergyman we were told was anything but complimentary the previous Sunday in the Church at the intended invasion of his parish by teetotallers, but thank God his power ended there & his influence by the way his parishioners spoke of him was not much more to be feared than his wrath, as far as the Cardington BWTA Branch was concerned. The strains of the Mission Band playing a March announced that our friends were on their way from the Station, & it soon appeared at the head of a following of about 340 marching briskly through the village & on through M^r Wootton's farm gates until they took up their station in the field where all were glad to seat themselves under the shade of the trees, the day being beautifully fine & in every respect most favorable. Hattie helped well at the tea (this being the first time she has had an opportunity of doing so) as did many others & all expressed great satisfaction & enjoyment. The Minister from the neighbouring village of Cotton End was present with his wife & addressed the gathering very forcibly as did M^rs Carter, M^rs Ransom & M^r Sutcliffe. The Band led the singing & enlivened at frequent intervals during the afternoon & evening, until we marched again from the train homeward, bidding us good night with 'God save the Queen' in the Midland R^d about 9 o'clock.

The packing of Lottie's presents & belongings was quite an affair. 17 cases were sent off to Nottingham a few days before Hattie & I left home July 30^th to distribute the contents of them in Charnwood House.[46] We took the maid that Lottie had previously engaged, with us. On arriving at Alexandra Park we found the woman whom Alex had arranged to be at the house to receive us had done her best in making it as clean & tidy as possible, & had prepared refreshment for us, after partaking of which about 3 o'clock, we began at once the work of unpacking, in which I did not expect we should accomplish much without the assistance of a man. However Hattie found a screw-driver, & hammer in the house & with these managed to open all but about half a dozen of the strongest & most stubborn cases, & by bed time we managed to get the Establishment in working order sufficient for our immediate necessities.

*October*

The Brewsters' Sessions, our holiday, & some other noteworthy events have passed since I last opened this record. As to the first we were thankful that sufficient influence was brought to bear upon the Magistrates to induce them to refuse to transfer any old licences or grant any new ones, excepting one which was granted provisionally last year to an unbuilt house, at the disastrous Brewsters' Sessions at which everything was granted that was applied for. Amongst others the removal of a licence from a very small Public House to the large house adjoining it in which the Brewer who owned it formerly lived. Drink had done its worst for the male members of his family & when the Widow & two daughters removed from the premises a foolish

---

[46] Lottie continued to live in Charnwood House until her death 60 years later in 1951. Alexandra Park is the road in which Charnwood House lies.

young man who was doing well as an Aerated Water Manufacturer was induced to buy the place nominally, in a few months after the alterations were made, the heavy undertaking so weighed on his mind that his brain became affected & he died very suddenly, leaving the lawyer & others I am told in difficulty what to do with a place for which they cannot realize the fictitious value which the removal of the licence from the little adjoining place gave it. So the drink <u>Traffic</u> has slain one after another in that house. The plan the Brewers are now adopting is to apply for the transfer of licences from neighbourhoods where the amount consumed in some Public Houses, close to each other, has decreased, to new streets & districts that have sprung up further out of the town, & we were most thankful that in several cases this was refused this year. More Abstainers than ever were in the Court this Sessions, both ladies & gentlemen, to lend the weight of their presence to our opposing Solicitor, M$^r$ Stimson. The Magistrates appeared rather surprised at their audience, mixed with the Publicans who came to renew their liberty to carry on their death dealing trade. At the request of the GT Committee Hattie colored for them a very large plan of Bedford showing in red the numerous places at which strong Drink was sold, & this was brought into Court & much referred to both by the Bench & the Solicitors.

*Dec$^r$ 3$^{rd}$*

Our first work on returning home from our Welsh trip was that connected with the Mission organised by the General Temperance Committee to be held in the Corn Exchange [Bedford] from Monday 5$^{th}$ Oct$^r$ to Saturday 17$^{th}$ inclusive. Colonel Stenhouse had been indefatigable in corresponding with many Speakers, & had succeeded in obtaining an attractive list, although many to whom he applied (especially Wesleyans) were away in America, either to the great Methodist Ecumenical Council, just being held there or to the Convention of the World's Women's Temperance Association, to which the BWTA is affiliated, & to which our President, Lady H Somerset & some other of the British Women have gone as Delegates.[47]

The 12 days' Mission we considered a success although the numbers who took the Pledge was [*sic*] very much smaller than at the last; owing partly to the great increase in Temperance work continuously since that time, & partly to counter attractions in the form of a Circus which day after day, or rather nightly, drew crowds of young men & the very people we wished to influence. Canon Leigh, Canon Hull of Northampton, Sir Robert Phayre, M$^r$ & M$^{rs}$ W H Caine & other excellent Speakers did much to stir up the zeal of Total Abstainers, as well as to add to their numbers. Collections at the meetings at the Corn Exchange, & Subscriptions previously promised, met the whole expenses of the Mission without applying for any help from the Guarantors. M$^r$ & M$^{rs}$ Caine had luncheon with us before going to the afternoon meeting for Women at which M$^{rs}$ C spoke. After this I went with them to dinner at D$^r$ Carter's. M$^r$ Caine gave a magnificent address at night after which they at once returned to Town.

Hattie helped very much particularly in the preliminary visitation & distribution of handbills, & out of this has arisen a new work for her. The gravel pits opposite our house on the other side of the hedge are worked by gangs of men from the Midland Railway Co (whilst this house was being built in the summer of 1863 I

---

47 The President of the Association was Frances Willard, a friend of Lady Henry Somerset.

remember looking out of the unglazed windows on a great field of yellow flowers of turnip & mustard seed, & no Midland Railway existed here) & to these Hattie went with handbills & an invitation to the Mission. A day or two after one of the men came to the house & asked her whether she would come occasionally & talk with & read to them in the wooden hut in which they take their dinners, which they had finished by half past 12 o'clock, & had then half an hour to spare. She complied with their request, & was very pleased & the men so much so that they asked her to come twice a week. So now she regularly goes to them Tuesdays & Fridays for half an hour, when she is at home & when she is not I have taken her place. The number present usually is from twelve to twenty. The time is filled first by singing a Sankey's Hymn of their own choice, then a few verses of Scripture with short comments, another Hymn, & perhaps a short temperance or other story, or a conversation, the conclusion a short prayer. One of the men begins the times,[48] & at times offers the prayer.

Nothing could be a greater proof of the power of real religion, than the effect it has on the lives & manners of these rough navvies, several Christian men amongst them exercising just the influence on their fellows that Godliness should manifest. All quiet & respectful, & Hattie as safe amongst them as with her Father. She calls them 'Her dear men' & they sent 'their best love to her' when she went to London to stay.

Early in Nov[r] Lottie paid us a short visit, stopping here on her way to London to choose a Piano. The first sight of her old home for a few moments overcame her, & made her quite hysterical but she soon regained her equilibrium, & delighted herself by going round the house to every room, to see whether any alterations had been made in her absence, & then settled down to the quiet pleasure of telling us about her new home, her doings, her friends, & her Husband whom she declared to be 'the best in the world'. She seemed as full of happiness as it was possible for her to be. God grant that it may be continued to her. Hattie accompanied her to London; they went direct to John's Office, & thence with him to a Piano Manufacturer's where she chose a beautiful Instrument; which will, with her love of music, make her home still more complete. After her shopping she went to see Edward & Clara & arranged to take their eldest boy, Alex, back with her on her return, after spending a day at Hendon. The next day she left by an early train with little Alex, just called here for an hour, to take flowers etc which had been promised, & left again to take advantage of the only train that goes through to Nottingham in the day without change.

## 1892

*Jan[y] 8th 1892*

The New Year has begun with many mercies. Amidst sickness & death around we are in health further than[49] Papa & Hattie have had colds which have kept them in. The dreaded Influenza has re-appeared it seems almost in every country as well

---

[48]  This is what is written; perhaps it should read 'begins the hymns'?
[49]  This is what is written. Perhaps she means 'other than that'.

as our own, but to-day's Paper gives a sad account of its prevalence & fatality in London & indeed throughout England & the same gives an account of the discovery by some German Drs of the bacilli supposed to cause the disease, & adds that D[r] Koch is investigating their discoveries.[50] This will also incite Edward to fresh effort in the same direction. He has now a large Laboratory over some new buildings close to the back of his house, & all the time he can spare from his Practice is spent in experimenting & carrying on his studies in Bacteriology (in which he has begun to give instruction to men older than himself) & also to pursue his Micro-Photography, in both of which he is now beginning to be look[ed] up to with respect, if not more, as an authority. He gave a lecture at a West End gathering whilst Hattie was in Town, on these subjects, at which both Will & John were also present, & all pronounced it excellent, as also it seemed to be considered by his other listeners who often loudly applauded. He wishes he could devote his whole time to science.

To return to Xmas. We quite hoped to have had John & Mattie with their two little girls with us, but the weather which had been unusually mild up to 10 days before Xmas day suddenly became excessively cold, the river being almost frozen over in a few days, but added to this such heavy fogs came on & lasted for nearly a week, making it dangerous for any to go out who were not compelled to do so. We therefore could not blame them for deciding the day before Xmas that they could not bring the children out, although we were very disappointed. I was the more so on Hattie's account, fearing she would feel very depressed without Lottie (who with Alex we willingly spared to cheer the bereft home at home at Chelmsford). She was however a capital girl. Busied herself in the morning with taking a few Xmas gifts to some of our neighbours, & after early luncheon went off alone to enjoy skating on the flooded ground close to the river, before it was crowded, as it was later, by thousands of skaters. Papa & I went to her after a time & enjoyed watching her and the animated scene generally; then we all had a walk together back by the Embankment to the town where she left us to go to D[r] Brown's to invite her old school fellows to meet Lottie who was to come to us the following Monday on her return journey. We spent the evening looking over a number of Xmas Numbers of the Illustrated Papers, read one or two of the stories in them, finishing by having the Maids in for one, & to listen to Hattie's singing to her Guitar, & then family worship. So ended a very quiet day. Only one bird left in the nest! This thought made me feel sad at times, but the time may come that all will have flown!

Lottie came with her Husband on Monday in time for early dinner looking well & happy but having the remains of a cold which she did not lose before returning. Alex stayed with her over Tuesday & that evening the three Daughters & two Sons of the Brown family came for the evening with a cousin Visitor. M[rs] Brown a little later. It was a time of great enjoyment specially to the girls who had been friends from childhood, but even Alex who rather disliked the thought of anything like 'a function' expressed pleasure.

On Thursday we invited all the Members of our little Church to take tea with us in the BR Room & as Lottie & Hattie were both with us entertained them to their evident satisfaction. The Singers were also invited & we presented Eates with a

---

[50] Dr Heinrich Koch (1843–1910) was a distinguished German bacteriologist and later a Nobel Prize winner in 1905 for his work on tuberculosis.

small recognition of his services at the Harmonium in the shape of a Stationery Case & Blotter. Being the last day of the year it was intended that Papa should as usual conduct a Watch Night Service, but he had so bad a cold that at the last moment I succeeded in getting him to stay in & M^r Sutcliffe took the meeting for him. The girls came in, almost against my wish & I fear Lottie increased her cold, which became worse, but I could not get her to stay longer than the following Monday. Since her return home she has been in bed several days & has had the D^r, who thinks she may have had Influenza, but the tendency now is to call most ailments by that name, those who really have it are not I think in much doubt. The distressing pain in the head, & the whole body generally, which are the early symptoms she certainly had not at home.

*Jan^y 16^th*

My last-born girlie would have been 23 years old to-day if her life had been prolonged, but at this distance of time from an event which cast a shadow over years past, I cannot wish her back. Whilst I am thinking of my babe that was taken so early, what overwhelming sorrow fills the homes & hearts of the first families in the land. Only two days ago the eldest Son of the Prince of Wales[51] suddenly passed away, whilst the whole country was preparing presents & rejoicings for his wedding the 27^th of next month with the Princess May, the eldest Daughter of the Duchess of Teck. Out shooting with the Prince of Wales & a large party at Sandringham on Wednesday with a cold on him, again on Thursday, walking home with his affianced bride 'to warm himself' it was said, retiring early to his room that night never to leave it again until carried out to his last home. On his birthday next day the 8^th he could not join the family dinner party, but was cheerful, & no danger was appre-hended, but inflammation of the lungs set in & in spite of the constant attendance of Drs & Nurses on Jan^y 13^th he breathed his last surrounded by his Parents, all his sisters, & the one brother Prince George, who now takes the position of Heir-Presumptive to the Crown. The Duke & Duchess of Teck with their poor Daughter were also there. The whole Country goes out in deep sympathy with all, especially with the young worse than Widow, whose love & hopes & brilliant prospects have all been so suddenly crushed.[52] May the bereft ones learn the solemn lesson which this keen affliction is intended to teach 'Be ye also ready'.

*March 16^th*

Hattie's birthday. She says it has been a very happy one. A fine day (the afternoon spent in the woods at Aspley, with Papa & myself) & various letters & presents have contributed to make it so no doubt, but a circumstance beyond these, which I have not yet had courage to note here has filled up the measure. My last home bird has become engaged, & to one whose addresses a few months since we could not

---

[51]  Prince Albert Victor. He died of pneumonia.
[52]  CEB refers to Princess May, properly Mary, whose 'brilliant prospects' were realised, as she went on in the following year to marry Albert's younger brother George, who became George V on the death of his father, Edward VII, in 1910. Princess May became Queen Mary, and was known as the model of regal propriety and formality. Years later, in 1928, when CEB was one hundred years old, she was presented to Queen Mary and her husband (see Postscript and Plate 17).

have sanctioned.[53] M[r] Hamilton is the fortunate winner. He frankly confesses that he is conscious of a great change in his views & feelings since he knew Hattie, & she is so satisfied with his present ones, & so hopeful that what is good & true in either of them will be mutually strengthened, that we have yielded to her judgment in a matter which involves so much, & withdrawn the opposition which at first we manifested.

Beyond this last family event, which for some weeks past has been very absorbing, little of importance has transpired with us, but in the outer world there has been much lamentation & sorrow since the year began. Sickness & death from Influenza & chest affections[54] have been unprecedented, & many whose lives seemed most valuable to the world have been taken. First & foremost of these is the Rev[d] CH Spurgeon[55] who after weeks of suffering at home had so far recovered as to be able to take the journey to Mentone[56] & seemed likely to return for continued usefulness in the Church & the world, such as scarcely ever has been accomplished by any other single individual, but a sudden relapse carried him off when his own hopes, & those of the people were highest. Father had a most kind but short letter, written by his own hand, from him only a week or two previously in which he spoke of his anticipated return in Feb[y], but alas! only to be laid in Norwood Cemetery.

*Saturday May 14th*

Tuesday morning I went to Norwood & had dinner with Grandma & Father, who was much as usual, at 3 o'clock left, calling at the Home on my way to OKR, where I changed my dress & on to the 'Welcome Home' of Lady H Somerset, who has just returned from six months stay in America. The Library at Memorial Hall was filled with Delegates & invited guests; these last chiefly gentlemen representing principal Temperance Associations. An address of welcome was read & presented to the BWTA President by the Treasurer M[rs] Stewart, & by her very graciously received, but from a few minutes conversation with Miss Docwra, I found great anxiety was felt by the Executive as to the next day's discussion of the Agenda, in which was introduced propositions 'forwarded from Chicago' by Lady H, evidently intended to alter the Constitution & scope of the Association. Her address & manner that evening scarcely foretold the events of the next day, but for some reason there were words of warning given with those of welcome (chiefly by the gentlemen) as to the introduction of new & American methods into the BWTA.

The next morning's meeting of Delegates was unusually large, & it appeared special means had been used by the President to make it so, by looking up all Branches not sending Delegates & urging their being sent. Lady H came on to the Platform accompanied by a stranger who took her seat close to the Presidential Chair on the left. After the preliminary business of reading reports etc the first symptoms of warfare began. With the most benignant smile Lady Somerset made a

---

[53] This is a veiled reference to CEB's opposition to Mr Hamilton (as she always called him) as a suitor. He did not see eye to eye with her religious views, was Scottish and an orphan, and did not enjoy an established career as yet.
[54] 'Affections' is a nineteenth-century usage, meaning infections.
[55] Charles Haddon Spurgeon (1834–1894), Baptist Minister, was the most popular preacher of his day.
[56] Mentone, or Menton, is a holiday/health resort on the French Mediterranean coast just by the Italian border.

proposal to elect the new Committee by ballot, instead as before by being named & voted for, this was over-ruled for this year but was followed by other propositions, one after another, all intending radical changes. Miss Docwra who has for several years chiefly led the business of the Association both in Committee & at Public Meetings, was continually obliged to interpose, & show that several proposals & resolutions were unconstitutional, & on one or two points her Ladyship had to yield, but the pertinacity with which she affirmed 'The Chair rules this in order', & persisted in having previously prepared resolutions of her own put to the meeting seemed to answer her end, & notwithstanding Amendments, & remonstrances, from the Executive & the older Delegates, her smile, & go ahead policy so carried away the majority that nearly all her propositions were agreed to, or postponed until next year for discussion.

The new ideas related to creating Departments for other than Temperance work. Women's Suffrage, Purity, etc etc were proposed to be carried on in the name of the BWTA & Superintendents for each appointed. This was strongly objected to by many of us, who feel that Temperance work only is that upon which we all think alike, & that to add others on which we are not all agreed is to introduce discord both into the Executive & the country Branches. Lady E Biddulph was exceeding warm in denouncing the new proposals, & I fear I made myself conspicuous in the same direction but we were in the minority. We discovered Lady H's attendant was an American who had returned with her & from Miss Willard's home, & on every occasion when the President was not on her feet (which was seldom) the two were engaged in a whispering which was evidently a prompting.[57] The intention is to assimilate the BWTA to the World's Women's Christian Association of which Miss Willard is President. Altogether the day was most exciting to me, & the discussion continued until some hours[58] beyond the allotted time. After a final protest against making Women's Suffrage a plank in the platform of our Temperance Association I left the adjourned meeting with Clara, about 8 o'clock, to go to the Converzasione at the Church Association, the chief attraction to which was its being held in the Institute of Painters in Water Color in Piccadilly. The Exhibition was open to the guests, & the gathering much more numerous & cheerful than that in Exeter Hall, but the Speeches that came between the music & refreshments, had the same ring of lamentation.

The excitement of this first week in London did not reach a climax until Saturday night. When I reached St Swithins in the morning Will was just leaving for North Hackney. I had not seen him when at the Temple, but his Clerk told me he was the selected Conservative candidate for that Division, & I read the Address he had issued, but knew little more. It was only when I got to Hendon that I found how rapid had been the march of events. The death of Sir Lewis Pelly the late Conservative Member had caused the vacancy in the constituency.[59] At the request of the Carlton Club,[60] Will consented to contest it, & with two other Candidates spoke at

---

[57] Miss Willard believed in the new approach, saying 'Everything is not in the Temperance movement, but the Temperance movement is in everything.'

[58] CEB inadvertently turned over 2 pages at this point – see later reference in text.

[59] General Sir Lewis Pelly was an officer in the Indian Army, and then served in the Diplomatic Service in the Persian Gulf and Afghanistan.

[60] The Carlton Club, founded in 1832, was effectively a Conservative party political organisation.

the first meeting the previous Friday, & having done so left. About 2 o'clock in the morning he was awakened by two ardent young politicians who made a journey of some dozen miles on bicycles to inform him he was the selected Candidate. The days of the following week he spent chiefly amongst the people in North Hackney, addressing sometimes five or six meetings in a day. (Fortunately he was not very busy in Chambers, although he was obliged to be in Court, part of two days.) This continued Monday & Tuesday on which last day the Writ was issued for the election to take place next day, Wednesday, May 11$^{th}$, only about 10 days from his first introduction to the Constituency! His Opponent (Gladstonian) M$^r$ Meates had, in view of the General Election, been 'nursing' it about 3 years. Will & Florence were expecting me to spend Sunday with them, so I determined to go to the meeting which was being held that night; & once fairly launched in the excitement, & the issue so near, resolved to see it through. For the details of these following days, I must turn back to the previous page, having inadvertently turned over two leaves!

It is now June 15$^{th}$, & I have not found opportunity to finish my record of the events of a month ago when Will was elected MP for North Hackney of which I have made mention on the pages following these.

On the Saturday I reached Hendon, I followed him at night to Hackney, found one of his Committee Rooms, & enquiring for the place of that night's meeting was told by the Chairman of the District M$^r$ Verry, to whom I introduced myself & went with him first calling at his house near the School-room in which it was to be held. His wife accompanied us, & we had seats on the Platform, meeting Will at the door & going to it with him. The meeting was very full & very orderly. A Barrister whose name I forget made a very witty speech after Will had spoken, & then an Irishman, who confirmed all my previous ideas against Home Rule or rather Rome Rule for Ireland. After the meeting the walk home from Finchley Station with my Son was very pleasant although near midnight. The weather being very fine & bright moonlight.

Monday morning Will was off to Chambers & thence to Hackney, whither I went later in the day to do some canvassing for him. M$^{rs}$ Verry had invited me to luncheon, & after it ordered a carriage & we went off together to do what we could for the Conservative Candidate so-called, but with so little of the old Tory type in him that some of that School would not have voted for him, but for helping to keep out the Gladstonian. Some said 'Why the man's a Radical' & truly to my thinking this was true, apart from the Irish question, & one or two standing Con principles in which I do not believe, Union of Church & State to whit. After getting our orders from the Committee Room we went off in the directions indicated to streets inhabited by working men & small shopkeepers, taking with us cards bearing a Cabinet size print of a very good Photo of Will surmounted by the Imperial crown, & surrounded by the Flags of England & Ireland in colors. It was very comical to see in windows on all sides, as one passed the streets, our Son's likeness, chiefly in private houses of his Supporters! The only place in which I was ashamed to see them was in the Public Houses, for the Publicans adopted him, because he believes in giving Compensation to a fair extent in compulsory extinction of Licences. His views on the Temperance question failed to satisfy either Publicans, Teetotallers or his Mother. Monday night M$^{rs}$ Fawcett spoke for him, first in a crowded meeting above, & then in an overflow meeting below the Hall. In canvassing we had some amusing incidents but very little incivility. Once our carriage was surrounded by half a dozen working men, standing about in the street several of them with little to do but drink but all professing to be ready to vote for him.

The following was the day of the Election & we went together, after early luncheon at St Swithins, to Dalston Station, found a grand Brake[61] & a pair of horses lent by some nobleman, ready to take any Voters who came by train to the polling Station. Into this we got, with but a single one, & were taken to a Committee Room. There we met Maidie [*sic*] Kelly who had been busy canvassing every day that week. We went to M^r Verry's together for a cup of tea, & leaving Papa (who was far from well) there I returned to do a little more canvassing a <u>second</u> time. When we had finished Will came driving by on his way to the Conservative Club. He took us into his carriage, & we went with him, & remained there until all was over. He seemed perfectly cool in the whole matter; had a cup of tea & then went down stairs with some of his ardent admirers to the Billiard Room where he played & won a game whilst the Votes were being counted in the Hall close by. I remained at the upstairs window watching the excited crowd of some thousands crowding around the Club & stretching far down the street opposite to it. These were kept amused by a Magic Lantern the slides of which were thrown through an open window on a large Screen that had been fixed outside the house. Various scenes representing Irish misery, <u>as it was</u> before M^r Balfour's reign,[62] then a likeness of him, which evoked great cheering, then Will's, at which there was still more, but the climax was reached when 'Majority 968' was thrown upon it, & when Will came back almost lifted from his feet by his new Constituents the cheers seemed enough to raise the roof. He had to make a Speech from the Hall Steps, then one down stairs & another from the Club window above; directly after which I took his arm on one side & Papa's on the other, & with the help of a double row of Policemen we managed to get through the crush to a D^rs carriage just outside it. The carriage was drawn up some distance from the Club & crowd to prevent any attempt to take out the horse. It was then near midnight & the last train from Dalston had gone, so we had to drive on to Finsbury Park, & reached that Station in time for the last train thence to Finchley, & again walked to St Swithins in bright moonlight. Such a majority was not anticipated by any but the most sanguine & Will was not one of them. Florence was in bed when we reached home, but waiting to hear what news we should bring, & of course was very pleased, & proud of her Husband.

Here I must not forget the fact of the birth of another Daughter[63] at St Swithins on May 27^th, our 11^th grandchild.

---

[61] A brake was an open-topped vehicle with four wheels and designed for country use. The form usually met, the shooting brake, was designed to carry the driver and a gamekeeper at the front, facing forward and up to six sportsmen on longitudinal benches, with their dogs, guns and game carried alongside in slat-sided racks.

[62] A.J. Balfour was Irish Secretary from 1887 to 1891 in Salisbury's second ministry (1886–1892). Politics were complicated, as after Gladstone's conversion to Home Rule, made public in December 1885, the Irish Nationalist MPs voted with the Liberals, but there was a migration of some 90 Liberal MPs who opposed Home Rule to vote with the Conservatives – it was their support which brought Salisbury to power in 1886. Because of this support, Salisbury adopted a more liberal approach, and this applied to Balfour's Irish policy, where coercion was reduced and the extension of peasant proprietorship of land was encouraged. Some thought that Balfour owed his promotion to the fact that Robert Cecil, Lord Salisbury, was his uncle – hence the phrase 'Bob's your uncle'.

[63] Charlotte Elspeth.

Papa returned home Thursday morning, but as our Son was to take his Seat in the House of Commons that afternoon I determined to stay & see the whole function to the end. I met him at Chambers after luncheon, & found he had endeavoured to secure an order for the Ladies' Gallery for me. My card was sent in, & after a little waiting the Attorney General came into the Lobby & very politely conducted me up to the box behind the lattice called the Ladies' Gallery, divided into two parts, the special one being appropriated for the Speaker's wife. It was then however only occupied by three or four ladies. Sir Richard Webster told me he was going to 'introduce' Will, with another London MP. Edward made his way to the Strangers' Gallery.

From about 3-30 to 5-30 the time was taken up by 'questions', these being put to the different Ministers by the Opposition Members; M$^r$ Balfour, M$^r$ Chaplin, & other Members of the Government, replying to them, according to the department to which they belonged. Very special interest has been taken by both Parties in this North Hackney election, which is the last that will take place before the General Election, so on the occasion of the new Member taking his seat (so said the Papers) the House was unusually full. He entered soon after 3-30, & took a place just within. Some time before 5 o'clock, the Attorney General & his other Introducer went to him (one on either side) & the three stood side by side, near the door until questions were finished, nearly ¾ hour later! These over, some Official called on the newly elected Member to come to the Table. The three made a low bow to the Speaker, & then advanced, stopped half way up the House & then bowed again; then the two retired, leaving Will to finish the journey alone. Another low reverence to the Speaker then the Oath was administered, & the Roll signed, after which the Speaker shook hands with the new MP as also did M$^r$ Balfour, amidst a great deal of cheering from the Government side of the House. Then he passed out behind the Chair, & soon re-entered as before & took a seat on the Conservative side.

After this [the] House went into Committee, to discuss the Small Holdings Bill. with M$^r$ Courtney in the Chair. This continued until about 7 o'clock, when there was an Adjournment, when M$^r$ Ambrose an MP & one of Will's neighbours, & friends came up to the Gallery & invited me to tea with himself & Will. I went down with him not into the Members tea-room, but into one to which they can take friends, where were several other ladies & gentlemen. We sat & chatted some time, but before we had finished tea, the Division bell rang, & both left me, promising to return as soon as they had performed their duty of voting. When they returned I was walking on the broad balcony overlooking the Thames. Will took me again to the Ladies' Gallery before returning to the House. I was very interested in the Debate on the Small Holdings bill on which there were several Divisions during the evening. 'Ayes to the right; Noes to the left' was followed by a general movement, in which many Liberal Unionists crossed over to the right, the Government side.[64] At about 10-30 we left, the talking & wrangling, seeming likely to go on much longer.

So the first day of Parliamentary duty for my Son ended, & in less than a month the whole bother & the whole expense will have to come over again. To Will this

---

[64] An example of the existence of the Conservative and Liberal Unionist co-operation mentioned above.

last has been over £613; to his Opponent rather more. The legal limit of Election expense is fortunately £650, but it seems a great shame that the Representative of a Constituency should in addition to the sacrifice of time & energy, bear the whole cost.[65] Truly the honor does not seem worth so much, & if that, or mere professional advancement, were the chief motives with Will (which I hope & believe they are not) I should hardly wish him success. His programme is not a perfect one, but calculated to benefit those who are the least cared for, the labouring & pauper classes. There is to be another contest at the General Election, by a local man a LCC,[66] & popular in the neighbourhood so that the fight will be much more difficult than the last, & may not be successful. May God grant success or failure as shall be for the carrying out of His purposes, not Will's.

*July 19th*

Nearly a fortnight has elapsed since I returned home after the excitement of Will's re-election for North Hackney, for that is an accomplished fact in spite of the Gladstonian Candidate being a resident in the Division, & his having had a special letter of request from Mr Gladstone, to allow himself to be nominated, as 'the only man who could recover the seat' for his party! The result of the contest was simply an increase of Will's majority from 969 to 1519, a result beyond our most sanguine expectations.

Friday morning I went to Hendon to see what could be done to rid Florence of the unfortunate woman she had from the Home as Cook, more than a year ago, who had returned to her old habit. I found her in a drunken heap on the floor of her bedroom, & much to Flo's relief arranged to take her back to the Home next morning. So, again & again, are our hopes for the restoration of these poor women blighted. There is no hope for them but total-abstinence, but how much more satisfactory is prevention by it, rather than waiting until the well-nigh useless attempt to cure.

Monday morning brought back all the electioneering bustle, my chief part in it was to make calls on some of Will's principal Friends & Supporters. He had no time either for this, or for canvassing, & Florence was not able to leave home until Tuesday when she came over with nurse & baby.

The day of the Election I drove with Will a good part of the morning, visiting his Committee rooms & the polling stations. We had an open carriage. Showing himself to his Constituents being one end in view. About 2 o'clock Florence was able to drive with him. They took me first of all to the Station, as I determined to go to the Home Committee meeting at Memorial Hall. I got back to find a large party of workers & Friends at Lenton Lodge[67] who sallied forth again & only ceased their labors when it was too near 8 o'clock to bring up any more voters. We knew there were working men who would have voted if there had been carriages to fetch them, but as the Election of the other two Members for the divisions of Hackney was going on the same day it was much more difficult than before to get these. Hattie

---

[65] Members of Parliament did not receive salaries until 1911 when a resolution was passed in the Commons that MPs should receive a payment of £400 *per annum*.

[66] LCC. It is not clear what this stands for; it could stand for London County Council(lor).

[67] Lenton Lodge was a large house in Lordship Road, Stoke Newington, within the North Hackney constituency, which Will was renting as his campaign headquarters.

was driving about in a D$^{rs}$ Victoria[68] most of the afternoon, but the day was cold & invalids who had promised would not come out. Greta like a brave girl marched 5 men to the polling station at one time, who would not have voted but for her offer to accompany them.[69]

The evening concluded with the same excitement as before only the Poll was declared at the Central Town Hall for all three Members at the same time. Will as having the largest majority of the three was called the senior Member & should have spoken first, but Sir Charles Russell had been Member for one Division some years, & was in everything but numbers so much his 'senior' that he insisted on giving place to him, the two QCs of opposite politics for the moment amicably yielding to each other. We could not hear or see anything of this at the Conservative Club where we were, but the crowd outside it was nearly as large as when Will's was the only election, & the news of his increased majority (which came before he could return) was as vociferously received. Then when he drove up to the Club this was if possible increased, & only ceased for a few moments whilst he congratulated them, rather than himself on 'the splendid victory they had achieved' etc. Will said he felt really sorry for his opponent M$^r$ M$^c$All who seemed much depressed, & said he did not expect such a beating. He could scarcely have felt grateful to M$^r$ Gladstone for inducing him to incur all the expense, by telling him 'he was the only man who could recover the Seat' when he would not otherwise have contested it.

### July 27$^{th}$

The General Election is now over & M$^r$ Gladstone has a majority of 42 in the country. Many are the conjectures as to what he will be able to do with it, & whether he will be able to carry his still undeclared Home Rule scheme. One great good has come out of these party conflicts. The Liberals have been forced to acknowledge the power of the Temperance vote, & have given so many pledges for Temperance Legislation that there is more hope than ever before that something will be done to check the dreadful drink Traffic, & help to make this nation (if not individuals) 'sober by Act of Parliament'. Amongst others our Bedford MP M$^r$ S Whitbread, a Brewer, has been educated by his Temperance Constituents to 'the Direct Veto' & has promised to support legislation for the suppression of Traffic in the article which he manufactures![70]

## 1893

### January 15$^{th}$ 1893

Another year has opened in circumstances of continued comfort & mercy for us as a family. Neither sickness nor sorrow for loss of dear ones has darkened our home. Some circumstances have caused disquiet & doubt, but we can afford to trust His

---

68   The Victoria was an elegant carriage style, very popular amongst wealthy families. There is one forward-facing seat for two passengers, and a driver's seat supported by an iron frame. This type of carriage became fashionable for riding in the park, especially with a stylish coachman installed.
69   Greta Cumming, a friend of Hattie's whose father was a master at Rugby School.
70   The 'Direct' or 'Local Veto' was part of the Gladstonian Liberals' election manifesto.

guidance this year, also who has hitherto done so much for us in those that have passed.

[CEB continues this entry without inserting a new date. The remaining paragraphs under this date heading, beginning 'Summer is gone', appear to have been written in September, as the next date entry, December 15th 1893, begins with the departure of Hattie for a holiday in the Isle of Wight in the first week in September.]

Summer is gone. It is a longer time than I thought since I have made an entry in my Diary. I have had little desire to chronicle events both of family & public life which have been painful. Amongst the first, anxiety on Hattie's account, both as to her health, & future.[71] Then up to April great difficulty with my valuable, but erring maid,[72] whom I first knew as an Inmate of the Home, but who after being with me four years fell back into a worse habit than that from which I had hoped she was rescued, finding means of obtaining laudanum, which at length brought her almost to madness, & myself to the verge of despair of ever being able to reclaim, or keep her, which however I have so far been able to do by constant watchfulness. Then came the greatest mortification I have ever experienced, in the action of the Secretaries of the Home, in reference to Edward as their Medical man. They professed not to be satisfied with his treatment of a poor unhealthy Patient, & instead of requesting him to call in another D$^r$ for consultation took it upon themselves to do so, with no better result for her, but made this the first pretext for a series of petty charges, which they brought to the Committee, but had not courage to read in my presence, but did so when I voluntarily withdrew, not knowing what was intended. Lady Elizabeth was not present, but at the next meeting of the Committee, at which Edward insisted on presenting himself, characterized what had been done & said at the previous one as altogether unworthy, & did the best she could to make an apology, but the evident design of Miss Bagster especially, to have the young Medical man, living near the Home, was so apparent & the Members of the Committee had been so influenced by her, that he sent in his resignation, & so ended his 7 years almost honorary service to the Home, without the least gratitude for his services, or recognition of them, excepting from Lady Elizabeth![73]

Nothing in my whole life has ever occasioned me so much pain & annoyance as the treatment of those who have had little or nothing to do with the work & difficulty of establishing that Home, especially the two present Secretaries, who were unknown to myself & the Committee until long after it was proved to be a success.

After these events came the May Meetings of the BWTA at which our worst fears were realized as to the result of Lady Henry Somerset's autocratic conduct as its President. The American methods which she learnt whilst under Miss Willard's influence in America were fully carried out. Women's Suffrage, The Labor Question, Purity & half-a-dozen other reforms were introduced into our Temperance work;

---

[71] See footnote to diary entry for 16 March 1892.

[72] Fanny, who has figured in these diaries several times before, and in whom CEB continued to have faith.

[73] A further blow to CEB, following her own enforced resignation three years earlier – see 25 April 1890.

those of the old Committee who were obnoxious to her, from their endeavours to moderate her wholesale proposals, & were those who had laboured for the Association years before Lady H S had anything to do with it, she got rid of by a swamping Committee of her own selection, & nomination, which, by methods as unconstitutional as her proposals she got elected, who were ready to do her bidding at any cost, carried away by her title, her fair speech, & the wonderful works that were put before them for accomplishment.

The former Executive finding their influence nullified after a short effort to co-operate, resigned their positions, & left the BWTA to begin the Women's Total Abstinence Union [WTAU]; many Branches did the same, in order to work on entirely temperance lines, affiliating to the new Union. Throughout the country disunion & discord have taken place amidst the once united body of women whose annual meetings were formerly seasons of happy intercourse looked forward to by all, but which, since the year of Lady Henry's advent, have become sorrowful gatherings in which two parties have been at strife, without a single effort on the part of the Arch-disturber of our peace to do other than carry out her own will, & remain President of the Association which she has rent in twain so mercilessly. The WTAU Committee is composed of the wisest & most experienced Members of the Association from which they were driven. They have taken Offices on Ludgate Hill, with the late Secretary of the BWTA, who had served many years & resigned when the split took place. In Bedford we are nearly in the same difficulties through the influence of a single Member of our Committee.

*Decr 15th*

The saddest event that has occurred to us as a family from the time I began to write these pages, took place in Sept[r], & in recalling the events of the last three months makes those that went before it comparatively small. Dear Grandma Collins who we fervently hoped would be spared to continue the loving devoted guardian of my poor Father until his end came, has been taken from him after nearly 18 years of faithful companionship, & comfort, such as seldom falls to the lot of so aged a man to enjoy. We decided that our holiday should be spent in the Isle of Wight, & Hattie left home with me the first week in Sept[r]. We spent a night at Norwood en route, & found Grandma slightly poorly, but about, almost as usual. Before we left the next morning to meet Papa at Waterloo I made her promise to let me hear from her when she had seen the D[r], at Father's wish rather than her own. We reached Totland Bay on Thursday, & on Saturday I had a letter from her saying she felt better & hoped soon to be quite well. The following Monday Father wrote to tell me that very day (Saturday) the D[r] discovered that an immediate operation was necessary, but that it had been successfully performed, & all was going on well. On Wednesday after along day out, we found on returning a telegram from Edward 'Grandma can only last a few hours'. It was not too late for the last boat that night. So leaving Papa & Hattie at our lodgings I crossed to Lymington & reached Waterloo soon after midnight & too late for a train to Norwood, so went to Edward's to sleep, & found from him that I should not see her again alive. Arriving at Penrith House, the worst was soon told. She passed away the previous day, before the telegram was received by me. M[rs] Doherty got to Norwood just in time to receive a look of recognition from her dying Sister, but about an hour later the end peacefully came. In one short week with little pain, & no anxiety excepting for her Husband, calmly expressing a few wishes as to the disposal of her watch, clothes etc the final scene was enacted, & the gentle loving spirit soared away, leaving on all sides testimonies, even from those who were not intimate friends, of her Christian character.

The more joyous events have been the safe arrival of another Son to Edward,[74] & a Daughter at Hendon, both born within the last two months, but the dates I do not recollect & now that we have over a dozen grandchildren, I do not take such note of their coming as when they were not so numerous.

Our eldest Grandson George has been here for the Grammar School education over 3 years, the last two terms having been almost exclusively occupied in preparing for an Exam for a Cadetship on board the training ship Britannia.[75] He has expressed so strong a wish, or rather determination, to go to sea that his Father applied for & obtained a nomination for him as one of about 50 boys whose friends have made similar applications. As only about a third of the number examined can be received he has a good chance of <u>not</u> passing, which would not be a matter of regret either to his Parents or to myself. He will have had an opportunity of carrying out his own wish under the most advantageous circumstances, no expense has been spared to specially prepare him for the examination, & if he has not succeeded in it, he will not have anyone to blame but himself. Adventure seems to be his great idea, in going to sea.

*Decr 30th*

With to-morrow (Sunday) the record of another year will close & I have only room to recall the mercies & pleasures that have filled the last days of this year & a little work done for the WTAU, but my old zest seems to have gone for all but home work, & I have not much concern for the working of either Association having had such painful experiences from the leading members of both. I find I have forgotten to write of what has happened in the Bedford Branch of the BWTA. Mrs Sampson, my coadjutor in its formation more than 10 years ago, has, with the Secretary Mrs Clark, after long continued disapproval of Lady Henry's tactics, entirely changed, & on a Resolution to dis-affiliate from the London Executive being proposed & carried (that we might not spend our time in Committee on discussing proposals from them, instead of carrying on our local temperance work) determined to leave our Committee, & with a few less influential Members of it have formed a separate society which they call the Bedfordshire Women's Gospel Temperance Union & taken about half the Members with them. We who remained have continued as if nothing had happened, further than calling our Association <u>Bedford</u> instead of British Women, still BWTA, holding our Prayer, Tea, & other meetings as usual.

We called as many of the Members as we could get together in August to explain the change that had taken place, & the retirement of the President & Secretary.

---

[74] 'Oct 20th' written in pencil above. Edward's son is Guy William John. The 'daughter at Hendon' is a mistake: CEB must be referring to Will's son John Keith.

[75] George, son of Will and Flo, is thirteen years of age, and is attending the Grammar School (now Bedford School). Many schoolboys at this time were fired with the excitement and romance of the British Empire, then in its heyday. It seems strange that the residence at Alpha Villa for three years of her eldest grandson should have been so infrequently noted by his grandmother before this. CEB does not seem very sympathetic to his ambitions. In the event, he did not pass and went on to become a doctor.

At this meeting without my having the least idea of what would take place, one lady proposed that I should be elected President, another seconded, & before I had really time to determine what would be best to do, this was put to the meeting & unanimously carried. Under the circumstances I accepted the position which I had before repeatedly refused, & have hitherto worked most happily with those of the Committee who, like myself, felt we had one object in view in our Association, & were determined to keep to it.

For our Annual Meeting in Oct[r] we invited Lady Elizabeth Biddulph to hold two meetings for us, she being in entire sympathy with the WTAU. She was not able to come until the first week in Nov[r]. I met her at the Station, brought her here for luncheon, after which she accompanied me to the Town Hall at 3 o'clock, where we found about 150 ladies assembled for the Drawing-room meeting to which they were invited. As President I had to preside & introduce Lady EB. She spoke well on the Temperance question, but created a slight feeling of annoyance in the minds of some by allusion to 'her class' in relation to it. After high tea with her at D[r] Goldsmith's we returned to the Hall where about 100 of our staunch members had in the meantime taken their tea. I was really surprised so many came after all the efforts we knew had been made by those who had left us, to draw the whole Association after them, but the evening meeting was even more successful. Quite a company of gentlemen as well as ladies surrounded Lady Elizabeth on the platform. The Chair was occupied by M[r] J Thomas, an earnest Abstainer CC & JP.[76] The Vicar of St Cuthbert's, M[r] Sharp, WM,[77] & M[rs] Thomas were the chief Speakers after her Ladyship, all of whom where at their best. The choir of Southend Chapel under M[r] Palmer had practised for this meeting & with a young Harpist whom I engaged, enlivened it between the speeches with songs & solos; the Hall was filled, & a good collection at the close defrayed all expenses; so we of the BWTA felt our troubles were almost at an end, & hoped we had taken out a new lease of prosperity from which we might go on with fresh courage. Lady Elizabeth was delighted with everything. She spent the night with us, & with her maid, left next morning.


## 1894

### Jany 24th 1894

Nearly the first month of the New year has passed before I have concluded my reference to the circumstances that transpired during the last weeks of 1893. A week before Xmas my Father came to spend a month with us. Two days later Lottie came home, & on the Saturday, Alex & M[r] Hamilton, who (with little Evelyn[78] who had been at Nottingham for some months) made up our Xmas party, & expressed themselves as having had a very happy time together. Four generations were represented. Grandpapa was very gently dealt with by all, & although much aged since Grandma's death, & making frequent allusions to her absence & loss, he was on the

---

[76] A County Councillor.
[77] There is nothing to indicate the identity of this person.
[78] Evelyn and her twin brother, Alec, were Edward and Clara's oldest children, born in 1886.

whole very happy & even jocular with his grand, & great-grandchildren. I returned to Norwood with him & his servant, & after seeing the rooms occupied well aired & comfortable, left him a week ago, with workmen in the house re-papering etc!

Once more I must refer to our Bedford WTA. At the first meeting in the year we invited all our Members to meet to elect their new Committee, after a social tea. I was unanimously chosen President for the year; several new Members joined the Committee, our numbers are continually increasing, & work extending to neglected, & new, parts of Bedford, in Cottage Meetings & Mothers' Meetings. Every member of the Committee seems very much in earnest, & we scarcely regret the disruption which has removed from our midst those who caused it, & has left us, a very united band of Workers.

### Feby 8th

Hattie has been in the house & under the Dr's care since New Year's day. He finds a weak spot in her lungs, which whilst not in itself serious requires great care against cold & has prevented her going to the Navvies' Hut on the Midland Railway, & all the work in which she helps me. We have decided to take her to Bournemouth in about a fortnight. She has thought a great deal too of being hindered in her home work, & when the D$^r$ suggested her amusing herself in her bed-room with her paints & brushes, asked him whether he would amuse himself with his drugs & bottles in like circumstances! She has however a picture to offer to the Academy, & a very successful Portrait of her Father, both of which, with several smaller ones, she nearly finished before her illness.

### August 16th /94

In my frequent visits to London I generally manage to see all my Sons either in going to or returning from Norwood. Will continues his arduous work in the Law Courts by day & in the House of Commons at night. On two occasions I have been to the latter with him, & on the last heard him speak in the House, on the Budget of Sir W$^m$ Harcourt, which has been the subject of an unusually long debate. I also heard Sir W$^m$ speak. M$^r$ Gladstone's retirement from parliamentary life some months since has made him Leader in the H of Commons, & he seems well able to sustain the position.[79] Will has had a long & lucrative Term but will be thankful when it ends, & will 'pair' with another Member, & go off with his numerous family to Shanklin as soon as possible instead of remaining until the end of the Session. Edward is busy as ever with his science work. His landlord has built him a Laboratory etc on to his house, much to his satisfaction. Clara & the children have been to Brighton but he cannot leave home. John was in entire charge of the business at South Place when I last called there M$^r$ Redfern being on holiday.

### Wednesday Dec$^r$ 19th

Lottie has been here to spend a week in the old home, & a very busy, if happy time she has had, in quite new work for her Mother, in which Hattie has also been

[79] Gladstone retired on 1 March 1894, and Queen Victoria offered the premiership to Lord Rosebery without consulting Gladstone, who would have preferred Harcourt, who became Leader of the House of Commons and Chancellor of the Exchequer. His Budget of 1894 was a memorable one, introducing a reform of death duties.

most helpful. This last has been in connection with a request which was made to me some weeks since, to allow myself to be nominated as Poor Law Guardian (or rather Candidate) on the Board here, 19 members of which have to retire at the end of the year. I gladly expressed my willingness to stand, as it seemed to me an Office of all others in which women were needed & I thought if only to care for the comfort of the women & children in the Workhouse, I should have great opportunity of usefulness.

There has of late been great complaint of 'irregularities' in its management by the Master, such as skimming the milk served to the children & inmates, giving them third rate flour, whilst he was himself living in luxury at the expense of the rate-payers. These & many other rumours have been hotly debated at the sittings of the Board & although to a great extent proved, by surprise visits to the Workhouse, by two of the Guardians, have been so extenuated, instead of investigated, by <u>every</u> other Member of the Board, that the two (M<sup>r</sup> Beckett a Clergyman, & M<sup>r</sup> Hull, a working man) determined to take steps to secure a new list of Candidates for the next Election. Amongst these there were six ladies which with 11 men & the two old Guardians made up the required 19. For the first time there has been great excitement in the town over the election of Guardians, & reports of the mismanagement under the previous ones being fully believed, especially by the rate-payers of the working-class, who form of course a majority, an unprecedented event has occurred. Every name on the new list has been elected, & a clean sweep made of the retiring Guardians excepting Messrs Beckett & Hull who were returned at the head of the poll in their respective Parishes. I am associated in St Mary's, with M<sup>r</sup> Wyatt the Vicar of St Leonard's, M<sup>r</sup> Sutcliffe our Town Missionary & M<sup>rs</sup> Grafton, the wife of an Engineer whose Works & house are in the Parish. The Election was yesterday, & we were returned, much to the surprise of those who had so long held the office of Guardians. I had only 22 votes above the most popular of these in this Parish, but am quite satisfied. My Total Abstinence principles did not add to my popularity amongst the drinking portion of the community, some of whom expressed the opinion that I should 'rob the poor men of their beer'. Possibly I may some day raise the enquiry what becomes of 36 gallons of ale weekly, as has been the case, & whether the Officials, or the poor men drink it at the Workhouse! Lottie & especially Hattie were very anxious that we should canvass & M<sup>r</sup> Wyatt was quite willing his name should appear with ours on the card to be left at Voters' houses but did not undertake any of the work so that I had to invite canvassers to met here & arrange for the whole of St Mary's.

The day after the Election Hattie invited 20 of 'her men' the navvies to a substantial tea in our BR Room. They came direct from their work on the line at 5 o'clock & were entertained until past 8 o'clock. Several accepted pledge cards. Lottie left next day to meet Alex at Chelmsford for Xmas.

**1895**

*Jany 12th 1895*

Will & Flo have spent a night with us this week as they also did rather more than a month ago. On the first occasion Florence came to speak for the Ladies early-closing League, & her Husband to support her. On the last Will, at the request of Mr Guy Pym[80] (the Conservative Candidate for Bedford at the next Election) came to assist him at a meeting to address Working men, & enlighten them as to what the Conservative party had done for their class! Hilda came with them to spend a fortnight with us.

The year has begun with much work in prospect. I have been asked to join the Executive of the Charity Organization Society[81] & this in addition to the duties of Guardian has already taken up every moment that I could spare from the ordinary round of temperance work & visitation. The new Guardians met the day before the Board meeting to consider what steps should be taken in reference to the investigation into the 'irregularities', which they had promised. Saturday Jany 5th I reached the Workhouse before 11 o'clock & found Mr Wyatt & a few others there before me. All had to sign a declaration as to faithful service on the Board, & when the later comers had done the same we adjourned from the Committee to the Board-room. There our places were indicated, the six Women Guardians were on the back elevated seat in a line with & at the right hand of the Chairman, the best that could be given us. My former BWTA friend Mrs Clark was elected in St Paul's Parish, & our old feud is almost forgotten in our new work together. We sit next to each other with only the Clerk (Mr Sharman) between us & the Chairman & have various little conferences with him & with each other.

Election of Chairman was the first business. Mr Charles Howard was unanimously recalled to that position which he had occupied many years.[82] There was more debate about the Vice-Chairman, the late one being displaced. Then came the election for Committees. All six ladies were elected on the Visiting Committee with a larger number of such & Mr Brown & myself on the Finance Committee with six or seven men. I volunteered for this last as giving an opportunity of looking into what has been supposed to be the extravagant expenditure of the Master.

*March 4th*

The extreme cold of the month of Feb^y & the preceding fortnight has been almost universal. An almost unbroken frost of six weeks has caused much distress to the poor & great inconvenience, the water supply having entirely ceased from the usual

---

Guy Pym was a member of a distinguished political family, a descendant of John Pym, who led the political opposition to Charles I in the Long Parliament and died in 1643. He is also related to Francis Pym, a prominent Conservative MP, who served under Prime Ministers Heath and Thatcher and held the offices of Secretary of State for Northern Ireland, Defence Secretary and Foreign Secretary.

81 The Charity Organisation Society was set up in 1869 by Henry Solly with the aim of improving the standard of administering charitable relief, emphasising the need for self help and accompanying it with personal care. It soon became involved in administering charity relief in London.

82 Charles Howard was the second son of John Howard (CEB's 'old Mr Howard') and now the senior Howard after the death of his brother James in 1889. He was regarded as a farming and livestock expert, lived at Biddenham and was chairman of Bedfordshire County Council from 1893 until his death in 1895.

sources. Water carts have been used to dole out a couple of buckets daily to our neighbours, & we should have been in the same case but for the independent arrangement which was necessary for our supply before the town system of water supply was laid on 34 years ago. In that long period we have never known the freezing up of the mains, nor such continued intense cold as has been experienced. Even at this date the river is not clear of ice, which has covered it for weeks. I intended to have visited my Father a month ago, but as he was tolerably well I could not make up my mind to face the bitter weather of the day on which I was to have gone to Norwood & the Home Committee Meeting.

My new work as Guardian has been very interesting & absorbing. Having been elected on three Committees, the Visiting, Finance, & Vagrancy, these take up time apart from the Board Meetings. All the six Women Guardians are on the first, Mrs Brown with myself on the second, & for the last I am the only one associated with the male Guardians. New wards have been built for the Casuals by the last Board, & the furnishing & fitting of them is left to us. Various reforms in the diet etc of the Workhouse Inmates have already been begun. The 'gruel' so called was we found made of flour, for which oatmeal has been substituted. The next will be the giving meat three or four times a week, instead of suet pudding only two days a week, & meat pudding two more, as now. The Dr has had an intimation that we are keeping an eye on the 36 gallon cask of beer which he alone has power to dispense, but which is at present used weekly, by his orders or sanction.

There is no need of 'an investigation' to discover that the Master's fortnightly 'requirements' for about 250 Inmates, & a dozen 'Officers' & Servants have been lavish in the extreme & entirely unchecked by the late Guardians who seem to have trusted him implicitly. The first Finance Committee I attended included the bills for the Xmas dinner & almost the first items I noticed were 'Turkey 24/- Fowls & sausages 28/-' together £2-12 of the rate payers' money to provide a repast for the Officials, which very few out of the Workhouse could have afforded, in Bedford!

*April 15th Easter Monday*
Lottie's birthday which she has spent with her Husband, Hattie, Mr Hamilton & myself at the Cottage, Aspley Heath. Her long illness has prevented her return home & she has now only so far recovered as to be unable to take up the ordinary run of domestic duties. To prevent her attempting this, Hattie will go to Nottingham with Alex, & direct these for her so that she may find her home in tolerable order after its being closed for nearly two months, & she is to return on Saturday.

On Saturday John came here quite unexpectedly only to find as he said 'his Mother had gone to the Workhouse'. I returned to tea after the Board meeting, & was very glad to have a couple of hours with him before he had to leave. He & Mattie are removing to a larger house just off the Finchley Rd in the course of a few weeks.

During Lottie's stay with us I have had to go twice to London. Difficulties have arisen at the Home & at a special request from the Secretary (Miss Bagster) I have attended this month's Committee meeting which I should not otherwise have done. On account of the Matron's illness she has been absent from the Tor & her substitute has also been ill there, & not wise in her management. In addition to this Miss Bagster has received a letter from the Solicitor of a former Patient (who after her supposed recovery was made assistant matron) charging her with having made statements in Committee to her disadvantage, & threatening an action for Libel. I was not at that meeting, but previous ones have been very exciting. The lady who succeeded me as Secretary has by a series of indiscretions & un-businesslike proceedings cost us first a long lawyer's bill, & then so muddled her accounts that she had to confess her deficiencies to us in Committee when we dealt most leniently with her but accepted her resignation. Now this fresh trouble has come to her co-secretary, which of course every Member of our Committee must share. I cannot help feeling thankful that amidst all the annoyance & sorrow I suffered through these very two ladies, on my own & Edward's account, nothing so great as they have experienced befell me & that I have been able to forgive & so to behave to Miss B that she looks to me for advice & help in the trouble now pending (which I am very glad to be able to give) & feel sincerely sorry for her.

### May 6th
At this date I intended to have written more but from some forgotten cause got no further, & it is now July 25th.

Many unexpected events have occurred since the first date was written. After the continual differences which have prevailed between the old & new Guardians for more than six months (several times causing stormy scenes at the Board) & the reiterated request on the part of some of the latter, to have the short hand Notes taken at the investigation into the charges against the Master & Matron read, there seemed no possibility of a change in the attitude of the two parties whilst these Officials, as also the Labour Master & Matron retained their position. Fortunately they have all at length realized that there was no probability of their former modes of proceeding being further tolerated, & have sent in their resignation, which was accepted by the majority of the Board, & they have all left, much to the satisfaction of those of us who have known most of their conduct & character. Mrs Brown & myself with four or five Men Guardians were elected as a Committee of management until new Officials could be appointed & also to select from the 86 applicants for the post of Master, those who from their testimonials it seemed most desirable to interview. Six applicants with their Wives were chosen & came at our request, through the Clerk, to meet the Board last Saturday week (20th inst). Of these two met with favorable consideration. One from Hull, the other from Whittlesey, Cambs. The latter for several reasons was the favorite of 5 of the Lady Guardians, & I took the first opportunity of proposing Mr Harvey, this was seconded by an old male Guardian, then the former was proposed & seconded, but after a rather excited counting & re-counting of votes Mr & Mrs Harvey were elected Master & Matron. With Mrs Harvey's kind face we were pleased, & her Husband is a fine stalwart man 6 feet high, whose bearing & appearance will command respect. I hope we have made a wise choice.

A fortnight at least must elapse before they can enter upon their work, & during this time our supervision must continue. I proposed that the Women Guardians should undertake all domestic management, & sleep in turn at the Workhouse. Mrs Brown undertook the two first nights, I, the two second; which gave me Saturday & Sunday & until after dinner on Monday. Mrs Clark succeeded me, & so on the others, as convenient to them. I slept soundly, found the day duties very continual, but not irksome by any means. Frequent applications for supplies, visiting the Wards, giving various directions to Cook, Nurses, & the two Male Officers left in charge with us, kept us moving. Sunday I went at 9-30 to the Church service in the Workhouse Chapel in the morning, & to the Nonconformist service at 3 p m, going between these to see the sick of which there are many, both men & women. After tea I spent more than an hour reading & talking to the old & infirm women who are not sick, & they expressed their pleasure as its being one of the happiest evenings they had passed there. Hattie is their Sunday visitor, & they seem to think very much of her. I had many enquiries after her as she is now away with Lottie & her Husband for their summer holiday in Scotland.

The knowledge which we are able to gain of the internal working of the House during this interregnum is most valuable to us who have the supervision, & I believe very beneficial to the Inmates. The diet needs great reform, & without waiting for formal permission to make any change, on Monday I got the Cook to substitute for the pea-soup (which the poor children especially hate, & often leave untasted) Irish-stew; & had the satisfaction of seeing the plates scraped clean, instead of having to be emptied into buckets & taken to the pigs in large quantities, as has been constantly the case. Our opportunity of observation of the internal working of domestic matters has been most useful & enabled us to offer suggestions in many ways, & to account to some extent for extravagant expenditure.

Amongst the unexpected events of the last few weeks has been the sudden resignation of the Liberal Government, & with that the hope of Temperance reform which it was intended by Sir Wm Harcourt to push forward. The election cry has been that he wished 'to deprive the poor man of his beer'! by his Local Veto Bill. Liberal Unionists & Conservatives alike have gone in on Beer by a tremendous majority, & the Brewers are triumphant. In Bedford the Liberal majority of 40 years (during which Mr Whitbread has been uninterruptedly returned) has been changed, & Guy Pym the Conservative Candidate returned.[83] Will is re-elected for North Hackney by a majority of over 2000, but we have not taken any part in his contest.

Home events have been visits from John & Mattie with their three little ones & Nurse. They are very proud of their baby-boy who is really a very fine child. My visitors had scarcely left when my unhappy servant, who for months past has been carrying on a course of dishonesty & continually under the influence of drink, broke out into such open drunkenness & abuse as quite unnerved me so that I felt quite ill, & finding every effort to restrain her useless after nearly 6 years' trial was compelled to send her away suddenly.

*Octr 10th*

Our autumnal holiday was begun rather later than usual this year so that I was able to attend the Brewsters' Sessions on Septr 8th. The only new licence applied for was refused. On the 9th I opened a small Sale of work for the Primitive Methodists; & on the 10th we left home for North Wales. The previous weeks had been filled with so much extra work, that we were more than usually glad of the rest & change. I determined not to have new Servants before going away, so with the

---

[83] Guy Pym replaced the Liberal Samuel Whitbread III, who had held the seat since 1852. Pym was re-elected in 1900, losing his seat in the Liberal landslide election of 1906.

help of a Char-woman Hattie & I managed to arrange household matters so that we had more order & comfort than for some time past, if with extra exertion. Our time however was not so entirely filled as to prevent my sitting some two hours or more several afternoons each week, in the month that elapsed between Hattie's first & second holiday, whilst she continued painting the portrait of myself which she began before going to Scotland. She has not finished it, but so far has been very successful. Her portrait of Miss Tottenham has been accepted for the Royal Academy Exhibition this year, the second time her work has been so fortunate as to be exhibited there.[84]

On Saturday 28th we left for Nottingham with Lottie & spent Sunday with her & Alex. Monday evening I left for Sheffield & Papa & Hattie for Bedford. My journey to Sheffield was to attend the Autumnal Meetings of the WTAU. I had entertainment at the house of Mr Langley the MP for one Division of Sheffield, but this, being nearly 2 miles from Montgomery Hall where our meetings were held, was little more than for sleeping & breakfast, leaving early & returning late. Neither the meetings nor the work were as pleasant as usual, but apart from these I was very glad for the opportunity of an introduction to Mr Wycliff Wilson the Chairman of the Sheffield Board of Guardians who was most kind to myself & 4 other Women Guardians all members of our Association. He placed his carriage at our disposal on two afternoons to visit the chief Workhouse just outside the town, & himself accompanied us over the Houses for the Pauper Children which he has been instrumental in establishing for them.

Business at the Board of Guardians here has not taken the peaceful turn that was hoped for by many of the Reform Guardians. Some of these seem to have abandoned that position, & are in many ways making ours more difficult. The new Master & Matron seem very satisfactory to all. Both appear to thoroughly understand their duties, & to be most anxious to fulfil them, and at the same time to meet the views & wishes of individual Guardians whenever they can legally do so, but in this last respect the Master is very particular, so that there is not much fear of further 'irregularities'. The principal causes of contention are the use that may be made of the short hand notes relating to these, under the late Master, before the Investigation Committee, they being required by the Solicitors for the defence in an Action which he is bringing against the 'Beds Times' for publishing a letter in reference to some of the charges that were brought against him, & also the continual efforts of the old Guardians to find fault with, & oppose, their new Colleagues. One of the two Board meetings from which I was absent last month was called 'a Stormy Meeting' in the Papers.

Since writing so far our late Chairman Mr Charles Howard has died, almost suddenly to those who knew little of him excepting in public life, but he had been a sufferer for some years, & only continued his offices at the earnest request of those who were associated with him in them. He was universally esteemed. I went with Papa to his funeral.

---

[84] The first was in 1893 with a painting entitled 'Lilies'. This one in 1895 was called 'Eileen'. Her third success was in 1911 with 'Robin'.

*Dec^r 31^st 1895*

So near to the close of another year, & also to the end of this book, I ought to be able to summarize many of the events of the past twelve months which would record successes & failures, which I have failed to note, but I should be ungrateful beyond measure if I failed to acknowledge the goodness & mercy that has been permitted to follow me & mine from the first day to the very last of this year. Personal difficulties & trials have been overcome, increase of health in Papa & Hattie, & no serious danger or illness has invaded the homes of my dear ones. My own strength although it has had some special strains, has been equal to every emergency, so that I can only sum up the whole in the words of the 103 Psalm, first 5 verses.

I have to-day returned from Hendon after a week's absence from home, called away in the first instance by duty to my aged Father, who has at length been induced to part with an over-bearing Servant, who, from having lived with him some years before the death of his late wife, had assumed so much, & had been yielded to so much by him, as to have been a great cause of anxiety & annoyance to me in all my recent visits to Norwood. That he might think less of her leaving, I went to him immediately to spend Xmas, sorely against my inclination I must acknowledge, for I left my Husband to make the best of his with Hattie & Mr Hamilton, who were excellent company for each other doubtless.

At our eldest Son's particular request a family meeting was arranged for at St Swithins, the day but one following Xmas day. Lottie & Alex were to go to Chelmsford for Xmas, & promised to join us in returning. I left Norwood with my Father on Friday, & arriving at Hendon, found Will somewhat disconcerted at a telegram from Bedford that Papa & Hattie would not arrive until the next day, which meant that unless they left by early train we should not see them until late in the afternoon. I sent them another telegram which had the desired effect of bringing them by early train next morning. Soon after them Alex & Lottie arrived. Then Edward & his family, & John & his excepting the baby boy, whom it was not thought safe to bring out after his recent illness. All were cordially welcomed by Will & Florence.

With the exception of the two youngest grandsons, we all sat down to early dinner together. Great-grand parent, Grand parents, 9 sons & daughters & 11 grand-children in all 25, with the two little ones in the nursery. Truly few Parents have more reason to be thankful for the temporal blessing bestowed on their children than we have. All enabled to meet in health & strength with the prospect of comparative prosperity before them, & in the present enjoyment of so much as falls to the lot of few families of the like number. During the nearly 17 years I have kept this record, death has not entered our ranks, excepting in the case of John's month old baby boy. Our eldest Son has enlarged & made his home, St Swithins, a charming place, & there was room & amusement for all. In the afternoon with my Husband I set our 13 grand-children in a row, according to their height, & beginning at the top put a halfcrown into the hand of each one, which small token may help to make the older ones at least remember an occasion that may never be repeated.

Edward & Clara & John & Mattie with their little ones returned home at night, but not until we had united in family worship & thanksgiving, led by Papa, & finished by uniting heart & voice in singing 'Praise God from whom all blessings flow'. The remainder of Will's family guests remained until Monday (Sunday also being a very happy day). Then the scattering began by Papa & Alex leaving, Lottie & Hattie to John's next day & I to Bedford with my Father.

Now it is January 1896. Lottie has returned with Hattie & spent a week at home, after the same time between her Brothers. Grandpapa has gone back to Norwood, & we are alone with our one chick. That will probably be for only a little while, for Mr Hamilton has asked to carry her off the end of May. My Diary began with the engagement of my eldest, & ends with the marriage of the youngest, if this page should be concluded as I expect. I dread the day.

# 1896

*June 12th /96*

It has come, & gone. A week yesterday (June 4th) the last bird flew from our nest & now I & my Husband are as much alone as we were when we began life together more than 43 years ago. Hattie's time & thoughts have been almost entirely occupied in preparation for the important event of her marriage, & few girls could leave their home & birthplace under more auspicious circumstances than she has done, as far as we her Parents could conduce to them. She has paid farewell visits to each of her Brothers, before making final arrangements for her wedding, taking with her to Will the portrait of myself for which he gave her a commission some months ago, & to put the finishing touches on this was her last home work.

The weather was most fortunate for her wedding day. A tent in the garden accommodated about 30 friends, many of whom came from a distance, to lunch at 1 o'clock, before the ceremony at 2-30, in our little Chapel, which was filled by friends & neighbours when we entered it. Mr Hamilton with his best man Dr M[85] arrived from Nottingham the same morning & with Dr Brown & Charles Moore awaited the coming of his Bride, who looked very sweet, & both went through the ordeal very bravely. C Moore read some portion of the beginning of the service, Dr Brown the remainder with a little homily at the end. When we returned to the garden Edward took photos of the Bridal party, then of relatives with them, & finally of all with the guests, numbering about forty. The four little Bridesmaids, Hilda, Evelyn & Maud, with Mr Hamilton's niece, looked very proud & pretty, holding their baskets of flowers.[86] We adjourned to the Drawing-room for afternoon tea, & Hattie had a little time with her friends (among whom were Miss Coles & Miss Jackson) before cutting her Cake; after which she had to prepare at once for her journey, & left en route for Scotland about 5 o'clock.

Mr Hamilton's Uncle, & his Aunt, who had been his nearest friends, since he lost his Mother when quite a child, came from Glasgow on the previous evening & slept here, as also his Sister-in-law & her daughter, who was the bridesmaid.[87] Our

---

[85] Dr Macnair, a boyhood – and lifelong – friend from Glasgow.

[86] Hilda is Will and Flo's eldest daughter, born 1884; Evelyn is Edward and Clara's twin, two years younger, and Maud is John and Mattie's daughter, born in 1888.

[87] William Robert Hamilton, to give him the Christian names which CEB never accords him, had a complex upbringing in Glasgow. His mother died when he was two and, his father then decamping to the USA, he was brought up by his mother's brother, the Rev. Samuel Connell.

neighbours were very kind in taking in friends for the night, Miss Risley accommodating Aunt Jenny, Fanny Moore, & Mattie, whilst Will & Florence were lodged next door. The gathering of our dear ones & friends seemed a time of happiness to them all, but less so to me, although it was a great pleasure to see all our children together in their old home once more. Lottie gave herself up to preparing & then entertaining, & it was only when she left with her Husband for Aspley Heath on Tuesday that I realized how empty the house was & wandered from one bed-room to another thinking how little use there would be for them.

On Friday evening we entertained about 80 of our poorer neighbours all of whom had shared in presenting Hattie with a beautiful oak tea-tray mounted, & with a plate for the inscription in the centre. The men from the railway whom she has so long been accustomed to visit in their Hut also sent their offerings of a framed text & a workbox. These also joined us at tea & John did his best to give them enjoyment in the shape of cigars afterward. If we may judge of the esteem in which both Mr Hamilton & Hattie are held by the quantity & quality of their wedding gifts they are fortunate indeed in deserving it. Over 100 were sent to them. May they so live as to secure His favor whose loving kindness is better than life. Amen & Amen.

# Postscript

Edward and Charlotte stayed on in Bedford until their Golden Wedding anniversary in 1903. After some discussion within the family it had been agreed that, as they were now well into their seventies, they should move close to their two surviving daughters, now both living in Nottingham. Accordingly they moved immediately after the anniversary celebrations. When the time came to leave Bedford 'a presentation to my husband' Charlotte noted in her fourth diary begun at the time, 'was made by a deputation of workmen from the Britannia Works ... a beautifully illuminated and framed address which they presented with kind words'.

Once in Nottingham Charlotte remained very active with a variety of good works, and they both went twice more on energetic holidays in Switzerland, as well as returning to their old haunts in the woods around Woburn. Lottie and Hattie had both married professional men in the 1890s and settled in Nottingham with their respective husbands Alex Morton and William Hamilton. Hattie quickly started a family, but Lottie remained childless. By 1900 the two families each occupied one of a pair of large late Victorian semi-detached houses in an exclusive development then on the northern edge of the city.

In the summer of 1916, at the height of the First World War, first Edward and then William Hamilton died. A year later Charlotte went to live with her daughters, who had connecting doors built between the two parts of their joint home. She continued to write her diary, now much concerned with current events, right through until the end of the war. On 11 November 1918 she rejoiced to be able to write: 'What a wonderful record ... that with 8 Grandsons all with one exception on active service ... not one of my children are amongst the mourners!' She ended in her ninety-first year with the sad news of the death of her beloved Florence, Will's wife, from Spanish flu in 1919. Will himself had lost his parliamentary seat in the Conservative debacle of 1906, and turned his great talents to his scientific researches – being elected a Fellow of the Royal Society in 1916 – and later on to psychology. Among many other appointments he became Chairman of the Harpur Trust.[1] Always sociable and open-handed he generously subsidised the education of several of his younger relatives. He never remarried and eventually retired to Devon, where he died in 1943 at the age of 89. He had been wheelchair-bound for some years.

Ted died in 1921. Somewhat in the shadow of his elder brother, he had struggled to find success. Though an excellent doctor, general practice was not his metier.

---

[1]  The Harpur Trust, known also as the Bedford charity, is the largest of Bedford's local charities, and one of the largest in the UK. It was founded by William Harpur in 1566 and its purpose is the making of grants for the promotion of education, the relief of hardship and need, and the support of recreation with a social welfare purpose. It also runs four independent schools in the town, the two schools attended by the Bousfield brothers, Bedford School and Bedford Modern School (both boys' schools until 2003, when Bedford Modern School became co-educational), and the two girls' schools, Bedford High School and Dame Alice Harpur School. Its income derives from land in Holborn which formed part of the original endowment.

Instead he preferred to concentrate on his researches in microbiology. He built his own laboratories and began to investigate bacteria. In 1898 he was appointed bacteriologist to the London Borough of Camberwell – the first such appointment in the country – examining samples for bacteriological contamination. He also conducted research for Burroughs Wellcome, but his contribution to public health seems to remain largely unacknowledged. The most religious of the brothers, Ted was a fervent Methodist like his father, serving as both a Class Leader and Circuit Steward.

John, after a slow start to his career, became a successful patent agent, but little survives of his history. He died aged only 63.

Hattie, a widow after 1916, Lottie and her husband lived out the rest of their lives in their adjoining houses. Both continued to support their mother in her Temperance and other good works. Hattie died in 1942 but Lottie lived on until 1951, dying at the age of 90, the last of the siblings. Charlotte herself seemed indestructible. At the age of 100 she was presented to King George and Queen Mary on the occasion of their visit to Nottingham in 1928. In deference to her great age they requested that she remain seated. She did so but inwardly was furious at the implication that she was unable to stand and show proper respect to Their Majesties. She made her last public speech the following year, survived an attack of flu and finally died in 1933 at the age of 105.

*John Hamilton*

# Appendix 1

## The Cox, Collins and Bousfield families

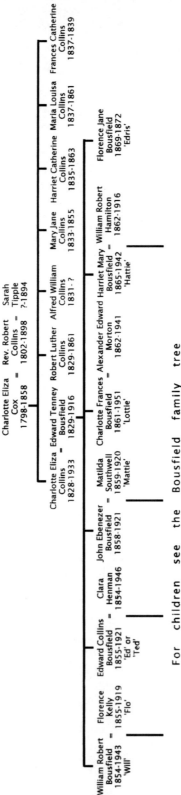

# The Bousfield family

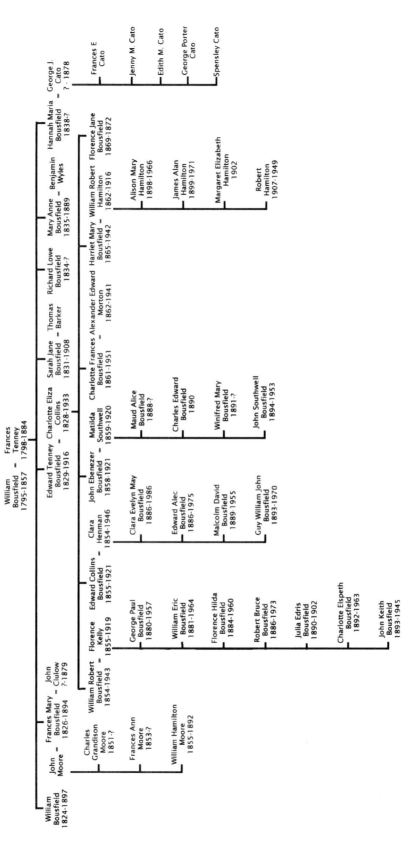

# Appendix 2
# Who's Who in the Bousfield family

| Name | Known as | Living at | Date |
|---|---|---|---|
| **Charlotte (CEB) and Edward Bousfield** | | | |
| Edward | 'Papa', later 'my Husband' | Newark, Notts | c. 1850–1856 |
| | | Sticklepath, Devon | c. 1856–1858 |
| | | 41 Cauldwell Street, Bedford | 1858–1863 |
| | | **Alpha Villa**, 44 Ampthill Road, Southend, Bedford | **1863–1903** |
| | | Aspley Heath (a rented house) | 1887–1890 |
| | | Aspley Heath (a rented cottage) | 1890–? |
| **CEB and Edward Bousfield's children** | | | |
| William (b. 1854, m. Florence Kelly 1879) | 'Will' | Clifton, Bristol | 1878–1879 as a tutor |
| | | Westbury, near Bristol | 1879 after marriage |
| | | Westbury Villa, 9 Cricklewood Lane, Cricklewood | 1880–1889 |
| | | St Swithins, Hendon | 1889 onwards |
| Edward (b.1855, m. Clara Henman 1882) | 'Ted', 'Ed', 'Eddie' Edward | Tewkesbury | 1878 |
| | | Winchester | 1879 assistant to a doctor |
| | | Wandsworth | 1879–1880 assistant to a doctor |
| | | Cotham, Bristol | 1881–1884 assistant to a doctor |
| | | Wellesley House, 363 Old Kent Rd, South London | 1884–1909 home and surgery |
| John (b.1858, m. Matilda Southwell 1887) | 'John' | Chelmsford | ?–1878 with the Mortons |
| | | Alpha Villa, Bedford | 1878–1882 |
| | | 8 Claremont Road, Cricklewood | 1882–1887 lodgings near Will |

| Name | Known as | Living at | Date |
|------|----------|-----------|------|
| | | Glenrock, 47 Hillfield Road West, South Hampstead | 1887–1895 |
| | | 9 Parsifal Road, South Hampstead | 1895 onwards |
| Charlotte (b.1861, m. Alex Morton 1891) | 'Lottie' | Alpha Villa | to 1891 |
| | | Charnwood House, Alexandra Park, Nottingham after marriage | 1891 onwards |
| Harriet (b.1865, m. William Hamilton 1896) | 'Hattie' | Alpha Villa | to 1895 |
| | | Alexandra Park, Nottingham after marriage | 1895 onwards |
| Florence Jane (b.1869, d.1872) | 'Edris' | Alpha Villa | 1869–1872 |

**CEB's parents and parents-in-law**

| | | | |
|------|----------|-----------|------|
| Rev. Robert Collins (father) and Mrs Sarah Collins (step-mother) | 'Father', 'Grandpapa' 'Grandmama Collins' | Penrith House/Lodge, 109 Belvedere Road, Upper Norwood, South London near Crystal Palace | ?–1898 |
| Mrs Bousfield (b.1798, d.1884) | 'Grandma Bousfield' | 41 Cauldwell Street, Bedford | 1863 to c. 1879 |
| | | 10, Saunders Street, Southport, with her daughter | c. 1879–1884 |

**CEB's sons- and daughters-in-law**

| | | | |
|------|----------|-----------|------|
| Florence Kelly | 'Flo' | Shanklin, Isle of Wight and 9 Sutherland Gardens (later called Avenue), Maida Vale, London | Until marriage in 1879 |
| Clara Henman | 'Clara' | Sutton Cottage, Bromham, Bedfordshire | Until marriage in 1882 |
| Matilda Southwell | 'Mattie' | Gurrey Lodge, Finchley Rd, Cricklewood, London | Until marriage in 1887 |
| Alex Morton | 'Alex' | Chelmsford Nottingham | |
| William Hamilton | 'Mr Hamilton' | Nottingham | |

# Bibliography

*Manuscript source*
'The Diary of Charlotte Eliza Bousfield', 3 volumes, transcribed and edited by John and Hilary Hamilton

*Printed sources*
Bell, Patricia, 'Aspects of Anglo-Indian Bedford', in *Worthington George Smith and Other Studies*, BHRS vol. 57 (Bedford: The Society, 1978), pp.181–203

Brown, Neville, *Dissenting Forbears: The Maternal Ancestors of J.M. Keynes* (Chichester: Phillimore, 1988)

Bushby, D.W., *Elementary Education in Bedford, 1868–1903* and *The Ecclesiastical Census, Bedfordshire, March 1851*, BHRS vol. 54 (Bedford: The Society, 1975)

Collett-White, James, *Bedfordshire in the 1880s* (Bedford: BLARS, 2006)

Dingle, A.E., *The Campaign for Prohibition in Victorian England* (London: Croom Helm, 1980)

Godber, Joyce, *The Harpur Trust 1552–1973* (Bedford: The Harpur Trust, 1973)

Godber, Joyce, *The Story of Bedford* (Luton: White Crescent Press Ltd, 1978)

Graham, Halina, Richard Wildman and Min Dinning, *Bedford Portrayed: Eighteenth and Nineteenth Century Bedford through Artists' Eyes* (Bedford: Cecil Higgins Art Gallery and Museum, 1992)

Hamilton, John, *Glad for God: A History of the Bousfields of Newark and Bedford to 1903* (Loughborough: Heart of Albion Press, 2003)

Keynes, Geoffrey, *The Gates of Memory* (Oxford: Oxford University Press, 1983)

Shiman, Lilian Lewis, *Crusade against Drink in Victorian England* (Basingstoke: Macmillan, 1988)

Welch, Edwin, ed., *Bedfordshire Chapels and Meeting Houses: Official Registration 1672–1901*, BHRS vol. 75 (Bedford: The Society, 1996)

Wildman, Richard, *Bedford: A Pictorial History* (Chichester: Phillimore, 1991)

# INDEX

CEB refers to Charlotte Bousfield; n following a page number refers to footnotes; Pl. refers to plates, between pages 96 and 97. Appendices 1 and 2 have not been indexed.